RSF: The Russell Sage Foundation Journal of the Social Sciences

Spatial Foundations of Inequality

VOLUME 3 · NUMBER 2 · FEBRUARY 2017

RSF: The Russell Sage Foundation Journal of the Social Sciences

ISSN 2377-8261

The Russell Sage Foundation

The Russell Sage Foundation, one of the oldest of America's general purpose foundations, was established in 1907 by Mrs. Margaret Olivia Sage for "the improvement of social and living conditions in the United States." The foundation seeks to fulfill this mandate by fostering the development and dissemination of knowledge about the country's political, social, and economic problems. While the foundation endeavors to assure the accuracy and objectivity of each book it publishes, the conclusions and interpretations in Russell Sage Foundation publications are those of the authors and not of the foundation, its trustees, or its staff. Publication by Russell Sage, therefore, does not imply foundation endorsement.

Board of Trustees

Sara S. McLanahan, *Chair*
Larry M. Bartels
Karen S. Cook
W. Bowman Cutter III
Sheldon H. Danziger
Kathryn Edin
Michael Jones-Correa
Lawrence F. Katz
David Laibson
Nicholas Lemann
Martha Minow
Peter R. Orszag
Claude M. Steele
Shelley E. Taylor
Hirokazu Yoshikawa

Mission Statement

RSF: The Russell Sage Foundation Journal of the Social Sciences is a peer-reviewed, open-access journal of original empirical research articles by both established and emerging scholars. It is designed to promote cross-disciplinary collaborations on timely issues of interest to academics, policymakers, and the public at large. Each issue is thematic in nature and focuses on a specific research question or area of interest. The introduction to each issue will include an accessible, broad, and synthetic overview of the research question under consideration and the current thinking from the various social sciences.

RSF Journal Editorial Board

Elizabeth O. Ananat, Duke University
Annette Bernhardt, University of California, Berkeley
Karen S. Cook, Stanford University
Sheldon H. Danziger, RSF President
Janet C. Gornick, The CUNY Graduate Center
Jennifer Hochschild, Harvard University
Douglas S. Massey, Princeton University
Mary E. Pattillo, Northwestern University
James Sidanius, Harvard University
Mary C. Waters, Harvard University
Bruce Western, Harvard University

Copyright © 2017 by Russell Sage Foundation. All rights reserved. Printed in the United States of America. No part of this publication may be reproduced, stored in a retrieval system, or transmitted in any form or by any means, electronic, mechanical, photocopying, recording, or otherwise, without the prior written permission of the publisher. Reproduction by the United States Government in whole or in part is permitted for any purpose.

Opinions expressed in this journal are not necessarily those of the editors, editorial board, trustees, or the Russell Sage Foundation.

We invite scholars to submit proposals for potential issues through the *RSF* application portal: https://rsfjournal.onlineapplicationportal.com/. Submissions should be addressed to Suzanne Nichols, Director of Publications.

To view the complete text and additional features online please go to **www.rsfjournal.org**.

Russell Sage Foundation
112 East 64th Street
New York, NY 10065

ISSN (print): 2377-8253
ISSN (electronic): 2377-8261
ISBN: 978-0-87154-739-2

RSF: *The Russell Sage Foundation*
Journal of the Social Sciences

VOLUME 3 NUMBER 2
FEBRUARY 2017

Spatial Foundations of Inequality

ISSUE EDITORS
George Galster, Wayne State University
Patrick Sharkey, New York University

CONTENTS

Spatial Foundations of Inequality: A Conceptual Model and Empirical Overview **1**
George Galster and Patrick Sharkey

A Continuous Measure of the Joint Distribution of Race and Income Among Neighborhoods **34**
Sean F. Reardon, Joseph Townsend, and Lindsay Fox

Racial Residential Segregation of School-Age Children and Adults: The Role of Schooling as a Segregating Force **63**
Ann Owens

Defensible Spaces in Philadelphia: Exploring Neighborhood Boundaries Through Spatial Analysis **81**
Rory Kramer

Urban Income Inequality and the Great Recession in Sunbelt Form: Disentangling Individual and Neighborhood-Level Change in Los Angeles **102**
Robert J. Sampson, Jared N. Schachner, and Robert D. Mare

From Bad to Worse: How Changing Inequality in Nearby Areas Impacts Local Crime **129**
John R. Hipp and Charis E. Kubrin

Segregation as a Source of Contextual Advantage: A Formal Theory with Application to American Cities **152**
Lincoln Quillian

How Living in the 'Hood Affects Risky Behaviors Among Latino and African American Youth **170**
Anna Maria Santiago, Eun Lye Lee, Jessica L. Lucero, and Rebecca Wiersma

Socioeconomic Segregation of Activity Spaces in Urban Neighborhoods: Does Shared Residence Mean Shared Routines? **210**
Christopher R. Browning, Catherine A. Calder, Lauren J. Krivo, Anna L. Smith, and Bethany Boettner

Spatial Foundations of Inequality: A Conceptual Model and Empirical Overview

GEORGE GALSTER AND PATRICK SHARKEY

Inequalities among individuals and households in achieved socioeconomic status (income, wealth, and so on) in the United States have reached levels not observed for almost a century. We believe that a corresponding evolution of geographic inequalities in socioeconomic, environmental, institutional, and political domains both reflect and—more importantly from our perspective—contribute to these inequalities across individuals.[1] It is this belief that motivated the Russell Sage Foundation to devote an issue of *RSF: The Russell Sage Foundation Journal of the Social Sciences* to this topic.

Our primary purpose in this introductory article is to develop a holistic, multilevel conceptual model for comprehending how space can be considered a foundation of U.S. socioeconomic inequality. Our secondary aim is to provide a synthetic review of the evidence on various dimensions of inequality of opportunity and outcomes in America, and the empirical scholarly literature that provides plausibly causal estimates of the impact of space on individual socioeconomic outcomes. We do not advance new empirical research but rather a framing of the issues that will be sufficiently robust and comprehensive to permit integration of all the papers in this issue as illustrations and amplifications. Moreover, we hope that our model will be useful in generating hypotheses and thereby stimulating further research on this crucial topic.

In overview, our conceptual model contends that the variations in geographic context across multiple scales (neighborhood, jurisdiction, metropolitan region)—what we call *spatial opportunity structure*—affects the socioeconomic outcomes that individuals can achieve in two ways by altering the payoffs that will be gained from the attributes individuals have during any given period and the bundle of attributes that individuals will acquire (both passively and actively) during their lifetimes.

In the first mechanism, the spatial opportunity structure serves as a mediating factor,

George Galster is Clarence Hilberry Professor of Urban Affairs at Wayne State University. **Patrick Sharkey** is professor of sociology at New York University.

© 2017 Russell Sage Foundation. Galster, George, and Patrick Sharkey. 2017. "Spatial Foundations of Inequality: A Conceptual Model and Empirical Overview." *RSF: The Russell Sage Foundation Journal of the Social Sciences* 3(2): 1–33. DOI: 10.7758/RSF.3.2.01. The authors thank Maren Toft for her comments on an earlier draft and Sylvia Tatman-Burruss for research assistance. Participants at the Russell Sage Foundation conference "Spatial Foundations of Inequality" and two anonymous reviewers provided valuable feedback on early drafts of this article. Direct correspondence to: George Galster at george.galster@wayne.edu, Department of Urban Studies and Planning, Room 3198, Faculty-Administration Building, Wayne State University, Detroit, MI 48202; and Patrick Sharkey at patrick.sharkey@nyu.edu, Department of Sociology, New York University, 295 Lafayette St., Room 4102, New York, NY 10012.

1. We are not the first to make such claims, of course. A similar theme is advanced in numerous seminal works (for example, Wilson 1987; Jencks and Mayer 1990; Brooks-Gunn et al. 1993; Briggs 1995; Brooks-Gunn, Duncan, and Aber 1997).

translating a given bundle of individual attributes into achieved status depending on geography of the individual's residence, work, and routine activity spaces. In the second mechanism, the spatial opportunity structure serves as a modifying factor affecting the bundle of attributes that individuals develop over time in three ways. First, it directly influences the attributes over which individuals may exercise little or no volition, such as exposure to environmental pollutants or violence. Second, it directly influences the attributes over which they exercise considerable volition by shaping what they perceive is the most desirable, feasible option. It does so by influencing what information about the individual's options is provided, what the information objectively indicates about payoffs from these options, and how the individual subjectively evaluates the information. These decisions early in life lead people into various path-dependent trajectories of achieved socioeconomic status and subsequent life decisions, in cumulatively reinforcing processes that can stretch across lifetimes and generations. Third, in the case of children and youth, the spatial opportunity structure indirectly influences their attributes through induced changes in the resources, behaviors, and attitudes of their caregivers.

INEQUALITIES IN THE SPATIAL OPPORTUNITY STRUCTURE

The first basic claim that motivates this issue is that various dimensions of inequality are organized in space. The spatial organization of inequality is, in part, simply a manifestation of inequality occurring at the level of individuals, families, and groups that is mapped on to spaces. However, spatial inequality also is due to intentional efforts to organize physical space in ways that maintain or reinforce inequality (Dreier, Mollenkopf, and Swanstrom 2001). As a result of both sets of processes, variation is tremendous in economic status, labor market opportunities, core institutions such as schools, environmental hazards, and social networks across city blocks, neighborhoods, cities and towns, metropolitan areas, and regions. We begin with a descriptive portrait of several different dimensions of the spatial opportunity structure, focusing on the distribution across space of different segments of the population as classified by racial-ethnic background and income, economic opportunities, environmental hazards, and violence.

Segregation by Economic Status and Race-Ethnicity

Trends in household income and wealth inequality, which have been well documented in academic work and the popular press, are mirrored by trends in the degree to which low- and high-income families live apart from each other, as measured by economic segregation (Bischoff and Reardon 2014; Jargowsky 1996, 2003, 2015; Reardon and Bischoff 2011, 2016; Watson 2009). No matter how economic segregation is measured, trends show steady growth in the degree of segregation by income since the 1970s. Sean Reardon and Kendra Bischoff (2016) use a straightforward measure of the proportion of families living in neighborhoods that have median income at least 50 percent above or 50 percent below the metropolitan area median to document changes in the degree to which American families have begun to sort into separate communities stratified by economic status. They find that, in 1970, about 15 percent lived in neighborhoods that were either extremely affluent or extremely poor. By 2012, that figure had risen to 34 percent.

Although the growth of affluent neighborhoods is an important contributor to the rise of economic segregation (Reardon and Bischoff 2011), much of the concern about the issue stems from the long-term rise of concentrated poverty. Paul Jargowsky (2003, 2015) documents trends in the proportion of all Americans and poor Americans living in neighborhoods with a poverty rate of 40 percent or greater in a series of reports, showing substantial growth in concentrated poverty from 1970 to 1990, a decline of high-poverty neighborhoods in the 1990s, and a subsequent increase in concentrated poverty from 2000 to the most recent years in which data were available (from 2009 through 2013). Since 2000, the number of extreme poverty neighborhoods has risen by more than 75 percent and the number of Americans living in such neighborhoods by more than 90 percent, from 7.2 million to 13.8 million (Jargowsky 2015).

Economic inequality in American neighborhoods overlaps with persistent racial and ethnic inequality. Residential segregation of African Americans from Anglo Americans is most commonly measured two ways: the dissimilarity index, which captures the comparative evenness of the overall distribution of two racial or ethnic groups across the neighborhoods of a city or metropolitan area, and the isolation index, which captures the degree to which members of a particular racial or ethnic group live in neighborhoods occupied by members of the same group.[2] According to both measures, the segregation of blacks from whites continues to be extremely high in many urban areas, although black-white segregation has declined steadily since 1970 (Glaeser and Vigdor 2012; Logan and Stults 2011; Logan, Stults, and Farley 2014). Measures of evenness in the distribution of both Hispanics and Asian Americans relative to whites show slight increases in the level of segregation over time, whereas measures of their isolation show larger increases over time, consistent with the rapid population growth of both groups (Logan 2011).

Beyond the separation of racial and ethnic groups from one another is the question of the average economic status in the neighborhoods of each group. Economic segregation within racial and ethnic groups has been rising over time, particularly for black and Hispanic families since 2000 (Bischoff and Reardon 2014). This trend has led to more inequality within groups; however, between-group inequality continues to be extreme. Jargowsky (2015) shows that roughly five million blacks live in neighborhoods with poverty rates of at least 40 percent, a figure that is higher than any other racial or ethnic group. Among the poor, 25 percent of blacks live in concentrated poverty, versus 7 percent of poor whites and 17 percent of poor Hispanics. These figures reflect a broader set of findings in the literature demonstrating that different racial and ethnic groups continue to live in highly unequal residential environments than other groups even after accounting for group differences in economic status. The gaps are most notable when blacks and whites are compared. In all urban areas across the country, Patrick Sharkey (2014) finds that black families with household income of $100,000 or more live in and are surrounded by neighborhoods with higher levels of disadvantage than white families with income of $30,000 or less (see also Logan 2011; Reardon, Fox, and Townsend 2015).

Schools and School Districts

The research described in the previous section indicates that inequality in residential environments (especially in its economic composition) has been growing for all American families. These same trends are amplified for families with children. Evidence using several measures of racial and economic segregation shows that households with children are distributed less evenly across neighborhoods of different racial-ethnic composition and economic status, respectively, than are households without children (Logan et al. 2001; Jargowsky 2015; Owens 2016). The relatively high level of residential segregation among children has important implications for schooling and academic achievement.

Trends in economic segregation in schools are not as clear as trends in residential segregation by income, mainly because of the absence of precise data on student economic status in schools across the country (Reardon and Owens 2014). Research using student eligibility for free lunch as a proxy for low economic status has documented trends from 1990 to 2010, and found growing segregation of low-income students between school districts within the same urban area, and growing segregation of low-income students between schools within the same district in the 1990s but not the 2000s (Owens, Reardon, and Jencks 2016). An alternative approach focuses on the overall population of families living within school districts (available from 1970) or on families with children in public schools (available since 1990).

2. The exposure index also is used frequently, but this measure is essentially the opposite of the isolation index and is designed to capture the degree to which members of a particular group are exposed to members of another group in their neighborhoods.

Using this approach, trends in the degree of segregation between school districts are largely consistent with the trends in economic segregation across neighborhoods. Economic segregation between school districts rose for all families in the 1970s and 1980s, and continued to rise for families with children in public schools in the 1990s and 2000s (Owens, Reardon, and Jencks 2016).

Levels and trends in school racial segregation are more difficult to summarize. From the late 1960s through the end of the 1970s, the segregation of black and white students within school districts, measured by evenness and exposure, declined substantially (Reardon and Owens 2014). However, segregation between school districts rose, particularly in the north. Since 1980, exposure of black students to white students has fallen (Orfield and Lee 2007), a pattern largely explained by the fact that the population of students in the United States has grown more diverse over time. Focusing on evenness, trends in black-white school segregation depend on the exact time frame under study, but most studies report modest increases since 1980 (Reardon and Owens 2014).

Jobs and Economic Opportunities
Early research on spatial inequality in access to jobs focused on the shift of employment opportunities away from central cities and into the suburbs, arguing that changes in urban economies had contributed to growing racial gaps in joblessness and welfare receipt (Kain 1968; Wilson 1987). In putting forth his spatial mismatch theory, John Kain (1968) argued that the combination of racial segregation, group variation in skills and human capital, discrimination in the labor and housing markets, and lack of access to employment networks and employment opportunities helped explain the relatively high rates of joblessness among black Americans in central cities. Subsequent research by William Julius Wilson (1996) focused on the growth of joblessness as a primary explanation for a set of changes and deteriorating conditions in high-poverty, central city neighborhoods.

Descriptive evidence generally supports the argument that spatial proximity to jobs contributes to racial and ethnic disparities in joblessness and economic status (Holzer 1991; Kain 1992). However, the original focus on the location of jobs in central city versus suburban areas applied primarily to large urban centers in the Northeast and Midwest (Ihlanfeldt and Sjoquist 1998). Judith Hellerstein, David Neumark, and Melissa McInerney (2008) argue for a more refined perspective that focuses on the importance of access to jobs held by black Americans, particularly those held by blacks with the same level of education. The overall prevalence of jobs is shown to be less important than the prevalence of jobs held by other blacks, suggesting that discrimination and employment networks may be more relevant than the raw presence of jobs in explaining racial gaps in employment (see also Hellerstein, Kutzbach, and Neumark 2014; Waldinger 1996).

Recent research focuses on spatial inequality in wages, well-paid jobs, and economic growth across urban areas. From 1980 to 2010, metropolitan areas that initially had high shares of college-educated workers have experienced greater growth and demand for well-paid workers, leading to growing inequality across metropolitan areas over time as the returns to college education have grown and urban economies have become increasingly bifurcated (Lindley and Machin 2014). Two sets of consequences have arisen. On the one hand, inequality between cities and metropolitan areas has grown as employment opportunities have shrunk absolutely and real wages have stagnated or fallen in places that are geographically and economically isolated from high-demand global cities. On the other hand, inequality within high-demand urban areas has widened as the growing returns to higher education have created widening gaps between highly educated and less-educated workers (Florida 2010).

An additional strand of evidence documents geographical variation in economic mobility across commuting zones (sets of contiguous counties that surround central cities and cover the entire nation), using data from tax records for all Americans over time. Raj Chetty and colleagues (2014) show that a single, national measure of economic mobility or persistence obscures the tremendous variation across regions of the United States and across specific commuting zones. Subsequent research exploiting sibling differences in time spent in low- and high-mobility commuting zones suggests that places themselves have causal effects on the probability of upward mobility, although less progress has been made in identifying characteristics of places that facilitate or impede upward mobility (Chetty and Hendren 2015).

The idea that places exert independent effects on the economic outcomes of residents receives further support from recent research focusing on the magnitude of the employment shock experienced by local areas during the Great Recession. Danny Yagan (2016) compares workers at the same level and in the same retail firm but located in areas of the country that were hit more or less hard by the economic downturn that began in 2008. Workers in areas hit harder by the recession were 1 percentage point less likely to be employed in 2014, several years after the recession had ended.

Environmental Hazards

In the 1980s, attention began to be focused on the siting of environmental hazards in communities across the country, revealing a pattern in which hazardous waste sites were disproportionately located in communities occupied primarily by racial and ethnic minority groups (Bryant and Mohai 1992). Since that time, research has proliferated on spatial variation in air pollution, environmental toxins like lead, siting of manufacturing plants, and the location of chemical accidents and hazardous waste.

This research has found consistent evidence that, within most metropolitan areas, different forms of environmental hazards are more common in low-income communities and in communities of color, though the degree of inequality by economic status and race-ethnicity varies depending on the specific type of hazard under study. Liam Downey and Brian Hawkins (2008) analyze variation in the concentration of air pollutants released from industrial facilities by neighborhood racial-ethnic composition and income; they find that black Americans live in neighborhoods with concentrations of toxic releases 1.45 times greater than those in white neighborhoods and 1.7 times greater than in Hispanic neighborhoods. The greater exposure of blacks to air pollution is particularly pronounced for very low-income blacks compared with their white and Hispanic counterparts, but is present at every level of income. Downey and Hawkins show that, just as middle- and upper-income black Americans live in neighborhoods with levels of disadvantage comparable to poor whites, black households with income equal to or greater than $50,000 live in neighborhoods with more air pollution than white households making less than $10,000 per year.

Although racial and economic gaps in exposure to environmental toxins are present at the national level, Downey (2007) documents tremendous variation in the degree of environmental inequality across U.S. metropolitan areas. In some urban areas, black and Hispanic residents are exposed to much higher levels of environmental hazards than whites, while in others there is no disparity. Even as more attention has been paid to pollution and environmental hazards, racial and ethnic gaps have persisted. Kerry Ard (2015) analyzes air pollution from 1995 to 2004 and finds sharp declines in average levels of pollution over time nationally, although declines in central cities were less pronounced. However, the gap in exposure to air pollution between blacks and whites has not changed over time, suggesting the persistent, important role of geography.

Persistent racial and ethnic gaps in exposure to environmental toxins relate closely to a large literature on inequality in health and well-being, which is reviewed elsewhere (Diez-Roux and Mair 2010; Kawachi and Berkman 2003; Sampson 2003). Recent research documents spatial variation in especially harmful toxins, notably lead. At the county level, Paul Stretesky (2003) documents an association between the percentage of black children and air lead concentrations. The few studies conducted at the neighborhood level in specific places document similar links between racial composition and elevated blood lead levels (for example, Lanphear et al. 1998). Robert Sampson and Alex Winter (forthcoming) use detailed data from Chicago children measured from 1995 to 2013 to track changes in elevated blood lead levels in block groups across the city, documenting enormous gaps in elevated blood lead by race and ethnicity in the mid-1990s; in some predominantly black neighborhoods, more than 90 percent of tested children had elevated levels of blood lead. These rates, however, dropped precipitously over the period for all groups. Although black and Hispanic neighborhoods continued to have higher rates of elevated blood lead, prevalence was well below 10 percent in all communities by the end of the period under study. Sampson and Winter argue that the patterns reveal both the enormous spatial disparities in exposure to environmental toxins as well as the power of public health intervention to reduce or eliminate the consequences of environmental inequality.

Violence

Among the developed nations of the world, the United States has a relatively high violent crime rate and an extremely high homicide rate (UNODC 2013). However, the national rate of homicides obscures the variation in the prevalence of violence across cities and neighborhoods. Whereas many cities are remarkably safe, cities such as St. Louis, Detroit, and Baltimore have homicide rates that rival the most violent, war-torn places in the world (Federal Bureau of Investigation 2015). Within cities, violent crime is unevenly distributed across neighborhoods. For example, in a city like Chicago with a high average violent crime rate, some communities in the northern part of the city are largely untouched. In the neighborhoods of the city's south and west sides, however, violence is concentrated in communities characterized by poverty, ethnic isolation, and institutional decay (Papachristos 2013; Sampson 2012).

The spatial concentration of violence is not unique to Chicago. Research from cities with low or average crime rates, such as Seattle and Boston, shows that a disproportionate share of violent crime takes place within a few city blocks and street segments (Braga, Papachristos, and Hureau 2010; Braga, Hureau, and Papchristos 2011; Weisburd et al. 2004).

A growing strand of evidence suggests that violence may be one of the central mechanisms by which growing up in a disadvantaged neighborhood affects the life chances of children (Sharkey and Sampson 2015). However, violent crime is one of the few dimensions of spatial inequality that has changed in a positive way over time. Over the past twenty years, the national rates of violent crime and homicide have roughly halved. The cities with the highest rates of violence in the 1990s, which had disproportionately high prevalence of racial and ethnic minority populations and high levels of poverty, have seen the greatest declines in violent crime since then (Ellen and O'Regan 2009).

Only limited evidence is available on trends in crime at the level of neighborhoods. Michael Friedson and Sharkey (2015) draw on data from six cities where it is possible to track neighborhood-level trends in crime over at least a decade, and find that the greatest absolute declines in violent crime occurred in the most violent neighborhoods. In four of the six cities, the relative decline of violence was also largest in the cities' most violent neighborhoods; in the remaining two, the proportional decline of violent crime was roughly equivalent in the most violent neighborhoods and in the rest of the cities. In these six cities, the trends mean that the level of inequality in community violent crime has declined over time, though it remains severe. The degree to which poor and nonpoor residents, and white and nonwhite residents, are exposed to violent crime in their neighborhoods has converged.

An Interim Summary

Our first claim in this paper is that various dimensions of inequality are organized in space. We review available evidence and document the degree of spatial inequality in economic status, access to well-paid jobs, exposure to environmental hazards, and exposure to community violence. We find that spatial inequality frequently is overlaid with racial and ethnic segregation of neighborhoods and schools. Where possible, we track changes over time in spatial inequality, and show that neighborhood economic segregation, concentrated poverty, ethnic residential segregation between whites and both Hispanics and Asians, and economic and ethnic segregation of schools have risen over time. By contrast, racial residential segregation between whites and blacks and spatial inequality in community violence have declined.

This review suggests that the fault lines for spatial inequality may be gradually shifting in the United States. Whereas the peak of racial segregation, joblessness, and violent crime may have passed several decades ago, the rise of economic segregation may suggest that economic status will become an increasingly important dimension of urban inequality. Further, the focus on trends in spatial inequality should not distract from the finding that U.S. neighborhoods continue to feature severe levels of racial, ethnic, and economic segregation and high levels of inequality in violence, environmental hazards, and other features of communities thought to be most directly linked to the life chances of residents. In the following section, we present a conceptual model designed to explain the processes and mechanisms behind the causal effect of such unequal places on individuals' socioeconomic opportunities.

A MODEL OF HOW VARIATIONS IN THE SPATIAL OPPORTUNITY STRUCTURE GENERATE INEQUALITIES IN INDIVIDUALS' ACHIEVED SOCIOECONOMIC STATUS

We are interested in understanding how the space or spaces in which individuals are embedded influences their socioeconomic outcomes. We conceptualize this aspect of space as *spatial opportunity structure*, the panoply of markets, institutions, services, and other natural and human-made systems that have a geographic connection and play important roles in people's socioeconomic status achievements.[3] The spatial opportunity structure includes labor, housing, and financial markets; criminal justice, education, health, transportation, and social service systems; the natural and built environment; public and private institutional resources and services; social networks; forces of socialization and social control (collective norms, role models, peers); and local political systems. By achieved socioeconomic status here we mean earnings, wealth, and occupational attainment.

Various elements of the spatial opportunity structure operate at and vary across spatial scales, as demonstrated. This variation occurs across at least three distinct scales. Across neighborhoods, variations in safety, natural environment, peer groups, social control, institutions, social networks, and job accessibility occur. Across local political jurisdictions, health, education, recreation, and safety programs vary. Across metropolitan areas, the locations of employment of various types and associated wages, working conditions, and skill requirements vary and housing and other market conditions that affect individuals' opportunities for advancement differ.[4]

We view the spatial opportunity structure as affecting socioeconomic outcomes via *structuring opportunity* both directly and indirectly. It directly affects how, during a given span of time, a given set of personal attributes will pay off in terms of socioeconomic status achievements. The spatial opportunity structure indirectly affects over a longer span the set of attributes individuals bring to the opportunity structure. Some of these indirect effects require little or no individual volition to acquire, such as aspects of mental and physical health that may be passively acquired merely by living in the natural, built, and social environment and collective norms and local networks that influence what information people receive and how they evaluate it. In the case of children and youth, other indirect effects transpire through influences on the caregivers that affect the resources and parenting behaviors brought to bear in the household. A final indirect effect occurs by molding individual volition involved in decisions related to education, risky behaviors, marriage, fertility, labor force participation, illegal activities, and sociopolitical participation. Decisions regarding these domains are so crucial in determining socioeconomic

---

3. Similar notions of *opportunity structure* and *geography of opportunity* were first introduced by George Galster and Sean Killen (1995).

4. Of course, within any of these three scales contextual variations in all noted domains are entirely possible.

outcomes in our society that we label them *life decisions*. In the following section, we amplify and illustrate these concepts and relationships with the aid of a heuristic visual model.

A Heuristic Model of Achieved Socioeconomic Status

A visual model of our conceptual framework for understanding how space provides a foundation for inequalities in achieved status is presented in figure 1. To begin with the most basic and obvious relationship, an individual's attributes will play a fundamental role in producing markers of achieved socioeconomic status; this is represented by path A in figure 1. If the individuals in question are adults, we would expect that interpersonal variations in their current bundles of achievement-influencing attributes would explain substantial variation in their contemporaneously measured achieved socioeconomic status; in the case of children, current attributes would be predictive (though less precisely) of future achieved socioeconomic status at some point or points as adults. Some personal characteristics are essentially fixed over the lifetime of the individual, inasmuch as they are associated with the vagaries of conception and birth. Such fixed attributes would include, for example, genetic signature, place and year of birth, and many (though not all) characteristics of the individual's parents and ancestors. Other personal characteristics are (potentially) more malleable over a lifetime. Some may be acquired passively, such as through child-rearing activities of one's parents, as is portrayed in path B in figure 1. Other malleable attributes will be the product of previous decisions and actions by the given individual even though, once acquired, may no longer be malleable; this is portrayed as path C in figure 1. Some decisions—our life decisions just mentioned—are especially important in establishing a trajectory for achieved status outcomes.[5] These include actions related to employment, crime, child-rearing, cognitive and vocational skills, educational credentials, smoking, drinking, substance abuse and other aspects of health, and social networks. Of course, the norms, aspirations, information, and resources individuals bring to bear in a particular life decision-making situation is substantially influenced by multiple inputs supplied by their parents or caregivers, both currently and perhaps previously in their lives, as represented by path D in figure 1.

Spatial Opportunity Structure as Mediator Between Personal Attributes and Achieved Status

At this point in our exposition, we take all these fixed and malleable attributes as predetermined so we can isolate one crucial role played by the space where the individual is currently embedded. We posit that the spatial opportunity structure serves as a *mediator* between individuals' current characteristics and their socioeconomic status outcomes (see path A in figure 1). Because the spatial opportunity structure varies dramatically across and within metropolitan areas in the ways that it evaluates personal attributes in the process of translating them into achieved status, one's chances for such achievements will be enhanced or eroded depending on place of residence, work, and routine activity space. Several illustrations make our point. Metro areas with labor market actors that are more prone to discriminate on the bases of gender or ethnicity against those who have decided to apply for jobs will diminish the expected socioeconomic payoffs from

---

5. We recognize the voluminous literature on human decision-making and considerable debate over the most appropriate model (see review in Galster and Killen, 1995). We think it irrelevant for our model which particular view is taken, so long as one rejects the notion that these choices are purely instinctual or random, having no relationship with the social construction of a current and prospective reality. We think these choices may generally be described as based on *bounded rationality*: imperfect (perhaps even incorrect) information, subjective assessments, and varying degrees of dispassionate, analytical thought versus impulse and snap judgments contingent on personal context. Though our model has many features in common with the "rational actor" model of Erikson and Jonsson (1996) and Becker (2003) we stress that socio-spatial context is a prime source of information and values related to an individual's assessments of expected benefits and costs.

Figure 1. Conceptual Framework

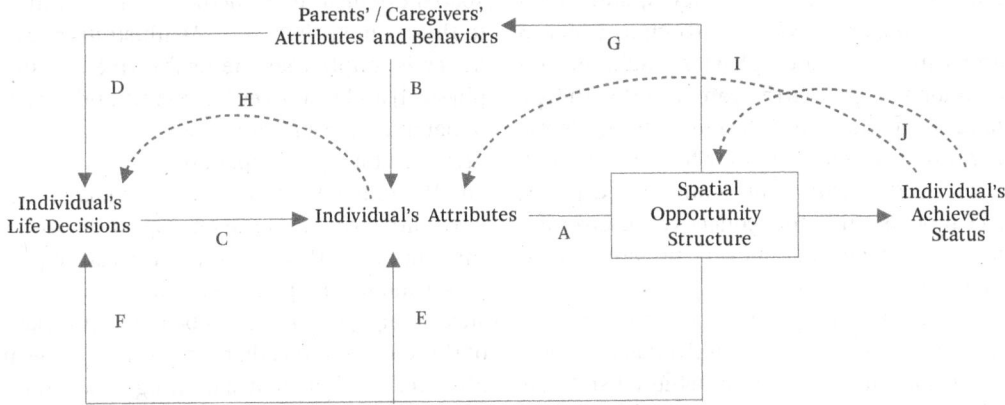

Source: Authors' compilation.

whatever attributes women and ethnic minorities bring to the workplace. Even the most attractive attributes from an employer's perspective may not yield a high income if the potential employee lives far from potential workplaces and cannot find a suitably fast and reliable form of commuter transportation. Under-resourced, poorly administered schools with weak teachers and a cadre of disruptive, violent peers will be less likely to leverage students' curiosity and native intelligence into literary and numerical competence and, ultimately, marketable educational credentials for those who have decided to get a diploma. Those with little to no work experience may find that neighborhoods dominated by illegal or underground markets will favorably evaluate some of their attributes (such as present orientation, predilection for violence) that were discounted in mainstream labor markets. Women living in neighborhoods dominated by patriarchal norms and collective socialization into rigid gender roles will be less able to convert even the most productive personality attributes and educational credentials into socioeconomic achievements in the larger society.

Spatial Opportunity Structure as a Modifier of Personal Attributes

As potent as the effects of the spatial opportunity structure as mediator may be, we think an often-overlooked yet powerful influence is exerted in three distinct ways through the passive and active acquisition or modification of personal attributes over time. First, through environmental exposure, it directly influences some attributes of individuals over which they may exercise little or no volition. Second, it directly influences the attributes of individuals over which they exercise considerable volition by shaping what they perceive is the most desirable, feasible option in the process of making life decisions. Third, in the case of children and youth, the spatial opportunity structure indirectly influences their attributes through induced changes in the resources, behaviors, and attitudes of their caregivers. Diagrammatically, we now turn our attention to paths E, F, and G portrayed in figure 1.

Personal attributes are constantly being molded by the physical and social environments in which a person lives, even if such molding has not been consciously chosen and may be unobserved by the individual; this is represented by path E in figure 1. Several examples for the physical and social scientific literature illustrate our point. We know, for example, how variations in air pollution can be associated with a range of health outcomes (McConnell et al. 2010; Lovasi et al. 2011). Lead associated with neighborhoods with older housing stock has been shown to cause permanent damage to children's cognitive functions and attention spans (Rau, Reyes, and Urzúa 2013). Exposure to violence (both as a victim and witness) creates physical, mental, and emotional responses that, among other things, have been shown to interfere with academic performance (Sharkey 2010; Sharkey et al. 2012, 2015). Neighborhood or school-based peers, role models, and other collective socialization forces can shape one's norms, preferences, aspirations, and behaviors.

As noted, an individual's attributes are also modified as a result of the individual's actions. Of primary importance for achieved status is what we termed life decisions. The spatial opportunity structure affects such decisions by shaping individuals' perceptions of what is the most desirable, feasible course of action; this relationship is portrayed in path F in figure 1. These decision-shaping effects of the spatial opportunity structure are transmitted by influencing: what information about the individual's options is provided, what the information objectively indicates about payoffs from these options, and how the information is subjectively evaluated by the individual. Local networks can affect the quantity and quality of information that an individual can access regarding the opportunity set. The notion of social isolation associated with minority neighborhoods of concentrated disadvantage (Wilson 1987) is illustrative. The collective norms operating within these networks can also shape which media of information transmission are considered more reliable sources of data about the opportunity structure. Neighborhood or school-based peers, role models, and other collective socialization forces can shape a person's norms and preferences, thereby altering the perceived prospective payoffs associated with various life decisions.

Finally, the spatial opportunity structure indirectly affects the attributes children and youth will exhibit by shaping the resources, attitudes, health, and parenting behaviors of their adult caregivers; this portrayed as path G in figure 1. In our discussion of paths E and F, we describe the various mechanisms of how spatial context can affect a person's attributes; our point here is simply to note that when such persons happen to be caregivers they become the medium through which the impacts of the spatial opportunity structure are transmitted to those under their care. As illustration, evidence is ample that the health (mental and physical) and resources (economic and social) of parents have a profound effect on how children develop in multiple domains (Haveman and Wolfe 1994). Thus, should the spatial opportunity structure have an impact on any of these domains through any of the causal processes modeled, the indirect causal link to the succeeding generation will be made. A variant of this connection is that caregivers have been observed to alter their parenting styles in response to their perceptions of the spatial context in which their children must operate (Galster and Santiago 2006).

Feedback Effects
To complete our conceptual model we consider several feedback effects (see dotted lines in figure 1). Once a particular life decision has been made, the associated attribute becomes part of the individual's "résumé" (path H in figure 1). This change in the portfolio of attributes will affect the individual's opportunities in the future, perhaps irreversibly, depending on the life decision in question. Certainly the acquisition of educational credentials provides a lifelong change in one's feasible set of opportunities; so does being convicted of a felony. Less obviously, prior life decisions may reshape individuals' aspirations, preferences, and evaluative frames. For example, a decision to raise children may intensify aversion to risky entrepreneurial ventures or participation in illegal activities. Similarly, if choices to seek long-term employment have consistently been frustrated, willingness to invest in human capital development for the future and respect for civil authority may wane, leading to a reevaluation of feasible options in the opportunity set. A decision to participate in gang activities may expose those individuals to different attitudinal and aspirational norms that likely alter their assessments of many options in life decision set.

What one has achieved at a given moment in terms of markers of socioeconomic status (income, wealth, and occupation) also generates two feedback effects. The first is that the degree of achieved status shapes the bundle of attributes the person will develop in the future by altering the degree of financial constraint on obtaining certain attributes (path I in figure 1). For example, greater accumulated wealth by a certain time in life permits people henceforth to buy superior training and credentials, maintain better health and free themselves from constraints on employment by offloading some child-care responsibilities on to hired caretakers. One will be exposed to different sources of information, collective norms, peer effects, and role models in the workplace depending on occupation.

Finally, and perhaps most fundamentally, achieved status affects what spatial opportunity structure one confronts (path J in figure 1). Clearly, for most households in the United States that do not receive subsidies for housing, their residential location and associated characteristics of the spatial opportunity structure will depend on their ability to pay for housing. Residential sorting on the bases of income and wealth is to be expected in an economy in which the market performs the main resource allocation functions. Other exposures to the spatial opportunity structure (via interfaces with schools, transportation systems, retail shopping, and workplaces) are similarly molded by ability to pay for products and services. Households with the greatest financial means select what they perceive as the most desirable niches in which to live and undertake their routine activities, which are ceteris paribus the most highly priced. The financial exclusivity of these spaces can be abetted by a variety of zoning codes and other development restrictions if the well-heeled can politically dominate a local jurisdiction to serve their interests. At the other extreme, households with little to no market power are relegated by default to the least expensive, residual pockets of the spatial opportunity structure: slums, ghettos, and the streets.

Cumulative Causation and Path Dependencies
This model should make it obvious that we view the processes involved in achieving socioeconomic status as cumulative, path dependent, and (typically) mutually reinforcing over time. One's stock of attributes measured at any given time will be shaped by the niche or niches of the spatial opportunity structure they have experienced in the past, both directly and indirectly through its influence on previous life decisions and actions by caregivers. Going forward, this set of attributes will constrain (to a greater or lesser extent depending on the attribute bundle and past socioeconomic achievements) the perceived life decision options and associated expected payoffs. By way of illustration, a person who has dropped out of high school and served jail time for being convicted of a felony will have far fewer options in the future for socioeconomic status achievements than a person who has a graduate degree and no brushes with the law; and expected financial payoffs associated with any similar life decision options they share (such as working full time) will differ significantly. These differences in opportunities will in turn lead both people down different paths of sequential life decisions in the future. Abetting this mutually reinforcing sequence of decisions over the life course is the financial effect on what parts of space one can afford to access. Those whose paths have resulted in substantial achievements in status early in life can afford to occupy more privileged niches later on, providing themselves and their offspring with even better attributes and opportunities, which in turn will spawn even more productive life decisions.

Evolution of the Spatial Opportunity Structure
This description has taken the housing market, a prime driver of the spatial opportunity structure, as given. From the perspective of an individual decision-maker, the assumption is reasonable. From a longer-term, general equilibrium perspective, the housing market in particular and the spatial opportunity structure in general is constantly evolving, partly in response to how the population has been sorting themselves as housing demanders across the metropolitan area. As documented earlier, this sorting process has produced a considerable racial and economic segregation and wide variations in many other contextual indicators. It is beyond the scope of this model to consider

all these forces shaping the spatial opportunity structure; a few illustrative comments are in order regardless.

Some of the alterations in the spatial opportunity structure may be exogenous to households, such as a technologically or international trade-induced industrial restructuring. Other alterations, however, may be influenced by the aggregate behaviors of households within a metropolitan area that have been produced by a previous period's opportunity structure. For example, the poor quality of the local public school system serving a neighborhood may constrain children's ability to gain good skills and credentials. Yet, if many parents decide to participate in a collective political process, the result may be a reallocation of fiscal resources to improve the local schools. The educational background of the parents of students living in the district is also an important constraint on school outcomes. Inasmuch as better-educated parents create more intellectually stimulating home environments, better monitor the completion of homework, and demonstrate more interest in what goes on in school, the quality of the classroom environment will be improved for all students. So if, in response to inferior public education, better-educated parents move out of the district or enroll their children in private schools, the constraints on all parents who remain in the public school system becomes tighter. For example, housing developers may cater to parents with substantial status by building new, high-quality subdivisions that create exclusive niches in the spatial opportunity structure. After incorporation, these niches may provide a wide range of attractive amenities and public services that encourage the success of the children living there.

Thus, those who are successful in one round of spatial status competition are in a better financial position in the next round in the evolving structure, thereby improving their and their children's odds of perpetuating this success and of generating market forces that alter the structure itself over time. Conversely, those who early in life make little headway in their status are relegated to inferior niches in the spatial opportunity structure, where their subsequent choices tend to perpetuate their inferior status. When society as a whole views some of these decisions as social problems concentrated in low-status niches, the larger opportunity structure can be altered in many ways. Those with financial means move away from neighborhoods and schools of concentrated disadvantage, weakening the local retail sector and the entry-level job opportunities they provide. The same moves may strain the financial capacity of the local political jurisdiction, forcing a retrenchment in public services. Certain locales can thus generate a self-reinforcing spiral of spatial decline and individual impoverishment.

Interim Summary of Heuristic Model
Within the framework summarized in figure 1, it is easy to comprehend how space plays a vital role not only as a foundation for inequality but also for perpetuating intergenerational inequality. Through cumulative causation and path dependency, those with the greatest status achieved early in life can situate themselves in a segment of the opportunity structure that enhances their prospects for continued success and provides their offspring with improved chances for doing the same. Over time, the spatial opportunity structure in turn evolves in ways that further benefit those with the greatest achieved status. By contrast, those who start with little typically are stuck in place, both geographically and socioeconomically, as Sharkey and Elwert (2011) document.[6]

EVIDENCE ON EFFECTS OF SPATIAL CONTEXT ON INDIVIDUAL OUTCOMES
The second claim motivating this paper is that the spatial organization of social and economic inequality maintains or reinforces inequalities across multiple domains of social and economic status. Obtaining unbiased, meaningful estimates of the independent, causal effect of spatial components of an individual's existential context is challenging (for an extensive discussion, see Galster 2008). Per-

---

6. The normative underpinnings of the geographic opportunity structure are presented by Dawkins (forthcoming).

haps the most contentious aspect, however, is the issue of geographic selection bias (Manski 1995, 2000; Duncan, Connell, and Klebanov 1997; Ginther, Haveman, and Wolfe 2000; Dietz 2002). The central issue is that individuals being studied (or their parents) likely have unmeasured motivations, behaviors, and skills related to their own (or their children's) socioeconomic prospects and move from and to certain types of places as a consequence of these unobserved characteristics. Any observed relationship between geographic conditions and outcomes for adults or their offspring may therefore be biased.[7] Skeptics may rightly argue that what is being measured is simply another impact of (unmeasured) individual attributes, not the impact of the space in which the individual resides.

Estimating Causal Impacts of Spatial Context

Three general empirical approaches have been adopted in response to the challenge of geographic selection bias. The most common approach consists of a variety of econometric techniques applied to observational (nonexperimentally generated) longitudinal datasets involving individuals and their spatial contexts. The two other, less common approaches use natural or experimental designs to generate quasi-random or random assignments of households to neighborhoods.

Econometric Models Based on Observational Data

Most studies of spatial context effects have used observational data collected from surveys of individual households in a variety of places as a result of mundane factors associated with normal market transactions. The subset that has tried to overcome geographic selection bias uses one or more of the following approaches (Galster and Hedman 2013):

- Difference models based on longitudinal data. The biases from unobserved, time-invariant individual characteristics are eliminated by measuring differences between two periods in outcomes and spatial contexts (Bolster et al. 2007; Galster et al. 2008; Musterd et al. 2008; van Ham and Manley 2009; Galster, Andersson, and Musterd 2010).

- Fixed-effect models based on longitudinal data. Unobserved, time-invariant characteristics of individuals that may lead to both geographic selection and outcomes are measured by individual dummy variables (Weinberg, Reagan, and Yankow 2004; Musterd, Galster, and Andersson 2012).

- Instrumental variables for spatial context characteristics. Proxy variables for geographic characteristics are devised that only vary according to attributes exogenous to the individual and thus are uncorrelated with their unobserved characteristics (Duncan, Connell, and Klebanov 1997; Crowder and South 2003; Crowder and Teachman 2004; Galster et al. 2007; Kling, Liebman, and Katz 2007; Ludwig et al. 2008; Cutler, Glaeser, and Vigdor 2008; Sari 2012; Hedman and Galster 2013; Damm 2014).

- Residents of same block. If sorting on individual unobservables at the census block level is minimal, then the impacts of networks among these very localized neighbors should be free of geographic selection bias (Bayer, Ross, and Topa 2008)

- Timing of events. Individuals moving into certain, well-defined types of places (such as public housing developments) after an event being investigated (such as a school achievement test) are likely to share common unobservable characteristics with individuals moving into the same places just before the event, so the short-term effect of the place can be measured by comparing the two groups' outcomes (Weinhardt 2014); analogously, Sharkey (2010) and Sharkey et al. (2012, 2014) address the selection bias

---

7. The direction of the bias has been the subject of debate, both Christopher Jencks and Susan Mayer (1990) and Marta Tienda (1991) arguing that measured contextual impacts are biased upward, and Jeanne Brooks-Gunn, Greg Duncan, and Lawrence Aber (1997) arguing the opposite. Lisa Gennetian, Lisa Sanbonmatsu, and Jens Ludwig (2011) show that these biases can be substantial enough to seriously distort conclusions about the magnitude and direction of context effects.

problem by exploiting the variation in the timing of local homicides compared with interview assessments for a sample of children in families that have previously selected the same neighborhood.

- Propensity score matching. Individuals who are closely matched on a wide variety of observable characteristics that predict their similar residential mobility behavior are likely to be well matched on their unobservable characteristics as well; comparisons between matches of differences in their spatial contexts and individual outcomes should thus provide unbiased causal evidence (Harding 2003).
- Inverse probability of treatment weighting (IPTW). Like propensity score matching, IPTW uses a model of selection into the treatment status to predict the probability that an individual is in the treatment state in which the individual is observed. A weighted pseudo-sample is then constructed in which the treatment and control groups are balanced on observables. IPTW models selection into treatment status at multiple time points, allowing for unbiased estimates of treatment effects over time in the presence of observed confounders that vary over time and may be endogenous to the treatment. Sharkey and Felix Elwert (2011) use this method in combination with a formal sensitivity analysis to estimate the cumulative effect of multigenerational exposure to neighborhood poverty on cognitive development.
- Nonmovers. Analyzing how exogenous neighborhood changes induce different outcomes for individuals who do not move during the analysis period arguably avoids the mobility selection issue (Sharkey 2012; Galster and Hedman 2013; Gibbons, Silva, and Weinhardt 2013, 2014).

None of these econometric fixes to observational datasets are without challenge. For example, difference models reduce statistical power by shrinking variation in the outcome variable and assume that change relationships are independent of starting conditions. Fixed-effect models assume that the individual dummies adequately capture the bundle of unobservables for all times during the panel and that the effect of this bundle remains constant during the panel. Instrumental variables must be both valid and strong. Micro-scale investigations are limited to neighborhood effect mechanisms than operate only at the small geographic scales and assume no residential sorting on unobservables at that scale. Relying on the timing of moves immediately before and after and event assumes that context effects operate quickly after exposure. Propensity score matching requires assumptions about the strong relationship between unobservable and observable characteristics of individuals. Those who do not move may be exhibiting residential selection based on unobserved characteristics.

Quasi-Random Assignment
Natural Experiments
It is sometimes possible to observe nonmarket interventions into households' residential locations that mimic random assignment. In the United States, such experiments typically have been based on court-ordered, public housing racial-ethnic desegregation programs (Rosenbaum 1991; Briggs 1997; Fauth, Leventhal, and Brooks-Gunn 2007), regional fair-share housing requirements (Schwartz 2010; Casciano and Massey 2012) or scattered-site public housing assignments (Santiago et al. 2014). In Canada and Europe, they have involved allocation of tenants to social housing (Oreopoulos 2003; Damm 2009, 2014; Rotger and Galster 2015) or placement of refugees in particular locales (Edin, Fredricksson, and Åslund 2003; Åslund and Fredricksson 2009).

Although these natural experiments may indeed provide some exogenous variation in locations, the geographic selection problem is unlikely to be avoided completely. In most cases, program staff makes assignments and participants have some nontrivial latitude in which locations they choose, both initially and subsequent to original placement. Moreover, programs that involve rental vouchers (Gautreaux, for example) entail selection in who succeeds in locating rental vacancies in qualifying locations and signing leases within the requisite period. These various potential selection processes raise the possibility that low-income families who succeed in living persistently in low-poverty neighborhoods were especially motivated, resourceful and, perhaps, courageous—traits poorly measured by researchers but likely ones that would help them and their children succeed irrespective of their spatial contexts. Additional empirical problems can arise if sampled subjects move quickly from their quasi-randomly assigned dwellings to another location, thereby minimizing exposure to measured context and potentially confounding consequences because moving itself can be disruptive. As time passes, the randomness of location can erode as selection of who stays in initially assigned places and who moves away comes into play. Finally, limitations are possible in the range of places to which study participants moved or were assigned because of where available private rental or subsidized housing was located, thereby reducing the power of statistical tests to discern context effects.

Random Assignment Experiments
Many researchers advocate a random assignment experimental approach for best avoiding biases from geographic selection. Data on outcomes that can be produced by an experimental design whereby individuals or households are randomly assigned to different geographic contexts is indeed, in theory, the preferred method. In this regard, the U.S. Moving to Opportunity (MTO) demonstration has been touted conventionally as the study from which to draw conclusions about the magnitude of neighborhood effects (Smolensky 2007; Sanbonmatsu et al. 2011; Ludwig 2012). The MTO research design randomly assigned public housing residents who volunteered to participate in one of three groups: controls that got no voucher but stayed in public housing in disadvantaged neighborhoods, recipients of rental vouchers with no restrictions, and recipients of rental vouchers and relocation assistance who had to move to census tracts with less than 10 percent poverty rates and remain for at least a year.

Debate over the power of MTO as an unambiguous test of spatial context effects has been considerable (see Clampet-Lundquist and Massey 2008; Sampson 2008; Burdick-Will et al. 2011; Briggs, Popkin, and Goering 2010; Briggs et al. 2008, 2011; Sanbonmatsu et al. 2011; Ludwig 2012). The debate focuses on five domains. First, although MTO randomly assigned participants to treatment groups, it randomly assigned characteristics neither of neighborhoods initially occupied by voucher holders (except maximum poverty rates for the experimental group) nor of neighborhoods in which participants in all three groups moved subsequently. Thus, a question remains about the degree to which geographic selection on unobservables persists. Second, MTO may not have created adequate duration of exposure to neighborhood conditions by any group at any location to observe much treatment effect. Third, MTO overlooked the potentially indelible developmental effects on adult experimental group participants who spent their childhoods in disadvantaged neighborhoods. Fourth, it appears that even experimental MTO movers rarely moved out of predominantly African American–occupied neighborhoods near those of concentrated disadvantage and achieved only modest changes in school quality and job accessibility. Thus, they may not have experienced sizable enhancements in their geographic opportunity structures. For these reasons, MTO may not have provided definitive evidence about the potential effects on low-income families from prolonged residence in multiply advantaged neighborhoods, despite its theoretical promise and conventional wisdom.

In summary, none of the three approaches to measuring effects of spatial context has proven limitation-free and unambiguously superior. Nevertheless, they as a group offer the strongest, plausibly causal evidence to date on the topic at hand. In our review, therefore, we synthesize findings only from these methodologically rigorous studies that use one or more of the approaches.

An Overview of the Scientific Literature on Spatial Context Effects
We organize our review by six outcome domains that clearly are related to socioeconomic opportunity: cognitive and behavioral development, educational performance and attain-

ment, teen fertility, physical and mental health, labor force participation and earnings, and crime. We emphasize at the outset that the scope, diversity and complexity of the relevant literature is vast in comparison with the length imitations of this paper. Thus, we do not attempt to review findings in any detail, reconcile conflicting results, nor attempt any formal meta-analysis. Instead, our aim is basic: in each outcome domain we tally the number of (methodologically rigorous) studies that find substantial, statistically significant effects of at least some aspect of spatial context (for at least some set of individuals) and those that do not.

Cognitive Skills and Academic Performance

Recent meta-analysis of the international literature (Niewenhuis and Hooimeijer 2014) and a comprehensive review of the U.S. literature (Sharkey and Faber 2014) find nontrivial neighborhood effects on the development of cognitive skills, academic performance, and educational attainment. Our assessment of the methodologically sophisticated literature reaches a similar conclusion, though the magnitude of the neighborhood effect likely varies across individuals and groups.

Measures of cognitive skills have been used to assess evidence for neighborhood effects frequently over the past twenty years (for reviews, see Sastry 2012; Sharkey and Faber 2014), but fewer studies have taken steps to address the problem of selection bias. Two studies have modeled selection into poor neighborhoods and then used inverse probability of treatment weighting to identify the impact of long-term exposure to neighborhood poverty on cognitive skill development. Using data from Chicago, Sampson, Sharkey, and Stephen Raudenbush (2008) find that living in neighborhoods of concentrated disadvantage leads to substantial declines in reading and language skills assessed years later. Sharkey and Elwert (2011) use national data from the Panel Study of Income Dynamics and find that family exposure to neighborhood poverty over consecutive generations reduces children's performance on tests of broad reading skills and applied problems skills by more than half of a standard deviation. A formal sensitivity analysis showed that the effect of multigenerational neighborhood poverty was robust to substantial potential bias arising from unobserved selection processes.

As described, Sharkey and his colleagues exploit the timing of incidents of violence to identify the acute impact of exposure to violence in children's environments on their performance on cognitive skills assessments. Sharkey (2010) finds that exposure to a recent homicide within close proximity to a child's home reduced the performance of African American children on tests of reading, language, and applied problems by more than a third of a standard deviation. In a subsequent study, Sharkey and his colleagues (2012) find similar impacts of recent exposure to nearby homicides on children's performance on vocabulary assessments as well as impacts on assessments of impulse control and attention.

Experimental evidence comes from the Moving to Opportunity program, and shows mixed and complex results. Several years after the experiment began and ten to fifteen years later, no effects of the intervention were found for the full sample on assessments of cognitive skills (Sanbonmatsu et al. 2006, 2011). However, the experiment generated positive effects on the reading assessments of African Americans across all cities four to seven years after implementation (Sanbonmatsu et al. 2006); positive effects on reading and math scores for the full sample of boys and girls among families that remained in low-poverty neighborhoods for longer durations of time (Turner et al. 2012); and strong positive effects for children in the Baltimore and Chicago sites, which persisted over ten to fifteen years only for the Chicago sample (Burdick-Will et al. 2011; Ludwig, Ladd, and Duncan 2001; Sanbonmatsu et al. 2011).

The research literature on academic outcomes and educational attainment is also large. Many studies using one or more of the described econometric techniques to obtain plausibly causal estimates from observational datasets have been conducted. Methods include propensity score matching (Harding 2003), sibling comparisons (Aaronson 1998; Plotnick and Hoffman 1999), fixed-effects (Plotnick and Hoffman 1999; Vartanian and Gleason

1999; Jargowsky and El Komi 2011), instrumental variables (Duncan, Connell, and Klebanov 1997; Crowder and South 2003; Galster et al. 2007), nonmovers (Gibbons, Silva, and Weinhardt 2014), and timing of events (Sharkey et al. 2014; Weinhardt 2014; Carlson and Cowan 2015). All of these find strong residential neighborhood effects on variously measured educational outcomes, with only two exceptions: Plotnick and Hoffman (1999), using U.S. data and Gibbons, Silva, and Weinhardt (2013) and Weinhardt (2014) using U.K. data.

Numerous studies based on natural experiments also are relevant in this outcome domain. These include data based on Gautreaux and Yonkers public housing desegregation programs (Rosenbaum 1995; Fauth, Leventhal, and Brooks-Gunn 2007; DeLuca et al. 2010), public housing revitalization programs (Jacob 2004; Clampet-Lundquist 2007), assignment to public housing waiting lists (Ludwig et al. 2011), inclusionary zoning mandates (Schwartz 2010; Casciano and Massey 2012), combined assisted housing-education programs (Tach et al. 2016) and public housing assignments (Santiago et al. 2014; Galster et al. 2015, 2016; Galster, Santiago, and Stack 2015; Galster and Santiago, forthcoming). These natural quasi-experiments provided only one example of no observed context effects (Jacob 2004),[8] though several of the observed effects in other studies were contingent on gender or ethnicity.

Recent evidence from MTO on college attendance is relevant to the discussion of neighborhood effects on educational attainment. Chetty, Nathaniel Hendren, and Lawrence Katz's (2015) reanalysis of MTO data found that moving to a lower-poverty neighborhood significantly increased college attendance rates for children who were younger than thirteen when their families moved to the neighborhoods, compared with experimental group children who moved when they were older or children in the other study groups.

Risky Behaviors and Violence
We now turn to evidence on developmental disorders and risky behaviors. The Denver public housing natural experiment is exploited by Anna Maria Santiago and her colleagues (2014) to estimate neighborhood effects on the hazard of low-income African American and Latino children being diagnosed with a neurodevelopmental disorder (retardation, learning disabilities, developmental delays, autism, ADD-ADHD). Several aspects of neighborhood context (especially safety, prestige, nativity and ethnic mix, neurotoxin pollution) proved strongly and robustly predictive. Neurocognitive developmental disorders were not investigated directly.

As for risky behaviors, we find only six studies of context effects involving the described econometric approaches to overcoming geographic selection; most identified effects on risky behaviors except smoking. Using propensity score matching, Jennifer Ahern and her colleagues (2008) find that an individual's propensity to drink was related to the neighborhood's culture of alcohol use; Scott Novak and his colleagues (2006), however, find only a small, barely discernable effect of retail tobacco outlet density on youth cigarette smoking. Markus Jokela (2014) uses the fixed-effect modeling approach and finds no impact of neighborhood disadvantage on the probability of smoking. Stephen Gibbons, Olmo Silva, and Felix Weinhardt (2013) also used fixed effects but find that the share of neighbors from lower-status backgrounds increases the chances of teen boys engaging in anti-social behaviors like graffiti, vandalism, shoplifting, fighting, or public disturbance. Two approaches using inverse probability weighting (marginal structural model) methods find that neighborhood poverty is strongly related to the odds of binge drinking (Cerdá et al. 2010) and drug injecting (Nandi et al. 2010).

Only three examples of either the random or quasi-random neighborhood assignment approaches are relevant to risky behaviors. Strong context effects on risky behaviors appear in both studies but are contingent on gender, ethnicity, and timing. Early MTO findings suggest that substantial reductions on girls' rates of risky behaviors and boys' drug use can

---

8. Little context effect was observed here because the experimental households did not use their housing vouchers to change their neighborhood characteristics significantly.

be attributed to residence in lower-poverty neighborhoods. However, after initial declines in risky behavior, boys living in lower-poverty neighborhoods four to seven years after their first move were more likely to reengage in risky behaviors (Sanbonmatsu et al. 2011). By the end of the demonstration project, girls assigned to low-poverty neighborhoods were less likely to have serious behavioral problems. No group differences in more serious antisocial behaviors were significant, however (Sanbonmatsu et al. 2011). Santiago and her colleagues' analysis of data from a Denver natural experiment reveals that cumulative exposure to multiple dimensions of neighborhood context (especially safety, social status, and ethnic and nativity composition) affected the hazard of adolescents running away from home, using aggressive or violent behavior, or initiating marijuana use, though with substantial ethnic heterogeneity of relationships. Finally, Magdalena Cerdá and her colleagues (2012) examine the impact of a new transportation infrastructure intervention in Medellin, Colombia, on violent behavior. and find that investment decreased violence significantly.

Teen Fertility

Very few studies have used any of the described statistical techniques to account for potential geographic selection bias confounding observational data on the fertility patterns of youth and their neighborhood contexts. The two exceptions are Robert Plotnick and Saul Hoffman (1999) and David Harding (2003). Plotnick and Hoffman find that neighborhood effects on teen childbearing disappeared when using a model of fixed effects with only observations of sisters, whereas Harding finds that neighborhood effects remained significant despite propensity score matching and argues that selection bias would need to be unreasonably large to rule out causal effects of neighborhood socioeconomic conditions on teen childbearing.

The evidence from natural and random assignment experiments is more consistent. Santiago and her colleagues (2014) find that hazards of teenage childbearing and fathering were greater in neighborhoods with higher property crime rates, lower occupational prestige and higher percentages of Latinos, though strength of effect depended on gender and ethnicity. Results from the MTO demonstration show that girls in the experimental group whose parent or parents moved to low-poverty neighborhoods felt safer and less pressured to engage in early sexual activity (and thus, by implication, early pregnancy and childbearing) in their new neighborhoods (Popkin, Leventhal, and Weismann 2010; Sanbonmatsu et al. 2011). Chetty, Hendren, and Katz (2015) analyze the subset of MTO experimental children who moved to low-poverty neighborhoods before they were thirteen and observe that they, indeed, were less likely to become single parents.

Physical and Mental Health

Michael Oakes and his colleagues (2015) recently completed a comprehensive review of the empirical literature related to neighborhood effects on health. After reviewing 1,369 articles, using criteria similar criteria to ours, they conclude that only about 1 percent produced plausibly causal estimates. A handful use the described statistical techniques applied to observational data and find that the results, though somewhat inconsistent, do not point to strong context effects on health. Three studies based on propensity score methods demonstrated no or barely discernable effects on minority infant mortality using different measures of neighborhood (Schootman et al. 2007; Johnson, Oakes, and Anderton 2008; Hearst, Oakes, and Johnson 2008). Based on inverse probability weighting (marginal structural model) methods, researchers have determined that neighborhood poverty was related to mortality in a strong but nonlinear way (Do, Wang, and Elliott 2013) but had mixed effects on self-assessed health and disability (Glymour et al. 2010). Finally, Jokela (2014) uses the fixed-effect modeling approach and finds no impact of neighborhood disadvantage on self-rated health, mental health and physical functioning, and amount of physical activity, instead finding evidence of selection of those with poorer health into more disadvantaged neighborhoods.

The random assignment experimental evidence here is also mixed but shows impacts on some health outcomes. MTO results show no significant differences in child asthma rates among groups assigned to neighborhoods with differing poverty rates, but does show effects on adult obesity and diabetes rates (Ludwig et al. 2011) and much lower stress levels among adults and children among those assigned initially to low-poverty neighborhoods (Sanbonmatsu et al. 2011). Findings for mental health suggested neighborhood effects but their size and direction were extremely varied, depending on lag of measurement after assignment, gender, and age (see Leventhal and Brooks-Gunn 2003; Kessler et al. 2014). Stephanie Moulton, Laura Peck, and Keri-Nicole Dillman (2014) analyze the subset of MTO experimental households who lived for substantial periods in low-poverty neighborhoods and conclude that health benefits may be much larger for that group.

The few natural experiments involving health outcomes consistently find neighborhood effects, at least on selected health indicators. Debra Cohen and her colleagues (2006) use exogenous shocks in neighborhood alcohol outlet density associated with the 1992 Los Angeles riots as a causal identification strategy and find strong impacts on neighborhood gonorrhea rates. Mark Votruba and Jeffrey Kling (2009) analyze data from the Gautreaux public housing relocation program. They find that when young, low-income African American men relocated to higher-education neighborhoods their all-cause and homicide mortality rates dropped relative to those moving to more disadvantaged areas. Finally, Santiago and her colleagues (2014) find strong neighborhood effects on the diagnoses of several child and adolescent health problems (asthma, obesity) using data from the Denver public housing natural experiment, although the relationships often depended on gender and ethnicity and in some cases manifested nonlinear thresholds. Asthma problems, for example, arose sooner for low-income, minority children residing in neighborhoods that had more property crime, lower occupational prestige, and higher concentrations of air pollution.

Labor Force Participation and Earnings
Most investigators find neighborhood effects on labor market outcomes when using one of the discussed econometric techniques on nonexperimental, observational datasets. Several studies using U.S. data (Weinberg, Reagan, and Yankow 2004; Dawkins, Shen, and Sanchez 2005; Cutler, Glaeser, and Vigdor 2008; Bayer, Ross, and Topa 2008; Sharkey 2012), several using Swedish data (Galster et al. 2008; Galster, Andersson, and Musterd 2010, 2015, 2016; Musterd, Galster, and Andersson 2012; Hedman and Galster 2013), one Danish study (Damm 2014) and one French study (Sari 2012) find nontrivial neighborhood effects on various adult labor market outcomes such as income and employment rates. One U.S.-based study (Plotnick and Hoffman 1999) and three U.K.-based analyses (Bolster et al. 2007; Propper et al. 2007; van Ham and Manley 2010) find minor, if any, neighborhood effects, and instead suggest geographic selection dominates.

Several researchers have probed the effect of spatial context on labor market outcomes exploiting the quasi-random assignment occurring in natural experiments. Studies in the United States (Rosenbaum 1991, 1995; Rubinowitz and Rosenbaum 2000; DeLuca et al. 2010; Galster, Santiago, and Lucero 2015a, 2015b; Galster et al. 2015; Chyn 2016), in Sweden (Edin, Fredriksson, and Åslund 2003; Åslund and Fredricksson 2009), and in Denmark (Damm 2009, 2014) all find evidence of strong neighborhood effects on several measures of adult and teen labor market outcomes in their analyses. The only finding of a trivial neighborhood effect using this approach came from a Canadian natural experiment study (Oreopoulos 2003).

Virtually no investigations using MTO data uncovered any substantial short- or long-term context effects on teen or adult labor market outcomes (for example, Ludwig, Duncan, and Pinkston 2005; Katz, Kling, and Liebman 2001; Ludwig, Ladd, and Duncan 2001; Ludwig, Duncan, and Hirschfield 2001; Orr et al. 2003; Kling, Leibman, and Katz 2007; Ludwig et al. 2008; Sanbonmatsu et al. 2011; Ludwig 2012). Three exceptions are notable. Susan Clampet-Lundquist and Douglas Massey (2008) and Margery Turner and her colleagues (2012) analyze the subset of MTO experimental households who lived for extended periods in low-poverty neighborhoods and find that their adult employment and earnings outcomes are substantially better than those of the control group. Chetty, Hendren, and Katz (2015) analyze the subset of MTO experimental children who moved to low-poverty neighborhoods before they were thirteen and observed that they had significantly higher earnings as young adults than either experimental group children who moved after age thirteen or children from the other study groups.

Crime

Six recent studies provide consistent evidence concerning the strong (if heterogeneous by gender) causal impact of geographic context on criminality. Mark Livingston and his colleagues (2014) use temporal lags and neighborhood fixed effects identify the effect of the share of criminal offenders resident in Glasgow postal code areas. They find that higher neighborhood shares of residents committing offenses during a quarter strongly predicted the probability of first-time violent and property offenses among residents in the subsequent quarter.

Four natural experiments are relevant here. Exploiting the quasi-randomness of assignment to public housing in Denver, Santiago and her colleagues (2014) find that low-income Latino and African American youth had greater hazards of engaging in violent behaviors in neighborhoods with lower occupational prestige and higher property crime rates, though with gendered impacts. Anna Damm and Christian Dustmann (2014) use the Danish dispersed settlement policy for refugees to identify causal impacts of municipal characteristics on youth criminality. They find that the share in a municipality of those age fifteen to twenty-five who were convicted of a crime during the year the family was assigned there strongly raised the probability of young male (but not female) refugees being convicted of a crime (especially for violent crimes and younger teens) during subsequent years. Gabriel Rotger and Galster (2015) use exogenous assignment to social housing in Copenhagen to identify strong causal effects of the prior drug offending characteristics of the housing development's residents at time of assignment on the odds of individuals ages fifteen through twenty-five who had just moved in committing property and drug crimes over the next two years. Stephen Billings, David Deming, and Stephen Ross (2016) study with natural experimental data the determinants of youth crime of fourteen-year-old students in Mecklenburg County, North Carolina. They demonstrate that peer effects on criminal behavior only arise when school peers (of the same race and gender) live less than a half-mile from each other and that the effects are stronger when neighbors are assigned to the same grade.

Finally, modest evidence indicates context effects on male criminality from MTO. Early impact evaluations indicate fewer arrests among males from families randomly assigned to low-poverty neighborhoods (Katz, Kling, and Liebman 2001; Ludwig, Duncan, and Hirshfeld 2001). These effects appeared to diminish and even reverse over time, however (Kling, Ludwig, and Katz 2005; Sanbonmatsu et al. 2011).

Findings

Table 1 summarizes the findings on the number of (methodologically rigorous) studies that have found substantial, statistically significant effects of spatial context (for at least some set of individuals) and those that have not, by outcome domain. The tally makes it clear that the preponderance of evidence in every outcome domain is that multiple aspects of spatial context exert important causal influences over a wide range of outcomes related to socioeconomic opportunity, though which aspects are most powerful depends on the outcome and the gender and ethnicity of the individuals in question.

EMPIRICAL GAPS IN THE STUDY OF SPATIAL INEQUALITY

Trends showing the rise of inequality in income and wealth have reached the mainstream as national and world leaders, policymakers, and the public have become increasingly focused on inequality in economic status as a defining issue of our time. Our goal in this introduction, and in the issue as a whole, is to shed light on the spatial dimensions of inequality. We argue that space is a particularly severe, and underappreciated, dimension of

Table 1. Conclusions from Causal Analyses of Neighborhood Effects

Significant Effects	No Effects
Cognitive and behavioral development	
Ahern et al. 2008; Cerda et al. 2010; Nandi et al. 2010; Sanbonmatsu et al. 2011; Cerda et al. 2012; Gibbons, Silva, and Weinhardt 2013; Santiago et al. 2014, this volume	Novak et al. 2006; Jokela 2014
Educational performance and attainment	
Rosenbaum 1995; Duncan, Connell, and Klebanov 1997; Vartanian and Gleason 1999; Crowder and South 2003; Clampet-Lundquist 2007; Fauth, Leventhal, and Brooks-Gunn 2007; Galster et al. 2007; DeLuca et al. 2010; Schwartz 2010; Sharkey and Sampson 2010; Jargowsky and El Komi 2011; Sharkey et al. 2012, 2014; Casciano and Massey 2012; Gibbons, Silva, and Weinhardt 2014; Santiago et al. 2014; Carlson and Cowan 2015; Chetty, Hendren, and Katz 2015; Galster et al. 2015, 2016; Galster, Santiago, and Stack 2015; Tach et al. 2016; Galster and Santiago, forthcoming	Plotnick and Hoffman 1999; Ludwig, Ladd, and Duncan 2001; Jacob 2004; Sanbonmatsu et al. 2006, 2011; Kling, Liebman, and Katz, 2007; Gibbons, Silva, and Weinhardt 2013; Weinhardt 2014
Teen fertility	
Harding 2003; Popkin, Leventhal and Weismann 2010; Sanbonmatsu et al. 2011; Santiago et al. 2014; Chetty, Hendren and Katz 2015; Galster and Santiago, forthcoming	Plotnick and Hoffman 1999
Physical and mental health	
Leventhal and Brooks-Gunn 2003; Cohen et al. 2006; Votruba and Kling 2009; Glymour et al. 2010; Ludwig et al. 2011; Sanbonmatsu et al. 2011; Do et al. 2013; Kessler et al. 2014; Moulton, Peck, and Dillman 2014; Santiago et al. 2014	Schootman et al. 2007; Hearst et al. 2008; Johnson et al. 2008; Jokela 2014
Labor force participation and earnings	
Rosenbaum 1991, 1995; Rubinowitz and Rosenbaum 2000; Edin, Fredricksson, and Åslund 2003; Weinberg, Reagan, and Yankow 2004; Dawkins, Shen, and Sanchez 2005; Cutler, Glaeser, and Vigdor 2008; Bayer, Ross, and Topa 2008, Clampet-Lundquist and Massey 2008; Galster et al. 2008; Åslund and Fredricksson 2009; Damm 2009, 2014; DeLuca et al. 2010; Galster, Andersson, and Musterd 2010, 2015, 2016; Musterd, Galster, and Andersson 2012; Sari 2012; Sharkey 2012; Turner et al. 2012; Hedman and Galster 2013; Damm 2014; Galster, Santiago, and Lucero 2015a, 2015b; Chetty, Hendren, and Katz 2015; Galster et al. 2015; Chyn 2016; Galster and Santiago, forthcoming	Plotnick and Hoffman 1999; Ludwig, Duncan, and Pinkston 2005; Katz, Kling, and Liebman 2001; Ludwig, Ladd, and Duncan 2001; Ludwig, Duncan, and Hirschfield 2001; Orr et al. 2003; Oreopoulos 2003; Bolster et al. 2007; Kling, Leibman, and Katz 2007; Propper et al. 2007; Ludwig et al. 2008; van Ham and Manley 2010; Sanbonmatsu et al. 2011; Ludwig 2012
Crime	
Katz, Kling, and Liebman 2001; Ludwig, Duncan, and Hirshfeld 2001; Livingston et al. 2014; Santiago et al. 2014; Damm and Dustmann 2014; Rotger and Galster 2015; Billings, Deming, and Ross 2016	Kling, Ludwig, and Katz, 2005; Sanbonmatsu et al. 2011

Source: Authors' compilation.
Note: Only techniques yielding plausibly causal estimates are summarized.

inequality in the United States. We argue, further, that a focus on space is crucial to understanding inequality in social and economic status because, as summarized in figure 1, space plays both mediating and modifying roles in the relationship between individual attributes and achieved status.

The articles in this issue fill in important gaps in what we know about spatial inequality and its relationship to other dimensions of the U.S. stratification system. Specifically, the contributions provide theory and evidence on three questions.

First, what are the scale and dimensions of spatial inequality in the United States, and how does the stratification of space emerge and change? The first article in this issue, from Sean Reardon, Joseph Townsend, and Lindsay Fox, may well become a seminal contribution to this question by developing what the authors refer to as "a general approach to describing the joint distribution of race and income among neighborhoods." Over time, researchers have published research that describes the average neighborhood characteristics of different racial and ethnic groups at different levels of income, but these studies have offered piecemeal evidence on the way that race and ethnicity and economic status overlap across the nation's neighborhoods. This article develops a systematic approach to characterizing the joint distribution of race and income in American communities, and opens the way for a wide range of different analyses that can offer more refined insights into the nature of spatial inequality.

The approach Reardon, Townsend, and Fox develop can be used as a flexible tool to analyze how, for instance, the average racial composition of neighborhoods changes for white, black, Hispanic, or Asian families at the bottom and the top of the income distribution. The authors suggest that the results presented in the article could be used to characterize the way that neighborhood income changes as household income rises, and how this varies across racial and ethnic groups. Applying this set of methods to counties, metropolitan areas, or commuting zones across the United States, the results presented in this article can become an extremely valuable resource for understanding geographic variation in the joint distribution of neighborhood race-ethnic composition and economic status. But the article also contains substantive conclusions that stand on their own as meaningful contributions to our understanding of the way that race and income interact in neighborhoods across America. It reinforces findings from other research showing that black and Hispanic households live in lower-income communities after considering their own household income, and it reveals that black and Hispanic neighbors tend to have lower incomes than white or Asian neighbors for all racial groups, regardless of income. The authors note how this simple finding may shed light on the way that within-neighborhood racial gaps in income could "play a role in shaping racial stereotypes."

The article from Ann Owens moves beyond much of the existing literature on residential segregation by pointing to the unique segregation of households with children and to the role of schools in contributing to the uneven distribution of racial and ethnic groups. Owens links the literature on neighborhood and school segregation by analyzing segregation within and between school districts, providing "evidence on the degree to which school options, operationalized here as residence in a particular school district boundary, contributes to racial residential segregation." She demonstrates that children live in more unequal residential environments than adults, meaning any consequences of racial segregation will be more pronounced among young people. At the same time, the growing diversity of the United States population is most pronounced among young people, which means all children will continue to be exposed to a rising share of neighbors from different racial and ethnic backgrounds, particularly Hispanics.

In a particularly novel contribution to the literature, Owens provides evidence suggesting that school boundaries play an important role in explaining why households with children are more segregated than those without. Segregation between school districts is higher among children than among adults, indicating that the school boundary takes on added importance for families with children. To understand neighborhood segregation, Owens argues, it is crucial to consider the way that parents use the boundaries of school districts when they make decisions about where to live.

Rory Kramer's article shifts from the nation as a whole to a single city, Philadelphia. He focuses on the way that physical attributes of geographic spaces can be used to form clear boundaries in order to maintain racial segregation in this highly stratified city that has experienced substantial demographic change, arguing for a theoretical focus on boundaries as a natural means to measure and understand the spatial scale of neighborhoods. Kramer puts forth an innovative method to define and measure spatial boundaries, using spatial analytic tools to observe salient geographic boundaries in Philadelphia that serve as markers separating communities from each other.

Although this method is effective in identifying the boundaries that maintain racial segregation, it is less effective in assessing why and how those boundaries change (or do not change) over time. For this task, local history is crucial. Kramer goes on to present a historical analysis outlining the factors that shape the rigidity and salience of geographic boundaries in specific neighborhoods in Philadelphia. He argues that the collective response of whites to the potential for neighborhood racial and ethnic change helps explain why some boundaries persist but others fade away. The conclusion to the article provides a powerful theory linking the features of physical space, demographic change, local history, and collective action in an attempt to understand how the stratification of a city's neighborhoods emerges and changes over time.

Like most of the papers in this volume, both the Kramer and the Owens articles move from descriptive science toward explanation; they thus make a contribution not only to questions of scale and dimensions of spatial inequality but also to *our second major question addressed in this issue: what are the processes that generate and reproduce spatial inequality?* Robert Sampson, Jared Schachner, and Robert Mare address this question with an analysis of the mechanisms linking individual residential trajectories with aggregate patterns of neighborhood inequality. Although much of the literature on neighborhood poverty is based on the image of poor, crime-ridden neighborhoods of the deindustrialized cities of the Northeast and Midwest, Sampson, Schachner, and Mare draw on a unique dataset that has followed families and neighborhoods in Los Angeles from 2000 to 2013, and focus their attention on processes of change in a city that looks nothing like the places that are the settings for most of the literature on urban inequality. By following families over the course of a severe economic downturn, they shed light on how change arises, both through residential mobility and as an external shock to stationary families across neighborhoods.

Although the stability of neighborhood inequality in Los Angeles is similar to that in Chicago, the traditional laboratory for the study of urban poverty, the dynamics leading to urban inequality are very different in Los Angeles. The most disadvantaged neighborhoods are occupied by both black and Latino families, and the rigid boundaries between central city and suburbs that characterize cities like Chicago are much less salient in Los Angeles. Residential mobility does not disrupt the rigid racial and ethnic hierarchy of neighborhoods in this city, nor does the shock of the Great Recession. Despite differences in the positioning of groups within this hierarchy, the persistence of urban inequality in Los Angeles bears striking resemblance to that in older industrial cities like Chicago.

Continuing the California-based studies, John Hipp and Charis Kubrin ask how levels and changes in the racial, ethnic, and economic composition of the area that surrounds a neighborhood—what they call an *egohood*—is associated with levels and changes in crime within the focal community. The idea and operationalization of egohoods is itself an important contribution, an improvement on the default conception of neighborhoods as distinct areas separated by an administrative boundary. Hipp and Kubrin consider the unique area surrounding every block within the city of Los Angeles. It is not just the level of disadvantage that influences criminal activity, the authors argue, but also the mix of people within the surrounding area, the potential for interactions between low-income and high-income

Angelenos, that predicts the probability of a crime. And it is not simply the mix of people at a given time but also the changes that are unfolding within and around a community that matter when considering the likelihood that crime will begin to rise or fall in a particular area. Hipp and Kubrin make several methodological advancements in the study of urban dynamics and crime, and in doing so generate new substantive insights into the social processes that make criminal activity more or less likely. Their article is likely to become a major contribution to the study of spatial inequality and crime.

A third question addressed in this issue is how space can serve as a mechanism to maintain, reinforce, or reproduce inequality. Again, it is a question addressed, in many ways, by the articles already described, but three additional studies address it directly. Lincoln Quillian develops a formal model that allows for a more refined understanding of the conditions under which the separation of different segments of any two groups, classified by any dimension of status or advantage, is likely to result in an amplification or reduction of inequality. One natural application is to understand how changes in the joint distribution of race and income in the United States has influenced overall racial inequality in terms of spatial exposure to disadvantaged neighbors. Quillian's contribution thus provides a clear theoretical model of how racial segregation is related to racial inequality, and his application to urban areas in the United States is an excellent complement to the contribution from Reardon, Townsend, and Fox.

Anna Maria Santiago, Eun Lye Lee, Jessica Lucero, and Rebecca Wiersma exploit a natural experiment whereby families receiving housing assistance in Denver were assigned to apartment units through a system that appears to be close to random. The authors document patterns of movement for families in the program, and show persuasively that assignment to apartments in different neighborhoods can be considered exogenous if it is analyzed within racial and ethnic groups. They examine how various dimensions of the neighborhood environment are linked with three risky behaviors during adolescence, including running away from home, engaging in violent or aggressive behavior, and using marijuana. They find that neighborhood racial and ethnic composition, social and economic composition, and safety are strongly connected with elevated levels of these risk behaviors, all of which have the potential to generate long-term and to have severe impacts on young people's developmental trajectories.

The study takes seriously the idea that processes of sorting into neighborhoods across Denver work differently for black and Latino families, even if they are all receiving housing assistance from the city. By estimating the impact of neighborhood conditions separately for black and Latino adolescents, the research not only allows for stronger causal inferences but also provides unique insight into the impact of neighborhoods for Latino youths, a group not well represented in the literature. The study allows for a more refined look at the specific aspects of neighborhoods that are most salient for adolescent risky behaviors, and does so in a way that generates important insights that can be used to guide housing policy.

In the final article, Christopher Browning, Catherine Calder, Lauren Krivo, Anna Smith, and Bethany Boettner take a novel approach to analyzing neighborhood effect mechanisms by examining the extent to which individuals from different social and economic backgrounds share space when they carry out routine activities such as going shopping or going to work. Using data from Los Angeles, the authors find that families with higher social and economic status are less likely to share common spaces with a diverse set of neighbors, and particularly in highly unequal neighborhoods. The analysis allows one to see beyond the socioeconomic composition of neighborhoods to the set of interactions that residents have with each other. In this way, this article presents evidence on interaction-based mechanisms of neighborhood effects that have been posited for several decades, yet rarely tested empirically.

Our hope is that this collection of articles advances the literature on the spatial foundations of inequality and generates additional research taking seriously the idea of space as a core dimension of stratification in the United States and beyond. We are grateful for the chance to edit such high-quality articles and to be able to work with this group of impressive scholars.

REFERENCES

Aaronson, Daniel. 1998. "Using Sibling Data to Estimate the Impact of Neighborhoods on Children's Educational Outcomes." *Journal of Human Resources* 33(4): 915–46.

Ahern, Jennifer, Sandro Galea, Alan Hubbard, Lorraine Midanik, and S. Leonard Syme. 2008. "'Culture of Drinking' and Individual Problems with Alcohol Use." *American Journal of Epidemiology* 167(9): 1041–49.

Ard, Kerry 2015. "Trends in Exposure to Industrial Air Toxins for Different Racial and Socioeconomic Groups: A Spatial and Temporal Examination of Environmental Inequality in the U.S. from 1995 to 2004." *Social Science Research* 53: 375–90.

Åslund, Olaf, and Peter Fredriksson. 2009. "Peer Effects in Welfare Dependence: Quasi-Experimental Evidence." *Journal of Human Resources* 44(3): 798–825.

Bayer, Patrick, Steven Ross, and George Topa. 2008. "Place of Work and Place of Residence: Informal Hiring Networks and Labor Market Outcomes." *Journal of Political Economy* 116(6): 1150–96.

Becker, Rolf. 2003. "Educational Expansion and Persistent Inequalities of Education." *European Sociological Review* 19(1): 1–24.

Billings, Stephen, David Deming, and Stephen Ross. 2016. "Partners in Crime: Schools, Neighborhoods and the Formation of Criminal Networks." NBER working paper no. 21962. Cambridge, Mass.: National Bureau of Economic Research.

Bischoff, Kendra, and Sean Reardon. 2014. "Residential Segregation by Income, 1970–2009." In *Diversity and Disparities: America Enters a New Century*, edited by John R. Logan. New York: Russell Sage Foundation.

Bolster, Anne, Simon Burgess, Ron Johnston, Kelvyn Jones, Carol Propper, and Rebecca Sarker. 2007. "Neighbourhoods, Households and Income Dynamics: a Semi-Parametric Investigation of Neighbourhood Effects." *Journal of Economic Geography* 7(1): 1–38.

Braga, Anthony, David Hureau, and Andrew Papachristos. 2011. "The Relevance of Micro Places in Citywide Robbery Trends: A Longitudinal Analysis of Robbery Incidents at Street Corners and Block Faces in Boston." *Journal of Research in Crime and Delinquency* 48(1): 7–32.

Braga, Anthony, Andrew Papachristos, and David Hureau. 2010. "The Concentration and Stability of Gun Violence at Micro Places in Boston, 1980–2008." *Journal of Quantitative Criminology* 26(1): 33–53.

Briggs, Xavier, ed. 1995. *The Geography of Opportunity*. Washington, D.C.: Brookings Institution Press.

Briggs, Xavier. 1997. "Moving Up Versus Moving Out: Researching and Interpreting Neighborhood Effects in Housing Mobility Programs." *Housing Policy Debate* 8(1): 195–234.

Briggs, Xavier, Elizabeth Cove, Cynthia Duarte, and Margery Austin Turner. 2011. "How Does Leaving High-Poverty Neighborhoods Affect the Employment Prospects of Low-Income Mothers and Youth?" In *Neighborhood and Life Chances: How Place Matters in Modern America*, edited by Harriet Newburger, Eugenie Birch, and Susan Wachter. Philadelphia: University of Pennsylvania Press.

Briggs, Xavier, Kadija Ferryman, Susan Popkin, and Maria Rendon. 2008. "Why Did the Moving to Opportunity Experiment Not Get Young People into Better Schools?" *Housing Policy Debate* 19(1): 53–91.

Briggs, Xavier, Susan Popkin, and John Goering. 2010. *Moving to Opportunity*. New York: Oxford University Press.

Brooks-Gunn, Jeanne, Greg J. Duncan, and J. Lawrence Aber, eds. 1997. *Neighborhood Poverty*, vol. 1: *Context and Consequences for Children*. New York: Russell Sage Foundation.

Brooks-Gunn, Jeanne, Greg J. Duncan, Pamela Klebanov, and Naomi Sealand. 1993. "Do Neighborhoods Influence Child and Adolescent Development?" *American Journal of Sociology* 99(2): 353–95.

Browning, Christopher, Catherine Calder, Lauren Krivo, Anna Smith, and Bethany Boettner. 2017. "Socioeconomic Segregation of Activity Spaces in Urban Neighborhoods: Does Shared Residence Mean Shared Routines?" *RSF: Russell Sage Foundation Journal of the Social Sciences* 3(2): 210–31. doi: 10.7758/RSF.3.2.09.

Bryant, Bunyan, and Paul Mohai, eds. 1992. *Race and the Incidence of Environmental Hazards*. Boulder, Colo.: Westview Press.

Burdick-Will, Julia, Jens Ludwig, Stephen Raudenbush, Robert Sampson, Lisa Sanbonmatsu, and Patrick Sharkey. 2011. "Converging Evidence for Neighborhood Effects on Children's Test Scores: An Experimental, Quasi-Experimental, and Observational Comparison." In *Whither Opportunity: Rising Inequality, Schools, and Children's Life Chances*, edited by Greg J. Duncan and Richard J. Murnane. New York: Russell Sage Foundation / Chicago: Spencer Foundation.

Carlson, Deven, and Joshua Cowen. 2015. "Student Neighborhoods, Schools, and Test Score Growth: Evidence from Milwaukee, Wisconsin." *Sociology of Education* 88(1): 38–55.

Casciano, Rebecca, and Douglas Massey. 2012. "School Context and Educational Outcomes: Results from a Quasi-Experimental Study." *Urban Affairs Review* 48(2): 180–204.

Cerdá, Magdalena, Ana Diez-Roux, Eric Tchetgen Tchetgen, Penny Gordon-Larsen, and Catarina Kiefe. 2010. "The Relationship Between Neighborhood Poverty and Alcohol Use: Estimation by Marginal Structural Models." *Epidemiology* 21(4): 482–89.

Cerdá, Magdalena, Jeffrey Morenoff, Ben Hansen, Kimberly Tessari Hicks, Luis Duque, Alexandra Restrepo, and Ana Diez-Roux. 2012. "Reducing Violence by Transforming Neighborhoods: A Natural Experiment in Medellin, Colombia." *American Journal of Epidemiology* 175(10): 1045–53.

Chetty, Raj, and Nathaniel Hendren. 2015. "The Effects of Neighborhoods on Children's Long-Term Outcomes: Quasi-Experimental Estimates for the United States." Unpublished paper. Stanford University, Palo Alto, Calif.

Chetty, Raj, Nathaniel Hendren, and Lawrence Katz. 2015. "The Effects of Exposure to Better Neighborhoods on Children: New Evidence from the Moving to Opportunity Experiment." NBER working paper no. 21156. Cambridge, Mass.: National Bureau of Economic Research.

Chetty, Raj, Nathaniel Hendren, Patrick Kline, and Emmanuel Saez. 2014. "Where Is the Land of Opportunity? The Geography of Intergenerational Mobility in the United States." NBER working paper no. 19843. Cambridge, Mass.: National Bureau of Economic Research.

Chyn, Eric. 2016. "Moved to Opportunity: The Long-Run Effect of Public Housing Demolition on Labor Market Outcomes of Children." Unpublished paper. University of Michigan, Ann Arbor.

Clampet-Lundquist, Susan. 2007. "No More 'Bois Ball: The Impact of Relocation from Public Housing on Adolescents." *Journal of Adolescent Research* 22(3): 298–323.

Clampet-Lundquist, Susan, and Douglas Massey. 2008. "Neighborhood Effects on Economic Self-Sufficiency: A Reconsideration of the Moving to Opportunity Experiment." *American Journal of Sociology* 114(1): 107–43.

Cohen, Deborah, Bonnie Ghosh-Dastidar, Richard Scribner, Angela Miu, Molly Scott, Paul Robinson, Thomas Farley, Ricky Bluthenthal, and Didra Brown-Taylor. 2006. "Alcohol Outlets, Gonorrhea, and the Los Angeles Civil Unrest: a Longitudinal Analysis." *Social Science and Medicine* 62(12): 3062–71.

Crowder, Kyle, and Scott South. 2003. "Neighborhood Distress and School Dropout: The Variable Significance of Community Context." *Social Science Research* 32(4): 659–98.

Crowder, Kyle, and Jay Teachman. 2004. "Do Residential Conditions Explain the Relationship Between Living Arrangements and Adolescent Behavior?" *Journal of Marriage and the Family* 66(3): 721–38.

Cutler, David, Edward Glaeser, and Jacob Vigdor. 2008. "When Are Ghettos Bad? Lessons from Immigrant Segregation in the United States." *Journal of Urban Economics* 63(3): 759–74.

Damm, Anna Piil. 2009. "Ethnic Enclaves and Immigrant Labor Market Outcomes: Quasi-Experimental Evidence." *Journal of Labor Economics* 27(2): 281–314.

———. 2014. "Neighborhood Quality and Labor Market Outcomes: Evidence from a Quasi-Random Neighborhood Assignment of Immigrants." *Journal of Urban Economics* 79(January): 139–66.

Damm, Anna Piil, and Christian Dustmann. 2014. "Does Growing Up in a High Crime Neighborhood Affect Youth Criminal Behavior?" *American Economic Review* 104(6): 1806–32.

Dawkins, Casey. Forthcoming. "Putting Equality in Place: The Normative Foundations of Geographic Equality of Opportunity." *Housing Policy Debate*.

Dawkins, Casey, Qing Shen, and Thomas Sanchez. 2005. "Race, Space and Unemployment Duration." *Journal of Urban Economics* 58(1): 91–113.

DeLuca, Stefanie, Greg Duncan, Ruby Mendenhall, and Michere Keels. 2010. "Gautreaux Mothers and Their Children." *Housing Policy Debate* 20(1): 7–25.

Dietz, Robert. 2002. "The Estimation of Neighborhood Effects in the Social Sciences." *Social Science Research* 31(4): 539–75.

Diez-Roux, Ana, and Christina Mair. 2010. "Neighborhoods and Health." *Annals of the New York Academy of Sciences* 1186(1): 125–45.

Do, Phuong, Lu Wang, and Michael Elliott. 2013. "Investigating the Relationship Between Neighborhood Poverty and Mortality Risk: A Marginal Structural Modeling Approach." *Social Science and Medicine* 91(August): 58–66.

Downey, Liam. 2007. "US Metropolitan-Area Variation in Environmental Inequality Outcomes." *Urban Studies* 44(5–6): 953–77.

Downey, Liam, and Brian Dawkins. 2008. "Race Income, and Environmental Inequality in the United States." Sociological Perspectives 51(4): 759–81.

Dreier, Peter, John Mollenkopf, and Todd Swanstrom. 2001. *Place Matters: Metropolitics for the Twenty-First Century*. Lawrence: University Press of Kansas.

Duncan, Greg J., James Connell, and Patricia Klebanov. 1997. "Conceptual and Methodological Issues In Estimating Causal Effects of Neighborhoods and Family Conditions on Individual Development." In *Neighborhood Poverty*, vol. 1, *Context and Consequences for Children*, edited by Jeanne Brooks-Gunn, Greg J. Duncan, and J. Lawrence Aber. New York: Russell Sage Foundation.

Edin, Per-Anders, Peter Fredriksson, and Olof Åslund. 2003. "Ethnic Enclaves and the Economic Success of Immigrants: Evidence from a Natural Experiment." *Quarterly Journal of Economics* 118(1): 329–57.

Ellen, Ingrid, and Katherine O'Regan. 2009. "Crime and U.S. Cities: Recent Patterns and Implications." *Annals of the American Academy of Political and Social Science* 626(1): 22–38.

Erikson, Robert, and Jan Jonsson. 1996. "Explaining Class Inequality in Education: The Swedish Test Case." In *Can Education Be Equalized? The Swedish Case in Comparative Perspective*, edited by Robert Erikson and Jan Jonsson. Boulder, Colo.: Westview Press.

Fauth, Rebecca, Tama Leventhal, and Jeanne Brooks-Gunn. 2007. "Welcome to the Neighborhood? Long-Term Impacts of Moving to Low-Poverty Neighborhoods on Poor Children's and Adolescents' Outcomes." *Journal of Research on Adolescence* 17(2): 249–84.

Federal Bureau of Investigation. 2015. "Uniform Crime Reports, 1960–2012." Uniform Crime Reporting Data Tool. Washington: U.S. Department of Justice. Accessed June 21, 2016. https://www.fbi.gov/about-us/cjis/ucr/.

Florida, Richard. 2010. *The Great Reset: How New Ways of Living and Working Drive Post-Crash Prosperity*. Toronto: Random House Canada.

Friedson, Michael, and Patrick Sharkey. 2015. "Violence and Neighborhood Disadvantage after the Crime Decline." *The Annals of the American Academy of Political and Social Science* 660(1): 341–58.

Galster, George. 2008. "Quantifying the Effect of Neighbourhood on Individuals: Challenges, Alternative Approaches and Promising Directions." *Journal of Applied Social Science Studies* [Schmollers Jahrbuch/ Zeitschrift fur Wirtschafts- und Sozialwissenschaften] 128(1): 7–48.

Galster, George, Roger Andersson, and Sako Musterd. 2010. "Who Is Affected by Neighbourhood Income Mix? Gender, Age, Family, Employment, and Income Differences." *Urban Studies* 48(13): 2915–44.

———. 2015. "Are Males' Incomes Influenced by the Income Mix of Their Male Neighbors? Explorations into Nonlinear and Threshold Effects in Stockholm." *Housing Studies* 30(2): 315–43.

———. 2016. "Neighborhood Social Mix and Adults' Income Trajectories: Longitudinal Evidence from Stockholm." *Geografisker Annaler*, Series B, *Human Geography*.

Galster, George, Roger Andersson, Sako Musterd, and Timo Kauppinen. 2008. "Does Neighborhood Income Mix Affect Earnings of Adults?" *Journal of Urban Economics* 63(3): 858–70.

Galster, George, and Lina Hedman. 2013. "Measuring Neighborhood Effects Non-experimentally: How Much Do Alternative Methods Matter? *Housing Studies* 28(3): 473–98.

Galster, George, and Sean Killen. 1995. "The Geography of Metropolitan Opportunity: A Reconnaissance and Conceptual Framework." *Housing Policy Debate* 6(1): 7–44.

Galster, George, David Marcotte, Marvin Mandell, Hal Wolman, and Nancy Augustine. 2007. "The Impact of Childhood Neighborhood Poverty on Young Adult Outcomes." *Housing Studies* 22(5): 723–52.

Galster, George, and Anna Santiago. 2006. "What's the 'Hood Got to Do with It? Parental Perceptions About How Neighborhood Mechanisms Affect Their Children." *Journal of Urban Affairs* 28(3): 201–26.

———. Forthcoming. "Neighborhood Ethnic Composition and Outcomes for Low-Income Latino and African American Children." *Urban Studies.*

Galster, George, Anna Santiago, Jackie Cutsinger, and Lisa Stack. 2016. "Neighborhood Effects on Secondary School Performance of Latino and African American Youth: Evidence from a Natural Experiment in Denver." *Journal of Urban Economics* 93(May): 30–48.

Galster, George, Anna Santiago, and Jessica Lucero. 2015a. "Adrift at the Margins of Urban Society: What Role Does Neighborhood Play?" *Urban Affairs Review* 51(1): 10–45.

———. 2015b. "Employment of Low-Income African American and Latino Teens: Does Neighborhood Social Mix Matter?" *Housing Studies* 30(2): 192–227.

Galster, George, Anna Santiago, Jessica Lucero, and Jackie Cutsinger. 2015. "Adolescent Neighborhood Context and Young Adult Economic Outcomes for Low-Income African Americans and Latinos." *Journal of Economic Geography* 16(2): 471–503. doi: 10.1093/jeg/lbv004.

Galster, George, Anna Santiago, and Lisa Stack. 2015. "Elementary School Difficulties of Low-Income Latino and African American Youth: The Role of Geographic Context." *Journal of Urban Affairs* 38(4): 477–502. doi: 10.1111/juaf.12266.

Gennetian, Lisa A., Lisa Sanbonmatsu, and Jens Ludwig. 2011. "An Overview of Moving to Opportunity: A Random Assignment Housing Mobility Study in Five U.S. Cities." In *Neighborhood and Life Chances: How Place Matters in Modern America*, edited by Harriet B. Newburger, Eugenie L. Birch, and Susan M. Wachter. Philadelphia: University of Pennsylvania Press.

Gibbons, Stephen, Olmo Silva, and Felix Weinhardt. 2013. "Everybody Needs Good Neighbours? Evidence from Students' Outcomes in England." *The Economic Journal* 123(571): 831–74.

———. 2014. "Neighbourhood Turnover and Teenage Achievement." *IZA* discussion paper no. 8381. Bonn: Institute for the Study of Labor.

Ginther, Donna, Robert Haveman, and Barbara Wolfe. 2000. "Neighborhood Attributes as Determinants of Children's Outcomes." *Journal of Human Resources* 35(4): 603–42.

Glaeser, Edward, and Jacob Vigdor. 2012. *The End of the Segregated Century: Racial Separation in America's Neighborhoods, 1890–2010.* New York: Manhattan Institute for Policy Research.

Glymour, M. Maria, Mahasin Mujahid, Qiong Wu, Kellee White, and Eric J. Tchetgen Tchetgen. 2010. "Neighborhood Disadvantage and Self-Assessed Health, Disability, and Depressive Symptoms: Longitudinal Results from the Health and Retirement Study." *American Journal of Epidemiology* 20(11): 856–61.

Harding, David. 2003. "Counterfactual Models of Neighborhood Effects: The Effect of Neighborhood Poverty on Dropping Out and Teenage Pregnancy." *American Journal of Sociology* 109(3): 676–719.

Haveman, Robert, and Barbara Wolfe. 1994. *Succeeding Generations: On the Effects of Investments in Children.* New York: Russell Sage Foundation.

Hearst, Mary, Michael Oakes, Pamela Johnson. 2008. "The Effect of Racial Residential Segregation on Black Infant Mortality." *American Journal of Epidemiology* 168(11): 1247–54.

Hedman, Lina, and George Galster. 2013. "Neighborhood Income Sorting and the Effects of Neighborhood Income Mix on Income: A Holistic Empirical Exploration." *Urban Studies* 50(1): 107–27.

Hellerstein, Judith, Mark. Kutzbach, and David Neumark. 2014. "Do Labor Market Networks Have an Important Spatial Dimension?" *Journal of Urban Economics* 79(1): 39–58.

Hellerstein, Judith, David Neumark, and Melissa McInerney. 2008. "Spatial Mismatch or Racial Mismatch?" *Journal of Urban Economics* 64(2): 464–79.

Hipp, John, and Charles Kubrin. 2017. "From Bad to Worse: How Changing Inequality in Nearby Areas Impacts Local Crime" *RSF: Russell Sage Foundation Journal of the Social Sciences* 3(2): 129–51. doi: 10.7758/RSF.3.2.06.

Holzer, Harry J. 1991. "The Spatial Mismatch Hypothesis: What Has the Evidence Shown?" *Urban Studies* 28(1): 105–22.

Ihlanfeldt, Keith R., and David L. Sjoquist. 1998. "The Spatial Mismatch Hypothesis: A Review of Recent Studies and Their Implications for Welfare Reform." *Housing Policy Debate* 9(4): 849–92.

Jacob, Brian. 2004. "Public Housing, Housing Vouchers, and Student Achievement: Evidence from Public Housing Demolitions in Chicago." *American Economic Review* 94(1): 233–58.

Jargowsky, Paul. 1996. "Take the Money and Run: Economic Segregation in U.S. Metropolitan Areas." *American Sociological Review* 61(6): 984–98.

———. 2003. "Stunning Progress, Hidden Problems: The Dramatic Decline of Concentrated Poverty in the 1990s." *Living Cities Census Series* no. 24. Washington, DC: Brookings Institution Press.

———. 2015. "The Architecture of Segregation." New York: The Century Foundation.

Jargowsky, Paul, and Mohamed El Komi. 2011. "Before or After the Bell? School Context and Neighborhood Effects on Student Achievement." In *Neighborhood and Life Chances: How Place Matters in Modern America*, edited by Harriet B. Newburger, Eugenie L. Birch, and Susan M. Wachter. Philadelphia: University of Pennsylvania Press.

Jencks, Cristopher, and Susan Mayer. 1990. "The Social Consequences of Growing Up in a Poor Neighborhood." In *Inner-City Poverty in the United States*, edited by Lawrence Lynn and Michael MacGeary. Washington, D.C.: National Academy Press.

Johnson, Pamela Jo, J. Michael Oakes, and Douglas L. Anderton. 2008. "Neighborhood Poverty and American Indian Infant Death: Are the Effects Identifiable?" *American Journal of Epidemiology* 18(7): 552–59.

Jokela, Markus. 2014. "Are Neighborhood Health Associations Causal? A 10-Year Prospective Cohort Study with Repeated Measurements." *American Journal of Epidemiology* 180(8): 776–84.

Kain, John F. 1968. "Housing Segregation, Negro Employment, and Metropolitan Decentralization." *Quarterly Journal of Economics* 83(2): 175–97.

———. 1992. "The Spatial Mismatch Hypothesis: Three Decades Later." *Housing Policy Debate* 3(2): 371–460.

Katz, Lawrence, Jeffrey Kling, and Jeffrey Leibman. 2001. "Moving to Opportunity in Boston: Early Results of a Randomized Mobility Experiment." *Quarterly Journal of Economics* 116(2): 607–54.

Kawachi, Ichiro, and Lisa Berkman, eds. 2003. *Neighborhoods and Health*. New York: Oxford University Press.

Kessler, Ronald, Greg Duncan, Lisa Gennetian, Lawrence Katz, Jeffrey Kling, Nancy Sampson, Lisa Sanbonmatsu, Alan Zaslavsky, and Jens Ludwig. 2014. "Associations of Housing Mobility Interventions for Children in High-Poverty Neighborhoods with Subsequent Mental Disorders During Adolescence." *Journal of the American Planning Association* 311(9): 937–48.

Kling, Jeffrey, Jeffrey Liebman, and Lawrence Katz. 2007. "Experimental Analysis of Neighborhood Effects." *Econometrica* 75(1): 83–119.

Kling, Jeffrey, Jens Ludwig, and Lawrence Katz. 2005. "Neighborhood Effects on Crime for Female and Male Youth: Evidence from a Randomized Housing Voucher Experiment." *Quarterly Journal of Economics* 120(1): 87–131.

Kramer, Rory. 2017. "Defensible Spaces in Philadelphia: Exploring Neighborhood Boundaries Through Spatial Analysis." *RSF: Russell Sage Foundation Journal of the Social Sciences* 3(2): 81–101. doi: 10.7758/RSF.3.2.04.

Lanphear, Bruce P., Robert S. Byrd, Peggy Auinger, and Stanley J. Schaffer. 1998. "Community Characteristics Associated with Elevated Blood Lead Levels in Children." *Pediatrics* 101(2): 264–71.

Leventhal, Tama, and Jeanne Brooks-Gunn. 2003. "Moving to Opportunity: An Experimental Study of Neighborhood Effects on Mental Health." *American Journal of Public Health* 93(9): 1576–82.

Lindley, Joanne, and Stephen Machin. 2014. "Spatial Changes in Labour Market Inequality." *Journal of Urban Economics* 79: 121–138.

Livingston, Mark, George Galster, Ade Kearns, and Jon Bannister. 2014. "Criminal Neighborhoods: Does the Density of Prior Offenders in an Area Encourage Others to Commit Crime?" *Environment and Planning A* 46(10): 2469–88.

Logan, John. 2011. "Separate and Unequal: The Neighborhood Gap for Blacks, Hispanics and Asians in Metropolitan America." *Project US2010* report. Providence, R.I.: Brown University. Accessed June 20, 2016. http://www.s4.brown.edu/us2010/Data/Report/report0727.pdf.

Logan, John, Deirdre Oakley, Polly Smith, Jacob Stowell, and Brian Stults. 2001. "Separating the Children." *Lewis Mumford Center* working paper. Albany: State University of New York.

Logan, John, and Brian Stults. 2011. "The Persistence of Segregation in the Metropolis: New Findings from the 2010 Census." *Project US2010* census brief. Providence, R.I.: Brown University. Accessed June 20, 2016. http://www.s4.brown.edu/us2010/Data/Report/report2.pdf.

Logan, John, Brian Stults, and Reynolds Farley. 2014. "Segregation of Minorities in the Metropolis: Two Decades of Change." *Demography* 41(1): 1–22.

Lovasi, Gina, James Quinn, Virginia Rauh, Frederica Perera, Howard Andrews, Robin Garfinkel, Lori Hoepner, Robin Whyatt, and Andrew Rundle. 2011. "Chlorpyrifos Exposure and Urban Residential Environment Characteristics as Determinants of Early Childhood Neurodevelopment." *American Journal of Public Health* 101(1): 63–70.

Ludwig, Jens. 2012. "Moving to Opportunity: Guest Editor's Introduction." *Cityscape* 14(2): 1–28.

Ludwig, Jens, Greg J. Duncan, and Paul Hirschfield. 2001. "Urban Poverty and Juvenile Crime: Evidence from a Randomized Experiment." *Quarterly Journal of Economics* 116(2): 655–79.

Ludwig, Jens, Greg J. Duncan, and Joshua Pinkston. 2005. "Neighborhood Effects on Economic Self-Sufficiency: Evidence from a Randomized Housing-Mobility Experiment." *Journal of Public Economics* 89(1): 131–56.

Ludwig, Jens, Helen F. Ladd, and Greg J. Duncan. 2001. "Urban Poverty on Educational Outcomes." *Brookings-Wharton Papers on Urban Affairs* 2: 147–201. Accessed June 20, 2016. http://home.uchicago.edu/ludwigj/papers/Ludwig_BWPUA_2001.pdf.

Ludwig, Jens, Jeffrey Liebman, Jeffrey Kling, Greg J. Duncan, Lawrence Katz, Ronald Kessler, and Lisa Sanbonmatsu. 2008. "What Can We Learn About Neighborhood Effects from the Moving to Opportunity Experiment?" *American Journal of Sociology* 114(1): 144–88.

Ludwig, Jens, Lisa Sanbonmatsu, Lisa Gennetian, Adam Emma, Greg J. Duncan, and Lawrence Katz. 2011. "Neighborhoods, Obesity, and Diabetes—A Randomized Social Experiment." *New England Journal of Medicine* 365(16): 1509–19.

Manski, Charles. 1995. *Identification Problems in the Social Sciences* Cambridge, Mass.: Harvard University Press.

———. 2000. "Economic Analysis of Social Interactions." *Journal of Economic Perspectives* 14(3): 115–36.

McConnell, Rob, Talat Islam, Ketan Shankardass, Michael Jerrett, Fred Lurmann, Frank Gilliland, Jim Gauderman, Ed Avol, Nino Künzli, Ling Yao, John Peters, and Kiros Berhane. 2010. "Childhood Incident Asthma and Traffic-Related Air Pollution at Home and School." *Environmental Health Perspectives* 118(7): 1021–26.

Moulton, Stephanie, Laura Peck, and Keri-Nicole Dillman. 2014. "Moving to Opportunity's Impact on Health and Well-Being Among High-Dosage Participants." *Housing Policy Debate* 24(2): 415–45.

Musterd, Sako, Roger Andersson, George Galster, and Timo Kauppinen. 2008. "Are Immigrants' Earnings Influenced by the Characteristics of Their Neighbours?" *Environment and Planning A* 40(4): 785–805.

Musterd, Sako, George Galster, and Roger Andersson. 2012. "Temporal Dimensions and the Measurement of Neighbourhood Effects." *Environment and Planning A* 44(3): 605–27.

Nandi, Arijit, Thomas Glass, Stephen Cole, Haitao Chu, Sandro Galea, David Celentano, Gregory Kirk, David Vlahov, William Latimer, and Shruti Mehta. 2010. "Neighborhood Poverty and Injection Cessation in a Sample of Injection Drug Users." *American Journal of Epidemiology* 171(4): 391–98.

Nieuwenhuis, Jaap, and Pieter Hooimeijer. 2014. "The Association between Neighbourhoods and Educational Achievement: A Systematic Review and Meta-Analysis." In *Neighbourhood Effects on Youth's Achievements: The Moderating Role of Personality*, edited by Jaap Nieuwenhuis. PhD diss. Utrecht University.

Novak, Scott, Sean Reardon, Stephen Raudenbush, and Stephen Buka. 2006. "Retail Tobacco Outlet Density and Youth Cigarette Smoking: A Propensity-Modeling Approach." *American Journal of Public Health* 96(4): 670–76.

Oakes, J. Michael, Kate Andrade, Ifrah Biyoow, and Logan Cowan. 2015. "Twenty Years of Neighborhood Effect Research: An Assessment." *Current Epidemiology Reports* 2(1): 1–8.

Oreopoulos, Philip. 2003. "The Long-Run Consequences of Living in a Poor Neighborhood." *Quarterly Journal of Economics* 118(4): 1533–75.

Orfield, Gary, and Chungmei Lee. 2007. "Historic Reversals, Accelerating Resegregation, and the Need for New Integration Strategies." Los Angeles: University of California, Civil Rights Project.

Orr, Larry, Judith Feins, Robin Jacob, Eric Beecroft, Lisa Sanbonmatsu, Lawrence Katz, Jeffrey Liebman, and Jeffrey Kling. 2003. *Moving to Opportunity: Interim Impacts Evaluation*. Washington: U.S. Department of Housing and Urban Development.

Owens, Ann. 2016. "Inequality in Children's Contexts: The Economic Segregation of Households with and Without Children." *American Sociological Review* 81(3): 549–74.

———. 2017. "Racial Residential Segregation of School-Age Children and Adults: The Role of Schooling as a Segregating Force." *RSF: Russell Sage Foundation Journal of the Social Sciences* 3(2): 63–80. doi: 10.7758/RSF.3.2.03.

Owens, Ann, Sean Reardon, and Christopher Jencks. 2016. "Income Segregation between Schools and Districts, 1990 to 2010." Stanford Center for Education Policy working paper no. 16–04. Palo Alto, Calif.: Stanford University.

Papachristos, Andrew. 2013. "48 Years of Crime in Chicago: A Descriptive Analysis of Serious Crime Trends from 1965 to 2013." *ISPS* working paper 13-023. Chicago: University of Chicago.

Plotnick, Robert, and Saul Hoffman. 1999. "The Effect of Neighborhood Characteristics on Young Adult Outcomes: Alternative Estimates." *Social Science Quarterly* 80(1): 1–18.

Popkin, Susan, Tama Leventhal, and Gretchen Weismann. 2010. "Girls in the 'Hood: How Safety Affects the Life Chances of Low-Income Girls." *Urban Affairs Review* 45(6): 715–44.

Propper, Carol, Simon Burgess, Anne Bolster, George Leckie, Kelvyn Jones, and Ron Johnston. 2007. "The Impact of Neighbourhood on the Income and Mental Health of British Social Renters." *Urban Studies* 44(2): 393–415.

Quillian, Lincoln. 2017. "Segregation as a Source of Contextual Advantage: A Formal Theory with Application to American Cities." *RSF: Russell Sage Foundation Journal of the Social Sciences* 3(2): 152–69. doi: 10.7758/RSF.3.2.07.

Rau, Tomás, Loreto Reyes, and Sergio Urzúa. 2013. "The Long-Term Effects of Early Lead Exposure: Evidence from a Case of Environmental Negligence." *NBER* working paper no. 18915. Cambridge, Mass.: National Bureau of Economic Research. Accessed June 20, 2016. http://www.nber.org/papers/w18915.

Reardon, Sean, and Kendra Bischoff. 2011. "Income Inequality and Income Segregation." *American Journal of Sociology* 116(4): 1092–153.

———. 2016. "The Continuing Increase in Income Segregation, 2007–2012." Palo Alto, Calif.: Stanford Center for Education Policy Analysis. Accessed June 20, 2016. http://cepa.stanford.edu/content/continuing-increase-income-segregation-2007-2012.

Reardon, Sean, Lindsay Fox, and Joseph Townsend. 2015. "Neighborhood Income Composition by Race and Income, 1990–2009." *Annals of the American Academy of Political and Social Science* 68(1): 78–97.

Reardon, Sean, and Ann Owens. 2014. "60 Years After Brown: Trends and Consequences of School Segregation." *Annual Review of Sociology* 40: 199–218.

Reardon, Sean, Joseph Townsend, and Lindsay Fox. 2017. "Characteristics of the Joint Distribution of Race and Income Among Neighborhoods." *RSF: Russell Sage Foundation Journal of the Social Sciences* 3(2): 34–62. doi: 10.7758/RSF.3.2.02.

Rosenbaum, James. 1991. "Black Pioneers: Do Moves to the Suburbs Increase Economic Opportunity for Mothers and Children?" *Housing Policy Debate* 2(4): 1179–213.

———. 1995. "Changing the Geography of Opportunity by Expanding Residential Choice: Lessons from the Gautreaux Program." *Housing Policy Debate* 6(1): 231–69.

Rotger, Gabriel Pons, and George Galster. 2015. "Neighborhood Context and Criminal Behaviors of the Disadvantaged: Evidence from a Copenhagen Natural Experiment." Presented at the European Network for Housing Research meetings. Lisbon. (June 28, 2015).

Rubinowitz, Leonard, and James Rosenbaum. 2000. *Crossing the Class and Color Lines: From Public Housing to White Suburbia*. Chicago: University of Chicago Press.

Sampson, Robert. 2003. "The Neighborhood Context of Well Being." *Perspectives in Biology and Medicine* 46(3): S53–73.

———. 2008. "Moving to Inequality: Neighborhood Effects and Experiments Meet Social Structure." *American Journal of Sociology* 114(11): 189–231.

———. 2012. *Great American City: Chicago and the Enduring Neighborhood Effect*. Chicago: University of Chicago Press.

Sampson, Robert, Jared Schachner, and Robert Mare. 2017. "Urban Income Inequality and the Great Recession in Sunbelt Form: Disentangling Individual and Neighborhood-Level Change in Los Angeles." *RSF: Russell Sage Foundation Journal of the Social Sciences* 3(2): 102–28. doi: 10.7758/RSF.3.2.05.

Sampson, Robert, Patrick Sharkey, and Stephen Raudenbush. 2008. "Durable Effects of Concentrated Disadvantage on Verbal Ability Among African-American Children." *Proceed-*

ings of the National Academy of Sciences 105(3): 845–52.

Sampson, Robert, and Alex Winter. Forthcoming. "The Racial Ecology of Lead Poisoning: Toxic Inequality in Chicago, 1995–2013." *Du Bois Review: Social Science Research on Race*.

Sanbonmatsu, Lisa, Lawrence Katz, Jens Ludwig, Lisa Gennetian, Greg J. Duncan, Ronald Kessler, Emma Adam, Thomas McDade, and Stacy Tessler Lindau. 2011. *Moving to Opportunity for Fair Housing Demonstration Program—Final Impacts Evaluation*. Washington: U.S. Department of Housing and Urban Development.

Sanbonmatsu, Lisa, Jeffrey Kling, Greg J. Duncan, and Jeanne Brooks-Gunn. 2006. "Neighborhoods and Academic Achievement: Evidence from the Moving to Opportunity Experiment." *Journal of Human Resources* 41(4): 649–91.

Santiago, Anna Maria, George Galster, Jessica Lucero, Karen Ishler, Eun Lye Lee, Georgios Kypriotakis, and Lisa Stack. 2014. *Opportunity Neighborhoods for Latino and African American Children*. Washington: U.S. Department of Housing and Urban Development.

Santiago, Anna Maria, Eun Lye Lee, Jessica Lucero, and Rebecca Wiersma. 2017. "How Living in the 'Hood Affects Risky Behaviors Among Latino and African American Youth." *RSF: Russell Sage Foundation Journal of the Social Sciences* 3(2): 170–209. doi: 10.7758/RSF.3.2.08.

Sari, Florent. 2012. "Analysis of Neighbourhood Effects and Work Behaviour: Evidence from Paris." *Housing Studies* 27(1): 45–76.

Sastry, Narayan. 2012. "Neighborhood Effects on Children's Achievement: A Review of Recent Research." In *Oxford Handbook on Child Development and Poverty*, edited by Rosalind B. King and Valerie Maholmes. New York: Oxford University Press.

Schootman, Mario, Elena Andresen, Fredric Wolinsky, Theodore Malmstrom, Philip Miller, and Douglas Miller. 2007. "Neighbourhood Environment and the Incidence of Depressive Symptoms Among Middle-Aged African Americans." *Journal of Epidemiology and Community Health* 61(6): 527–32.

Schwartz, Heather. 2010. *Housing Policy Is School Policy: Economically Integrative Housing Promotes Academic Achievement in Montgomery County, MD*. New York: Century Foundation.

Sharkey, Patrick. 2010. "The Acute Effect of Local Homicides on Children's Cognitive Performance." *Proceedings of the National Academy of Sciences* 107(26): 11733–38.

———. 2012. "An Alternative Approach to Addressing Selection into and out of Social Settings: Neighborhood Change and African American Children's Economic Outcomes." *Sociological Methods and Research* 41(2): 251–93.

———. 2014. "Spatial Segmentation and the Black Middle Class." *American Journal of Sociology* 119(4): 903–54.

Sharkey, Patrick, and Felix Elwert. 2011. "The Legacy of Disadvantage: Multigenerational Neighborhood Effects on Cognitive Ability." *American Journal of Sociology* 116(6): 1934–81.

Sharkey, Patrick, and Jacob Faber. 2014. "Where, When, Why, and for Whom Do Residential Contexts Matter? Moving Away from the Dichotomous Understanding of Neighborhood Effects." *Annual Review of Sociology* 40(1): 559–79.

Sharkey, Patrick, and Robert Sampson. 2010. "The Acute Effect of Local Homicides on Children's Cognitive Performance." *Proceedings of the National Academy of Sciences* 107(26): 11733–38.

———. 2015. "Neighborhood Violence and Cognitive Functioning." In *Social Neuroscience: Brain, Mind, and Society*, edited by Russell Schutt, Larry Seidman, and Matcheri Keshavan. Cambridge, Mass.: Harvard University Press.

Sharkey, Patrick, Amy Schwartz, Ingrid Ellen, and Johanna Lacoe. 2014. "High Stakes in the Classroom, High Stakes on the Street: The Effects of Community Violence on Students' Standardized Test Performance." *Sociological Science* 1(May): 199–220.

Sharkey, Patrick, Nicole Tirado-Strayer, Andrew Papachristos, and C. Cybele Raver. 2012. "The Effect of Local Violence on Children's Attention and Impulse Control." *American Journal of Public Health* 102(12): 2287.

Smolensky, Eugene. 2007. "Children in the Vanguard of the U.S. Welfare State." *Journal of Economic Literature* 45(4): 1011–23.

Stretesky, Paul B. 2003. "The Distribution of Air Lead Levels Across U.S. Counties: Implications for the Production of Racial Inequality." *Sociological Spectrum* 23(1): 91–118.

Tach, Laura, Sara Jacoby, Douglas Wiebe, Terry Guerra, and Therese Richmond. 2016. "The Effect of Microneighborhood Conditions on Adult

Educational Attainment in a Subsidized Housing Intervention." *Housing Policy Debate* 26(2): 380–97.

Tienda, Marta. 1991. "Poor People and Poor Places: Deciphering Neighborhood Effects on Poverty Outcomes." In *Macro-micro Linkages in Sociology*, edited by Joan Huber. Newbury Park, Calif.: Sage.

Turner, Margery Austin, Jennifer Comey, Daniel Kuehn, and Austin Nichols. 2012. *Residential Mobility, High-Opportunity Neighborhoods, and Outcomes for Low-Income Families: Insights from the Moving to Opportunity Demonstration*. Washington: U.S. Department of Housing and Urban Development.

United Nations Office on Drugs and Crime (UNODC). 2013. "Global Study on Homicide 2013." Vienna: UNODC.

van Ham, Maarten, and David Manley. 2009. "The Effect of Neighbourhood Housing Tenure Mix on Labor Market Outcomes: A Longitudinal Perspective." *IZA discussion paper no. 4094*. Bonn: Institute for the Study of Labor.

———. 2010. "The Effect of Neighborhood Housing Tenure Mix on Labour Market Outcomes: A Longitudinal Investigation of Neighborhood Effects." *Journal of Economic Geography* 10(2): 257–82.

Vartanian, Thomas, and Philip Gleason. 1999. "Do Neighborhood Conditions Affect High School Dropout and College Graduation Rates?" *Journal of Socio-Economics* 28(1): 21–24.

Votruba, Mark Edward, and Jeffrey Kling. 2009. "Effects of Neighborhood Characteristics on the Mortality of Black Male Youth: Evidence from Gautreaux, Chicago." *Social Science and Medicine* 68(5): 814–23.

Waldinger, Roger. 1996. *Still the Promised City? African Americans and New Immigrants in Postindustrial New York*. Cambridge Mass.: Harvard University Press.

Watson, Tara. 2009. "Inequality and the Measurement of Residential Segregation by Income." *Review of Income and Wealth* 55(3): 820–44.

Weinberg, Bruce, Patricia Reagan, and Jeffrey Yankow. 2004. "Do Neighborhoods Affect Work Behavior? Evidence from the NLSY79." *Journal of Labor Economics* 22(4): 891–924.

Weinhardt, Felix. 2014. "Social Housing, Neighborhood Quality and Student Performance." *Journal of Urban Economics* 82(1): 12–31.

Weisburd, David, Shawn Bushway, Cynthia Lum, and SueMing Yang. 2004. "Trajectories of Crime at Places: A Longitudinal Study of Street Segments in the City of Seattle." *Criminology* 42(2): 283–322.

Wilson, William Julius. 1987. *The Truly Disadvantaged: The Inner City, the Underclass, and Public Policy*. Chicago: University of Chicago Press.

———. 1996. *When Work Disappears: The World of the New Urban Poor*. New York: Alfred A. Knopf.

Yagan, Danny. 2016. "The Enduring Employment Impact of Your Great Recession Location." Unpublished working paper. Department of Economics, University of California, Berkeley.

A Continuous Measure of the Joint Distribution of Race and Income Among Neighborhoods

SEAN F. REARDON, JOSEPH TOWNSEND, AND LINDSAY FOX

We develop and illustrate a general and innovative method for describing in detail the joint distribution of race and income among neighborhoods when only coarse income data are available. The approach provides estimates of the average income distribution and racial composition of the neighborhoods of households of a given racial category and specific income level. We illustrate the method using 2007–2011 tract-level data from the American Community Survey. We show, for example, that blacks and Hispanics of any given income typically live in neighborhoods substantially poorer than those of whites and Asians of the same income. Our approach provides a general method for fully characterizing the joint patterns of racial and socioeconomic segregation, and so may prove useful in understanding the spatial foundations and correlates of racial and socioeconomic inequality.

Keywords: race, income, neighborhood composition, segregation, exposure

Although racial and socioeconomic segregation are persistent features of the residential landscape, both have changed over the last four decades in the United States. Racial segregation has declined moderately, particularly segregation between white and black households, but remains high in many places (Logan and Stults 2011; Logan, Stults, and Farley 2004). Segregation by income has risen sharply since 1970, mostly in the 1980s and the 2000s (Reardon and Bischoff 2011; Bischoff and Reardon 2014; Jargowsky 1996, 2003; Watson 2009). Less clear, however, are the trends and patterns of the joint distribution of neighborhoods' racial and socioeconomic characteristics. That is, we do not have a clear description of how much neighborhoods differ, in terms of racial and economic composition, among households with the same income but differing race, or same race but differing income. Without such a description, it is unclear whether and how changes in racial and economic segregation have altered disparities in neighborhood conditions.

In U.S. census and American Community Survey (ACS) data, income is tabulated—by race and census tract—by a set of ordered income categories. Exact information on the

Sean F. Reardon is professor of poverty and inequality in education at Stanford University. **Joseph Townsend** is a PhD candidate and Institute of Education Sciences predoctoral fellow at Stanford University. **Lindsay Fox** is a researcher at Mathematica Policy Research.

© 2017 Russell Sage Foundation. Reardon, Sean F., Joseph Townsend, and Lindsay Fox. 2017. "A Continuous Measure of the Joint Distribution of Race and Income Among Neighborhoods." *RSF: The Russell Sage Foundation Journal of the Social Sciences* 3(3): 34–62. DOI: 10.7758/RSF.3.2.02. An earlier version of this paper was presented at the Russell Sage Foundation conference "The Spatial Foundations of Inequality" on February 11–12, 2015. We thank George Galster, Patrick Sharkey, two anonymous reviewers, and the conference participants for helpful feedback. Direct correspondence to: Sean F. Reardon at sean.reardon@stanford.edu, Graduate School of Education, Stanford University, 520 Galvez Mall, #526, Stanford, CA 94305, 650-736-8517; Joseph Townsend at jtownsen@stanford.edu, Graduate School of Education, Stanford University, 520 Galvez Mall, #407, Stanford, CA 94305; and Lindsay Fox at lfox@mathematica-mpr.com, Mathematica Policy Research, 505 14th Street, Suite 800, Oakland, CA 94612.

means, medians, and variances of these income distributions is generally not available. As a result, the spatial patterns of the full joint distribution of race and income are also not readily available, making a complete description of racial and economic segregation difficult to obtain.

In this paper, we demonstrate an innovative approach to describing the joint distribution of race and income among neighborhoods when only coarse income data are available. We are not the first to suggest methods of describing features of this joint distribution (see, for example, Logan 2002), but the innovation of our approach is that it is much more general and versatile than existing techniques. It yields an estimate of the complete cumulative income distribution function, averaged among neighborhoods, by race and income. This makes it possible to make meaningful comparisons of the joint distribution across time and place despite differences in income distributions or differences in how income is coarsened. We show that estimating a set of multidimensional exposure functions is sufficient to generate a wide range of useful statistics regarding the joint distribution of racial and economic composition of neighborhoods, including many of the measures proposed and used in a more ad hoc fashion in much of the literature. We also explain how these measures can be used by other researchers and why it is beneficial to have a fully continuous measure of inequality.

Our interest in developing these methods derives from the theoretical and empirical literature describing the ways in which neighborhoods affect their residents' educational, socioeconomic, and health outcomes. In much of the neighborhood effects research, neighborhood poverty (or socioeconomic conditions more generally) is hypothesized to be a key distal driver of neighborhood effects, operating by directly or indirectly affecting housing conditions, school and childcare quality, access to healthy food, green spaces, safe playgrounds, social networks, the prevalence of adult role models, and a range of other institutional and collective resources that are beneficial for child development (Acevedo-Garcia and Lochner 2003; Brooks-Gunn, Duncan, and Aber 1997; Leventhal and Brooks-Gunn 2000; Sampson 2008; Sampson, Raudenbush, and Earls 1997; Wodtke, Harding, and Elwert 2011).

Although some research has suggested that neighborhoods have no significant effect on many aspects of children's development, educational success, and social, behavioral, or economic outcomes (Ludwig et al. 2013; Kling, Liebman, and Katz 2007; Sanbonmatsu et al. 2006), recent experimental and quasi-experimental research suggests that neighborhood socioeconomic conditions can have substantial effects on such outcomes, particularly as a result of sustained exposure during childhood (Chetty, Hendren, and Katz 2015; Burdick-Will et al. 2011; Harding 2003; Wodtke, Harding, and Elwert 2011; Santiago et al. 2014). Indeed, Raj Chetty and his colleagues' (2015) analysis of the Moving to Opportunity experiment shows that children in families who used a (randomly assigned) housing voucher to move to a low-poverty neighborhood have substantially higher college attendance rates and 31 percent higher earnings by their mid-twenties than those in a control group not assigned a voucher, a finding that suggests that neighborhood poverty (or its correlates and sequelae) is harmful to young children's development.

These findings highlight the importance of precisely measuring average neighborhood socioeconomic conditions, and differences in these conditions across time, racial or ethnic group, and households of varying incomes. Yet many of the measures currently used in the literature lack features that would allow for meaningful comparisons across these dimensions. For example, many measures lack detail on how conditions differ across the income distribution, instead relying on broad, arbitrarily defined categories such as low-, middle-, or high-income. These same measures tend to be limited to the income categories available in the source data. Finally, these measures can be difficult to compare across place, due to differences in the income distributions; and across time, due to changes in the categories available in the data. By describing the joint distribution of race and income among neighborhoods using percentile terms, our new measures avoid these issues. Our approach describes the average neighborhood racial and income composition for households of a given race and income level. Measuring neighborhood conditions with such sensitivity not only permits more detailed analyses of neighborhood effects, but also offers an opportunity to understand the spatial foundations of racial and socioeconomic inequality.

We develop and demonstrate in this paper a highly general approach to measuring the joint patterns of racial and economic neighborhood composition. In effect, this approach relies on estimating the average race-specific income distribution in the neighborhoods of individuals of any specific income and race. The functions describing these distributions can be used for a wide range of types of descriptive analyses, and provide a detailed account of the joint distribution of race and income across neighborhoods. Although we provide some example findings that result from our estimated functions, a full description and explanation of the joint distribution is beyond the scope of this paper. Our goal is to elucidate and illustrate this new approach so that others may use it or the data we produce in settings where a richer description of the interaction between race and income across neighborhoods is fruitful (see, for example, Reardon, Fox, and Townsend 2015).

Using the methods we develop here, we can construct a dataset containing detailed estimates of the joint distribution of race and income in each county, commuting zone, metropolitan area, and state in the United States and for each year for which census or ACS data are available. These provide both a detailed description of spatial inequality and a resource for studying spatial inequality. Our measures can be merged to other data to analyze the trends, causes, and consequences of segregation. For example, Chetty provides estimates of average adult earnings and other outcomes, conditional on childhood family income, for every county and commuting zone in the United States (www.equality-of-opportunity.org). Merging these data with our estimates of average neighborhood income distributions, conditional on family income, for each commuting zone, one might investigate the links among childhood family income, childhood neighborhood income distribution, and adult earnings, educational attainment, and childbearing. Because both our measures and Chetty's mobility measures are available for families of any specific income percentile, they allow a detailed investigation of the extent to which neighborhood segregation mediates patterns of social immobility. This is but one example of the ways that detailed estimates of the joint spatial distribution of race and income might help research develop a more nuanced understanding of the spatial foundations of inequality.

MEASURING SEGREGATION

Hundreds of articles have been devoted to developing and describing ways of measuring racial and economic segregation; hundreds more are devoted to describing their trends (for example, James and Taeuber 1985; Massey and Denton 1988, 1993; Reardon and Firebaugh 2002; Reardon and Bischoff 2011; Reardon and Owens 2014). The welter of methodological approaches to measuring segregation is partly due to academics' penchant for methodological hair-splitting. Nonetheless, important theoretical and conceptual distinctions among dimensions of segregation do lead to different measurement approaches.

Despite the abundance of ways of measuring segregation, most approaches are limited to measuring segregation along a single population dimension at a time. We know, for example, how to measure segregation among two or more racial groups (James and Taeuber 1985; Massey and Denton 1988; Reardon and Firebaugh 2002), among ordered occupational or educational groups (Reardon 2009), and by income or any other single continuous dimension (Reardon 2011; Reardon and Bischoff 2011; Jargowsky 1996). Methods of measuring multidimensional patterns of segregation, such as the joint distribution of race and income among neighborhoods, however, are less well developed.

Three approaches have been used to describe features of the joint distribution of racial and economic segregation patterns. One measures racial segregation among households of similar income (Adelman 2004; Denton and Massey 1988; Darden and Kamel 2000; Farley 1995; Iceland, Sharpe, and Steinmetz

2005; Iceland and Wilkes 2006; Massey and Fischer 1999), or income segregation among households of the same race (Farley 1991; Jargowsky 1996; Bischoff and Reardon 2014; Reardon and Bischoff 2011; Massey and Fischer 2003). Typically, this approach relies on evenness measures of segregation, such as the dissimilarity index or similar measures (James and Taeuber 1985). Some of these studies allow the comparison of overall racial segregation levels with within-income category segregation levels as a way of testing hypotheses about the role of income in shaping racial segregation levels; they do not provide a clear description of the joint distribution of race and income across neighborhoods, however.

A second approach looks at the distribution of neighborhoods along a variety of typologies and the interaction of those typologies. For example, Margery Turner and Julie Fenderson (2006) categorize neighborhoods according to how mixed they are on measures of race, ethnicity, nativity, and income. Cross-tabulating these categorizations shows the patterns of interaction between neighborhood racial and income composition. This approach shows the extent to which tracts with very low proportions of low-income residents are predominantly white or predominantly minority. Edward Goetz, Tony Damiano, and Jason Hicks (2015) take a similar approach, using it to identify what they call racially concentrated areas of wealth (RCAWs). They define RCAWs as tracts in which at least 90 percent of residents are white and more than half exceed an income threshold of four times the cost of living adjusted poverty threshold. Such approaches are useful for their specificity, but provide only partial descriptions of the joint distribution of race and income and depend on how racial and income distributions are dichotomized.

A third approach relies on so-called exposure measures of segregation to describe the average exposure of households of a given race-by-income category to those of another such category. Most commonly, these studies compute racial groups' exposure to poverty: the average proportion of poor residents in the neighborhoods of members of different racial groups (Timberlake 2002, 2007; Timberlake and Iceland 2007; Logan 2002, 2011; Massey and Fischer 2003). These measures provide a much more interpretable description of differences in average neighborhood socioeconomic conditions than the evenness measures. John Logan (2011), for example, categorizes households by race and three income categories (poor, middle, and affluent) and measures the exposure of various race-by-income groups to other groups. This approach results in descriptive statements such as "Affluent blacks are currently less [exposed to black neighbors] than poor blacks (36.3 versus 42.9), and also somewhat more exposed to whites (42.9 versus 39.8)" (Logan 2011, 3). A related approach compares groups' exposure with some measure of neighborhood quality. Samantha Friedman, Joseph Gibbons, and Chris Galvan (2014) use data from the American Housing Survey to compare neighborhood conditions among middle- and upper-class households of different races or ethnicities; they find that affluent blacks and Hispanics experience inferior neighborhood circumstances relative to affluent whites. Like the neighborhood typology measures, such approaches depend on the definition of income categorizations used.

The more general drawback of all these approaches is that, unless fine-grained income information is available, they are limited to comparisons based on the income categories reported in the data, which may be relatively crude. Moreover, these categories may change over time (for example, the Census Bureau has often changed the number and definition of the income categories reported in published tables). Even if they do not change, their location in the income distribution will vary across time and place because of differences in income distributions. Finally, even within a given place and time, the categories are not necessarily exactly comparable across groups. Suppose we define *poor* as having an income below $20,000. By this definition, the average poor black household will generally have a lower income than the average poor white household, simply because the black income distribution is lower than the white distribution. So a comparison of the neighborhoods of poor whites and blacks may be misleading when we base the comparison on broad income categories rather than exact income.

We adopt an approach similar to the third one here, but our innovation is to develop methods of estimating the joint distribution of racial and economic neighborhood composition in ways that are not sensitive to the definitions of income categories provided in the census or ACS. Our approach allows one to describe the average racial and income distributions in neighborhoods of households of different incomes, the average racial and income distributions in the neighborhoods of households of different income levels and race, and the average race-specific income distributions in the neighborhoods of households of different income levels and race. These measures are similar to the more standard exposure measures used by others (for example, the exposure of poor blacks to middle-class neighbors), but differ in that they are fully continuous, rather than categorical, measures of exposure. In effect, they describe the average joint distribution of race and income in the neighborhoods of individuals of any specific income and race. As a result, they can be used for a wide range of types of descriptive analyses, and provide a detailed account of the joint distribution of race and income across neighborhoods.

ESTIMATING AVERAGE NEIGHBORHOOD INCOME DISTRIBUTIONS, BY RACE AND INCOME

In this paper, we use g and h to denote racial groups (or other categorical groups); we use p and q to denote income levels, expressed as percentiles (scaled from 0 to 1, for convenience) of the population income distribution; and we use i to index neighborhoods. The function $\rho_x(p)$ describes the income density function in some population x, where x may refer to a specific group or neighborhood; correspondingly, the function $R_x(p) = \int_0^p \rho_x(r) dr$ denotes the cumulative income distribution function in population x. Finally, we use T_x to denote the count of households in population x, and π_{gi} to indicate the proportion of households in neighborhood i that are in group g.

Primary Estimand and Estimation Approach

Our goal, in general, is to estimate the function $f_g^h(p,q)$ that describes the average cumulative income distribution function of group h in the neighborhoods of members of group g with income p. That is,

$$f_g^h(p,q) = \sum_i \left[\frac{T_i \cdot \pi_{gi} \cdot \rho_{gi}(p)}{T \cdot \pi_g \cdot \rho_g(p)} \cdot \pi_{hi} \cdot R_{hi}(q) \right]. \quad (1)$$

Note that $f_g^h(p,q)$, defined this way, is interpreted as the weighted average proportion of the households in a neighborhood that are members of group h and have incomes less than or equal to q, where the weights are the number of households of group g with income p in each neighborhood. In the segregation literature, such measures are called *exposure* measures because they describe the average extent to which members of one group (in this case members of group g with income p) are exposed to members of another group (members of group h with incomes less than or equal to q) in their local context (neighborhood in this case) (Massey and Denton 1988; Lieberson 1981). In appendix A, we describe how to estimate the functions $f_g^h(p,q)$ by assuming they can be approximated by a set of multidimensional polynomials of p and q.

Other Quantities of Interest

If we know $f_g^h(p,q)$ for all groups g and h, we can derive a number of additional useful quantities:

Functions describing exposure to overall (not race-specific) neighborhood income distributions, conditional on race and income. The average cumulative income distribution in the neighborhoods of members of group g with incomes p is simply the sum of the corresponding group-specific functions:

$$f_g^t(p,q) = \sum_h f_g^h(p,q). \quad (2)$$

Functions describing exposure to race-specific neighborhood income distributions, conditional on income. The typical household with income p lives in a neighborhood where members of group h have an income distribution given by

$$f_t^h(p,q) = \sum_g \left[\pi_g \cdot \rho_g(p) \cdot f_g^h(p,q) \right]. \quad (3)$$

The function describing exposure to overall neighborhood income distributions, condi-

tional on income. Combining equations (2) and (3), we can derive the function $f_t^t(p,q)$ which describes the average cumulative income distribution function in the neighborhoods of households with income p:

$$f_t^t(p,q) = \sum_h f_t^h(p,q) = \sum_g \pi_g \rho_g(p) f_g^t(p,q)$$
$$= \sum_g \pi_g \rho_g(p) \sum_h f_g^h(p,q). \quad (4)$$

Average neighborhood racial composition, conditional on race and household income. The average racial composition of the neighborhoods of members of group g with income p (the exposure of members of group g and income p to members of group h) is simply $f_g^h(p,1)$. The average racial composition in the neighborhoods of households with income p is likewise given by the functions $f_t^h(p,1)$. Note that $f_g^t(p,1) = f_t^t(p,1) = 1$ by definition (because all households in a neighborhood have incomes less than or equal to 1 by definition).

Average neighborhood race-specific income density functions, conditional on race and income. Because $f_g^h(p,q)$ is a cumulative distribution function, we can obtain the corresponding density function, denoted $\rho_g^h(p,q)$, by taking the derivative of f_g^h with respect to q:

$$\rho_g^h(p,q) = \frac{d}{dq} f_g^h(p,q). \quad (5)$$

The formula holds when g or h or both g and h is replaced by t as well.

Percentiles of average neighborhood race-specific income distributions, conditional on race and income. First define

$$f_g^{*h}(p,q) = \frac{f_g^h(p,q)}{f_g^h(p,1)}. \quad (6)$$

Now $f_g^{*h}(p,q)$ describes, for members of group g with incomes p, the weighted average proportion of the households in a neighborhood that are members of group h with incomes less than or equal to q relative to the weighted average proportion of the households in a neighborhood that are members of group h, where the weights are defined as above. If we wanted to know the median income among the group h neighbors of a member of group g with income p, we would find q such that $f_g^{*h}(p,q) = 0.50$. More generally, the $100 \cdot c^{th}$ percentile of the income distribution of members of group h in the neighborhoods of members of group g with income p is $f_g^{*h-1}(p,c)$, where $f_g^{*h-1}(p,c)$ returns the value q such that $f_g^{*h}(p,q) = c$.

Note that $f_g^t(p,1) = f_t^t(p,1) = 1$ by definition, but $f_t^h(p,1) \neq 1$ in general, so

$$f_g^{*t}(p,q) = f_g^t(p,q)$$
$$f_t^{*t}(p,q) = f_t^t(p,q)$$
$$f_t^{*h}(p,q) = \frac{f_t^h(p,q)}{f_t^h(p,1)}. \quad (7)$$

Thus, estimating $f_g^h(p,q)$ is sufficient to obtain a number of useful functions describing the joint neighborhood distribution of race and income. A number of other standard exposure measures, as well as measures of between-group differences in income, can be readily computed from the $f_g^h(p,q)$ functions, as we describe in appendix C.

DATA

In this paper, we use data from the 2007–2011 ACS to illustrate the types of descriptive patterns that can be obtained from our approach. We use census tracts as our definition of neighborhoods. The ACS provides partial cross-tabulations of household counts by income and racial-ethnic categories. The 2007–2011 ACS data include sixteen categories of income, seven race categories, and one indicator for whether the household is of Hispanic origin. We focus here on five mutually exclusive and exhaustive race-ethnic groups: non-Hispanic Asian, non-Hispanic black, Hispanic, non-Hispanic white, and non-Hispanic other. We use an iterative proportional fitting (IPF) process to estimate the full cross-tabulations of these five race-ethnic categories by income within each census tract, using Public Use Microdata Samples (PUMS) data to seed the IPF tables (for complete details on the construction of the cross-tabulations and a discussion of the accuracy of the IPF process, see Reardon, Fox, and Townsend 2015). The result is a dataset containing estimated counts of the number of households in each race-ethnic group that are in each income category for each tract in the United States between 2007 and 2011.

Illustrative Application of the Approach

The purpose of this paper is to illustrate a new way of describing the joint distribution of race and income across neighborhoods. To do so, we use the 2007–2011 ACS data and the estimation methods described in the appendix to compute eighty observed values of $\rho_g(p)$ and 6,400 values of $f_g^h(p,q)$ for each of the values of g, h, p, and q observed in the ACS data. We fit multidimensional polynomials to these data to estimate the continuous functions $\rho_g(p)$ and $f_g^h(p,q)$. Using these, we derive the other functions described and construct a set of illustrative figures to demonstrate a number of ways that the estimates can be used to describe the joint neighborhood distributions of race and income. All of our calculations use income percentiles scaled from 0 to 1 (as noted), but the illustrative figures below show income on a percentile scale from 0 to 100 for ease of interpretation.

A first step in estimating the exposure measures is calculating race-specific household income densities, described by the functions $\rho_g(p)$. These density functions are presented (stacked) in figure 1, which shows the proportion of households of a given race at each percentile of the national household income distribution. The horizontal axis measures household income in percentiles (with corresponding dollar amounts noted) of the national household income distribution. The vertical axis is population proportion. Reading the figure vertically, then, describes the proportion of households of each race among all households at a given income percentile. The shaded area for each group describes the group's income distribution.

Figure 1 illustrates the unequal income distributions among white, black, Hispanic, and Asian households in the United States. Black households are disproportionately concentrated at the lower end of the income distribution, Hispanics in the bottom half, and white and Asian households above the national median. Nonetheless, a majority of low-income households are white in the United States, by virtue of their much larger population share. Although the patterns in figure 1 have been demonstrated in previous research, our estimation approach facilitates the presentation of these patterns in terms of percentile ranks of the national income distribution.

Figure 2 presents the 25th, 50th, and 75th percentiles of the average neighborhood income distributions of households at each point in the income distribution. These distributions are described by the function $f_t^t(p,q)$. Rather than plot the full surface described by $f_t^t(p,q)$, however, figure 2 plots selected percentiles of neighborhood income distributions. To compute these values, we construct the function $f_t^{t-1}(p,c)$ (by numerically inverting $f_t^t(p,q)$) for the values $c \in \{.25, .50, .75\}$ and for $p \in \{.01, .02, \ldots, .99\}$. For example, to identify the 50th percentile income in the typical neighborhood of a household with 5th percentile income, we set $f_t^t(.05,q)$ equal to 0.50 and solve for q via numerical interpolation. The horizontal axis represents a household's income; the vertical axis represents neighborhood household income.[1]

As an example of how to read this figure, consider households with income of $20,000, which is approximately at the 18th percentile of the national income distribution. Such households, on average, live in neighborhoods where 25 percent of households have incomes at or below the 20th percentile of the national household income distribution (about $22,000); where the median of the average neighborhood household income distribution is roughly equal to the 42nd percentile of the national household income distribution (about $44,000); and where the 75th percentile of the average neighborhood household income distribution

---

1. Although the exposure measures themselves are calculated in percentiles, the axes need not be presented in percentiles. The axes can be rescaled and shown in dollars, or even log dollars. The dollar figures here, as well as in all following figures, are 2012 dollars and correspond directly to the thresholds of the sixteen income categories in the ACS data. For convenience, here and elsewhere, the axes are labeled in terms of both income percentiles and dollars.

Figure 1. Race-Specific Income Distributions, All Households, 2007–2011

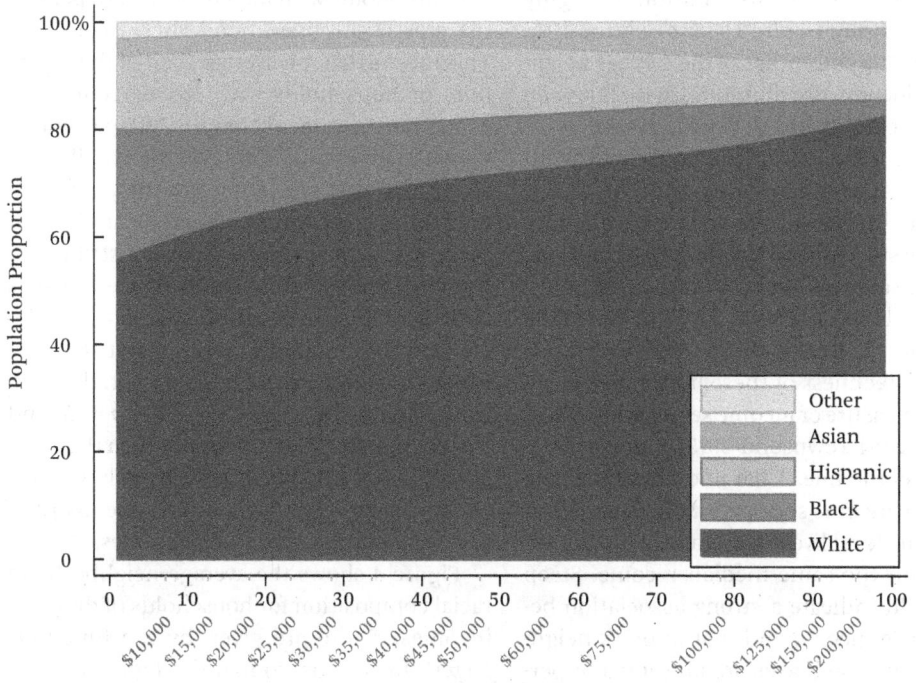

Source: Authors' calculations from ACS.

Figure 2. Average Neighborhood Household Income Distributions, 2007–2011

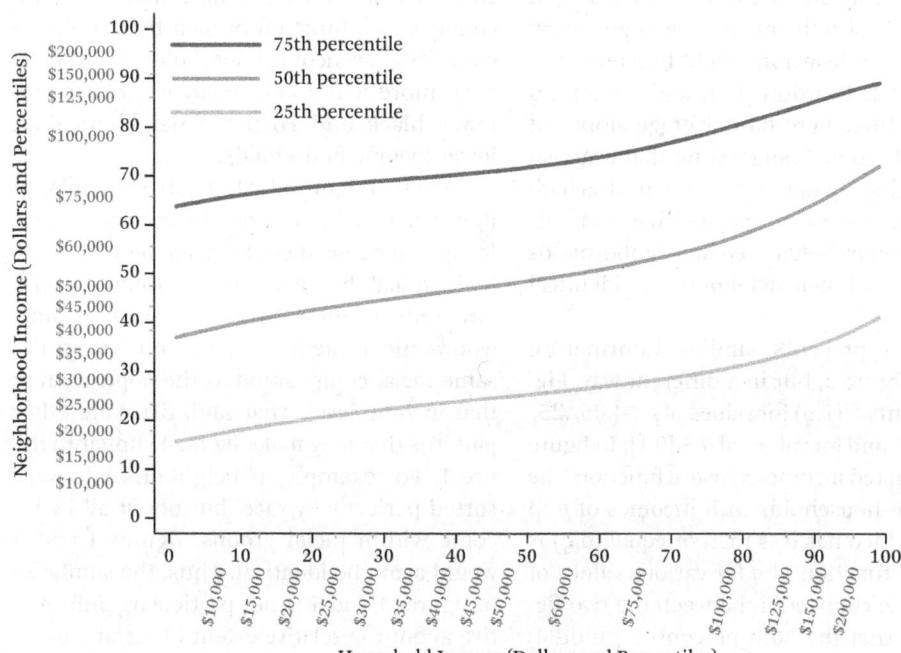

Source: Authors' calculations from ACS.

is at about the 68th percentile of the national household income distribution (roughly $77,000). Although figure 2 shows only the 25th, 50th, and 75th percentiles of the average neighborhood income distributions, these lines can be constructed for any desired percentile.

Figure 2 makes clear that households with higher incomes live, on average, in neighborhoods with higher household income distributions. The steepness of the lines in figure 2 describes the association between a household's income and the 25th, 50th, and 75th percentile household income in the neighborhood. Indeed, the steepness of these lines provides an intuitive measure of income segregation (Reardon, Fox, and Townsend 2015). Consider the 50th percentile line. A flat line would indicate no or little income segregation: households at any income level live, on average, in neighborhoods with the same median income. Steep lines would indicate a strong association between one's income and that of one's neighbors. Because both axes are presented in percentile terms, the maximum value of the slope, averaged over the range of percentiles, is one. The lines are steeper in the right side of figure 2, indicating that segregation among upper-income households is moderately larger than among lower-income households, consistent with other research on income segregation (Bischoff and Reardon 2014; Reardon and Bischoff 2011; Reardon, Fox, and Townsend 2015). The lines here have average slopes of roughly 0.25 to 0.35, suggesting that segregation is roughly one-quarter to one-third as high as its theoretical maximum, which would only occur if all households lived in neighborhoods where they and their neighbors had identical incomes.

Figure 3 presents similar information to that in figure 2, but in a different way. Figure 3 presents $f_t^i(p,q)$ for values of $p \in \{.05, .25, .50, .75, .95\}$ and for values of $q \in [0,1]$. In figure 3, the estimated income exposure function (the exposure of households with incomes of p to those with incomes less than or equal to q) is drawn as a function of q for various values of p. To see the connection between the two figures, note that the 50th percentile (middle) line in figure 2 corresponds to where each of the lines in figure 3 crosses the value 50 on the vertical axis. The top line in figure 3, representing households with income at the 5th percentile, crosses this line around where q equals 38. This means that, on average, half of the neighbors of households with 5th percentile incomes have incomes below the 38th percentile. Figure 2 shows this as well: on the middle line, when p (scaled here from 0 to 100) equals 5, median neighborhood income is at the 38th percentile of the national income distribution. Drawing the functions as in figure 3 makes clear again that segregation between the affluent and the middle class is greater than between the middle class and the poor: the horizontal spaces between the $p = 50$, $p = 75$, and $p = 95$ lines are greater than between the $p = 5$, $p = 25$, and $p = 50$ lines, indicating larger discrepancies in neighborhood income distributions as household income increases.

Figure 4 shows the average neighborhood racial composition for households of different incomes. These are given by the functions $f_t^h(p,1)$. In contrast to figure 1, figure 4 shows the average racial composition of households' neighborhoods, not the population racial composition. On the vertical axis, the typical racial composition of the neighborhood sums to 100 percent, and the figure shows how the racial composition of the average neighborhood changes as a function of own household income. Higher-income households, on average, have more white and Asian neighbors and fewer black and Hispanic neighbors than lower-income households.

Note that figure 4 looks relatively similar to figure 1. If neighborhoods were sorted perfectly by income, then these two figures would be identical, because every household would have only neighbors with their same income, who would, by definition, have on average the same racial composition as the population at that income level. That said, there are other patterns that may make figure 4 similar to figure 1. For example, if neighborhoods were sorted perfectly by race, but not at all by income within racial groups, figures 1 and 4 would again be identical. Thus, the similarity of figures 1 and 4 is not particularly informative about the relative extent of racial and income segregation that underlie them.

What is not clear from figure 4 is whether

Figure 3. Average Cumulative Neighborhood Income Distributions, 2007–2011

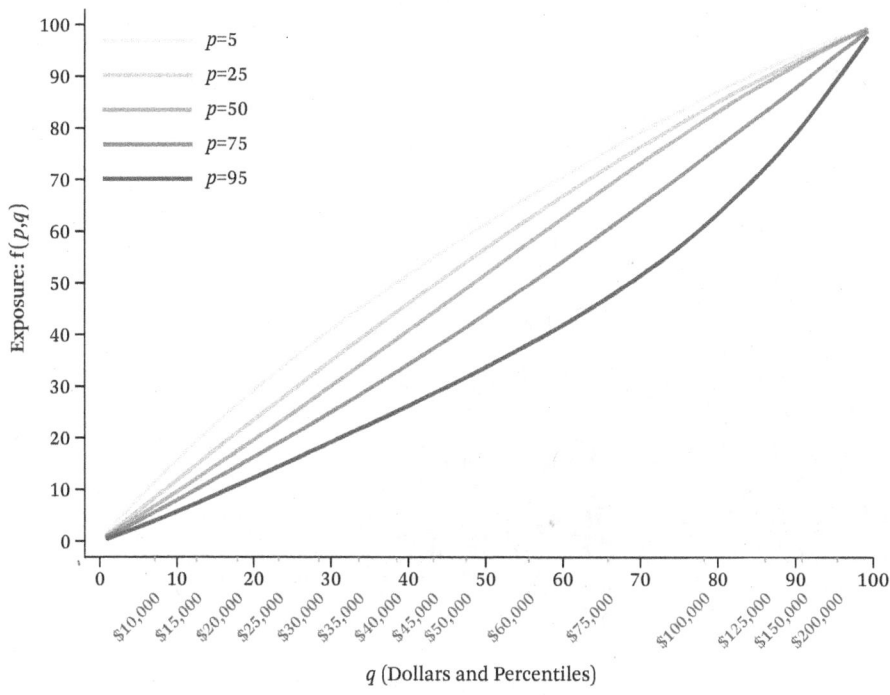

Source: Authors' calculations from ACS.

Figure 4. Average Neighborhood Racial Composition, by Household Income, All Households 2007–2011

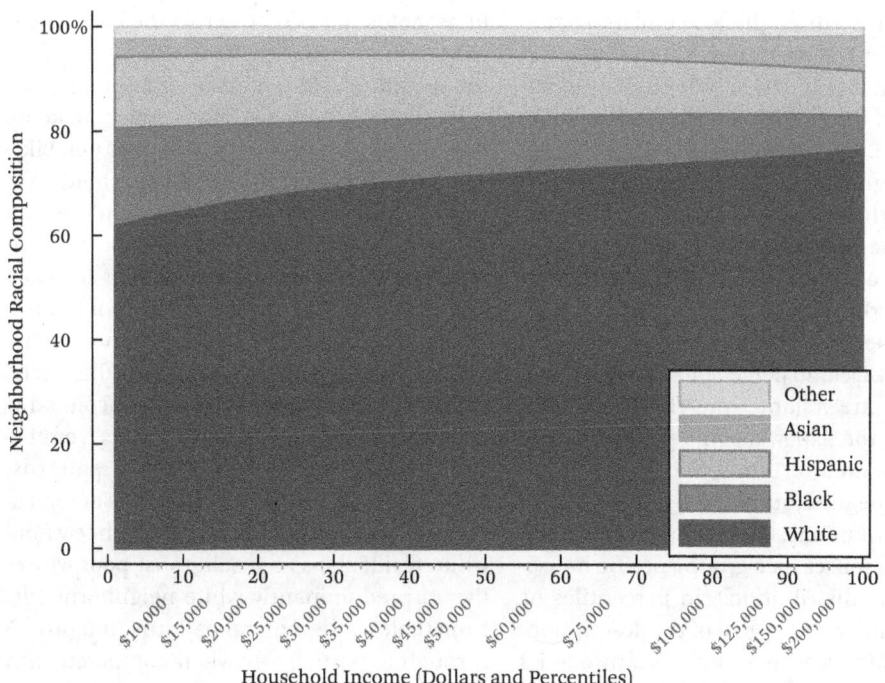

Source: Authors' calculations from ACS.

Figure 5. Average Neighborhood Racial Composition, by Household Income, Asian Households, 2007–2011

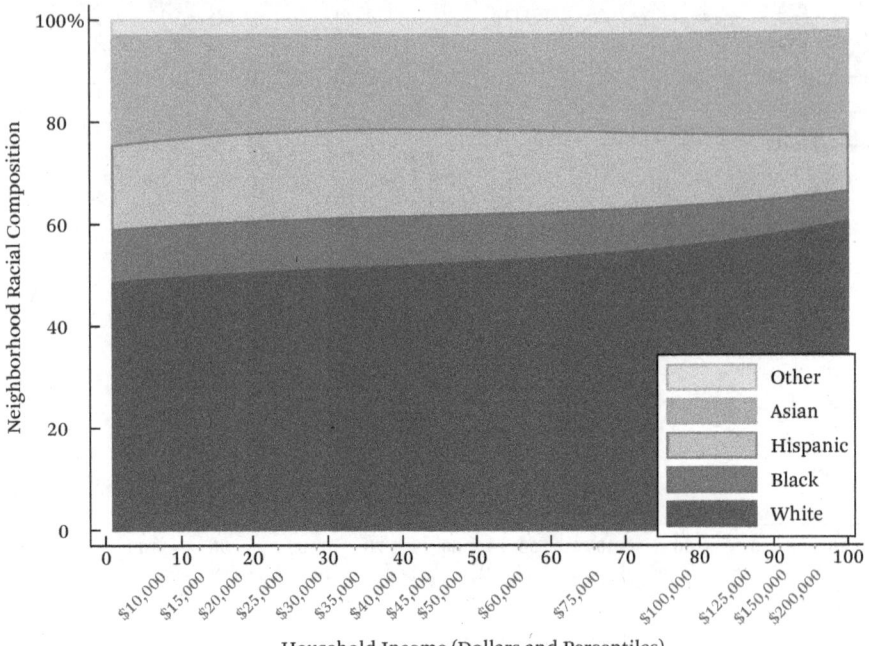

Source: Authors' calculations from ACS.

households of different races but the same income typically live in racially similar neighborhoods. Figures 5 through 8 are similar to figure 4, but present average neighborhood racial composition as a function of both householders' race and income, as described by the functions $f_g^h(p,1)$. For example, figure 5 shows the average neighborhood racial composition for Asian households, conditional on their household income percentile. Asian households at the 50th percentile of the income distribution live in neighborhoods where, on average, roughly 50 percent of households are white, 10 percent are black, 20 percent are Hispanic, and 20 percent are Asian. Note that here, and throughout the paper, income percentiles are always measured in terms of the overall national income distribution, not group-specific income distributions. Of course, the axes could be scaled to reflect race group-specific household income distributions, in percentiles or dollars, if that were the goal of the description.

One striking feature of figures 5 through 8 is the high proportion of same-race households in the neighborhoods of each race group, regardless of income. For example, the average neighborhood racial composition for Asian households shows that, across the income distribution, nearly 20 percent of households in the neighborhood are Asian households, despite the fact that Asian households make up only roughly 5 percent of the population. Likewise, even high-income black households typically live in neighborhoods that are more than 40 percent black and less than 50 percent white. Similar patterns are evident for each race group, but are most extreme for whites. White households live in neighborhoods that are around 80 percent white, and this racial isolation is consistent across the income distribution. In part this pattern results from between-region racial composition patterns. Many low-income white households are in rural areas and parts of the country with few non-white residents; as a result, most poor whites live in predominantly white neighborhoods. Nonetheless, the general patterns in figures 5 through 8, particularly when compared with figure 4, indicate high levels of racial segregation, even conditional on income.

Figure 6. Average Neighborhood Racial Composition, by Household Income, Black Households, 2007–2011

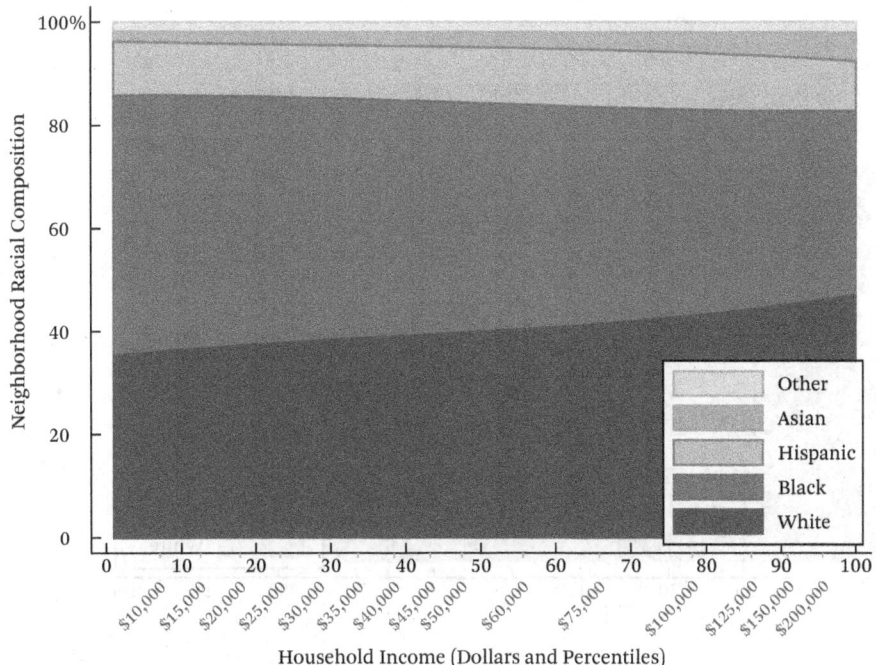

Source: Authors' calculations from ACS.

Figure 7. Average Neighborhood Racial Composition, by Household Income, Hispanic Households, 2007–2011

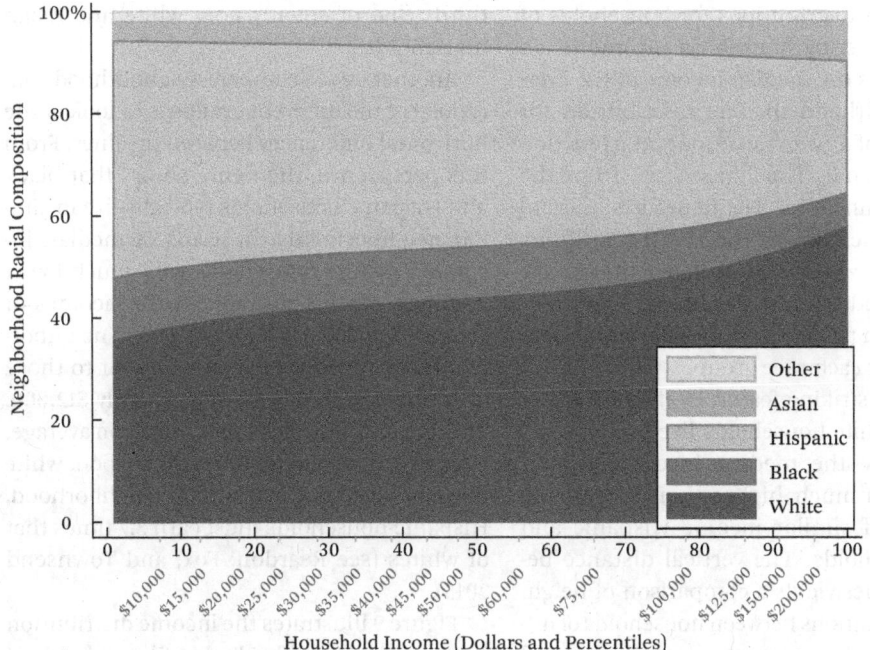

Source: Authors' calculations from ACS.

Figure 8. Average Neighborhood Racial Composition, by Household Income, White Households, 2007–2011

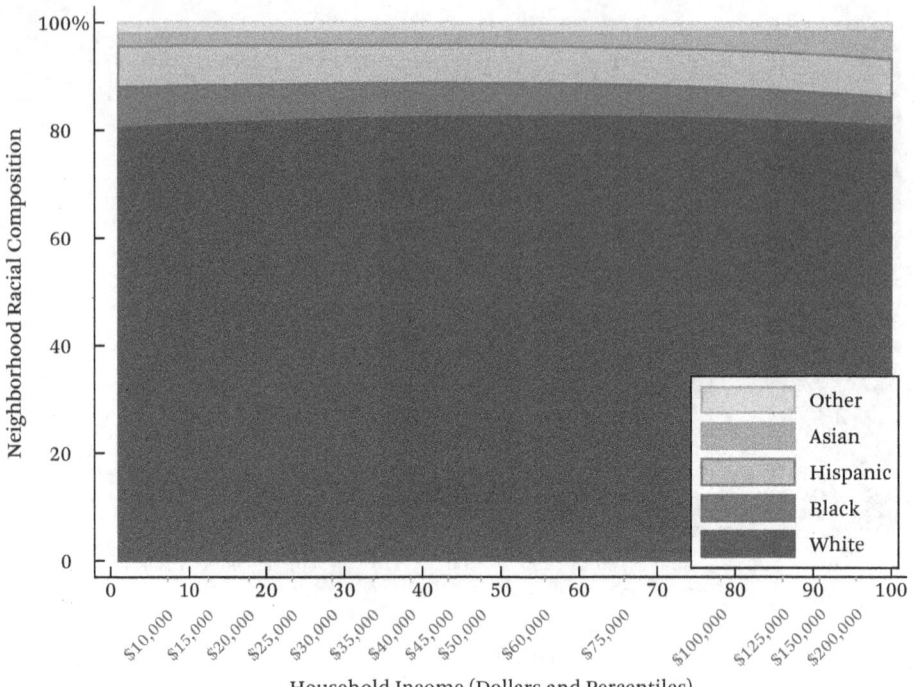

Source: Authors' calculations from ACS.

Figure 9 describes the average neighborhood income distributions for households of different races, by household income. Each line describes the median income of the average neighborhood income distribution for households of a given race group, as a function of their income. The lines come from the $f_g^{t-1}(p,0.50)$ functions. The figure is similar to figure 2 (which shows the $f_t^{t-1}(p,0.50)$ function), but shows only the median of the average neighborhood income distribution (not the 25th and 75th percentiles), and presents a separate line for each race group.

The most striking feature of figure 9 is that Asian and white households live in neighborhoods where the median income of their neighbors is much higher than that of the neighbors of similar income Hispanic and black households. The vertical distance between the lines yields a comparison of neighborhood conditions between households of different races. For example, poor black and Hispanic households live in neighborhoods where the median income is roughly two-thirds that of equally poor white and Asian households.

Another way to compare neighborhood conditions of the different groups is to look at the horizontal differences between the lines. From this perspective, the figure shows that black and Hispanic households typically live in similar neighborhoods (in terms of median income) as white households with much lower incomes. Black households with incomes of roughly $60,000, for example, live in neighborhoods with median incomes similar to those of white households earning roughly $12,000. This means that black households, on average, need to earn about five times that of poor white households to live in a similar neighborhood. Hispanic households must earn 3.7 times that of whites (see Reardon, Fox, and Townsend 2015).

Figure 9 illustrates the income distribution in the typical neighborhood of households of different races. Figure 10, in contrast, illus-

Figure 9. Neighborhood Median Income, by Household Race and Income, 2007–2011

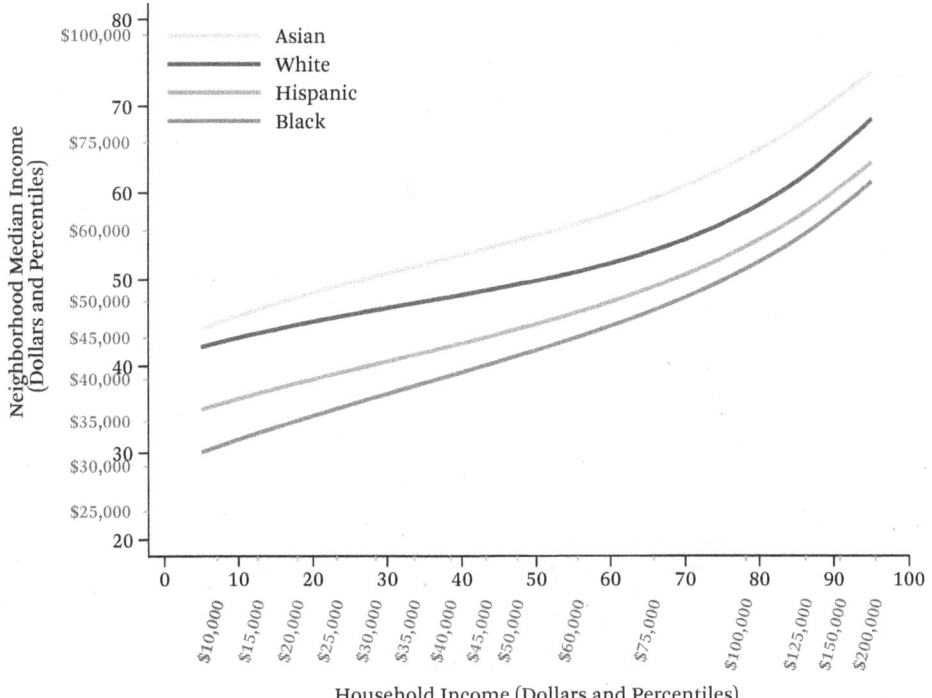

Source: Authors' calculations from ACS.

trates the opposite: the income distributions of each race in the average neighborhood of households of a given income. Specifically, figure 10 plots the functions $f_t^{*h-1}(p, 0.50)$. Each line represents the median of the neighborhood income distribution of a specific group for typical households of specific incomes. For example, a typical household at the 25th percentile of the income distribution lives in a neighborhood where the median black income is at roughly the 30th percentile of the national income distribution and the median white income is at roughly the 47th percentile. The figure shows that, on average, Asian and white income distributions are higher than those of blacks and Hispanics for all values of household income, indicating that, for most households in the United States, black and Hispanic neighbors are poorer than Asian and white neighbors. Indeed, across the income distribution, the typical household's black neighbors have median incomes roughly $20,000 less than those of white neighbors—a substantial difference. These patterns have important implications for perceptions of racial differences. If households were sorted only by income, the average household would experience no racial differences in income among their neighbors. The patterns here (as well as in figures 5 through 9) indicate that households are sorted not only on income, but on race as well. The average person looking at his or her neighbors experiences blacks and Hispanics as poorer than whites and Asians.

Figures 11 through 14 are similar to figure 10, but show race-specific median incomes in the neighborhoods of Asian, black, Hispanic, and white households, respectively. Specifically, each line in figures 11 through 14 is one of the $f_g^{*h-1}(p, .50)$ functions. For example, the third (Hispanic) line in figure 11 indicates that the typical Asian household at the median of the national income distribution lives in a neighborhood where the median income among Hispanic households is around the 46th percentile of the national income distribution. As in the other figures showing the f^{-1} functions, one could choose other percentiles

Figure 10. Race-Specific Neighborhood Median Income, All Households, 2007–2011

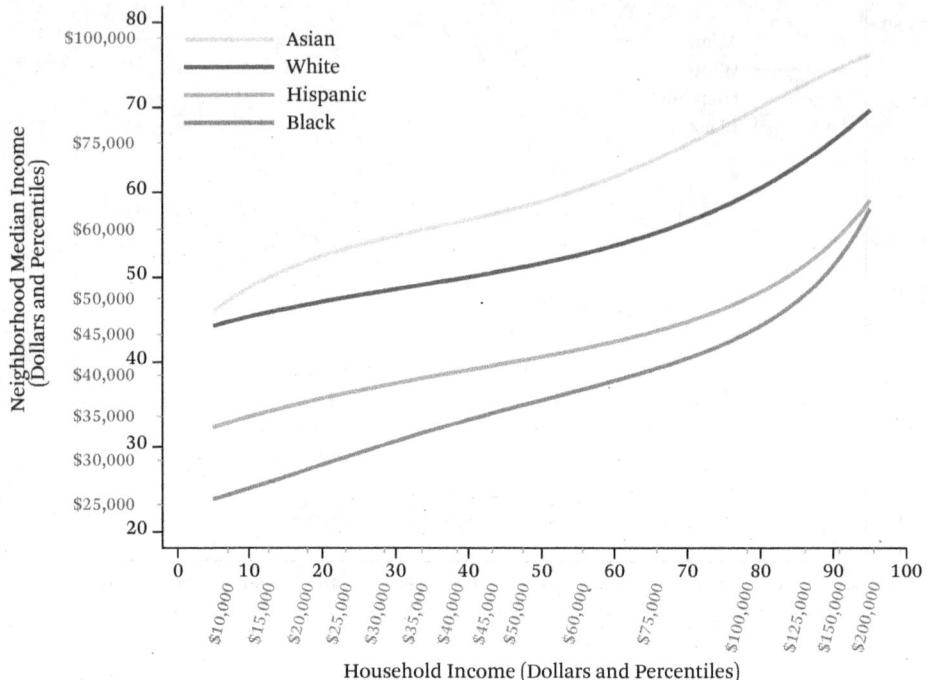

Source: Authors' calculations from ACS.

Figure 11. Race-Specific Neighborhood Median Income, Asian Households, 2007–2011

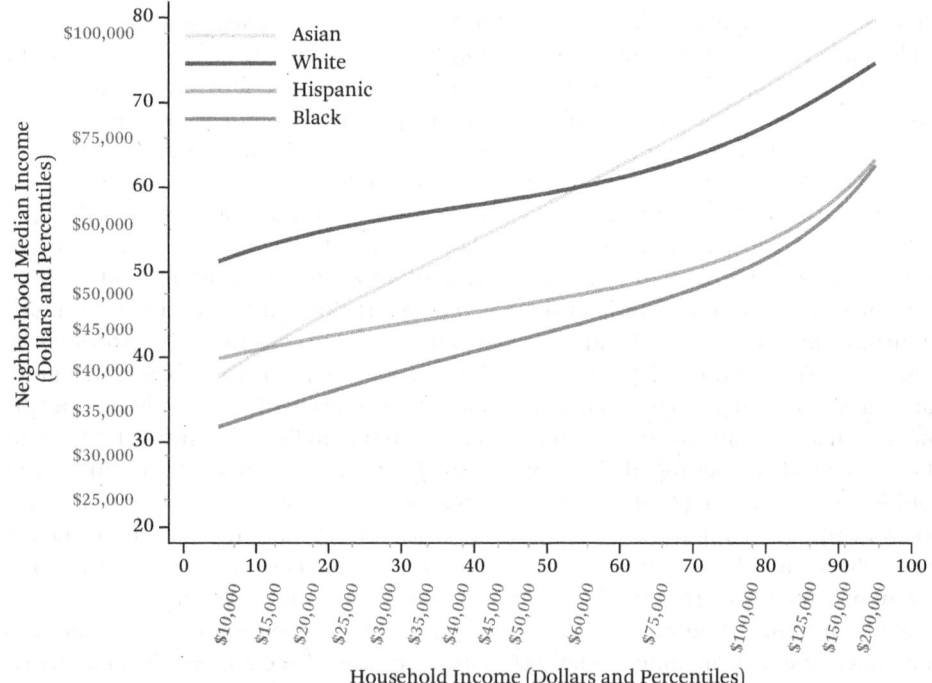

Source: Authors' calculations from ACS.

Figure 12. Race-Specific Neighborhood Median Income, Black Households, 2007–2011

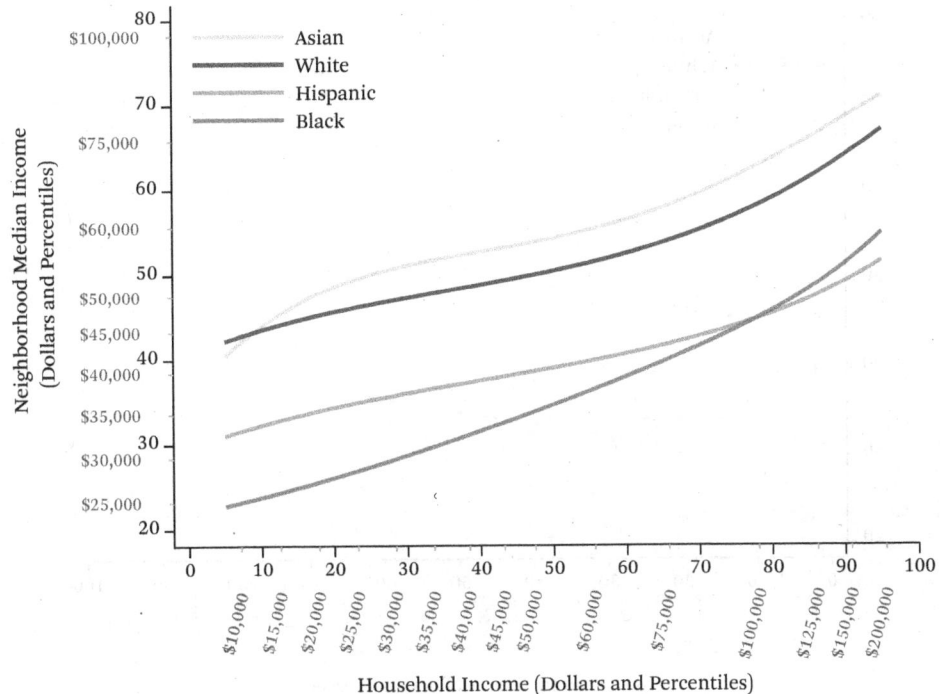

Source: Authors' calculations from ACS.

Figure 13. Race-Specific Neighborhood Median Income, Hispanic Households, 2007–2011

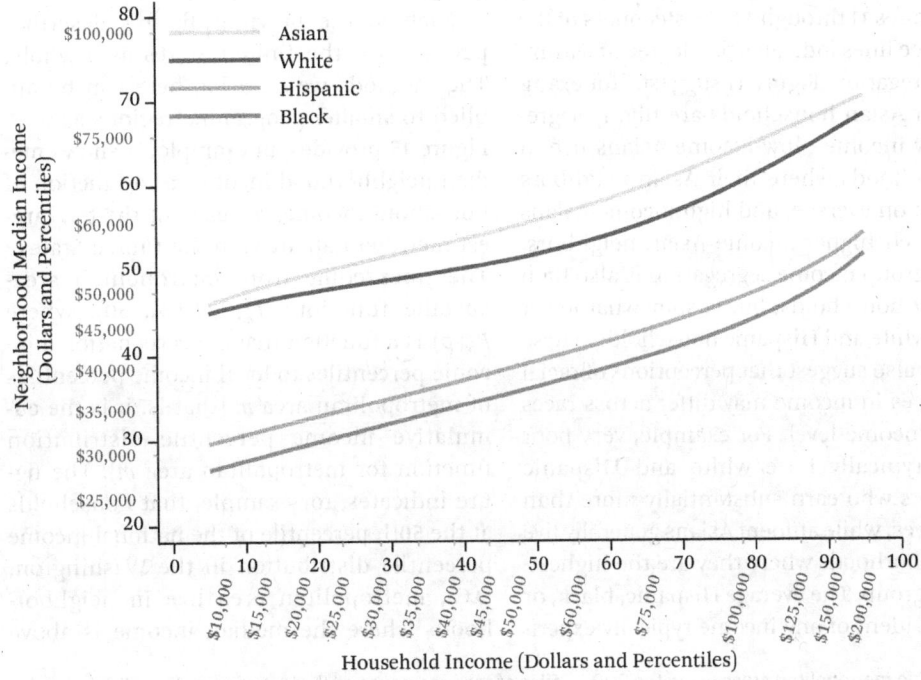

Source: Authors' calculations from ACS.

Figure 14. Race-Specific Neighborhood Median Income, White Households, 2007–2011

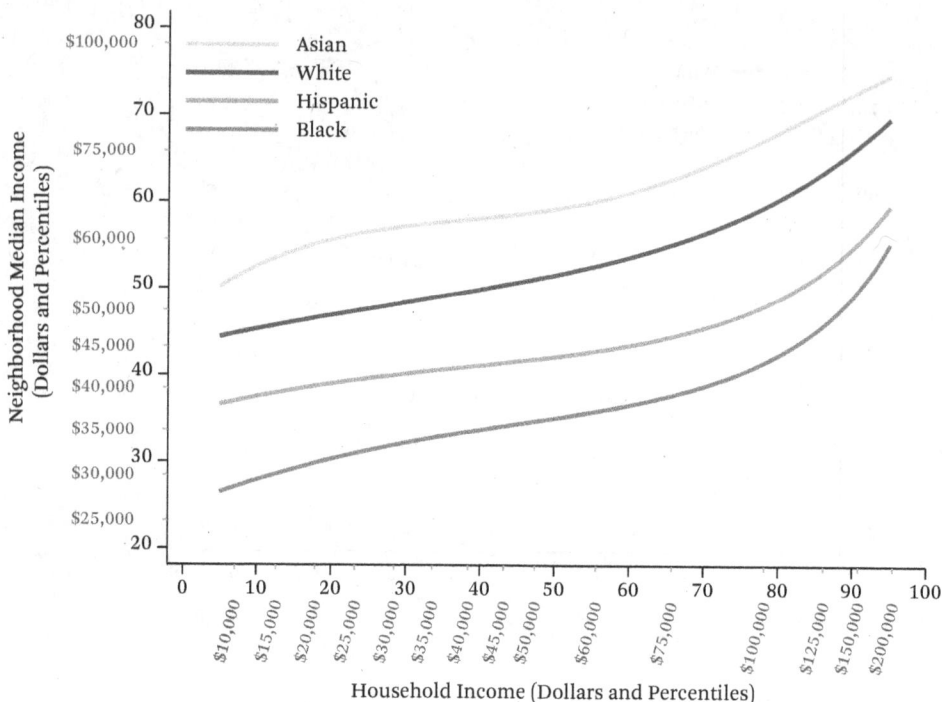

Source: Authors' calculations from ACS.

of these race-specific distributions to display as well.

In figures 11 through 14, the steepness of the same-race lines indicates the degree of within-race segregation. Figure 11 suggests, for example, that Asian households are highly segregated by income—low-income Asians live in neighborhoods where their Asian neighbors are poor, on average, and high-income Asians have much higher-income Asian neighbors. Within-group income segregation is also high for black households, but is somewhat lower among white and Hispanic households. These findings also suggest that perceptions of racial differences in income may differ across races and by income level. For example, very poor Asians typically have white and Hispanic neighbors who earn substantially more than themselves, while affluent Asians generally live in neighborhoods where they are the highest-income group. The average Hispanic, black, or white resident of any income typically experiences Asians as wealthier than all other race groups.

Each of the previous figures describes patterns for the United States as a whole. The methods we describe here can be applied to smaller geographic regions as well. Figure 15 provides an example. It shows median neighborhood income, as a function of household income, for each of the ten largest metropolitan areas in the United States.[2] The lines come from metropolitan area-specific functions $f_{mt}^{t\,-1}(R_m(p), .50)$, where $R_m(p)$ is a function that converts national income percentiles to local income percentiles of metropolitan area m (that is, it is the cumulative income percentile distribution function for metropolitan area m). The figure indicates, for example, that households at the 50th percentile of the national income percentile distribution in the Washington, D.C., metropolitan area live in neighborhoods where the median income is above

2. We define metropolitan areas using the 2003 Office of Management and Budget metropolitan division codes and rank these areas based on their total population in 2010.

Figure 15. Neighborhood Median Income, Ten Largest Metropolitan Areas, 2007–2011

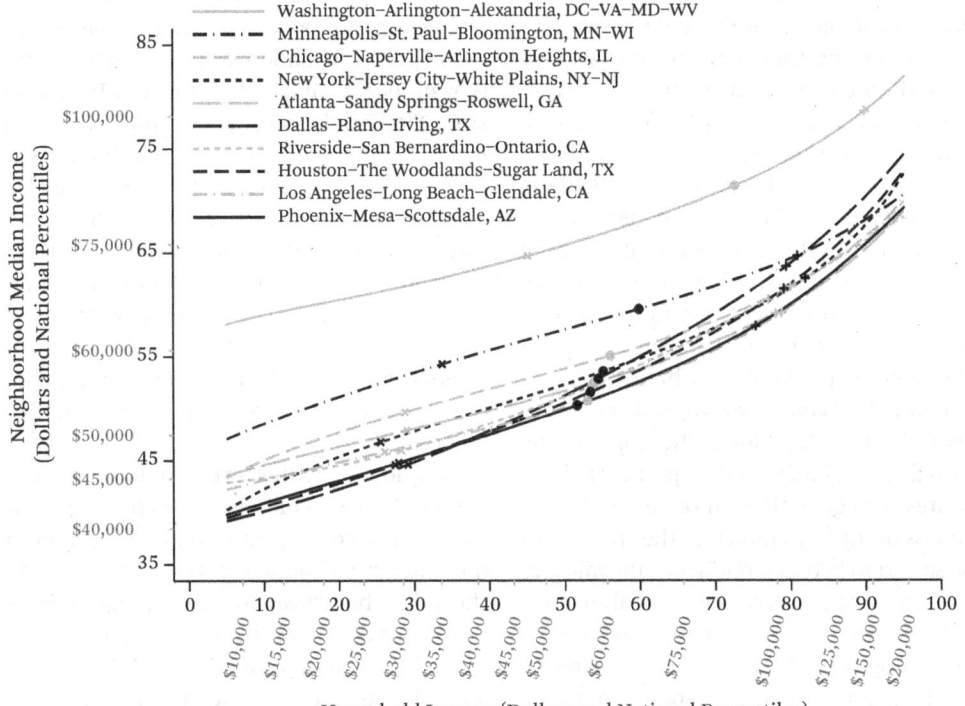

Source: Authors' calculations from ACS.

the 65th percentile of the national income distribution.

A notable feature of this figure is that both axes are shown in the national income distribution to allow for comparisons across metropolitan areas. Although the graph could be constructed using local income distributions, that would obscure comparisons among households of the same income in different metropolitan areas, because the 50th percentile of Chicago's income distribution is not the same as the 50th percentile of New York's income distribution. Using a common scale for income (percentiles of the national income distribution) makes evident that households in some metropolitan areas live, on average, in very different neighborhoods than similar income households in other areas. For example, Washington, D.C., households earning $60,000 live in much higher-income neighborhoods than similar income households in Los Angeles do; in fact, Washington, D.C., households earning $60,000 typically live in neighborhoods similar to those of Los Angeles households earning $150,000. For reference, the markers on the lines indicate the 25th, 50th, and 75th percentiles of each metropolitan area's own household income distribution.

Also evident in figure 15 is that income segregation varies across metropolitan areas. Again, the steepness of the lines in figure 15 provides an intuitive measure of income segregation. In the Minneapolis metropolitan area, for example, segregation is lower than in the Dallas or Houston areas. In Dallas and Houston, for example, high- and low-income households live, on average, in neighborhoods very different in median income levels; the difference in neighborhood conditions in Minneapolis, particularly between high- and middle-income households, is much less pronounced.

DISCUSSION

The approach we outline here provides a variety of ways of characterizing the joint patterns of racial and socioeconomic segregation. A full characterization of these patterns is provided by the group-specific income distributions (the ρ_g functions, in our notation) and the set of exposure functions that describe the average neighborhood income distributions conditional on race and income (the f_g^h functions), but simply reporting the parameters of these functions is neither feasible nor particularly informative (in our illustration here, these functions are together characterized by a total of 480 parameters). Instead, we have chosen to illustrate key features of these functions in a series of figures, each of which highlights a different aspect of the joint distribution.

One could, of course, derive additional statistics from these functions. The slopes of the lines in figure 2, for example, may be useful as measures of segregation. In other words, the steepness of the lines indicates the strength of the association between one's own income and that of one's neighbors. The vertical or horizontal distances between the lines in figure 9, likewise, might be thought of as measures of racial inequality in neighborhood conditions net of differences due to between-race differences in household income. Measures of between-group differences in racial composition of neighborhoods (evident in figures 5 through 8) may be useful for measuring and understanding racial segregation. Statistics of these types can be derived from the estimated ρ_g and f_g^h functions and then may be usefully compared across time or metropolitan areas to assess changes or variation in patterns of racial/economic segregation.

Our goal here is to describe a general approach to measuring joint patterns of racial and socioeconomic segregation. Given that, a discussion of the substantive implications of the patterns illustrated in our figures here is beyond the scope of this paper, but a few features of the figures are particularly striking. First, the figures clearly show large racial differences in neighborhood racial and economic composition, even conditional on income. That is, equally poor white, black, Hispanic, and Asian households are located in very different neighborhoods from one another; for example, black households typically live in neighborhoods similar to those of white households making $40,000 to 50,000 less. This is consistent with research showing that economic disparities are insufficient to explain racial segregation and that middle-class blacks live in poorer neighborhoods than most whites (Logan 2002, 2011; Reardon, Fox, and Townsend 2015; Timberlake 2002, 2007; Timberlake and Iceland 2007; Adelman 2004; Friedman, Gibbons, and Galvan 2014; Pattillo 1999; see also Pattillo 2005; for a useful review of this literature, see Lareau and Goyette 2014). If racial segregation were simply the result of racial differences in income, we would expect racial differences in neighborhood composition to disappear once we condition on household income. The figures here clearly show that they do not.

Second, the figures reveal something about the income levels of households that different racial and income groups might encounter in their neighborhood. Figures 10 through 14 show that the typical household, regardless of income level or race, lives in a neighborhood where black and Hispanic neighbors have lower incomes than white and Asian neighbors. Indeed, the black and Hispanic neighbors of high-income households have lower median incomes, on average, than the white and Asian neighbors of low-income households. This pattern may play a role in shaping racial stereotypes.

Third, figure 15 shows substantial variation among metropolitan areas in the patterns of exposure to high- and low-income neighbors, conditional on income. Not shown here, but straightforward to compute from the methods described, are metropolitan patterns of racial differences in neighborhood economic conditions. A full description of variation across metropolitan areas in the joint neighborhood distribution of race and income would likely reveal considerable variability.

Recent scholarship demonstrates that neighborhood economic conditions affect child development and opportunities for educational and economic success. For example, Chetty, Hendren, and Katz (2015) demonstrate that moving to a lower-poverty area has a substantial positive effect on the life-course trajectory of young children. Given this evidence, it is likely that variation in economic neighborhood conditions across racial groups, households of different incomes, and metropolitan areas may lead to disparities in developmental, educational, and economic outcomes. In other words, segregation matters for children's outcomes.

In general, children growing up in poor families face a double disadvantage. Their families have fewer private resources than richer families, and they tend to live in poorer neighborhoods, meaning they have access to fewer contextual resources as well. Even more troubling, figure 9 illustrates that low-income black and Hispanic children face a triple disadvantage relative to middle-class white children: not only do their families have fewer private resources and live in poorer neighborhoods, but they also live in much poorer neighborhoods than equally poor white children. Given that neighborhood conditions matter for children's development, the joint patterns of racial and economic segregation described here suggest that children of different races and incomes face dramatically different life opportunities. The stark racial disparities in neighborhood conditions may be one source of persistent racial inequality.

The methods described here provide a consistent way of quantifying disparities in neighborhood conditions that is largely independent of the specific income thresholds used in tabulating income in the ACS data. This innovation makes possible much more detailed comparisons of racial and economic neighborhood conditions across place, time, and population groups than has been used in prior work. We expect that these methods and the resultant datasets will enable researchers to more carefully investigate the patterns, causes, and consequences of racial and economic segregation.

APPENDIX A: ESTIMATING INCOME DENSITY AND EXPOSURE FUNCTIONS

Estimating the income density and exposure functions proceeds in three steps. First, we estimate the group-specific income density functions $\rho_g(p)$ and, from them, the group-specific cumulative income distribution functions $R_g(p)$. Second, we estimate the functions $f_t^h(p,q)$ and, from them, the function $f_t^t(p,q)$. Third, we estimate the functions $f_g^h(p,q)$ and, from them, the functions $f_g^t(p,q)$.[3] We do this because the parameter estimates from each step of the model are used to inform the estimation of each subsequent step. Once we have estimated each of these functions, we use them to compute the various exposure functions of interest, as described in the text.

Notation

We use g and h to denote G racial groups; we use p and q to denote income levels, expressed as percentiles (scaled from 0 to 1, for convenience) of the population income distribution; and we use i to index neighborhoods. We use $j, k = 1 \ldots, K$ to index the ordered income categories in which income is reported in the ACS. The ACS data we use in this paper includes five mutually exclusive racial-ethnic groups and sixteen income categories, so $G = 5$ and $K = 16$ here. Finally, we use T_x to denote the count of households in population x, and π_{gi} to indicate the proportion of households in neighborhood i that are in group g.

Data

The data consist of tract-level counts of households of race g with income in category k in census tract i. These counts are denoted T_{igk}. Let $T_{ig\cdot} = \sum_{j=1}^{K} T_{igj}$ denote the total number of households of group g in tract i, let $T_{i\cdot\cdot} = \sum_g T_{ig\cdot}$ denote the total number of households in tract i; and let $T_{\cdot g\cdot} = \sum_i T_{ig\cdot}$ denote the total number of households of group g in the population. The proportion of households of group g in tract i with incomes in income category k is

$$r_{igk} = \frac{T_{igk}}{T_{ig\cdot}}. \tag{A1}$$

---

3. One approach to estimating $f_g^h(p,q)$ is to estimate $\rho_{gi}(p)$ in each neighborhood i and to estimate $\rho_g(p)$. Then $R_{gi}(p)$ can be estimated as $\hat{R}_{gi}(p) = \int_0^p \hat{\rho}_{gi}(r)dr$. We then estimate $f_g^h(p,q)$ by substituting $\hat{\rho}_{gi}(p)$, $\hat{R}_{hi}(p)$, and the observed group counts and proportions into Equation (1). The potential drawback of this approach is that it requires us to estimate ρ_{gi} from small samples in each neighborhood i and group g. Instead, we adopt an alternative approach, which we describe in detail in this appendix.

The proportion of households of group g in the population with incomes in income category k is

$$r_{gk} = \frac{\sum_i T_{igk}}{T_{\cdot g \cdot}}. \quad (A2)$$

We denote the corresponding proportion of households with incomes in category k or below as $r_{ig\leq k} = \sum_{j=1}^{k} r_{igj}$ and $r_{\cdot g \leq k} = \sum_{j=1}^{k} r_{\cdot gj}$, respectively. Finally, the proportion of the total population of households that have income in income category k is denoted p_k or q_k:

$$p_k = q_k = \frac{\sum_i \sum_{g=1}^{G} T_{igk}}{\sum_i \sum_{g=1}^{G} \sum_{j=1}^{K} T_{igj}}. \quad (A3)$$

COMPUTING EXPOSURE MEASURES

From the ACS data, we compute $G^2 K^2 = 6{,}400$ values of f_{gj}^{hk} (for each combination of g, h, j, k, where g and h index five racial groups and j and k index sixteen income categories). Each f_{gj}^{hk} is an exposure index of members of group g with income in category j to members of group h in income category k or below. These are computed from the tract-by-group-by-income category counts as

$$f_{gj}^{hk} = \sum_i \left[\frac{T_{ig\cdot} \cdot r_{igj}}{T_{\cdot g \cdot} \cdot r_{\cdot gj}} \cdot \frac{T_{ih\cdot} r_{ih\leq k}}{T_{i\cdot\cdot}} \right]. \quad (A4)$$

We also compute $GK^2 = 1{,}280$ values of f_{tj}^{hk} (for each combination of h, j, k). Each f_{tj}^{hk} is an exposure index of members of the population with income in category j to members of group h in income category k or below. These are computed from the tract-by-group-by-income category counts as

$$f_{tj}^{hk} = \sum_i \left[\frac{\sum_g (T_{ig\cdot} \cdot r_{igj})}{\sum_g (T_{\cdot g \cdot} \cdot r_{\cdot gj})} \cdot \frac{T_{ih\cdot} r_{ih\leq k}}{T_{i\cdot\cdot}} \right]. \quad (A5)$$

Estimating $R_g(p)$ and $\rho_g(p)$

We assume the group-specific income density functions (the $\rho_g(p)$'s) can be well approximated as polynomials of order C:

$$\rho_g(p) \approx \sum_{c=0}^{C} \alpha_c^g p^c. \quad (A6)$$

This might be unrealistic if income were measured in dollars (because the long right tail of the cumulative income distribution function cannot be modeled well as a polynomial), but it is much less problematic when p measures income in percentiles of the population income distribution. In this case, the $\rho_g(p)$ functions must satisfy a few conditions. Specifically,

$$\int_0^1 \rho_g(r) dr = 1;$$

$$\sum_{g=1}^{G} \pi_g \rho_g(p) = \rho(p) = 1. \quad (A7)$$

The first condition in (A7) is simply the property that the density functions have integral 1. The second follows from the fact that the population income percentile distribution is, by definition, uniform. These two conditions imply, respectively, that

$$\sum_{c=0}^{C} \frac{1}{c+1} \alpha_c^g = 1 \,\forall\, g,$$

and

$$\sum_{g=1}^{G} \pi_g \alpha_c^g = \begin{cases} 1 \text{ if } c = 0 \\ 0 \text{ if } c \neq 0 \end{cases}. \quad (A8)$$

Therefore, we can estimate the $\rho_g(p)$ functions by fitting the following regression model to the $GK = 80$ points $(\rho_{\cdot gk}, m_k)$:

$$\rho_{gk} = \sum_{g=1}^{G} \sum_{c=1}^{C} \alpha_c^g \left(D_g \cdot m_k^c\right) + e_{gk}, \quad (A9)$$

where D_g is an indicator variable taking the value 1 if an observation pertains to group g and 0 otherwise. Let $m_k = \frac{1}{2}(p_{k-1} + p_k)$ be the percentile that falls in the middle of category k.[4] For the analyses reported in this paper, we set $C = 3$. Inspection of the fitted income density functions indicates very good fit with $C = 3$.

In fitting the model, we enforce the following $G + C + 1$ linear constraints:

$$\sum_{c=0}^{C} \frac{1}{c+1} \alpha_c^g = 1 \,\forall\, g,$$

and

$$\sum_{g=1}^{G} \pi_g \alpha_c^g = \begin{cases} 1 \text{ if } c = 0 \\ 0 \text{ if } c \in \{1, \ldots, C\} \end{cases}. \quad (A10)$$

---

4. In practice, when we fit (A9), we replace the midpoint m_j^c with $m_j^{c*} = m_j^c + z_{cj}$, where z_{cj} is defined as in appendix B. In addition, we fit (A9) using weighted least squares regression, with weights as detailed in appendix B.

This set of constraints is sufficient to satisfy the conditions in (A7). One of the constraints is redundant, so a total of $G + C$ constraints are used to estimate the density functions.

For each group g, the estimated income density function is then a Cth-order polynomial:

$$\hat{\rho}_g(p) = \sum_{c=0}^{C} \hat{\alpha}_c^g p^c. \quad (A11)$$

From $\hat{\rho}_g(p)$, it is straightforward to estimate the group-specific cumulative income distribution function $R_g(p)$ by taking the integral of $\hat{\rho}_g(p)$ on the interval $[0,1]$:

$$\hat{R}_g(p) = \int_0^1 \hat{\rho}_g(r) dr$$

$$= \sum_{c=0}^{C} \frac{1}{c+1} \hat{\alpha}_c^g p^{c+1}. \quad (A12)$$

Estimating $f_t^h(p,q)$ and $f_t^t(p,q)$

Before estimating the $f_t^h(p,q)$ and $f_t^t(p,q)$ functions, note that it follows from the definition of $f_t^h(p,q)$ (equation (3)) that

$$f_t^t(p,q) = \sum_{h=1}^{G} f_t^h(p,q). \quad (A13)$$

Next, note that the $f_t^h(p,q)$ and $f_t^t(p,q)$ functions must satisfy four conditions, by definition:

$$f_t^h(p,0) = 0$$

$$\int_0^1 f_t^h(r,q) dr = \pi_h R_h(q);$$

$$\frac{d}{dq} f_t^t(p,q) = f_t^{t'}(p,q) = f_t^{t'}(q,p) = \frac{d}{dp} f_t^t(q,p)$$

$$f_t^t(p,1) = \sum_{h=1}^{G} f_t^h(p,1) = 1. \quad (A14)$$

The first of these states that the exposure of any subset of households to the members of another group h with incomes less than or equal to 0, is by definition 0. The second says that, on average, neighborhoods have the same income distribution of each group h as the total population. The third is a symmetry condition that follows from the definition of $f_t^t(p,q)$.[5] The fourth says that the exposure of any subset of households to households with incomes less than or equal to 1, is by definition 1.

We assume the $f_t^h(p,q)$ functions are well approximated as polynomial surfaces of order A in p and B in q:

$$f_t^h(p,q) = \sum_{a=0}^{A} \sum_{b=0}^{B} \gamma_{ab}^{th} p^a q^b. \quad (A15)$$

We estimate these functions by fitting the following regression model to the GK^2 points (f_{tj}^{hk}, m_j, q_k):

$$f_{tj}^{hk} = \sum_{h} \sum_{a=0}^{A} \sum_{b=0}^{B} \gamma_{ab}^{th} \left[D_{th} \cdot m_j^a \cdot q_k^b \right] + u_{thpq}, \quad (A16)$$

where D_{th} is an indicator that an observation pertains to exposure to group h.[6]

To ensure that the estimated functions satisfy the conditions in (A14), we impose a set of constraints on the model:

$$\gamma_{a0}^{th} = 0 \; \forall a \in \{1,...,A\}, h \in 1\{1,...,G\}$$

$$A + 1 = B = C + 1;$$

$$\sum_{a=0}^{A} \frac{1}{a+1} \gamma_{ab}^{th} = \frac{1}{b} \pi_h \alpha_{b-1}^h$$

$$\forall b \in \{1,...,B\}, h \in \{1,...,G\};$$

$$\sum_{h=1}^{G} b \gamma_{ab}^{th} = \sum_{h=1}^{G} (a+1) \gamma_{(b-1)(a+1)}^{th}$$

$$\forall a \in \{1,...,A\}, b \in \{1,...,a\}. \quad (A17)$$

Together, these constraints ensure that the conditions in (A14) are met. The first constraint in (A17) implies the first condition of (A14) is met:

$$f_t^h(p,0) = \sum_{a=0}^{A} \sum_{b=0}^{B} \gamma_{ab}^{th} p^a 0^b$$

$$= \sum_{a=0}^{A} \gamma_{a0}^{th} p^a = \sum_{a=0}^{A} 0 \cdot p^a = 0. \quad (A18)$$

---

5. To see this, note that $\frac{d}{dq} f_t^t(p,q)$ is the exposure of individuals with income of exactly p to those with income of exactly q: $\frac{d}{dq} f_t^t(p,q) = \sum_i \left[\frac{T_i \rho_i(p)}{T_i \rho(p)} \cdot \frac{T_i \rho_i(q)}{T_i} \right] = \sum_i \left[\frac{T_i \rho_i(q)}{T_i \rho(p)} \cdot \frac{T_i \rho_i(p)}{T_i} \right] = \frac{d}{dp} f_t^t(q,p)$.

6. Again, in fitting this model, we replace the midpoints m_j^c with $m_j^c + z_j^c$ and use a weighted least squares regression as detailed in appendix B.

Note that the constraint that $y_{a0}^{th} = 0$ for all h and a implies that the y_{a0}^{th} terms can be omitted from (A16) going forward.

Second, the constraints in (A17), along with (A12) imply the second condition in (A14):

$$\int_0^1 f_t^h(r,q)dr = \sum_{b=1}^B \left[\sum_{a=0}^A \frac{\gamma_{ab}^{th}}{a+1}\right] q^b = \sum_{b=1}^B \left[\frac{\pi_h}{b} \alpha_{b-1}^h\right] q^b$$

$$= \pi_h \sum_{c=0}^C \frac{1}{c+1} \alpha_c^h q^{c+1} = \pi_h R_h(q). \quad (A19)$$

Third, the constraints in (A17) imply the third condition in (A14):

$$\frac{d}{dq} f_t^t(p,q) = \sum_{a=0}^A \sum_{b=1}^B b \gamma_{ab}^{tt} p^a q^{b-1}$$

$$= \sum_{a=0}^A \sum_{b=1}^B b \left[\sum_{h=1}^G \gamma_{ab}^{th}\right] p^a q^{b-1}$$

$$= \sum_{a=0}^A \sum_{b=1}^B (a+1) \left[\sum_{h=1}^G \gamma_{(b-1)(a+1)}^{th}\right] p^a q^{b-1}$$

$$= \sum_{a=0}^A \sum_{b=0}^A (a+1) \left[\sum_{h=1}^G \gamma_{b(a+1)}^{th}\right] p^a q^b$$

$$= \sum_{a=0}^A \sum_{b=0}^A (b+1) \left[\sum_{h=1}^G \gamma_{a(b+1)}^{th}\right] p^b q^a$$

$$= \sum_{a=0}^A \sum_{b=1}^B b \left[\sum_{h=1}^G \gamma_{ab}^{th}\right] p^{b-1} q^a$$

$$= \sum_{a=0}^A \sum_{b=1}^B b \gamma_{ab}^{tt} q^a p^{b-1}$$

$$= \frac{d}{dp} f_t^t(q,p). \quad (A20)$$

Finally, the constraints in (A17), in conjunction with (A8), ensure that the fourth condition in (A14) is met:

$$f_t^t(p,1) = \sum_{h=1}^G f_t^h(p,1)$$

$$= \sum_{h=1}^G \sum_{a=0}^A \sum_{b=1}^{A+1} \gamma_{ab}^{th} p^a 1^b$$

$$= \sum_{a=0}^A \sum_{b=1}^{A+1} \left[\sum_{h=1}^G \gamma_{ab}^{th}\right] p^a$$

$$= \sum_{a=0}^A \sum_{b=1}^{A+1} \left[\frac{a+1}{b} \sum_{h=1}^G \gamma_{(b-1)(a+1)}^{th}\right] p^a$$

$$= \sum_{a=0}^A \sum_{b=0}^A \left[\frac{a+1}{b+1} \sum_{h=1}^G \gamma_{b(a+1)}^{th}\right] p^a$$

$$= \sum_{a=0}^A \sum_{h=1}^G \left[\sum_{b=0}^A \frac{a+1}{b+1} \gamma_{b(a+1)}^{th}\right] p^a$$

$$= \sum_{a=0}^A \sum_{h=1}^G \left[\pi_h \alpha_a^h\right] p^a$$

$$= \sum_{a=0}^A \left[\sum_{h=1}^G \pi_h \alpha_a^h\right] p^a$$

$$= \sum_{a=0}^0 p^a$$

$$= 1. \quad (A21)$$

Thus, the constraints in (A17) and (A10) are sufficient to ensure the conditions in (A14) are satisfied. We satisfy the first set of constraints in (A17) by setting $y_{a0}^{th} = 0$ for all a and g. After we set $A + 1 = B = C + 1$, the last two conditions in (A17) contain an additional $GB + AB/2$ constraints that are required to estimate $f_t^h(p,q)$. Because $f_t^h(p,q)$ has GB^2 total parameters, there are a total of $AB\left[\frac{2G-1}{2}\right]$ free parameters in the model. With $G = 5$ and $A + 1 = B = 4$, $f_t^h(p,q)$ has 80 parameters, subject to 26 constraints, for a total of 54 freely estimated parameters.

Once we have estimated $f_t^h(p,q)$, it is straightforward to estimate

$$f_t^t(p,q) = \sum_h f_t^h(p,q). \quad (A22)$$

Estimating $f_g^h(p,q)$ and $f_g^t(p,q)$

Estimating the functions $f_g^h(p,q)$ and $f_g^t(p,q)$ follows the same logic, with some modifications. Recall that we require that $A + 1 = B = C + 1$. As before, we assume the functions $f_g^h(p,q)$ can be well approximated as polynomial surfaces of order A in p and $B = A + 1$ in q:

$$f_g^h(p,q) = \sum_{a=0}^A \sum_{b=0}^{A+1} \gamma_{ab}^{gh} p^a q^b. \quad (A23)$$

The $f_g^h(p,q)$ and $f_g^t(p,q)$ functions must satisfy several conditions:

$$f_g^t(p,0) = f_g^h(p,0) = 0;$$

$$f_g^t(p,1) = \sum_{h=1}^{G} f_g^h(p,1) = 1;$$

$$f_t^h(p,q) = \sum_{g=1}^{G} \pi_g \rho_g(p) f_g^h(p,q);$$

$$\int_0^1 f_t^h(r,q) dr = \sum_{g=1}^{G} \pi_g \int_0^1 \rho_g(r) f_g^h(r,q) dr$$

$$= \pi_h R_h(q). \qquad (A24)$$

These are satisfied with the following constraints:

$$\gamma_{a0}^{gh} = 0 \ \forall a, g, h;$$

$$\sum_{h=1}^{G} \sum_{b=1}^{A+1} \gamma_{ab}^{gh} = \begin{cases} 1 \text{ if } a = 0 \\ 0 \text{ if } a > 0 \end{cases} \forall g;$$

and

$$\gamma_{ab}^{th} = \sum_{g} \pi_g \sum_{c=\max(0,a-A)}^{\min(A,a)} \alpha_c^g \gamma_{(a-c)b}^{gh} \ \forall b \in \{1,\ldots,B\},$$

$$h \in \{1,\ldots,G\}, a \in \{0,\ldots\ldots,2A\}, \qquad (A25)$$

where $\gamma_{ab}^{th} = 0$ for all $a \in \{A+1,\ldots,2A\}$. The second and third lines of (A25) contain a total of $G(A+1)(2A+2) = 2GB^2$ constraints (160 constraints in our example with $G=5$ and $B=4$).

The first condition in (A24) follows from the constraint that $\gamma_{a0}^{gh} = 0$ for all a, g, and h:

$$f_g^h(p,0) = \sum_{a=0}^{A} \sum_{b=0}^{B} \gamma_{ab}^{gh} p^a 0^b = \sum_{a=0}^{A} \gamma_{a0}^{gh} p^a$$

$$= \sum_{a=0}^{A} (0 \cdot p^a) = 0. \qquad (A26)$$

As earlier, this implies we can omit the γ_{a0}^{gh} terms from the model. The second condition follows from second constraint:

$$\sum_{h=1}^{G} f_g^h(p,1) = \sum_{h=1}^{G} \sum_{a=0}^{A} \sum_{b=1}^{A+1} \gamma_{ab}^{gh} p^a 1^b$$

$$= \sum_{a=0}^{A} \left[\sum_{h=1}^{G} \sum_{b=1}^{A+1} \gamma_{ab}^{gh} \right] p^a = p^0 = 1. \qquad (A27)$$

The third condition follows from the third constraint:

$$\sum_{g=1}^{G} \pi_g \rho_g(p) f_g^h(p,q)$$

$$= \sum_{g=1}^{G} \pi_g \left[\sum_{c=0}^{A} \alpha_c^g p^c \right] \sum_{a=0}^{A} \sum_{b=1}^{A+1} \gamma_{ab}^{gh} p^a q^b$$

$$= \sum_{a=0}^{A} \sum_{b=1}^{A+1} \sum_{c=0}^{A} \sum_{g=1}^{G} \pi_g \alpha_c^g \gamma_{ab}^{gh} p^{a+c} q^b$$

$$= \sum_{a=0}^{2A} \sum_{b=1}^{A+1} \left[\sum_{g=1}^{G} \pi_g \sum_{c=\max(0,a-A)}^{\min(A,a)} \alpha_c^g \gamma_{(a-c)b}^{gh} \right] p^a q^b$$

$$= \sum_{a=0}^{A} \sum_{b=1}^{A+1} \gamma_{ab}^{th} p^a q^b$$

$$= f_t^h(p,q). \qquad (A28)$$

The fourth condition follows from (A28) and (A19):

$$\sum_{g=1}^{G} \pi_g \int_0^1 \rho_g(r) f_g^h(r,q) dr = \int_0^1 f_t^h(r,q) dr$$

$$= \pi_h R_h(q). \qquad (A29)$$

Although the constraints in (A25) are sufficient to satisfy the conditions in (A24), in practice, we use a subset of constraints implied by those in (A25) for computational ease. Specifically, we use the first and second sets of constraints from (A25) and an additional set of GB constraints implied by those in the third line of (A25) and the third line of (A17):

$$\sum_{a=0}^{A} \frac{1}{a+1} \sum_g \pi_g \sum_{c=0}^{a} \alpha_c^g \gamma_{(a-c)b}^{gh} = \frac{1}{b} \pi_h \alpha_{b-1}^h \ \forall b, h. \qquad (A30)$$

Once we have constrained $\gamma_{a0}^{gh} = 0$ for all a, g, h, the second line of (A25) implies GB constraints. One of the GB constraints in (A30) is redundant, so we invoke a set of $2GB - 1$ total constraints in fitting the $f_g^h(p,q)$ functions.

We estimate the $f_g^h(p,q)$ functions by simultaneously fitting a set of G^2 separate polynomial surfaces of order A in p and order $A+1$ in q through the G^2K^2 points (f_{gj}^{hk}, m_j, q_k), subject to the constraints described:

$$f_{gj}^{hk} = \sum_g \sum_h \sum_{a=0}^{A} \sum_{b=1}^{B} \gamma_{ab}^{gh} \left[D_{gh} \cdot m_j^a \cdot q_k^b \right] + u_{ghpq}, \qquad (A31)$$

where D_{gh} is an indicator variable taking the value 1 if an observation pertains to the exposure of group g to group h, and 0 otherwise.[7] Given $G = 5$ and $A + 1 = B = 4$, the functions have a total of 400 parameters, which are subject to 39 linear constraints (159 if we use the full set of constraints in (A25)).

Once we have estimated $f_g^h(p,q)$, it is straightforward to estimate

$$f_g^t(p,q) = \sum_h f_g^h(p,q), \tag{A32}$$

which implies that

$$\gamma_{ab}^{gt} = \sum_h \gamma_{ab}^{gh}. \tag{A33}$$

APPENDIX B: ESTIMATING A NONLINEAR ASSOCIATION WHEN THE REGRESSOR IS MEASURED ORDINALLY

This appendix describes one solution to the following general problem: we want to estimate a nonlinear polynomial function describing the conditional mean (given X) of a variable Y when X is measured in a set of ordered categories rather than continuously.

Some notation

Suppose income, a continuous variable denoted by X, is categorized into K categories, defined by $K - 1$ ordered thresholds $c_1, c_2, \ldots, c_{K-1}$. Instead of observing X, we instead observe $c \in \{1, \ldots, K\}$ where $c = j$ iff $c_{j-1} < X \le c_j$, where $c_0 = -\infty$ and $c_K = +\infty$. In addition, let p denote income in percentile ranks, scaled from 0 to 1 (so that $p = CDF(x)$ and $p_j = CDF(c_j)$ for $j \in \{0, \ldots, K\}$, where $CDF(x)$ is the cumulative income distribution function in the population of interest). Let $m_j = \frac{1}{2}(p_{j-1} + p_j)$ be the percentile that falls in the middle of category j. Let $w_j = \frac{1}{2}(p_j - p_{j-1})$ be half the width of income category j. Note that since p measures income percentile ranks in the population of interest, p is uniformly distributed on the interval $[0,1]$ and its density function is $\rho(p) = 1$, by definition.

Let Y measure some characteristic of an individual, where Y may be binary or continuous. Our goal is to estimate the function $f(p) = E[Y|p]$ describing the conditional expectation of Y given p, despite the fact that we only observe c and Y. Our approach is the following: first, estimate the mean value of Y (and its sampling variance) among individuals in each income category j; denote these $\hat{\bar{Y}}_j$ and $\hat{v}_j$, respectively; second, assign income category j a value of p equal to $m_j = \frac{1}{2}(p_{j-1} + p_j)$, the midpoint of the interval (p_{j-1}, p_j); and, third, regress $\hat{\bar{Y}}_j$ on a polynomial function of m_j using weighted least squares regression, weighting the observations by $1/\hat{v}_j$.

One complication that arises is that, if the function $f(p)$ is nonlinear, then $E[Y|c = j] \ne E[Y|p = m_j]$. That is, the mean value of Y within an income category will not necessarily equal the mean value of Y among those with incomes at the exact midpoint of the income category. If the curvature of $f(p)$ is substantial or the income categories are wide, simply regressing $\hat{\bar{Y}}$ on m may lead to bias in the estimated β_a's. To remedy this potential bias, we make an adjustment to the m_j^a's.

Suppose that $f(p)$ is well approximated by a polynomial of order A:

$$f(p) \approx \sum_{a=0}^{A} \beta_a p^a. \tag{B1}$$

We can express the average value of Y in category j as

$$\bar{Y}_j = \frac{\int_{p_{j-1}}^{p_j} \rho(r) f(r) dr}{\int_{p_{j-1}}^{p_j} \rho(r) dr}. \tag{B2}$$

Because $\rho(p) = 1$, this is

$$\bar{Y}_j = \frac{\int_{p_{j-1}}^{p_j} \sum_{a=0}^{A} \beta_a r^a dr}{p_j - p_{j-1}}$$

$$= \sum_{a=0}^{A} \beta_a \frac{(p_j^{a+1} - p_{j-1}^{a+1})}{(a+1)(p_j - p_{j-1})}$$

$$= \sum_{a=0}^{A} \frac{\beta_a}{(a+1)} \sum_{b=0}^{a} p_j^{a-b} p_{j-1}^b$$

---

7. In fitting this model, we replace the midpoints m_j^c with $m_j^c + z_j^c$ and use a weighted least squares regression as detailed in appendix B.

$$= \sum_{a=0}^{A} \frac{\beta_a}{(a+1)} \sum_{b=0}^{a} (m_j + w_j)^{a-b} (m_j - w_j)^b$$

$$= \sum_{a=0}^{A} \beta_a \left[m_j^a + \frac{1}{a+1} \sum_{b=0}^{a} (m_j + w_j)^{a-b} (m_j - w_j)^b - m_j^a \right]$$

$$= \sum_{a=0}^{A} \beta_a \left[m_j^{a*} \right], \quad (B3)$$

where $m_j^{a*} = m_j^a + z_{aj}$ and

$$z_{aj} = \frac{1}{a+1} \sum_{b=0}^{a} \left[(p_j)^{a-b} (p_{j-1})^b - m_j^a \right]$$

$$= \frac{1}{a+1} \sum_{b=0}^{a} \left[(m_j + w_j)^{a-b} (m_j - w_j)^b - m_j^a \right]. \quad (B4)$$

Note that the z_{aj}'s in (B4) can be simplified. For example, for $a \in (0,1,2,3,4)$, we get

$$z_{0j} = 0$$

$$z_{1j} = 0$$

$$z_{2j} = \frac{w_j^2}{3}$$

$$z_{3j} = m_j w_j^2$$

$$z_{4j} = 2m_j^2 w_j^2 + \frac{1}{5} w_j^4. \quad (B5)$$

(B3) implies that $\bar{Y}_j = E[Y|c=j]$ is not a simple polynomial function of m_j unless $A = 0$ or $A = 1$ (that is, unless $f(p)$ is a linear function). If $f(p)$ is nonlinear, $\bar{Y}_j$ is a linear combination of $m_j^{0*}, m_j^{1*}, \ldots m_j^{A*}$. As a result, we can estimate $f(p)$ by regressing $\hat{\bar{Y}}_j$ on the m_j^{a*}'s rather than on the m_j^a's:

$$\hat{\bar{Y}}_j = \sum_{a=0}^{A} \beta_a m_j^{a*} + u_j, \ u_j \sim N[0, \hat{v}_j]. \quad (B6)$$

In (A9), $\hat{\bar{Y}}_j = \pi_{gj}$, the proportion of households in income category j who are members of group g. In (A16) and (A33) $\hat{\bar{Y}}_j = f_{ij}^{hk}$, the average proportion one's neighbors who are members of group h and who have incomes at or below some category k. The sampling variance of $\hat{\bar{Y}}_j$ in either case will be proportional to the width of the income category (because this is proportional to the number of households in that category in the population) and $\hat{\bar{Y}}_j(1-\hat{\bar{Y}}_j)$ (the variance of a proportion). Because the estimates of WLS are invariant under a linear scaling of the weights, we set $\hat{v}_{gj} = w_j \hat{\bar{Y}}_{gj} \left(1 - \hat{\bar{Y}}_{gj}\right)$.

APPENDIX C: OTHER QUANTITIES OF INTEREST

Given $f_g^h(p,q)$ for all groups g and h, we can derive a number of additional useful quantities. Several of these are described in the text. Here, we describe two additional quantities of interest.

Standard exposure measures. We can obtain additional exposure measures, such as the exposure of members of group g with incomes between p_{min} and p_{max} to members of group h with incomes between some q_{min} and q_{max}, by computing

$$\frac{\int_{p_{min}}^{p_{max}} \rho_g(r) \left[f_g^h(r, q_{max}) - f_g^h(r, q_{min}) \right] dr}{\int_{p_{min}}^{p_{max}} \rho_g(r) dr}. \quad (C1)$$

A useful special case of this is the exposure of those in group g with income less than or equal to p to those in group h with income less than or equal to q. Denoted $F_g^h(p,q)$, this is

$$F_g^h(p,q) = \frac{\int_0^p \rho_g(r) f_g^h(r,q) dr}{\int_0^p \rho_g(r) dr}. \quad (C2)$$

For example, the exposure of group g to poor neighbors would be $F_g^t(1, q_{poverty})$, where $q_{poverty}$ is the income value that corresponds to the poverty line. Thus, measures of "exposure to poverty" used in much of the segregation literature (Logan 2011; Timberlake 2002) are special cases of the measurement approach we describe here. Note that in the special case where $p = q = 1$, $F_g^h(1,1)$ is a standard exposure measure of racial segregation, the exposure of group g to group h (usually denoted $_g P_h^*$). In our notation, this standard exposure measure can be written

$$_g P_h^* = F_g^h(1,1) = \int_0^1 \rho_g(r) f_g^h(r,1) dr. \quad (C3)$$

Standardized measures of between-group differences in neighborhood income distributions, conditional on household income. We might want to measure the difference between the average neighborhood income density functions for two groups g_1 and g_2, conditional on p; that is, for any given value of p, we want to measure the difference between the distributions $p_{g_1}^t(p,q)$ and $p_{g_2}^t(p,q)$. We could do this by measuring, for example, the difference in their medians (that is, by comparing $f_{g_1}^{t\,-1}(p,.50)$ and $f_{g_2}^{t\,-1}(p,.50)$), but this would not provide a summary measure of the overall difference in the distributions. A useful summary measure of the degree of overlap of two distributions is the probability that a randomly chosen value from one distribution is larger than a randomly chosen value from the other. In our case here, this is the probability that a randomly chosen member of the neighborhood of the typical group g_1 household with income p has an income higher than that of a randomly chosen member of the neighborhood of the typical group g_2 household with income p. This probability is equal to

$$Pr_{g_1 > g_2}(p) = \int_0^1 f_{g_1}^t\left(p, f_{g_2}^{t-1}(p,c)\right)dc. \quad (C4)$$

This probability can be converted to the V statistic, a nonparametric measure of the difference between two distributions:

$$V_{g_1 g_2}(p) = \sqrt{2}\Phi^{-1}\left(Pr_{g_1 > g_2}(p)\right), \quad (C5)$$

where $\Phi^{-1}(\cdot)$ is the probit function. Here $V_{g_1 g_2}(p)$ is a function of p that describes the extent of overlap between the typical neighborhood income distributions. V can be interpreted as the standardized difference between the means of two normal distributions with the same degree of overlap as the distributions of interest, so it is interpretable as a "pseudo effect size" (Ho and Haertel 2006; Ho and Reardon 2012; Holland 2002).

REFERENCES

Acevedo-Garcia, Dolores, and Kimberly A. Lochner. 2003. "Residential Segregation and Health." In *Neighborhoods and Health*, edited by Ichiro Kawachi and Lisa F. Berkman. New York: Oxford University Press.

Adelman, Robert M. 2004. "Neighborhood Opportunities, Race, and Class: The Black Middle Class and Residential Segregation." *City & Community* 3(1): 43–63.

Bischoff, Kendra, and Sean F. Reardon. 2014. "Residential Segregation by Income, 1970–2009." In *Diversity and Disparities: America Enters a New Century*, edited by John Logan. New York: The Russell Sage Foundation.

Brooks-Gunn, Jeanne, Greg J. Duncan, and J. Lawrence Aber, eds. 1997. *Neighborhood Poverty: Context and Consequences for Children*, vol. 1. New York: Russell Sage Foundation.

Burdick-Will, Julia, Jens Ludwig, Stephen W. Raudenbush, Robert J. Sampson, Lisa Sanbonmatsu, and Patrick Sharkey. 2011. "Converging Evidence for Neighborhood Effects on Children's Test Scores: An Experimental, Quasi-experimental, and Observational Comparison." In *Whither Opportunity? Rising Inequality and the Uncertain Life Chances of Low-Income Children*, edited by Greg J. Duncan and Richard J. Murnane. New York: Russell Sage Foundation.

Chetty, Raj, Nathaniel Hendren, and Lawrence F. Katz. 2015. "The Effects of Exposure to Better Neighborhoods on Children: New Evidence from the Moving to Opportunity Experiment." *American Economic Review* 106(4): 855–902.

Darden, Joe T., and Sameh M. Kamel. 2000. "Black Residential Segregation in the City and Suburbs of Detroit: Does Socioeconomic Status Matter?" *Journal of Urban Affairs* 22(1): 1–13.

Denton, Nancy A., and Douglas S. Massey. 1988. "Residential Segregation of Blacks, Hispanics, and Asians by Socioeconomic Status and Generation." *Social Science Quarterly* 69(4): 797–817.

Farley, John E. 1995. "Race Still Matters: The Minimal Role of Income and Housing Costs as Causes of Housing Segregation in St. Louis, 1990." *Urban Affairs Review* 31(2): 244–54.

Farley, Reynolds. 1991. "Residential Segregation of Social and Economic Groups Among Blacks, 1970–80." In *The Urban Underclass*, edited by Christopher Jencks and Paul E. Peterson. Washington, D.C.: Brookings Institution Press.

Friedman, Samantha, Joseph Gibbons, and Chris Galvan. 2014. "Declining Segregation Through the Lens of Neighborhood Quality: Does Middle-Class and Affluent Status Bring Equality?" *Social Science Research* 46: 155–68. doi: 10.1016/j.ssresearch.2014.03.003.

Goetz, Edward, Tony Damiano, and Jason Hicks. 2015. "American Urban Inequality: Racially Concentrated Affluence." Cambridge, Mass.: Lincoln Institute of Land Policy. Accessed June 27, 2016. http://www.lincolninst.edu/docs/979/1839_8%20Edward%20Goetz.pdf.

Harding, David J. 2003. "Counterfactual Models of Neighborhood Effects: The Effect of Neighborhood Poverty on Dropping Out and Teenage Pregnancy." *American Journal of Sociology* 109(3): 676-719.

Ho, Andrew D., and Edward H. Haertel. 2006. "Metric-Free Measures of Test Score Trends and Gaps with Policy-Relevant Examples." Los Angeles: University of California, National Center for Research on Evaluation, Standards, and Student Testing.

Ho, Andrew D., and Sean F. Reardon. 2012. "Estimating Achievement Gaps from Test Scores Reported in Ordinal 'Proficiency' Categories." *Journal of Educational and Behavioral Statistics* 37(4): 489-517.

Holland, Paul. 2002. "Two Measures of Change in the Gaps Between the CDFs of Test Score Distributions." *Journal of Educational and Behavioral Statistics* 27(1): 3-17.

Iceland, John, Cicely Sharpe, and Erika Steinmetz. 2005. "Class Differences in African American Residential Patterns in US Metropolitan Areas: 1990-2000." *Social Science Research* 34(1): 252-66. doi: 10.1016/j.ssresearch.2004.02.001.

Iceland, John, and Rima Wilkes. 2006. "Does Socioeconomic Status Matter? Race, Class, and Residential Segregation." *Social Problems* 53(2): 248-73.

James, David R., and Karl E. Taeuber. 1985. "Measures of Segregation." *Sociological Methodology* 14(1): 1-32.

Jargowsky, Paul A. 1996. "Take the Money and Run: Economic Segregation in U.S. Metropolitan Areas." *American Sociological Review* 61(6): 984-98.

———. 2003. Stunning Progress, Hidden Problems: The Dramatic Decline of Concentrated Poverty in the 1990s. In *Living Cities Census Series*. Washington, D.C.: Brookings Institution Press.

Kling, Jeffrey R., Jeffrey B. Liebman, and Lawrence F. Katz. 2007. "Experimental Analysis of Neighborhood Effects." *Econometrica* 75(1): 83-119.

Lareau, Annette, and Kimberly Goyette. 2014. *Choosing Homes, Choosing Schools*. New York: Russell Sage Foundation.

Leventhal, Tama, and Jeanne Brooks-Gunn. 2000. "The Neighborhoods They Live In: The Effects of Neighborhood Residence on Child and Adolescent Outcomes." *Psychological Bulletin* 126(2): 309-37.

Lieberson, Stanley. 1981. "An Asymmetrical Approach to Segregation." In *Ethnic Segregation in Cities*, edited by Cecil Peach, Vaugh Robinson, and Susan Smith. London: Croon Helm.

Logan, John R. 2002. "Separate and Unequal: The Neighborhood Gap for Blacks and Hispanics in Metropolitan America." Lewis Mumford Center report. Albany: State University of New York.

———. 2011. "Separate and Unequal: The Neighborhood Gap for Blacks, Hispanics and Asians in Metropolitan America." *US2010* Census Brief. Providence, R.I.: Brown University. Accessed June 27, 2016. http://www.s4.brown.edu/us2010/Data/Report/report0727.pdf.

Logan, John R., and Brian Stults. 2011. "The Persistence of Segregation in the Metropolis: New Findings from the 2010 Census." US2010 Report. Providence, R.I.: Brown University. Accessed June 27, 2016. http://www.s4.brown.edu/us2010/Data/Report/report2.pdf.

Logan, John R., Brian J. Stults, and Reynolds Farley. 2004. "Segregation of Minorities in the Metropolis: Two Decades of Change." *Demography* 41(1): 1-22.

Ludwig, Jens, Greg J. Duncan, Lisa A. Gennetian, Lawrence F. Katz, Ronald C. Kessler, Jeffrey R. Kling, and Lisa Sanbonmatsu. 2013. "Long-Term Neighborhood Effects on Low-Income Families: Evidence from Moving to Opportunity." *NBER* working paper no. 18772. Cambridge, Mass.: National Bureau of Economic Research.

Massey, Douglas S., and Nancy A. Denton. 1988. "The Dimensions of Residential Segregation." *Social Forces* 67(2): 281-315.

———. 1993. *American Apartheid: Segregation and the Making of the Underclass*. Cambridge, Mass.: Harvard University Press.

Massey, Douglas S., and Mary J. Fischer. 1999. "Does Rising Income Bring Integration? New Results for Blacks, Hispanics, and Asians in 1990." *Social Science Research* 28(3): 316-26.

———. 2003. "The Geography of Inequality in the United States, 1950-2000." *Brookings-Wharton Papers on Urban Affairs* 2003(January): 1-40. Accessed June 27, 2016. http://www.jstor.org/stable/i25067390.

Pattillo, Mary. 1999. *Black Picket Fences: Privilege*

and *Peril Among the Black Middle Class*. Chicago: University of Chicago Press.

———. 2005. "Black Middle-Class Neighborhoods." *Annual Review of Sociology* 31(1): 305–29. doi: 10.1146/annurev.soc.29.010202.095956.

Reardon, Sean F. 2009. "Measures of Ordinal Segregation." In *Occupational and Residential Segregation*, edited by Yves Flückiger, Sean F. Reardon, and Jacques Silber. Bingley, UK: Emerald Group Publishing.

———. 2011. "Measures of Income Segregation." *CEPA* working paper. Stanford, Calif.: Stanford Center for Education Policy Analysis.

Reardon, Sean F., and Kendra Bischoff. 2011. "Income Inequality and Income Segregation." *American Journal of Sociology* 116(4): 1092–153.

Reardon, Sean F., and Glenn Firebaugh. 2002. "Measures of Multi-Group Segregation." *Sociological Methodology* 32(1): 33–67.

Reardon, Sean F., Lindsay Fox, and Joseph Townsend. 2015. "Neighborhood Income Composition by Race and Income, 1990–2009." *Annals of the American Academy of Political and Social Science* 660(1): 78–97.

Reardon, Sean F., and Ann Owens. 2014. "60 Years After Brown: Trends and Consequences of School Segregation." *Annual Review of Sociology* 40(1): 199–218.

Sampson, Robert J. 2008. "Moving to Inequality: Neighborhood Effects and Experiments Meet Social Structure." *American Journal of Sociology* 114(1): 189–231.

Sampson, Robert J., Stephen W. Raudenbush, and Felton Earls. 1997. "Neighborhoods and Violent Crime: A Multilevel Study of Collective Efficacy." *Science* 277(5328)(June 15): 918–24.

Sanbonmatsu, Lisa, Jeffrey R. Kling, Greg J. Duncan, and Jeanne Brooks-Gunn. 2006. "Neighborhoods and Academic Achievement: Results from the Moving to Opportunity Experiment." *Journal of Human Resources* 41(4): 649–81.

Santiago, Anna Maria, George C. Galster, Jessica L. Lucero, Karen J. Ishler, Eun Lye Lee, Georgios Kypriotakis, and Lisa Stack. 2014. "Opportunity Neighborhoods for Latino and African American Children: Final Report." Washington: U.S. Department of Housing and Urban Development.

Timberlake, Jeffrey M. 2002. "Separate, but How Unequal? Ethnic Residential Stratification, 1980 to 1990." *City & Community* 1(3): 251–66.

———. 2007. "Racial and Ethnic Inequality in the Duration of Children's Exposure to Neighborhood Poverty and Affluence." *Social Problems* 54(3): 319–42.

Timberlake, Jeffrey M., and John Iceland. 2007. "Change in Racial and Ethnic Residential Inequality in American Cities, 1970–2000." *City & Community* 6(4): 335–65.

Turner, Margery Austin, and Julie Fenderson. 2006. "Understanding Diverse Neighborhoods in an Era of Demographic Change." Washington, D.C.: Urban Institute, Metropolitan Housing and Policy Center.

Watson, Tara. 2009. "Inequality and the Measurement of Residential Segregation by Income." *Review of Income and Wealth* 55(3): 820–44.

Wodtke, Geoffrey T., David J. Harding, and Felix Elwert. 2011. "Neighborhood Effects in Temporal Perspective: The Impact of Long-Term Exposure to Concentrated Disadvantage on High School Graduation." *American Sociological Review* 76(5): 713–36.

Racial Residential Segregation of School-Age Children and Adults: The Role of Schooling as a Segregating Force

ANN OWENS

Neighborhoods are critical contexts for children's well-being, but differences in neighborhood inequality among children and adults are understudied. I document racial segregation between neighborhoods among school-age children and adults in 2000 and 2010 and find that though the racial composition of children's and adults' neighborhoods is similar, exposure to own-age neighbors varies. Compared with adults' exposure to other adults, children are exposed to fewer white and more minority, particularly Hispanic, children. This is due in part to compositional differences, but children are also more unevenly sorted across neighborhoods by race than adults. One explanation for higher segregation among children is that parents consider school options when making residential choices. Consistent with this hypothesis, I find that school district boundaries account for a larger proportion of neighborhood segregation among children than among adults. Future research on spatial inequality must consider the multiple contexts differentially contributing to inequality among children and adults.

Keywords: racial segregation, racial inequality, neighborhood segregation, school districts, household composition

Racial residential segregation remains a significant stratifying force in America's cities. Segregation creates vastly unequal neighborhoods, with white residents typically living in safer neighborhoods with more socioeconomic resources than minority (particularly African American and Hispanic) residents. Where one lives shapes a person's everyday activities, social interactions, educational, occupational, and recreational opportunities, and aspirations and expectations. Neighborhoods are particularly important contexts for children's development and well-being. A large neighborhood effects literature demonstrates that growing up in an impoverished neighborhood reduces educational performance and attainment, increases the odds of teen parenthood, and may diminish cognitive and psychological well-being (for reviews, see Sharkey and Faber 2014; Leventhal and Brooks-Gunn 2000; Sampson, Morenoff, and Gannon-Rowley 2002; Jencks and Mayer 1990). Therefore, particular attention should be paid to whether children experience higher residential segregation, and thus more inequality in their neighborhood contexts, than adults.

When making residential choices, families with children may face different constraints and have different preferences than childless households. These different opportunities and priorities may interact with racial-ethnic inequalities to produce different levels of racial segregation for children than for adults. For example, racial inequality in economic re-

Ann Owens is assistant professor of sociology at the University of Southern California and an affiliate of the Spatial Sciences Institute, Population Research Center, and Sol Price Center for Social Innovation at USC.

© 2017 Russell Sage Foundation. Owens, Ann. 2017. "Racial Residential Segregation of School-Age Children and Adults: The Role of Schooling as a Segregating Force." *RSF: The Russell Sage Foundation Journal of the Social Sciences* 3(2): 63–80. DOI: 10.7758/RSF.3.2.03. The author acknowledges the reviewers and editors for constructive and helpful feedback. Direct correspondence to: Ann Owens at annowens@usc.edu, 851 Downey Way, HSH 204, Los Angeles, CA 90089.

sources may be larger among families with children (where more white than minority families have two parents and thus two incomes) than among households without children. In terms of preferences, one important residential consideration more relevant to households with children is school options. Even as school choice policies weaken the link between neighborhood residence and school attendance, the majority of public school students—73 percent in 2007—attend their neighborhood school (Grady and Bielick 2010), so school options may contribute to parents' residential decision-making. Research indicates that white and higher-income parents are sensitive to living in minority neighborhoods or those that feed into minority schools because of schooling and child well-being concerns (Krysan 2002), whereas minority and lower-income parents view trade-offs between schools and neighborhoods differently and evaluate schools based on leadership, safety, and culture rather than on racial composition (Rhodes and DeLuca 2014). These different school-related preferences between white and minority parents may lead to racial residential segregation, higher than among childless individuals who do not take school-related concerns into account.

This article innovates on past research in two ways to advance the study of spatial inequality. First, I disaggregate segregation by household composition, examining racial residential segregation among children and adults in 2000 and 2010. I estimate both the *exposure* of children and adults to neighborhoods of varying racial-ethnic composition and the *evenness* with which children and adults are sorted across neighborhood by race-ethnicity. I consider segregation between whites and several nonwhite groups (blacks, Hispanics, and Asians), as well as between nonwhite groups and multiracial segregation among many racial-ethnic groups. Investigating segregation separately by household composition reveals different trends in segregation, implying different causes and processes. Second, I consider how school concerns contribute to residential segregation among children and adults. I operationalize school concerns by examining how neighborhood racial segregation maps onto school district boundaries, comparing the proportion of children's and adults' segregation between neighborhoods that occurs within and between school districts.[1] This approach moves beyond research that considers only one administrative or political unit to examine how residential and school boundaries interact and overlap to produce segregation. Overall, results present a portrait of the racial residential inequality children and adults experienced from 2000 to 2010 and the role of schooling in shaping residential segregation, particularly for children.

RESIDENTIAL SEGREGATION AMONG CHILDREN AND ADULTS

A large body of research documents trends in racial residential segregation between neighborhoods (for a review, see Charles 2003). Segregation is typically measured with exposure indices that capture the degree of potential interaction between groups in neighborhoods, or with evenness indices that assess how similarly racial groups are distributed across neighborhoods of a larger area like the city or metropolitan area. From 1980 to 2000, black-white residential segregation declined in terms of both measures, though blacks remained hypersegregated from whites in many areas. Hispanics and Asians experienced declining exposure to whites as their populations grew, alongside small increases in segregation measured by evenness, though Hispanics and Asians remained less segregated from whites than blacks. From 2000 to 2010, these trends generally continued. Black and whites continued to be sorted more evenly across neighborhoods, while evenness between whites and other minority groups was more stable (Logan and Stults 2011). Hispanic and Asian residents continued to become more isolated (that is, exposed to more members of their own group) and exposed to fewer whites in the 2000s.

Few studies examine racial segregation separately among children and adults. John Logan and his colleagues (2001) estimate segregation

---

1. School attendance zone boundaries also likely affect residential decisions, but a lack of comprehensive data prevents a parallel analysis at the attendance zone, rather than district, level.

for children in 2000 using an exposure and an evenness index. The authors find that minority children are exposed to fewer white children than minority adults are to white adults. Children are also sorted by race more unevenly than adults across neighborhoods—compared with the larger metropolitan area context, children live in less diverse neighborhoods than adults. John Iceland and his colleagues (2010) conducted similar analyses at the household level, comparing households with and without children, and reach similar conclusions: households with children experienced higher levels of segregation and racial isolation than those without children in 2000. Paul Jargowsky (2014) documents residential segregation between neighborhoods in the late 2000s and finds that school-age children, particularly kindergarten- and pre-K children, are more racially segregated than all people using an evenness measure. Other research examines income segregation among adults and children and finds that economic segregation between neighborhoods both is higher among households with children than among those without and rose almost exclusively among households with children from 1990 to 2010 (Owens 2016). This article updates research on the unique residential segregation experiences of children by estimating racial segregation between neighborhoods with exposure and evenness indices for all racial groups among adults and school-age children in 2000 and 2010. I then move beyond past research to consider the role of school districts in contributing to residential segregation among children and adults.

Because the child population has more non-white members than the adult population does, exposure to minorities could be higher among children than adults simply because of these compositional differences.[2] However, research finds that evenness measures of segregation are also higher among children than adults, suggesting that higher levels of child segregation are not due only to compositional differences but also to different residential selection and sorting processes for households with children compared to those without. One reason racial sorting of households between neighborhoods may differ depending on whether they have children is inequality in economic resources with which to purchase housing. The disparity in economic resources between white and minority (black and Hispanic) households with children may be greater than the economic disparity between white and minority households without children (Iceland et al. 2010). White households with children are more likely than their minority counterparts to involve two parents, creating a large racial economic disparity given that two-parent households tend to have more economic resources. In contrast, white and minority households without children may have more similar economic resources. The gap in ability to pay for housing between whites and minorities may thus be larger among households with children than among those without, leading to higher residential racial segregation among households with children. Kris Marsh and John Iceland (2010) find this interaction between household structure, economic resources, and racial inequality in their comparison of segregation among single adults living alone with married-couple households—racial segregation is lower among single adults living alone in part because income differences between black and white households are smaller among this group than among married-couple households.

A second reason segregation may vary depending on the presence of children in the household is residential preferences. Families with children, particularly white families, may be more sensitive than those without children to living in minority neighborhoods if they use minority composition as a proxy for high-quality neighborhoods or for social problems such as crime (Krysan 2002; Goyette, Iceland, and Weininger 2014; Harris 1999). Research provides mixed evidence on whether households with children are more sensitive to neighborhood racial composition. Two studies indicate that households with children are not more sensitive than those without children to the racial composition of both the origin and

---

2. In 2010, 54 percent of the child population and 67 percent of the adult population was non-Hispanic white (U.S. Census Bureau 2010).

destination neighborhood when deciding where to move (Crowder 2000; South and Crowder 1998). Other research, however, indicates that households with young children are more likely than those without children to move when the proportion of minority neighbors in their neighborhood increases (Goyette, Iceland, and Weininger 2014). Higher sensitivity to racial diversity among households with children than among those without may lead to higher segregation among children in terms of both evenness and exposure.

THE ROLE OF SCHOOLS IN RESIDENTIAL SEGREGATION

Although only a few studies document residential segregation separately among children and adults, a large body of literature documents the racial segregation of children in another context: schools (see Reardon and Owens 2014). Measured by evenness, school segregation between black and white students declined—blacks and whites were more evenly represented across schools—during the 1990s and 2000s, though less than residential segregation did: 4.4 percent in school segregation versus 10 percent in residential for people of all ages (Stroub and Richards 2013; Logan and Stults 2011). School segregation measured by evenness increased slightly between whites and Asians and, particularly, between whites and Hispanics during this time. Exposure indices indicate that the isolation of minority students in schools has increased as their exposure to white students has declined over the past three decades (Orfield and Frankenberg 2014). These changes in exposure are larger than what would be expected given the decline in sorting between blacks and whites and the small increases in sorting between whites and Hispanics or Asians. Therefore, the rise in isolation of minority students is due in large part to the growth in the minority, particularly Hispanic, population.

School segregation estimates provide some suggestive evidence for the trend in residential segregation among children, but neighborhood and school composition do not always correspond. Research shows that schools tend to have higher proportions of minority and low-income students than the neighborhoods they draw from, suggesting that white and higher-income families select out of local neighborhood schools (Saporito and Sohoni 2007; Saporito 2003; Saporito and Hanley 2014). Choices among school sectors (public, private, charter, or magnet) and school choice policies within sectors mean that residential and school segregation patterns are related to one another but may not be perfectly aligned, and though they affect one another, both residential and school segregation have independent predictors as well.

When making residential choices, households consider a bundle of amenities, including location, transportation, housing unit characteristics, and—for households with children—school options. Parents face trade-offs across housing units, neighborhoods, and schools when making residential decisions. Some parents prioritize neighborhoods and do not send their children to the local schools. In other cases, parents avoid neighborhoods linked to unacceptable school options. In 2007, about a quarter of parents of public school students in neighborhood schools reported moving to a neighborhood for the school (Grady and Bielick 2010). School options contribute to residential segregation among households with children because white and higher-income parents weigh neighborhood and school options differently than minority and lower-income parents do when making residential choices. White and higher-income parents use race- and class-based assumptions to assess school desirability. White parents conflate minority racial composition with lower school quality (Krysan 2002) and use school and district racial composition in their residential, school sector (public or private), and school choice decisions (Holme 2002; Lareau 2014; Krysan 2002; Lankford and Wyckoff 2006; Saporito and Lareau 1999).

Minority and lower-income parents may consider schools differently than white parents. First, Anna Rhodes and Stefanie DeLuca's study (2014) of low-income African American parents suggests that, although parents care about their children's education, minority parents may not give schools the same weight in residential decisions that white families do. In addition to being priced out of some school districts, minority parents may privilege safety, housing unit amenities, and proximity to child care and employment over considerations about schools when making residential moves. Second, when minority parents do consider school options, they make different assessments than white parents. Minority parents may prefer schools where their children are not the minority (Henig 1996), and minority parents and students often consider safety, school leadership, a sense of belonging, and school culture rather than test scores or school composition (Wells 1996). Taken together, whites' school considerations contribute to their decisions to live in whiter, less integrated neighborhoods, and minority parents' school considerations, coupled with their economic limitations, may contribute to their residence in neighborhoods with more minority residents.

School options contribute to higher levels of racial segregation among households with children than among those without children because membership in a particular school district or school attendance zone is likely of more concern to households with children than those without when making residential choices. School quality is capitalized into home prices, creating high-cost and low-cost areas that affect all households regardless of whether they have children (Black 1999; Bayer, Ferreira, and McMillan 2007; Nguyen-Hoang and Yinger 2011). Still, childless households may not be willing to pay the additional costs associated with living near a particular school or in a particular district, even if high-quality schools may be good for their property value. Given the economic disparities between racial groups, racial segregation may be higher among households with children than those without if high-income white families with children use their resource advantage to purchase a home in an area linked to a particular school that is unaffordable to lower-income and minority families with children, and childless white and minority households both place less weight on school options.

In this study, I provide comprehensive evidence on racial segregation between neighborhoods among school-age children and adults in 2000 and 2010, considering segregation between non-Hispanic white, black, Asian, other race, and Hispanic residents. I examine the relationship between school options and racial segregation by identifying how much residential segregation occurs within and between school districts. This analysis provides evidence on the degree to which school options, operationalized here as residence in a particular school district, contributes to racial residential segregation.

DATA AND METHODS

Summary File 1 of the 2000 and 2010 U.S. Census provides full counts of residents by age and race by Hispanic ethnicity in each census tract (neighborhood).[3,4] I define two age groups: school-age children (six to seventeen years old) and adults (eighteen and older).[5] I distinguish between non-Hispanic whites, non-Hispanic blacks, non-Hispanic Asians (non-Hispanic people who identify as Asian, Native Hawaiian, or Pacific Islander), non-Hispanic other race individuals (non-Hispanic people who identify as other race, American Indian or Alaska Native, or multiracial), and Hispanic (any race).

---

3. Summary File 4 of the 1990 Census also provides this information, but estimates are based on the 1 in 6 sample rather than full population. As Logan and colleagues (2001) note in their technical documentation, when examining segregation by race-ethnicity by age group, segregation indices estimated from sample data differ nontrivially from full count data. I explored the 1990 data but could not produce credible segregation estimates compared to prior research. Therefore, I focus on 2000 and 2010 data.

4. Neighborhoods can be defined at a variety of geographic scales. I also estimated segregation between block groups among residents older and younger than eighteen (data on race by detailed age categories are not available at the block group level). Block group segregation results are consistent with those presented here, though segregation is higher overall between block groups than between tracts, consistent with past research (results available on request).

5. Results are substantively identical comparing adults with all children younger than eighteen.

For brevity throughout the rest of the article, I do not specify non-Hispanic when referring to racial groups and I use *child* or *children* to refer to school-age child or children. I examine racial-ethnic segregation between neighborhoods within metropolitan areas, using the 2003 definitions of Metropolitan Statistical Areas provided by the Office of Management and Budget. I limit analyses to the hundred largest (most populous) metropolitan areas as of 2010. Segregation indices can be biased if the population of a particular group is small. Following Iceland and his colleagues (2010), I aimed to analyze metropolitan areas with at least one thousand members in each racial-ethnic by age (adult or child) group. Among the hundred largest metropolitan areas, one—McAllen-Edinburg-Pharr, Texas—has slightly fewer than a thousand black and other race children. I retain all hundred largest metropolitan areas to have a consistent sample across comparisons and to follow other work on segregation examining the hundred largest metropolitan areas—excluding McAllen does not noticeably change results.

I measure segregation using both an exposure measure and an evenness measure. I estimate exposure using the interaction and the isolation indices. The two-group interaction index between members of racial group x and y within a metropolitan area is estimated as follows (Massey and Denton 1988):

$$_xP_y^* = \sum_{i=1}^n \left[\frac{x_i}{X}\right]\left[\frac{y_i}{t_i}\right]$$

where x_i, y_i, and t_i are the counts of members in racial-ethnic group x, y, and the total population of tract i, respectively. X is the total population of racial-ethnic group x in the metropolitan area. The interaction index can be interpreted as the probability that a randomly drawn member of racial-ethnic group x shares a neighborhood with a member of racial-ethnic group y. I separately estimate the interaction of whites, blacks, Asians, and Hispanics with all other groups (including those of other race).

The isolation index estimates the exposure of members of racial group x to other members of racial group x (the probability that a randomly drawn member of racial-ethnic group x shares a neighborhood with another member of x), and it is estimated as follows:

$$_xP_x^* = \sum_{i=1}^n \left[\frac{x_i}{X}\right]\left[\frac{x_i}{t_i}\right].$$

In the results, I present isolation and interaction indices for white, black, Asian, and Hispanic residents averaged across the hundred largest metropolitan areas, weighting the average by the number of members of the racial group in the metropolitan area. Weighting provides the exposure of the average person in that racial group to all other racial groups, allowing me to ascertain the neighborhood racial composition of the average member of each racial group in the hundred largest metropolitan areas.

I estimate interaction and isolation indices by age in two ways. First, I estimate interaction and isolation indices within an age group, considering only, for example, white children's exposure to white, black, Hispanic, Asian, and other race children (or white adults' exposure to white, black, Hispanic, Asian, and other race adults). This provides an estimate of exposure to neighborhood peer groups of children or adults, following Logan and his colleagues (2001). However, children's contexts are shaped by the racial composition of the adults in their neighborhoods as well. Therefore, I also estimate the interaction and isolation of children or adults to all people—for example, white children's exposure to all white, black, Hispanic, Asian, and other race residents (I estimate exposure to all same-racial-group members by combining the same-racial-group child isolation index and the interaction of children with same-racial-group adults).

I measure evenness using the entropy index H (Theil 1972; Theil and Finezza 1971; Massey and Denton 1988). H compares the entropy, or the extent of racial diversity, of each tract with that of the larger metropolitan area; it can be estimated with regard to two groups or among many racial groups. H ranges from 0 to 1, 0 indicating no segregation—the racial diversity in each tract is the same as the racial diversity in the metropolitan area—and 1 indicating complete segregation—each tract consists of only one racial group and the tract therefore has no racial diversity. I estimate age-group-specific H

to identify whether children are more unevenly sorted across neighborhoods by race than adults. H is less sensitive to racial composition than the exposure indices.

Entropy is estimated with the following equation (Reardon, Yun, and Eitle 2000):

$$E = \sum_{r=1}^{n} Q_r ln \frac{1}{Q_r},$$

where Q_r is the proportion of the population comprised of racial-ethnic group r and entropy is estimated by summing over each racial-ethnic group (either two or many). Entropy is estimated for each tract and for the metropolitan area. H measures the overall departure of tracts' entropy from the metropolitan area's entropy, using the equation

$$H = \frac{\sum_{i=1}^{k} \frac{t_i}{T}(E - E_i)}{E},$$

where T is total metropolitan area population, t_i is tract i's total population, E is metropolitan area entropy, and E_i is entropy in tract i. I estimate binary H between whites and each minority group (blacks, Asians, and Hispanics) separately, as well as between whites and all nonwhites. I also estimate binary H between blacks and Asians, blacks and Hispanics, and Asians and Hispanics. Finally, I estimate multiracial H to measure segregation among all groups: whites, blacks, Asians, those of other race, and Hispanics.

H can be decomposed to clarify the geographic source of segregation. Most metropolitan areas (ninety-five of the largest hundred) consist of more than one school district, so residential segregation can occur between neighborhoods within school districts or between neighborhoods in different school districts. Research measuring school segregation within metropolitan areas has decomposed H into its between- and within-district components, determining what proportions of school segregation in a metropolitan area are due to segregation between schools within the same district and to segregation between districts (Reardon, Yun, and Eitle 2000; Stroub and Richards 2013). Here, I decompose residential segregation into its between- and within-school district components—identifying what proportions of neighborhood segregation are due to segregation between neighborhoods within the same district and to segregation between districts—to explore the role of school districts in contributing to children's and adults' racial residential segregation.

I link tracts to school districts using the MABLE/Geocorr Geographic Correspondence Tool for 2000 and 2010 elementary and unified district boundaries (Missouri Census Data Center 2012). MABLE/Geocorr provides a crosswalk between tracts and school districts based on the proportion of each tract weighted by population that lies within a school district, if the tract is divided. About half the tracts are completely within a school district, but the other half are divided by two or more districts, creating partial tracts within districts. For divided tracts, I multiply the number of residents or households in each racial-ethnic group for each age group by the population proportion of the tract in the district. The decomposition assumes that the smaller geographic unit (neighborhoods) lies within the larger unit (districts), so I treat both tracts and partial tracts as neighborhoods and reestimate residential segregation within metropolitan areas. Then I sum population counts by racial-ethnic group and age among tracts and partial tracts to the district level. Based on these counts, I estimate residential racial segregation between districts within metropolitan areas. The decomposability properties of H allow me to ascertain the proportion of residential segregation that occurs between districts by dividing residential segregation between neighborhoods by residential segregation between districts (Theil 1972). If school district boundaries contribute more to the residential decisions of families with children than those without, a larger proportion of children's than adults' residential racial segregation will occur between districts.

RACIAL INTERACTION AND ISOLATION

Figure 1 presents the neighborhood racial composition (exposure) experienced by adults or school-age children of four racial-ethnic groups in 2010: Asian, black, Hispanic, and white. I present the average neighborhood composition across the one hundred largest

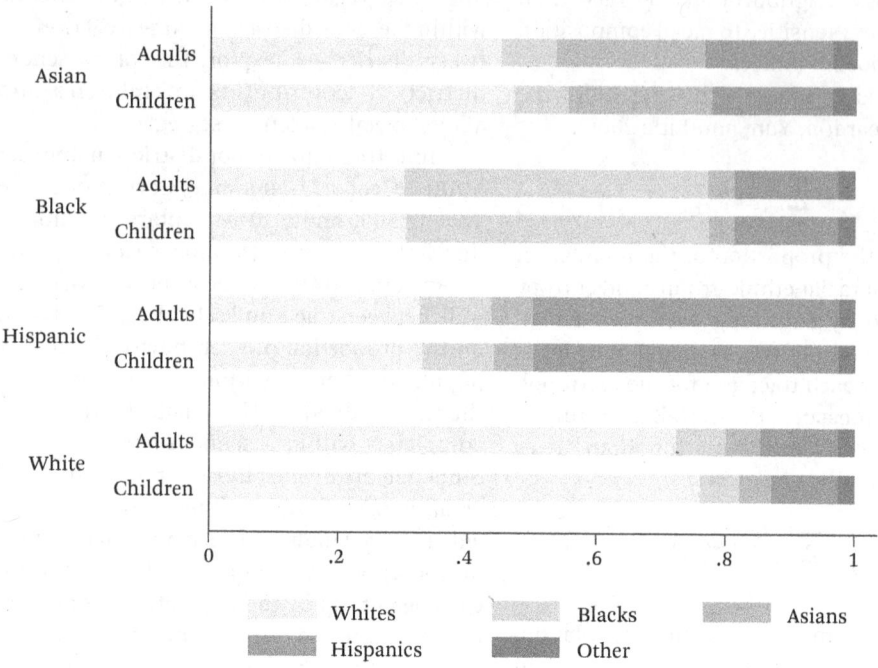

Figure 1. 2010 Neighborhood Racial Composition, All Residents

Source: Author's calculations based on U.S. Census Bureau 2010.
Note: Children denotes residents six to seventeen years old. All racial categories are non-Hispanic.

metropolitan areas. Estimates of neighborhood composition are derived from interaction and isolation indices, weighted by the population of the racial group. Figure 1 presents adults' and children's exposure to all residents of the neighborhood, not only to one's own age group, and differences between children and adults are minimal.[6] In 2010, across the hundred largest metropolitan areas, the average white child lived in a neighborhood that was 76 percent white, 6 percent black, 5 percent Asian, 10 percent Hispanic, and 3 percent other race; the average white adult lived in a neighborhood that was 72 percent white, 8 percent black, 6 percent Asian, 12 percent Hispanic, and 3 percent other race. Differences between adults' and children's neighborhood composition are smaller among other racial-ethnic groups—the proportion of one's own racial group in the neighborhood for the average black, Hispanic, and Asian child is within 1 percentage point of the proportion of own racial group exposure for adults. Asian children are exposed to slightly more whites than Asian adults—47 percent in a child's neighborhood versus 45 percent for adults. The difference between adults' and children's neighborhood racial exposure changed little from 2000 to 2010—no gap between children and adults in exposure to neighbors of any particular race grew more than 1.5 percentage points for any racial group during this decade (see table 1). The most notable change from 2000 to 2010 is growing exposure to Hispanic and, to a lesser extent, Asian neighbors among all groups and declining exposure to white neighbors among all groups except blacks.

In contrast, figure 2 presents neighborhood racial composition of (exposure to) one's age group peers (adult or children) in 2010. Here, larger differences in exposure emerge, particularly for minority children compared to minor-

---

6. I do not report statistical significance when discussing differences because the estimates draw from data on the full population of residents in the hundred largest metropolitan statistical area (for further discussion, see Sharkey 2014).

Figure 2. 2010 Neighborhood Racial Composition, Own Age Group

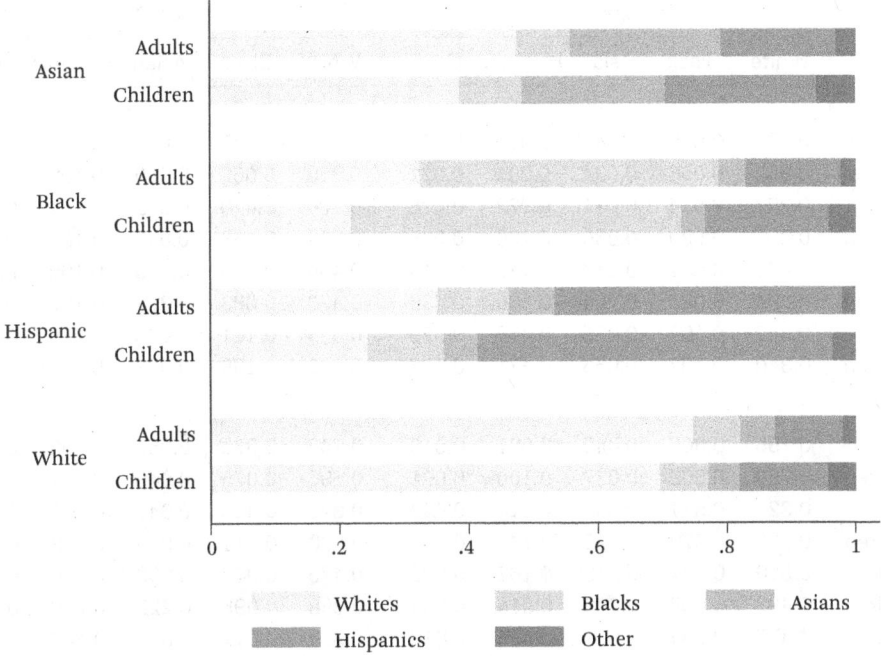

Source: Author's calculations based U.S. Census Bureau 2010.
Note: Children denotes residents six to seventeen years old. All racial categories are non-Hispanic.

ity adults. In the hundred largest metropolitan areas in 2010, the average black child lived in a neighborhood where 22 percent of children were white, 51 percent were black, 4 percent were Asian, 19 percent were Hispanic, and 4 percent were other race; the average black adult lived in one where 33 percent of adults were white, 46 percent were black, 4 percent were Asian, 15 percent were Hispanic, and 2 percent were other race. The average Hispanic child lived in a neighborhood where 55 percent of children were Hispanic and 25 percent of children were white; the average Hispanic adult lived in one where 45 percent of adults were Hispanic and 35 percent of adults were white. The average Asian child lived in a neighborhood where 39 percent of children were white, 22 percent were Asian, and 24 percent were Hispanic; the average Asian adult lived in one where 48 percent of adults were white, 23 percent were Asian, and 18 percent were Hispanic. Minority children are exposed to more minority children, in particular Hispanic, than minority adults are to minority adults. White children are also exposed to more Hispanic children (and live among fewer white children) than white adults are to Hispanic adults, but the difference in exposure to Hispanics between adults and children (3 percentage points) is smallest among whites.

From 2000 to 2010, exposure to Hispanics of one's own age group increased for all racial-ethnic and age groups, but the increase for children was greater than that for adults. Greater and growing exposure to Hispanic same-age peers among children than adults is due in part to the larger Hispanic child population than Hispanic adult population.[7] Same-age-group isolation indices (exposure to own racial group) declined for whites and blacks,

---

7. Rather than compositional differences (that Hispanic children are more numerous than Hispanic adults), an alternative explanation for greater exposure to Hispanics among children is differential residential patterns among households with and without children. To test this, I estimated the exposure of adults to children of dif-

Table 1. Average Neighborhood Racial Composition

		2000					2010				
		White	Black	Asian	Hispanic	Other	White	Black	Asian	Hispanic	Other
All neighbors											
White	Adult	0.777	0.068	0.043	0.091	0.022	0.723	0.077	0.055	0.120	0.026
	Children	0.805	0.056	0.037	0.081	0.021	0.760	0.062	0.050	0.103	0.025
Black	Adult	0.297	0.524	0.031	0.122	0.025	0.300	0.470	0.042	0.161	0.026
	Children	0.290	0.529	0.030	0.126	0.025	0.304	0.468	0.040	0.162	0.026
Asian	Adult	0.492	0.081	0.210	0.177	0.040	0.450	0.085	0.230	0.198	0.038
	Children	0.494	0.083	0.204	0.180	0.039	0.470	0.083	0.224	0.187	0.036
Hispanic	Adult	0.350	0.107	0.059	0.459	0.026	0.324	0.111	0.066	0.475	0.024
	Children	0.340	0.107	0.056	0.471	0.026	0.330	0.109	0.063	0.474	0.024
Own age group											
White	Adult	0.795	0.063	0.042	0.081	0.018	0.747	0.073	0.055	0.106	0.019
	Children	0.763	0.069	0.037	0.100	0.031	0.696	0.075	0.049	0.137	0.043
Black	Adult	0.321	0.511	0.032	0.114	0.022	0.325	0.463	0.043	0.148	0.021
	Children	0.222	0.579	0.028	0.140	0.031	0.220	0.511	0.036	0.193	0.040
Asian	Adult	0.516	0.077	0.212	0.162	0.033	0.475	0.083	0.233	0.180	0.029
	Children	0.423	0.098	0.209	0.214	0.056	0.388	0.095	0.222	0.236	0.059
Hispanic	Adult	0.377	0.104	0.061	0.435	0.023	0.352	0.111	0.070	0.447	0.020
	Children	0.271	0.119	0.051	0.527	0.032	0.245	0.117	0.053	0.550	0.035

Source: Author's calculations based on U.S. Census Bureau 2000, 2010.
Note: Children denotes residents six to seventeen years old. All racial categories are non-Hispanic. Racial composition for the average group member is estimated from isolation and interaction indices weighted by number of own group members in the MSA, averaged across the hundred largest MSAs.

more among children than adults, but increased for Asians and Hispanics. Table 1 presents a summary of the results described here, showing the average racial composition of children's and adults' neighborhoods with regard to all neighbors (the first panel, corresponding to figure 1) and own age group (the second panel, corresponding to figure 2) in 2000 and 2010.

Research draws on own-age-group exposure to conclude that segregation is higher among children than adults (Logan et al. 2001). Considering exposure to both own-age group and the entire neighborhood population, however, paints a more complex picture—racial composition of all of adults' and children's neighbors is fairly similar. Both types of neighborhood exposure—to all neighbors and to own-age neighbors—are important in creating social contexts that affect children's well-being. The racial composition of all neighbors may be associated with social and economic resources available in the neighborhood, including adult socialization and supervision and the tax base that funds schools and public goods. Exposure to own-age group may have consequences when children interact—for example, in neighborhood schools or adolescent peer groups. The high level of neighborhood isolation among Hispanic children (0.55 in 2010), for example, is consistent with the fact that the average Latino student attended school where 57

ferent racial groups, and I find that adults are also exposed to more Hispanic children than Hispanic adults (Hispanics make up 25 percent of the child population and 17 percent of the adult population to which the average adult is exposed). Therefore, compositional differences account for some of the greater exposure of children to Hispanic children, though as I discuss, children are also sorted more unevenly by race than adults (and households with children are sorted more unevenly than those without) across neighborhoods.

Table 2. Residential Segregation Measured by Evenness Between Neighborhoods

	2000			2010		
	Adults	Children	Difference	Adults	Children	Difference
White-black	0.354	0.435	0.081	0.316	0.401	0.085
White-Asian	0.126	0.168	0.042	0.134	0.174	0.040
White-Hispanic	0.197	0.245	0.048	0.197	0.250	0.053
White-nonwhite	0.252	0.313	0.061	0.225	0.271	0.046
Black-Asian	0.297	0.342	0.045	0.273	0.323	0.050
Black-Hispanic	0.233	0.246	0.013	0.195	0.205	0.010
Asian-Hispanic	0.206	0.243	0.037	0.209	0.243	0.034
Multiracial	0.238	0.280	0.042	0.211	0.239	0.028

Source: Author's calculations based on U.S. Census Bureau 2000, 2010.
Note: Children denotes residents six to seventeen years old. All racial categories are non-Hispanic. Multiracial segregation is estimated among non-Hispanic whites, non-Hispanic Asians, non-Hispanic blacks, non-Hispanic individuals of other race, and Hispanics.

percent of his peers were Latino in 2011 (Orfield and Frankenberg 2014).

Children's exposure to their age group provides insight into what neighborhood racial composition will look like in the coming decades, given ongoing demographic changes. Whites are projected to be a minority nationwide by 2044 (Frey 2014), though a majority-minority metropolitan population will likely occur even sooner. Total neighborhood racial composition will gradually become more similar to children's current same-age contexts than adults' due solely to population change. Whether individuals will sort by race between neighborhoods differently as the minority population grows is unclear, though white-Hispanic and white-Asian evenness indicators among all residents have been generally stable over the past several decades, indicating stalled integration amid demographic change (Logan and Stults 2011). The next section explores this second aspect of segregation: whether evenness indices vary between children and adults in 2000 and 2010.

Racial Evenness Across Neighborhoods

Table 2 presents estimates of segregation in terms of the evenness with which racial-ethnic groups are spread across neighborhoods among adults and children (H). Segregation between whites and each minority group (blacks, Asians, Hispanics, and all nonwhites) as well as between minority groups is higher among children than adults in both 2000 and 2010. The largest difference between children's and adults' segregation is in white-black segregation, for which H is more than 8 points higher among children than adults in 2000 and 2010.

Table 2 also indicates that whites and blacks became more evenly represented across neighborhoods (H declined) from 2000 to 2010 among both adults and children, consistent with research documenting declining black-white segregation. The adult-child gap, however, increased slightly, indicating that children experienced less integration than adults. Segregation measured by H between white and Asian adults and children increased, more among adults than children. White and Hispanic children became more unevenly distributed across neighborhoods over time, and the child-adult gap grew slightly because white-Hispanic adult segregation was stable. The increasing exposure of white children to Hispanic children documented in figure 2 and table 1 is thus due both to demographic changes and increased residential sorting between white and Hispanic children (though these estimates combine adults who live with and without children, as discussed below, complicating conclusions about sorting). In contrast, H between Hispanic children and black and Asian children declined or was stable, so the growing Hispanic child population, rather than increased sorting, accounts for the rising

Table 3. Proportion of Neighborhood Racial Segregation Occurring Between School Districts, Children and Adults

	2000			2010		
	Adults	Children	Difference	Adults	Children	Difference
White-black	0.457	0.536	0.079	0.490	0.561	0.071
White-Asian	0.472	0.480	0.008	0.486	0.496	0.010
White-Hispanic	0.438	0.497	0.059	0.462	0.524	0.062
White-nonwhite	0.477	0.560	0.083	0.505	0.576	0.071
Black-Asian	0.423	0.455	0.032	0.439	0.481	0.042
Black-Hispanic	0.361	0.400	0.039	0.385	0.427	0.042
Asian-Hispanic	0.406	0.429	0.023	0.419	0.456	0.037
Multiracial	0.458	0.528	0.070	0.484	0.544	0.060

Source: Author's calculations based on U.S. Census Bureau 2000, 2010.
Note: Children denotes residents six to seventeen years old. All racial categories are non-Hispanic. Multiracial segregation is estimated among non-Hispanic whites, non-Hispanic Asians, non-Hispanic blacks, non-Hispanic individuals of other race, and Hispanics. N=95 largest MSAs with more than one school district.

exposure to Hispanic children among minority children.

Overall, results indicate that white children are segregated from minority children more than white adults are segregated from minority adults. This suggests that white parents may be particularly sensitive to mixed-race neighborhood contexts and avoid neighborhoods with minority residents more than childless white households do. These analyses are at the individual level, but adults live in the same home, and thus same neighborhood, as their coresident children. Due to adult-child coresidence, estimating the evenness index separately for adults and children splits some households and does not place households into mutually exclusive groups. Therefore, children's segregation does not capture sorting preferences of future generations because adults are making the residential choices. This clouds future prediction and provides little insight into whether future generations will sort more or less by race. In the next section's exploration of the role of school districts in residential segregation, I consider evenness at the household level as well as the individual child or adult level to more clearly distinguish between households with and without children. Generally, the evenness index for adults estimated at the individual level as in table 2 provides an upwardly biased estimate of the evenness index for households without children, because adults who live with children (included in individual-level estimates) are more segregated than those who do not. The difference in evenness between households with and without children is therefore larger than the difference in adult and child evenness presented here.

Racial Evenness Across Neighborhoods Within and Between School Districts

School considerations may be one reason that children are more unevenly sorted by race across neighborhoods than adults. Parents may make residential choices with school options in mind, so school concerns are a sorting mechanism shaping the neighborhood outcomes of children more than childless adults. The decomposability properties of H allow me to estimate the proportion of neighborhood segregation in terms of evenness that occurs between districts, the remainder occurring between neighborhoods within school districts. I hypothesize that more neighborhood segregation occurs between school districts among children than among adults—residential sorting of children between districts is likely higher because the boundaries are more relevant to them and their families, so segregation between school districts accounts for more of the total residential sorting between neighborhoods. Table 3 presents the results.

Table 4. Proportion of Neighborhood Racial Segregation Occurring Between School Districts, Households with and Without Children

	2000			2010		
	Without Children	With Children	Difference	Without Children	With Children	Difference
White-black	0.425	0.528	0.104	0.464	0.546	0.082
White-Asian	0.431	0.484	0.053	0.461	0.488	0.027
Non-Hispanic			0.082			0.068
White-Hispanic	0.407	0.489		0.445	0.513	
White-nonwhite	0.439	0.549	0.110	0.478	0.561	0.083
Black-Asian	0.384	0.463	0.079	0.404	0.490	0.086
Multiracial	0.427	0.524	0.097	0.463	0.536	0.073

Source: Author's calculations based on U.S. Census Bureau 2000, 2010.
Note: Children denotes residents six to seventeen years old. All racial categories include Hispanic and non-Hispanic householders except the non-Hispanic white-Hispanic segregation estimate. Multiracial segregation is estimated among whites, Asians, blacks, and other race, regardless of Hispanic ethnicity. N=95 largest MSAs with more than one school district.

In 2000, about 54 percent of the residential segregation (in terms of evenness) between black and white children occurred between school districts on average across metropolitan areas (segregation between neighborhoods within districts accounts for the rest). About 46 percent of residential segregation between black and white adults occurred between districts. This large proportion among adults, for whom school district boundaries are less relevant, underscores that district boundaries often map onto municipality boundaries or geographic areas with other amenities attractive to adults without children that influence residential choices. Further, childless homeowners may pay attention to school district boundaries when buying a home because of the capitalization of school quality into home prices, and some currently childless households are empty-nesters who made residential choices when they did have children in the household or young householders planning to have children. However, more residential segregation occurred between school districts for children than for adults, and results are similar for segregation between other racial-ethnic groups. The proportion of neighborhood segregation attributable to between-district segregation is up to 8 percentage points greater among children, depending on the racial groups of interest. The greatest differences between children and adults in the proportion of neighborhood segregation attributable to segregation between districts are for white-black, white-nonwhite, and multiracial segregation. This suggests that school district boundaries play the biggest role in shaping the residential outcomes of white children, contributing to their segregation from minorities. In 2010, residential segregation between districts again accounts for a greater proportion of total residential segregation among children than among adults.

Of course, children do not live in households by themselves, so I also estimated residential segregation (evenness) between neighborhoods and the proportion attributable to between-district segregation at the household level, comparing households with and without school-age children. Table 4 presents these results.

Consistent with table 3, more residential segregation occurs between districts among households with children than among those without. The proportion of residential segregation occurring between districts for childless households is lower than the proportion for adults in table 3, as the individual-level analysis included adults who live in households with children. The difference in the proportion of residential segregation attributable to between-district segregation is thus larger between households with and without children than between adults and children—up to 11 percentage points. I prefer the individual-level results and present them throughout this article because, although the Census Bureau provides household counts by the presence of children age six to seventeen by householder race, the racial groups include both Hispanic and non-Hispanic householders. The only available race-by-ethnicity category is for non-Hispanic whites, so I can estimate segregation between non-Hispanic whites and Hispanics. Given the importance of the residential patterns of Hispanics throughout the results presented, I prefer the individual-level results where Hispanic ethnicity is identified.

The proportion of neighborhood racial unevenness due to sorting between districts grew from 2000 to 2010 among both adults and children for all racial group comparisons, in both individual- (table 3) and household-level (table 4) estimates. This growth could be due to changes in either between-neighborhood or between-district evenness. Table A1 presents estimates of average residential segregation between districts in these years: among most racial-ethnic groups, for both adults and children, it declined (exceptions are white-Asian, white-Hispanic, and Asian-Hispanic). Table 2 shows that residential segregation between neighborhoods also declined between most racial groups, so the growing proportion of neighborhood segregation between districts indicates that residential segregation declined less than between-district segregation. The adult-child gap in the proportion of residential segregation between districts increased for some racial-ethnic groups but declined for others during this time. Therefore, during the 2000s, school district boundaries have not necessarily become a stronger influence on the residential decision-making of parents than on that of childless adults. School districts may coincide with municipalities or clusters of neighborhoods comprising a section of a city or metropolitan area; recent research notes the importance of considering multiple geographic scales of segregation, finding that Hispanic-white and Asian-white macro-scale segregation grew in the 1990s (Reardon et al. 2009). Macro-scale segregation could correspond to school districts, and future research should investigate whether the geographic scale of segregation also varies by age group.

Among all racial-ethnic group comparisons, about half of children's residential segregation is due to children living in neighborhoods in different school districts. A higher proportion, about 60 percent, of children's school segregation is due to children attending schools in different school districts (Stroub and Richards 2013). This suggests that the residential population of school districts is more diverse than the student population of schools in the district. This disparity is consistent with the work of Saporito and his colleagues (Saporito and Sohoni 2007; Saporito 2003; Saporito and Hanley 2014) showing that public schools have a student body that is poorer and more minority than the child population in the school's attendance area. In part, this is due to white and higher-income parents opting out of the neighborhood school, sending their children to private or choice schools. White and higher-SES parents may be more willing to live in diverse residential settings than to send their children to diverse schools.

DISCUSSION

Children are exposed to higher racial residential segregation, and therefore face greater neighborhood inequality, than adults. Exposure to neighbors of all ages shapes children's outcomes through neighborhood effects on local institutional resources like schools and other public spaces, neighboring networks and social support, and adult supervision and socialization of children. In terms of exposure to all neighbors, children and adults experience fairly similar contexts. However, other neighborhood mechanisms including adolescent peer groups and neighborhood school composition depend on exposure to one's age group, and in this regard children face more segregation. Children of each racial-ethnic group are exposed to fewer whites and more minority children, particularly Hispanic, than adults are to adults of other racial groups. This difference is driven in part by the larger (and growing) ratio of Hispanic children to Hispanic adults. Examining the exposure of children to peers also emphasizes the rapidly changing demographic context that future generations will experience. Even if residential sorting processes do not change in ways that create more segregation, majority white neighborhoods may be obsolete for these subjects' children or grandchildren.

In terms of how evenly members of different racial-ethnic groups are represented across neighborhoods, children are also more segregated than adults, suggesting that children experience more homogeneous, less diverse neighborhoods than adults. Research on the importance of neighborhoods for children's well-being generally takes two approaches. First, most neighborhood effects research identifies an impact associated with living in a neighborhood of a certain composition. Higher segregation among children than adults suggests that more minority children than minority adults are exposed to neighborhoods of concentrated disadvantage, for example. Therefore, neighborhoods are a more critical context for the population of children than adults. Second, a smaller body of research takes an aggregate-level approach, identifying negative effects of neighborhood segregation, rather than composition, on children's outcomes (Quillian 2014). This research suggests that the degree of inequality between neighborhoods—not just the composition of immediate neighborhood—matters. My findings suggest that children's contexts are more unequal than adults', and that children thus bear the negative consequences. Future research should continue to investigate the absolute versus relative impact of neighborhood disadvantage.

One factor that contributes to higher segregation among children is the link between neighborhood residence and school attendance. Neighborhood residence is often pointed to as an explanation for school segregation, but concerns about schooling also contribute to neighborhood segregation. Parents consider trade-offs across school districts, neighborhoods, schools, and housing units when making residential decisions, and segregation between neighborhoods occurs both between and within school districts. Consistent with the hypothesis that school options are one driver of residential choices among families with children, I find that about half of children's racial residential segregation occurs between school district boundaries, a greater proportion than for adults' racial residential segregation. Concerns about school options may have aggregated into macro-scale patterns of inequality and spatial segregation. In particular, white parents seem to avoid living in school districts where black and Hispanic children live, perhaps because they use racial composition as a proxy for neighborhood—and local neighborhood school—quality (Harris 1999; Krysan 2002). Although school choice policies, charter schools, and magnet schools offer some families choice within districts, only a handful of voluntary interdistrict public school choice programs exist. As long as neighborhoods are demarcated by school district boundaries limiting enrollment options, parents will take these boundaries into account when making residential choices, which may contribute to segregation between white and minority children. School concerns also shape residential patterning within districts, and future research should investigate the role of school attendance zones and policies in contributing to residential segregation.

This study emphasizes the importance of jointly considering two critical social contexts for children's development: schools and neighborhoods. Considerable research documents school segregation, but less is known about the residential experiences of children versus those of adults. To design effective policies aimed at equalizing both neighborhood and school contexts, policymakers must understand the degrees to which neighborhood composition contributes to school segregation and to which school concerns contribute to neighborhood residential decisions and segregation. The two contexts are intertwined, and a policy that breaks the link between school attendance and neighborhood residence—beyond intradistrict school choice plans—is necessary to break the cyclical relationship and reduce inequality among both contexts. Understanding segregation in terms of multiple contexts is critical in identifying the degree to which children experience multiple disadvantages as they navigate their social worlds.

Table A1. Residential Segregation Between School Districts

	2000			2010		
	Adults	Children	Difference	Adults	Children	Difference
White-black	0.171	0.249	0.078	0.163	0.240	0.077
White-Asian	0.062	0.085	0.023	0.068	0.090	0.022
White-Hispanic	0.097	0.140	0.043	0.099	0.145	0.046
White-nonwhite	0.129	0.188	0.059	0.122	0.167	0.045
Black-Asian	0.135	0.171	0.036	0.129	0.170	0.041
Black-Hispanic	0.082	0.097	0.015	0.073	0.086	0.013
Asian-Hispanic	0.166	0.114	−0.052	0.168	0.120	−0.048
Multiracial	0.115	0.156	0.041	0.108	0.137	0.029

Source: Author's calculations based on U.S. Census Bureau 2000, 2010.
Note: Children denotes residents six to seventeen years old. All racial categories are non-Hispanic. Multiracial segregation is estimated among non-Hispanic whites, non-Hispanic Asians, non-Hispanic blacks, non-Hispanic individuals of other race, and Hispanics. Estimates in table 3 do not equal these estimates divided by those in table 2 because table 3 presents the average proportion, not the proportion of averages, and N for table 3 and this table is the ninety-five largest MSAs with more than one school district, not the hundred largest MSAs.

REFERENCES

Bayer, Patrick, Fernando Ferreira, and Robert McMillan. 2007. "A Unified Framework for Measuring Preferences for Schools and Neighborhoods." *Journal of Political Economy* 115(4): 588–638.

Black, Sandra E. 1999. "Do Better Schools Matter? Parental Valuation of Elementary Education." *Quarterly Journal of Economics* 114(2): 577–99.

Charles, Camille Zubrinsky. 2003. "The Dynamics of Racial Residential Segregation." *Annual Review of Sociology* 29(1): 167–207.

Crowder, Kyle D. 2000. "The Racial Context of White Mobility: An Individual-Level Assessment of the White Flight Hypothesis." *Social Science Research* 29(2): 223–57.

Frey, William H. 2014. "New Projections Point to a Majority Minority Nation in 2044." Washington, D.C.: Brookings Institution Press.

Goyette, Kimberly A., John Iceland, and Elliot Weininger. 2014. "Moving for the Kids: Examining the Influence of Children on White Residential Segregation." *City & Community* 13(2): 158–78.

Grady, Sarah, and Stacey Bielick. 2010. "Trends in the Use of School Choice: 1993 to 2007." NCES 2010-004. Washington: U.S. Department of Education.

Harris, David R. 1999. "'Property Values Drop When Blacks Move In, Because…': Racial and Socioeconomic Determinants of Neighborhood Desirability." *American Sociological Review* 64(3): 461–79.

Henig, Jeffrey. 1996. "The Local Dynamics of Choice: Ethnic Preferences and Institutional Responses." In *Who Chooses? Who Loses? Cluture, Institutions, and the Unequal Effects of School Choice*, edited by Bruce Fuller, Richard F. Elmore, and Gary Orfield. New York: Teachers College Press.

Holme, Jennifer Jellison. 2002. "Buying Homes, Buying Schools: School Choice and the Social Construction of School Quality." *Harvard Educational Review* 72(2): 177–206.

Iceland, John, Kimberly A. Goyette, Kyle Anne Nelson, and Chaowen Chan. 2010. "Racial and Ethnic Residential Segregation and Household Structure: A Research Note." *Social Science Research* 39(1): 39–47.

Jargowsky, Paul A. 2014. "Segregation, Neighborhoods, and Schools." In *Choosing Homes, Choosing Schools*, edited by Annette Lareau and Kimberly Goyette. New York: Russell Sage Foundation.

Jencks, Christopher, and Susan E. Mayer. 1990. "The Social Consequences of Growing Up in a Poor Neighborhood." In *Inner-City Poverty in the United States*, edited by Laurence E. Lynne and Michael G. H. McGreary. Washington, D.C.: National Academies Press.

Krysan, Maria. 2002. "Whites Who Say They'd Flee:

Who Are They and Why Would They Leave?" *Demography* 39(4): 675–96.

Lankford, Hamilton, and James Wyckoff. 2006. "The Effect of School Choice and Residential Location on the Racial Segregation of Students." In *Advances in Applied Microeconomics*, vol. 14. *Improving School Accountability*, edited by Timothy J. Gronberg and Dennis W. Jansen. Amsterdam: Elsevier.

Lareau, Annette. 2014. "Schools, Housing, and the Reproduction of Inequality." In *Choosing Homes, Choosing Schools*, edited by Annette Lareau and Kimberly A. Goyette. New York: Russell Sage Foundation.

Leventhal, Tama, and Jeanne Brooks-Gunn. 2000. "The Neighborhoods They Live in: The Effects of Neighborhood Residence on Child and Adolescent Outcomes." *Psychological Bulletin* 126(2): 309–37.

Logan, John R., Deirdre Oakley, Polly Smith, Jacob Stowell, and Brian Stults. 2001. "Separating the Children." *Lewis Mumford Center* report. Albany: State University of New York.

Logan, John R., and Brian J. Stults. 2011. "The Persistence of Segregation in the Metropolis: New Findings from the 2010 Census." *Project US2010* census brief. Providence, R.I.: Brown University. Accessed June 26, 2016. http://www.s4.brown.edu/us2010/Data/Report/report2.pdf.

Marsh, Kris, and John Iceland. 2010. "The Racial Residential Segregation of Black Single Living Alone Households." *City & Community* 9(3): 299–319.

Massey, Douglas S., and Nancy A. Denton. 1988. "The Dimensions of Residential Segregation." *Social Forces* 67(2): 281–315.

Missouri Census Data Center. 2012. "MABLE/Geocorr Geographic Correspondence Engine." Accessed June 26, 2016. http://mcdc.missouri.edu/websas/geocorr12.html.

Nguyen-Hoang, Phuong, and John Yinger. 2011. "The Capitalization of School Quality into House Values: A Review." *Journal of Housing Economics* 20(1): 30–48.

Orfield, Gary, and Erica Frankenberg. 2014. "Brown at 60: Great Progress, a Long Retreat, and an Uncertain Future." Los Angeles, Calif.: Civil Rights Project/Proyecto Derechos Civiles. Accessed June 23, 2016. https://civilrightsproject.ucla.edu/research/k-12-education/integration-and-diversity/brown-at-60-great-progress-a-long-retreat-and-an-uncertain-future/Brown-at-60-051814.pdf.

Owens, Ann. 2016. "Inequality in Children's Contexts: The Economic Segregation of Households with and Without Children." *American Sociological Review* 81(3): 549–74.

Quillian, Lincoln. 2014. "Does Segregation Create Winners and Losers? Residential Segregation and Inequality in Educational Attainment." *Social Problems* 61(3): 402–26.

Reardon, Sean F., Chad R. Farrell, Stephen A. Matthews, David O'Sullivan, Kendra Bischoff, and Glenn Firebaugh. 2009. "Race and Space in the 1990s: Changes in the Geographic Scale of Racial Residential Segregation, 1990–2000." *Social Science Research* 38(1): 55–70.

Reardon, Sean F., and Ann Owens. 2014. "60 Years After Brown: Trends and Consequences of School Segregation." *Annual Review of Sociology* 40: 199–218.

Reardon, Sean F., John T. Yun, and Tamela McNulty Eitle. 2000. "The Changing Structure of School Segregation: Measurement and Evidence of Multiracial Metropolitan-Area School Segregation, 1989–1995." *Demography* 37(3): 351–64.

Rhodes, Anna, and Stefanie DeLuca. 2014. "Residential Mobility and School Choice Among Poor Families." In *Choosing Homes, Choosing Schools*, edited by Annette Lareau and Kimberly A. Goyette. New York: Russell Sage Foundation.

Sampson, Robert J., Jeffrey D Morenoff, and Thomas Gannon-Rowley. 2002. "Assessing 'Neighborhood Effects': Social Processes and New Directions in Research." *Annual Review of Sociology* 28: 443–78.

Saporito, Salvatore. 2003. "Private Choices, Public Consequences: Magnet School Choice and Segregation by Race and Poverty." *Social Problems* 50(2): 181–203.

Saporito, Salvatore, and Caroline Hanley. 2014. "Declining Significance of Race?" In *Choosing Homes, Choosing Schools*, edited by Annette Lareau and Kimberly A. Goyette. New York: Russell Sage Foundation.

Saporito, Salvatore, and Annette Lareau. 1999. "School Selection as a Process: The Multiple Dimensions of Race in Framing Educational Choice." *Social Problems* 46(3): 418–39.

Saporito, Salvatore, and Deenesh Sohoni. 2007. "Mapping Educational Inequality: Concentrations of Poverty Among Poor and Minority Students in Public Schools." *Social Forces* 85(3): 1227–54.

Sharkey, Patrick. 2014. "Spatial Segmentation and the Black Middle Class." *American Journal of Sociology* 119(4): 903–54.

Sharkey, Patrick, and Jacob W. Faber. 2014. "Where, When, Why, and for Whom Do Residential Contexts Matter? Moving Away from the Dichotomous Understanding of Neighborhood Effects." *Annual Review of Sociology* 40: 559–79.

South, Scott J., and Kyle D. Crowder. 1998. "Leaving the 'Hood: Residential Mobility between Black, White, and Integrated Neighborhoods." *American Sociological Review* 63(1): 17–26.

Stroub, Kori J., and Meredith P. Richards. 2013. "From Resegregation to Reintegration: Trends in the Racial/Ethnic Segregation of Metropolitan Public Schools, 1993–2009." *American Educational Research Journal* 50(3): 497–531.

Theil, Henri. 1972. *Statistical Decomposition Analysis*, vol. 14. Amsterdam: North-Holland Publishing.

Theil, Henri, and Anthony J. Finezza. 1971. "A Note on the Measurement of Racial Integration of Schools by Means of Informational Concepts." *Journal of Mathematical Sociology* 1(2): 187–94.

U.S. Census Bureau. 2000. "Summary Tape File 1, Tables P4, P6, P26, P34, PCT12." Washington: U.S. Department of Commerce.

———. 2010. "Summary Tape File 1, Tables P9, P11, P18, P38, PCT12." Washington: U.S. Department of Commerce.

Wells, Amy Stuart. 1996. "African-American Students' View of School Choice." In *Who Chooses? Who Loses? Cluture, Institutions, and the Unequal Effects of School Choice*, edited by Bruce Fuller, Richard F. Elmore, and Gary Orfield. New York: Teachers College Press.

Defensible Spaces in Philadelphia: Exploring Neighborhood Boundaries Through Spatial Analysis

RORY KRAMER

Few spatial scales are as important to individual outcomes as the neighborhood. However, it is nearly impossible to define neighborhoods in a generalizable way. This article proposes that by shifting the focus to measuring neighborhood boundaries rather than neighborhoods, scholars can avoid the problem of the indefinable neighborhood and better approach questions of what predicts racial segregation across areas. By quantifying an externality space theory of neighborhood boundaries, this article introduces a novel form of spatial analysis to test where potential physical markers of neighborhood boundaries (major roads, rivers, railroads, and the like) are associated with persistent racial boundaries between 1990 and 2010. Using Philadelphia as a case study, the paper identifies neighborhoods with persistent racial boundaries. It theorizes that local histories of white reactions to black in-migration explain which boundaries persistently resisted racial turnover, unlike the majority of Philadelphia's neighborhoods, and that those racial boundaries shape the location, progress, and reaction to new residential development in those neighborhoods.

Keywords: segregation, boundaries, racial violence, spatial analysis

Urban theorists from Jane Jacobs (1961) to Mike Davis (1992) to David Harvey (2000) emphasize that the physical attributes of space identify who is welcome in an area, how that area can be used, and mark boundaries. Davis and Harvey argue that inequality can be perpetuated, reinforced, and created by land use patterns that isolate or connect neighborhoods, create "defended neighborhoods" (Suttles 1972), and identify cultural distinctions between otherwise adjacent neighborhoods.

At the same time, studies of ethnic groups or identities often focus on the boundaries between groups as opposed to within-group similarities (Brubaker 2002; Wimmer 2009) and studies of neighborhoods often theorize about the importance of boundaries to the neighborhood (Galster 1986; Grannis 2005; Martin 2003). However, research on neighborhood boundary making is practically nonexistent apart from a few rare exceptions (Ananat 2011; Grannis 2005; Legewie and Schaeffer 2016; Roberto 2015), even as scholars show that urban neighborhoods are unequally embedded in larger, interconnected social and geographic systems within the urban context (Peterson and Krivo 2010; Sampson 2012; Sharkey 2014). This line of research has shown that boundaries between neighborhoods are not impervious walls, but instead vary in their effects on indi-

Rory Kramer is assistant professor of sociology at Villanova University.

© 2017 Russell Sage Foundation. Kramer, Rory. 2017. "Defensible Spaces in Philadelphia: Exploring Neighborhood Boundaries Through Spatial Analysis." *RSF: The Russell Sage Foundation Journal of the Social Sciences* 3(2): 81–101. DOI: 10.7758/RSF.3.2.04. The author thanks Camille Charles, Tukufu Zuberi, Grace Kao, Tara Jackson, Lindsay Mack, and Brianna Remster for their comments on earlier drafts. The editors of this issue, participants at the Russell Sage Foundation conference "Foundations of Spatial Inequality," and two anonymous reviewers also provided important feedback on this article. Dana Tomlin provided invaluable support in writing and testing the python script utilized in this article. Direct correspondence to: Rory Kramer at rory.kramer@villanova.edu, Department of Sociology and Criminology, Villanova University, 800 E. Lancaster Avenue, Villanova, PA 19085.

vidual outcomes (Legewie and Schaeffer 2016). Left unanswered is why some neighborhoods are isolated while others experience significant spillover across their edges and what explains changes in those boundary effects between neighborhoods over time.

Combining those insights, this article studies how physical barriers affect racial segregation over time in an urban setting. The article presents an innovative way of conceptualizing and measuring segregation that focuses on the boundaries between racial groups that use kernel density estimation to measure residential segregation. It enhances that method by quantifying the externality space approach that George Galster (1986, 2001) developed for use in identifying racial segregation boundaries and attributes of the physical space (such as major roads, industrial land use, railroads, and rivers) that preserve those boundaries over time. It then leverages that innovation to illustrate in a case study the long-lingering association between localized responses to integrative efforts in the 1960s and 1970s and the location of persistent racial boundaries in Philadelphia in the twenty-first century.

Specifically, after reviewing the relevant research on segregation, urban communities, inequality, boundaries, and the appropriateness of Philadelphia as a case study, the article introduces an innovative method, non-Euclidean smoothing, to identify and compare neighborhood boundaries. I map the rate of change in local racial demographics over distance (that is, the slope) to identify where sharp demographic shifts occur when potential interaction barriers (physical topologies such as major roads, railroad tracks, and large, nonresidential areas) are incorporated into the mapping process. It examines the local histories of three unique areas—West Mount Airy, South Philadelphia, and Fishtown—to generate a hypothesis that neighborhood responses to civil rights era black migration—either embracing racial integration in the 1950s and 1960s (West Mount Airy) or violently rejecting efforts to integrate neighborhoods or schools (South Philadelphia and Fishtown)—continue to shape the relative location and strengths of racial boundaries at their borders across three decennial censuses (1990, 2000, and 2010).

LITERATURE REVIEW

Where one lives has long-ranging consequences for what George Galster and Patrick Sharkey (this volume) call one's *spatial opportunity structure*. For example, sociologists have highlighted the impact of residential segregation and neighborhoods more broadly on major forms of inequality including educational outcomes, crime victimization, wealth accumulation, employment opportunities, access to social services and government, and social capital (Charles 2003, 2006; Leventhal and Brooks-Gunn 2000; Morenoff 2003; Sampson, Sharkey, and Raudenbush 2008; Wodtke, Harding, and Elwert 2011). As Douglas Massey and Nancy Denton famously asserted in *American Apartheid*, residential segregation is the "institutional apparatus that supports other racially discriminatory processes and binds them together into a coherent and uniquely effective system of racial subordination" (1993, 8). In short, where racial residential segregation is, there are also related racial and spatial inequalities that rely on segregation to persist. For example, research details that residents in more segregated metro areas and neighborhoods were more likely to be offered subprime loans, more likely to experience foreclosures on those loans, and more adversely affected by the wave of foreclosures after the housing bubble burst (Rugh and Massey 2010; Hyra et al. 2013).

Efforts to appropriately define one's neighborhood and therefore one's spatial opportunity structure for the purpose of social scientific research have, however, faced serious difficulties. Traditionally, social scientists measure segregation by examining the demographics of individual neighborhoods as the unit of measurement and comparing them with an ideal, integrated hypothetical city. Yet, as some note, a common flaw in the neighborhood effects literature is the struggle to identify the geographic bounds of the neighborhood (Galster 2008; Durlauf 2004). This creates two problems. First, defining the neighborhood has largely been an exercise in comparing different, inadequate geographic proxies for an ambiguous but important social concept, one that often varies depending on individual residential histories (Hwang 2015). In part, that is because we know that individuals define their neighborhood not as singular, static entities but rather as shifting geographies based on the conceptual topic of interest, such as one's social networks, economic activity, or home valuation (Suttles 1972; Martin 2003; Hwang 2015). No matter the proxy used, the modifiable areal unit problem (MAUP) introduces a real but unknown degree of measurement error when defining neighborhoods that can have significant impacts on the identification of one's spatial opportunity structure (Downey 2006; Grengs 2007; Openshaw and Taylor 1979). For example, the neighborhood of Spring Garden in Philadelphia is split between four predominantly white (all > 75 percent white) census tracts and two majority black and Latino census tracts. Using census tracts as neighborhood proxies, it would appear to be an example of significant segregation. Using traditional spatial analytic techniques that Barrett Lee and his colleagues introduce (2008), it would appear to be an integrated area. One of those two findings would be an artifact of MAUP, but it is impossible for an analyst without local knowledge of the neighborhood to know which is correct.

Second, segregation research generally treats each neighborhood as completely insular and isolated. Some research has looked at "spillover effects" (Peterson and Krivo 2010; Sampson 2012; Sharkey 2014) between neighborhoods, but still treats each individual neighborhood as the unit of interest, albeit influenced by surrounding areas. Segregation does work at the neighborhood level—via social geographic processes such as redlining, localized housing markets, and school catchment areas—to structure individual opportunity. However, neighborhood boundaries are not walls around fortresses, and as the research on spillover effects on crime demonstrates, neighborhood effects are not necessarily caused only by the hyperlocal neighborhood, but also by proximate neighborhoods, or possibly the ones past that as well (Peterson and Krivo 2010; Crowder and South 2011). The impact of one's neighbors (or their neighbors) is not necessarily the same throughout a city. The clarity of borders between one neighborhood and another also can vary; many neighborhoods have clear, well-established boundaries that have lasted generations, but others shift gradually from one demographic to another without clear divisions (Hunter 1982).

Here, I argue that an *externality approach* to identifying important boundaries can resolve many of these difficulties (Galster 1986, 2001). Galster argues that a neighborhood is meaningful to individuals insofar as changes within an area "are perceived as altering the well-being (use value, psychological or financial benefits) the individual derives from the particular location" (2001, 2114). He defines that area as an externality space and identifies three key dimensions of an externality space or neighborhood—the *congruence* of an individual's externality space with predefined geographic boundaries; the *generality* of an externality space (for example, do the use value externalities map to the same areas as the financial or psychological externalities); and the *accordance* across multiple people's externality spaces (whether or not individuals agree on the boundaries of their externality spaces).

Where individuals do not share externalities with proximate others, is, axiomatically, a boundary between externality spaces or neighborhoods. Like a geographic market area in real estate, boundaries are identified in this schema not based on a priori definitions of neighborhoods but rather by identifying schisms in the social meaning or attributes of space at a given point, thus resolving the need to rely on proxies such as the census tract. In other words, Galster identifies how a researcher might systematically conceptualize one's sense of being a part of a place-based corporate entity in opposition to another, or, in Gerald Suttles's (1972) terms, a "defended neighborhood." For example, this paper theorizes that white racial violence (or organized support for integration in West Mount Airy) in the 1950s and 1960s created a lasting, contemporary sense of opposition between neighborhoods.

In lieu of a priori definitions of where one neighborhood begins or ends, an urban area is considered to lack internal neighborhood boundaries except where changes in key variables across a small space are noticeable. Those changes locate the edges or boundaries of an externality space. In terms of racial segregation, locations where the racial composition of the population changes quickly can be seen as the edges of racial externality spaces. A similar analysis looking at a different externality (such as income, family composition, or educational attainment) may identify different neighborhood cleavages for the same geographic space. For example, Rick Grannis's concept of a *t-community*, areas linked by small, tertiary streets, can be recast as an externality space measure of walkability (2005, 2009). Similarly, Ann Owens's research (this issue) demonstrating that school boundaries act as a sorting mechanism for racial segregation can be cast as the impact of one externality (shared school assignment) on another (racial residential segregation).

This analysis can be understood as a *slope-based approach* that focuses on the congruence and accordance of a single externality, in this case, racial segregation. Imagine a three dimensional map of a city. The x- and y-axes are the same geographic latitude and longitude coordinates as found on a traditional map and the z-axis is the measure of the externality of interest, in this case the percentage of a given race in that area. Racial externality boundaries would be those locations where that z-axis changes quickly, or, in other words, where its slope in z-x or z-y space is quite steep. Combining these literatures, this paper analyzes racial segregation externalities in Philadelphia, identifies those that are stable over time and those that are fleeting, and compares the two types to theorize about the causes of long-lasting, stable racial boundaries in Philadelphia. In the section that follows, I discuss why Philadelphia is a good case study for this project.

Philadelphia as Case Study

Although American urban sociology has traditionally centered on the Chicago school, its birth can be traced to Du Bois's pioneering *Philadelphia Negro* (1996; Morris 2015). Beyond Philadelphia's symbolic role as the birthplace of American urban sociology, its recent demographic changes provide an ideal case study for measuring how boundaries affect the pattern and location of racial change in an urban area. Like many other Rust Belt industrial cities, Philadelphia's population and economy began to shrink in the mid-twentieth century with increasing suburbanization and declines in urban manufacturing and industrial production. Overall, Philadelphia lost roughly five hundred thousand residents from its high of more than two million residents in the 1950s to barely over 1.5 million in the 2000 Census.

Because of economic weaknesses, Philadelphia was not an immigration destination until the 1990s. In 1990, the city was roughly 53 percent white, 39 percent black, 5 percent Hispanic, and 3 percent Asian. Although immigration began to increase in the 1990s, the city's total population continued to fall, primarily because the white population declined. In 2000, whites were only 45 percent of the population, blacks 43 percent, Hispanics 8 percent, and Asians 4.5 percent. In the 2000s, the white and black populations continued to fall, albeit more slowly, but the increase in Asian and Latino (as well as significant African and Caribbean) immigration led to the first increase in Philadelphia's total population between decennial censuses since the 1940s. In the 2000s, the Asian population of Philadelphia grew from under 5 percent of the total to roughly 7 percent (thirty thousand new residents); the Hispanic population grew from over 8 to over 12 percent (sixty thousand new residents) at the same time. The black population was stable between 2000 and 2010, but the white population shrank by 12.4 percent (more than eighty thousand). In sum, even as late as 2000, Philadelphia was a largely biracial city, split almost entirely between white and black residents, but ten years later was substantially more multiracial, and included a rapidly growing Hispanic and Asian population. By 2010, Philadelphia was the fiftieth most diverse county (of more than three thousand) in the country. Thus, during the period under study, racial segregation boundaries were under significant risk of change as Philadelphia's racial demographics shifted from a majority white biracial city in decline to a growing multiracial city with a black plurality.

This paper focuses on the city of Philadelphia and not the larger metropolitan statistical area (MSA), which includes eleven other counties spanning four states and encompassing nearly six million residents, for two substantive reasons. First, although the city accounts for only 25 percent of the MSA's population, it accounts for more than 45 percent of the area's total nonwhite population and more than half of the MSA's black population in 2010. Those numbers are even more dramatic in 1990 and 2000. Second, by focusing on one municipality, I avoid the potential for local municipal boundaries to act as segregation boundaries via political acts such as maximum density requirements (Rugh and Massey 2010; Rothwell and Massey 2009).

DATA AND METHODS

Block-level demographic data for this project come from the 1990, 2000, and 2010 Summary File 1 of the U.S. Census. Census blocks are formed by the combination of physical features that can be used as boundaries (streets, streams, railroads, etc.) or legal boundaries if relevant to that location, or both. To identify boundaries, I combine the TIGER shapefile definitions of major roads provided in the census (Grannis 2005) with data from the Pennsylvania Spatial Data Access clearinghouse to identify the locations of rivers, parks, and railroad tracks that can also serve as potential physical boundaries between neighborhoods.[1]

Spatial data can be organized two ways: vector and raster. Although vector maps, which use polygons, points, and lines to represent actual objects in space, at first glance seem a more intuitive form of mapping for social scientists, raster methodology is actually better for social analysis (Downey 2006). Raster maps are a cell-based spatial dataset in which each equal-sized grid cell is assigned a value for a given variable (population, altitude, type of vegetation, and so on) and provide greater opportunity to properly integrate space into sociological research because their size and layout are standardized.

Raster Smoothing

Similar to incorporating a moving average in a graph with noisy data, raster maps can be smoothed to better model changes across a space that may be obscured by noisy data. Kernel estimation (or kernel density analysis) was developed to obtain a smooth estimate of a probability density from an observed sample (Bailey and Gattrell 1995). When an entire population has been mapped (such as the decennial censuses used in this paper), kernel density analysis acts as a form of data smoothing. As Lee and his colleagues (2008) show, kernel density analysis can approximate the demographics of a local area around each raster cell in a given city or metro area. This paper builds on Lee and his colleagues' process by allowing a second variable (in this case, aspects of the physical environment) to affect the variable of interest (the demographics of a raster cell's local area). The smoothing technique I use is empirically identical to the kernel density analysis that Lee and his colleagues use but is slightly simplified. In the following section, I describe the innovative method that incorporates what I call friction into the kernel density analysis, which allows me to measure the consistency of neighborhood boundaries over time.

Non-Euclidean smoothing

Social space, in reality, is far from Euclidean. We expect physical attributes of a space to dramatically affect the ease of interaction in that space. For example, people who live along a small, tertiary street are likely to interact and be exposed to each other frequently, even if they live several blocks from each other, because they walk along the same sidewalks or frequent the same neighborhood shops and restaurants (Grannis 2009). On the other hand, people living across an interstate highway from each other may be physically closer than the residents described earlier but are much less likely to interact. We can consider these attributes of the physical space as a cost to travel—that is, it is easy to cross a small, tertiary street but takes more effort to find a way to cross a highway or railroad tracks. The only change is that the bandwidth, rather than being equal in all directions, is instead a function of a given friction (or cost) function of the space (for further details on the methodology, see Kramer 2012). As Trevor Bailey and Tony Gattrell note, the kernel estimate is "just a

1. The census defines major roads as arterial roads, often those with more than two lanes or that are highly trafficked.

more sophisticated version of the weighted moving average scheme" (1995, 161). A non-Euclidean kernel density analysis can be understood as a weighted moving average across space where the weighting depends on the cost of moving across a given space.

To date, although others have demonstrated the impact of physical barriers on residential segregation (Ananat 2011), no one has visually represented such barriers. Fortunately, representing these physical barriers is a conceptually simple task after incorporating non-Euclidean kernel density analysis. Imagine that the populations being smoothed are, in fact, a liquid slowly spreading evenly across a perfectly smooth and level field. Physical barriers to residential interaction in this extended metaphor can be seen as levels of particularly high or low friction on that previously level space. A park, where people may be more likely to share the social space and interact, would be a low friction area through which that liquid would move more quickly than across a level field (Jacobs 1961; Anderson 2011). Large highways or rivers would have high levels of friction that slow the movement and interaction of residents across that social space. In this case, the bandwidth is a function of physical barriers to social interaction.

This article reports all slopes, or rates of change over space, as a percentage change that is the average difference between racial compositions of all of the surrounding cells and the cell being analyzed. In other words, the slope can be interpreted as the expected difference between the value of a variable in that cell and a neighbor cell—thus, a black racial slope of 10 percent at a boundary represents a boundary between two neighborhoods that have a 20 percent difference in their proportions black.

CONSISTENT BARRIERS: LOCATIONS AND POSSIBLE EXPLANATIONS

Racial segregation and residential patterns are constantly evolving and changing, and the impact of individual barriers changes along with those demographic forces. Other urban scholars show that barriers are more commonly associated with white neighborhood boundaries. Architecture and city planning have been used to protect whites and their privileged spaces and neighborhoods (Davis 1992; Deener 2012). Many white residents have been moving out of the city, but those who remain are increasingly separated from nonwhite others by physical barriers.

Grannis's (2005, 2009) finding that pedestrian access is strongly related to local patterns of segregation can be leveraged to identify locations where racial externality spaces are bounded. Major roads and railroads are barriers to pedestrian access. However, as Grannis notes, not all major roads are racial segregation boundaries. Thus, to identify which potential barriers act as racial segregation boundaries, I treat all barriers as nearly impenetrable and then identify which are, in that scenario, locations characterized by steep racial slopes. Specifically, to test the impact of land use on racial boundaries, I incorporate non-Euclidean kernel density smoothing into the analysis and set the friction at a potential boundary raster cell (a raster cell on a major road, railway, river, or nonresidential space[2]) at one thousand times that of a nonboundary raster cell. That is, I assume that all potential boundaries act as barriers between neighborhoods that are one thousand times more difficult to cross than other spaces and then identify where those boundaries correspond to sharp racial cleavages in the city.

To illustrate the effect of non-Euclidean smoothing, figure 1 presents a map of the change in the percentage black for a neighborhood in South Philadelphia (Point Breeze), which I discuss in more detail later. Areas in where the map is shaded are locations where the percentage black grew or shrank substantially (at least 5 percent) simply due to the inclusion of the borders in the calculation. In

---

2. I define nonresidential spaces as any census block in which the population is zero. This includes large, block-sized commercial malls but not mixed-use spaces, industrial parks, hospitals, and other block-sized institutions like major government offices. Many of these spaces are adjacent to major roads or are single blocks in the middle of neighborhoods and thus have little impact on the results shown; some major industrial parks in the Southwest of Philadelphia (including oil refineries) and two major airports would otherwise bias results toward greater integration (Grengs 2007).

Figure 1. Change in South Philadelphia Black Population

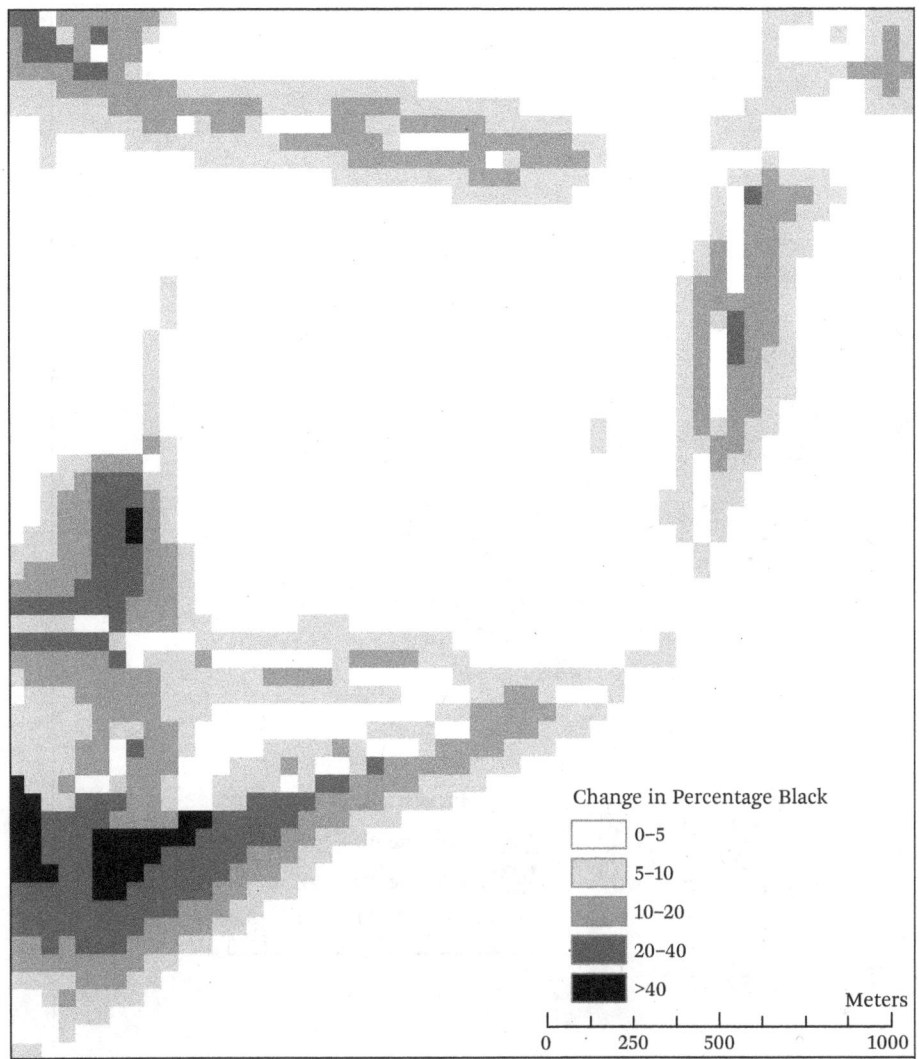

Source: Author's calculations based on U.S. Census Bureau 2011.
Note: Neighborhoods defined by one-thousand meter radius.

this example, the neighborhood's racial composition does not change (Point Breeze remains predominantly black and the surrounding neighborhoods remain predominantly white), but incorporating non-Euclidean smoothing heightens the contrast at borders between neighborhoods. Traditional kernel density smoothing visualizes artificially smooth transitions between majority black and majority white neighborhoods where non-Euclidean smoothing is able to identify the more sudden demographic shifts at neighborhood boundaries.

Although barriers normally change slopes over time, some barriers have consistently steep slopes. Identifying those barriers that are consistent racial boundaries may have implications for understanding why certain areas resist racial turnover and what may help spur desegregation efforts in those communities and neighborhoods. Figure 2 shows which barriers have high racial slopes between 1990 and

Figure 2. White-Nonwhite Racial Slopes at Barriers

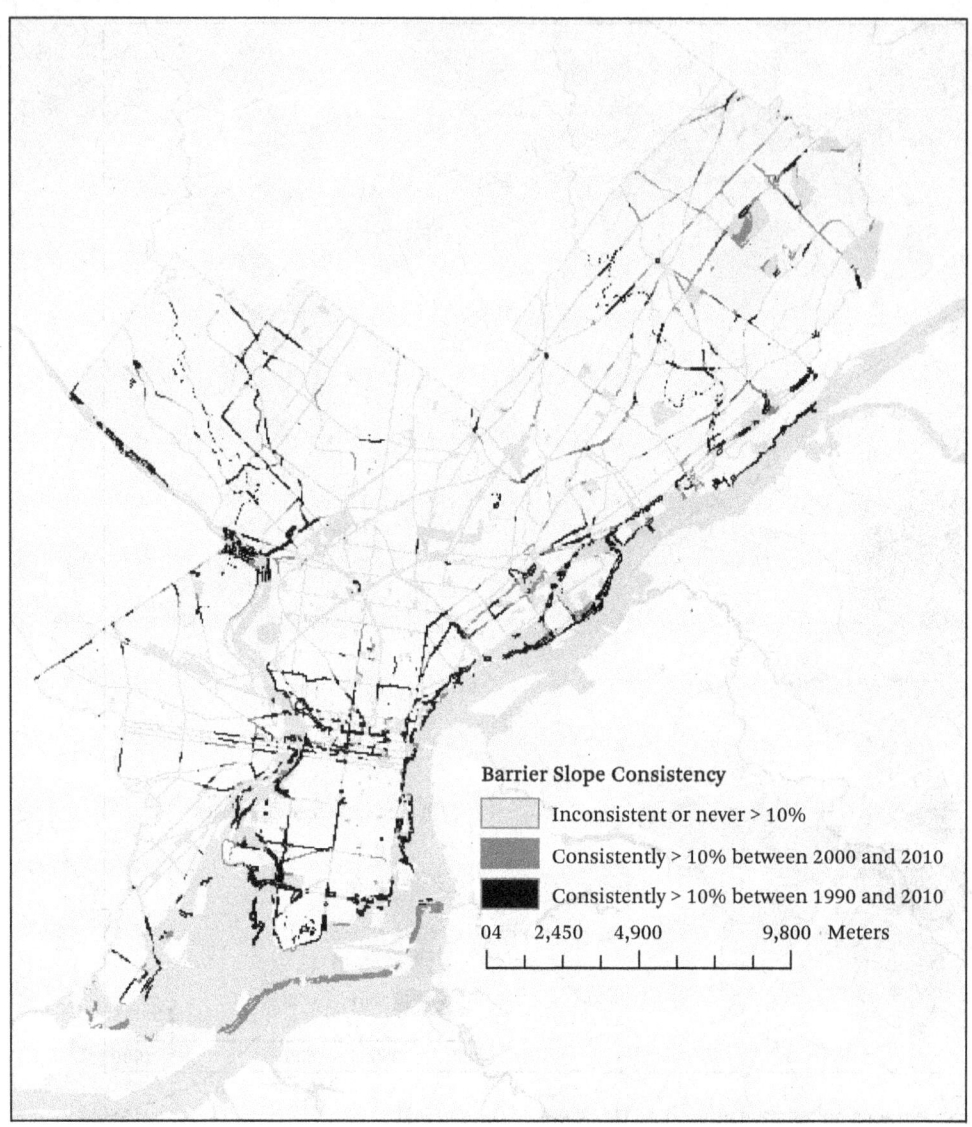

Source: Author's calculations based on U.S. Census Bureau 2011.
Note: Neighborhoods defined by one-thousand meter radius.

2010 (persistent slopes) or between 2000 and 2010 (newly formed, persistent slopes). I define a high slope as one above 10 percent. This means that crossing a barrier generally leads to a roughly 20 percent difference in the percentage nonwhite across both sides of the barrier. The large majority of barrier cells are not consistently high, especially in West Philadelphia and North Philadelphia—both highly segregated, predominantly black areas of the city.

Excluding those at the political boundaries of Philadelphia, few barriers act as consistent racial boundaries between 1990 and 2010. Due to that scarcity of consistently high slopes inside the city limits, it is hard to identify specific barriers of interest from figure 2, but some larger patterns do emerge. Generally, most barriers that were consistent in 1990 and 2000 stayed that way through 2010—about 85 percent of the cells identified as consistently high were categorized as such across all three decades (again, many of these barriers are located at Philadelphia's political boundaries and not between its neighborhoods). This indicates that racial boundaries are either easily overwhelmed over relatively brief periods (ten years) or are hardly penetrable, and few boundaries separate them. As an exploratory analysis, mapping boundaries can identify specific neighborhoods from whose history one can generate hypotheses about why some boundaries are consistent and others are readily crossed. Excluding political boundaries and the center city business area, where the extreme density of major roads and Philadelphia's Chinatown make it appear heavily bounded, three areas of the city have significant concentrations of consistent boundaries: West Mount Airy, Fishtown/Port Richmond, and South Philadelphia/Point Breeze. These areas were also sites of unique racial histories—specifically, collective white racial reactions to black in-migration in the 1950s and 1960s—that help explain the consistency of their barriers.

WEST MOUNT AIRY: CONSCIOUS INTEGRATION, BUT FOR HOW LONG?

Figure 3 focuses on West Mount Airy, a neighborhood that prides itself on being purposefully integrated since the 1950s; the United Nations sent delegates to the neighborhood to witness that integration in 1961 (Ferman, Singleton, and DeMarco 1998; Perkiss 2014). As large numbers of Philadelphia's black elite moved in, local groups in West Mount Airy went door to door to combat realtor efforts to blockbust the neighborhood (Perkiss 2014). West Mount Airy spent the 1950s and 1960s creating a collective identity as an integrated community; it consciously became a defended space of integration in a city otherwise actively segregating its growing black population (Hunter 1982; Massey and Denton 1993).

Unfortunately, West Mount Airy appears to be sliding toward internal segregation. The areas in the northern section of the map are the main dividing lines between Chestnut Hill, a wealthy white area, and West Oak Lane, a predominantly black, middle-class neighborhood. More importantly for West Mount Airy, the two black parts of West Mount Airy are isolated from the majority white area by barriers with steep slopes; Wissahickon Avenue is a consistent barrier across all three census periods and Lincoln Drive (the S-shaped curve in the middle of the map) becomes a steep racial boundary in 2000 and stays that way in 2010 (parts of Lincoln Drive were boundaries in 1990, but the whole stretch became a steep boundary only in 2000). Part of this divide corresponds to the type of housing stock available; the housing west of Lincoln Drive is generally large, detached single-family houses, and to the east it is generally smaller and attached row homes. Where Lincoln Drive is not a steep boundary near the southern edge of West Mount Airy, commuter train tracks replace Lincoln Drive as such. Importantly, although Wissahickon Avenue and Lincoln Drive also double as census tract boundaries, the SEPTA train tracts do not. Similarly, in South Philadelphia and Fishtown, I also identify racial boundaries—25th street, sections of Front Street, and Frankford Avenue—that do not double as census tract boundaries.

In West Mount Airy, class appears to be strongly associated with race, because local leaders have expressed concern over economic segregation leading to racial resegregation, even in an area nationally known for a proud history of integration (Smith 2014). The divide often corresponds to the type of housing stock available, as described in the previous paragraph. In areas where two groups with very disparate wealth statuses exist near one another, the wealthier group's advantages allow it to self-segregate. As income inequality and segregation has grown over time, West Mount Airy has grown more economically segregated, much like the rest of society (Reardon and Bischoff 2011), which has led to an emergence of racial segregation. In northwest Philadelphia, race and class are bounded together.

West Mount Airy's relatively privileged residents promoted integration and succeeded for at least two generations in perpetuating it, but the more common form of white collective action in Philadelphia and throughout the country in the 1960s was racial violence or flight in support of segregation. Philadelphia—and West Mount Airy—lost the majority of its white

Figure 3. Black-White Slope, West Mount Airy, Northwest Philadelphia

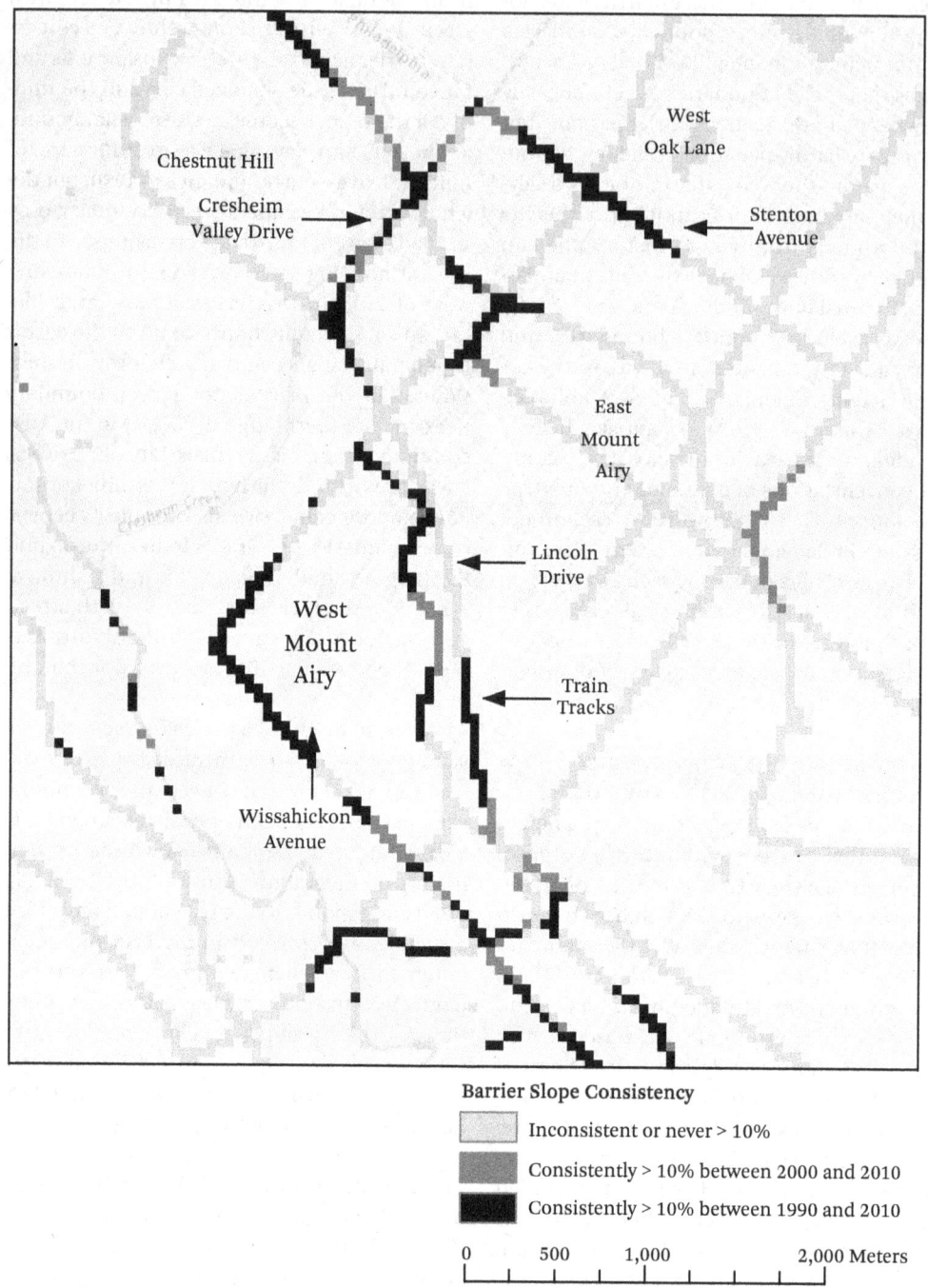

Source: Author's calculations based on U.S. Census Bureau 2011.
Note: Neighborhoods defined by one-thousand meter radius.

population to the suburbs beginning in the 1960s and, even as Philadelphia's population grew between 2000 and 2010, its white population continues to shrink. Because of this, most neighborhoods that experienced black in-migration in Philadelphia do not have consistent racial barriers because whites generally vacate those neighborhoods when nonwhite populations move in.

BATTLE LINES THEN AND NOW: SOUTH PHILADELPHIA AND FISHTOWN AS DEFENDED COMMUNITIES

The exceptions to that general pattern are the foci of the next figures; both neighborhoods were epicenters of the most aggressive white racial violence in Philadelphia in the 1960s and continued racial tensions since then. Echoing Owens's research in this volume, which shows how school boundaries act as a sorting mechanism for residential segregation, in South Philadelphia, that racial violence was in response to black efforts to integrate and white efforts to close Bok High School—then largely black and underachieving and closed in 2013 on the basis of school budget deficits—located five blocks east of Broad Street in the heart of Italian South Philadelphia, the political home of notorious law-and-order police commissioner turned mayor Frank Rizzo (Countryman 2005). In 1968, when Rizzo was police commissioner, it was the site of intense racial violence, of police protection for students using public transportation to attend school, and of veiled racial threats by local Italian American residents about making Bok "for South Philadelphians" (Countryman 2005, 245–53). At the height of the crisis, due to fears of further violence, fewer than 25 percent of Bok's majority black students and fewer than 20 percent of the predominantly white Southern High School attended school.

Figures 4 and 5 take a closer look at South Philadelphia, specifically focused on the boundaries surrounding the predominantly black and high-poverty Point Breeze section of the city. Figure 4 identifies steep black-white slopes, which starkly identifies Broad Street as a substantial racial boundary in South Philadelphia. The largely black Point Breeze neighborhood (west of Broad) is bounded to the South from the predominantly white Girard Estates neighborhood by two barriers, Snyder Avenue, which first became a census tract boundary in 2000, and West Passyunk Avenue, and the southern part of 25th Street, which does not extend far north. Broad Street is a consistently steep barrier as well for whites, who primarily live east of it, leaving Point Breeze economically neglected and isolated next to the reinvigorated, traditionally Italian eastern part of South Philadelphia. In sum, from figure 4, it appears that Point Breeze is hemmed in on three sides with regard to the white population in the area.

Unlike West Mount Airy, South Philadelphia has experienced substantial immigration, especially from Mexico and Southeast Asia. Figure 5, which focuses on black-nonblack boundaries, shows the impact of that immigration. The southern part of Broad Street where Snyder and Broad meet is now an inconsistent barrier because the large Asian immigration just west of Broad Street and the Hispanic and Asian immigration into the eastern side of South Philadelphia just north of Snyder Avenue have created a more multiracial area with gentler slopes, a potential example of the global neighborhoods that John Logan and Charles Zhang identify (2010, 2011). The lack of barriers to the north of Point Breeze helps explain why gentrification has slowly spread from north to south rather than from east to west. No major road separates the wealthy Rittenhouse area of center city from the southwest part of South Philadelphia. Because of this, gentrification and redevelopment followed a direct route from center city to the area now known as Graduate Hospital through to Point Breeze.

The final maps, figures 6 through 8, look at a third set of neighborhoods with historic identities. Port Richmond and Fishtown on the Delaware River have long histories as white working-class neighborhoods that included large Polish and Russian immigrant communities throughout the twentieth century. To their west lies Kensington, a previously white working-class community that experienced racial turnover in the 1950s and 1960s into a largely black and then Hispanic community. Even more overtly than South Philadelphia,

Figure 4. Racial Slopes, South Philadelphia and Center City, Black-White

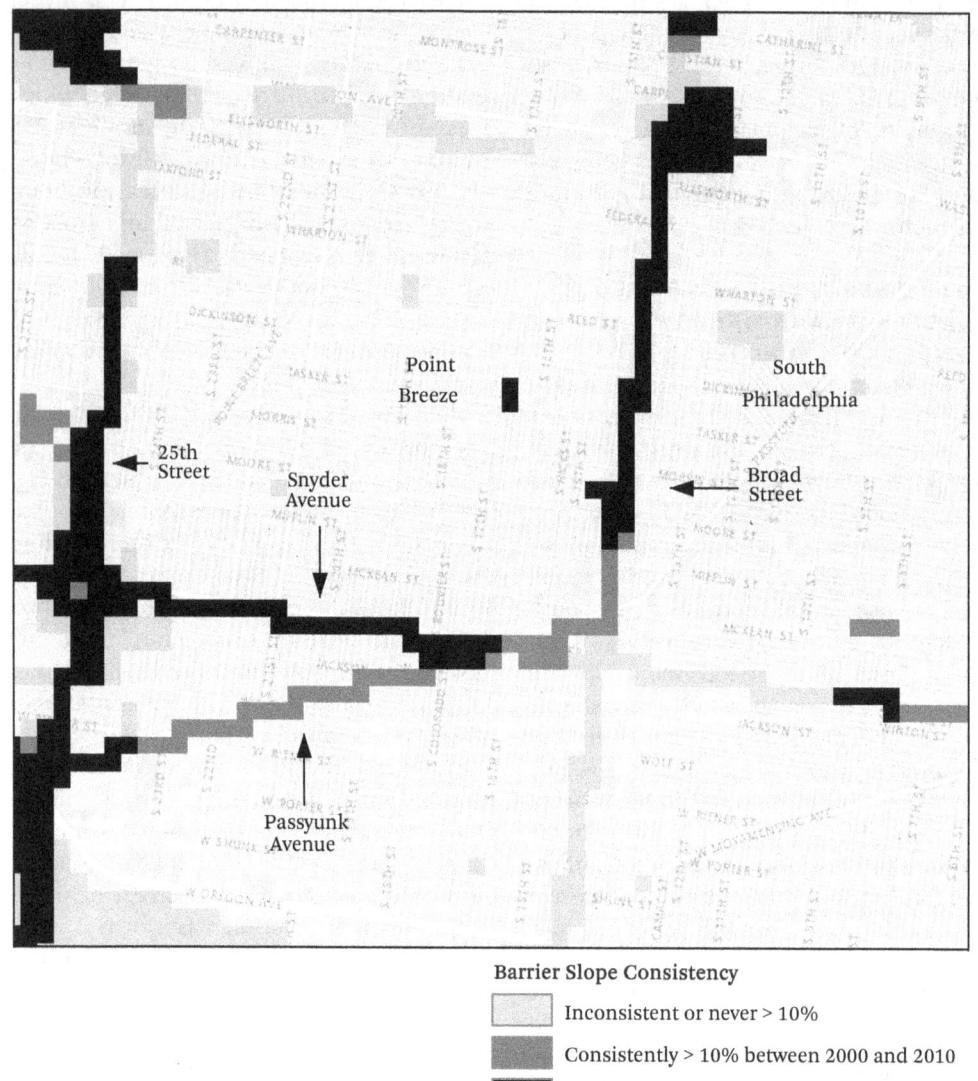

Barrier Slope Consistency
- Inconsistent or never > 10%
- Consistently > 10% between 2000 and 2010
- Consistently > 10% between 1990 and 2010

0   250   500   1,000 Meters

Source: Author's calculations based on U.S. Census Bureau 2011.
Note: Neighborhoods defined by one-thousand meter radius.

Fishtown and Port Richmond were the sites of significant racial protests against black in-migration and were notorious in Philadelphia for their insular community and "unofficial curfew" for blacks, and for a week-long riot in 1966 when a black family moved near Kensington Girls High (Wolfinger 2007, 185–86). Figure 6 shows that the white populations of Fishtown and Port Richmond are bounded by major roads, as Frankford Avenue and then Aramingo Avenue have consistently steep racial slopes. Frankford Avenue, along with the elevated subway line above North Front Street, is consistently steep from 1990 through 2010; Aramingo Avenue is only consistently steep in 2000 and 2010 because the eastern parts of Kensington were just beginning to see significant Hispanic in-migration in the late 1980s

Figure 5. Racial Slopes, South Philadelphia and Center City, Black-Nonblack

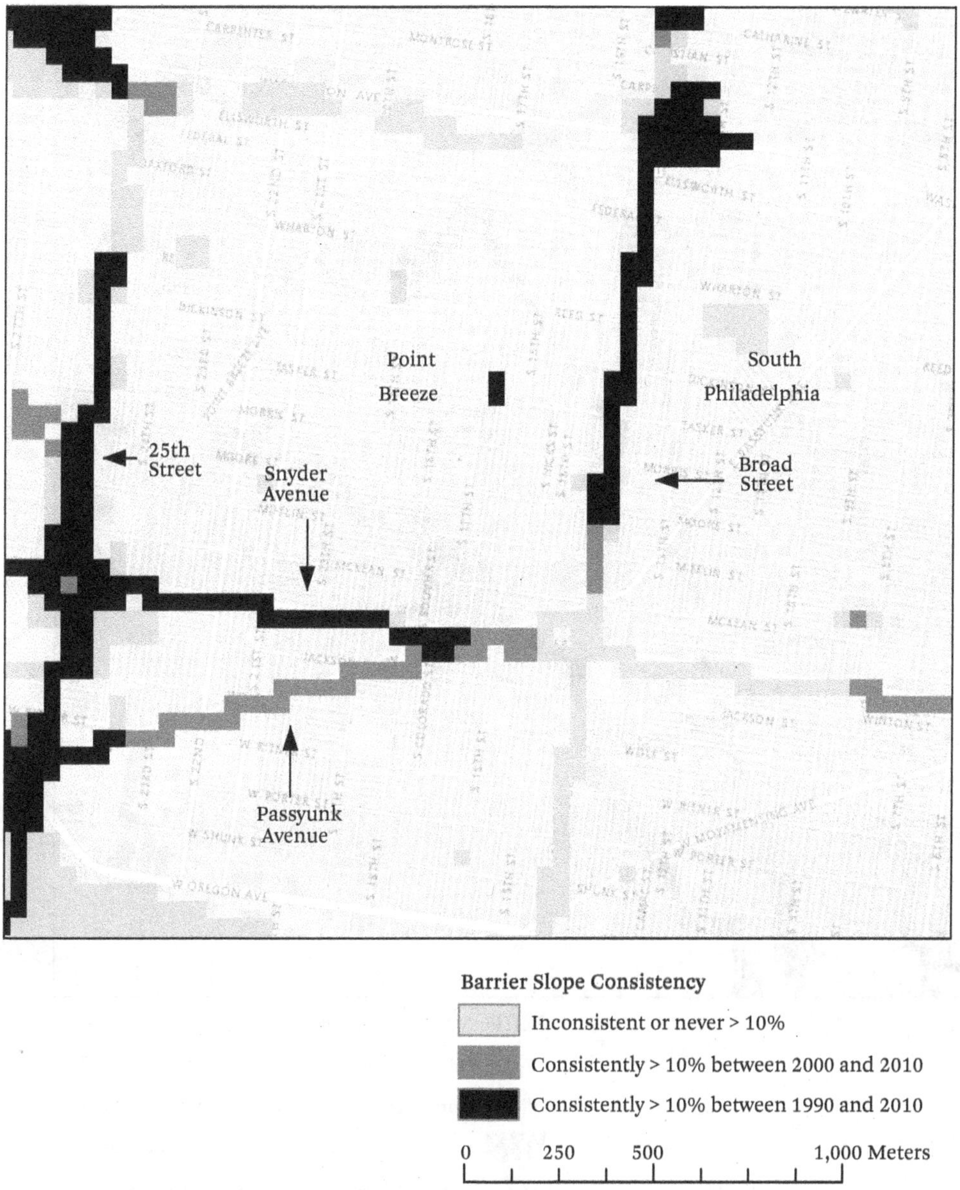

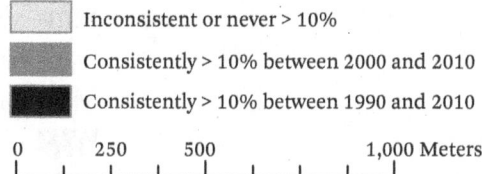

Source: Author's calculations based on U.S. Census Bureau 2011.
Note: Neighborhoods defined by one-thousand meter radius.

and 1990. That in-migration, too, was met with substantial racial and ethnic violence as the growing Latino population moved further east (Lin 1993). To the south, Girard Avenue divides Northern Liberties, a major hub of redevelopment and gentrification, from the blighted areas of South Kensington.

Figure 7 shows that the steep slopes for white-nonwhite racial change are not related to black-white divides. Most of the consistency found in figure 6 disappears. There is still a divide on Front Street, and the division between North Liberties and South Kensington is consistent. In addition, a new slope is identified in the north between the largely black and Hispanic Harrowgate neighborhood and

Figure 6. Racial Slopes, Fishtown, Port Richmond, and Kensington Neighborhoods, White-Nonwhite

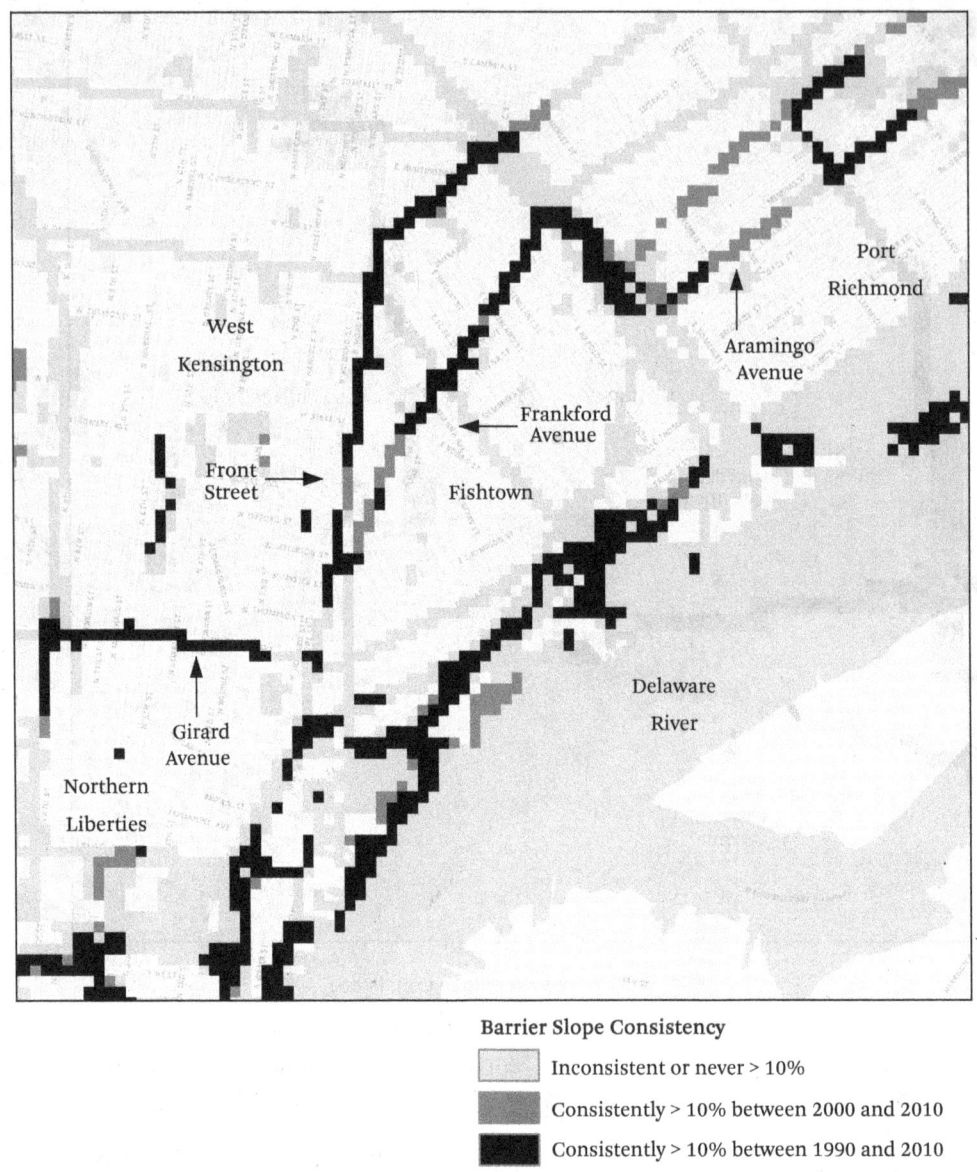

Source: Author's calculations based on U.S. Census Bureau 2011.
Note: Neighborhoods defined by one-thousand meter radius.

the rest of Northeast Philadelphia, a predominantly white area. This consistency was not identified in the white-nonwhite map because a growing Hispanic and Asian population has been moving into the areas north of Harrowgate—and the black population of Harrowgate has expanded northward.

Figure 8, which presents black-nonblack racial slopes, clarifies the role of neighborhood boundaries for the black population in North Philadelphia. Because the Kensington section of Philadelphia is a large hub of Hispanic immigration, the slopes protecting white neighborhoods like Port Richmond and Fishtown

Figure 7. Racial Slopes, Fishtown, Port Richmond, and Kensington Neighborhoods, Black-White

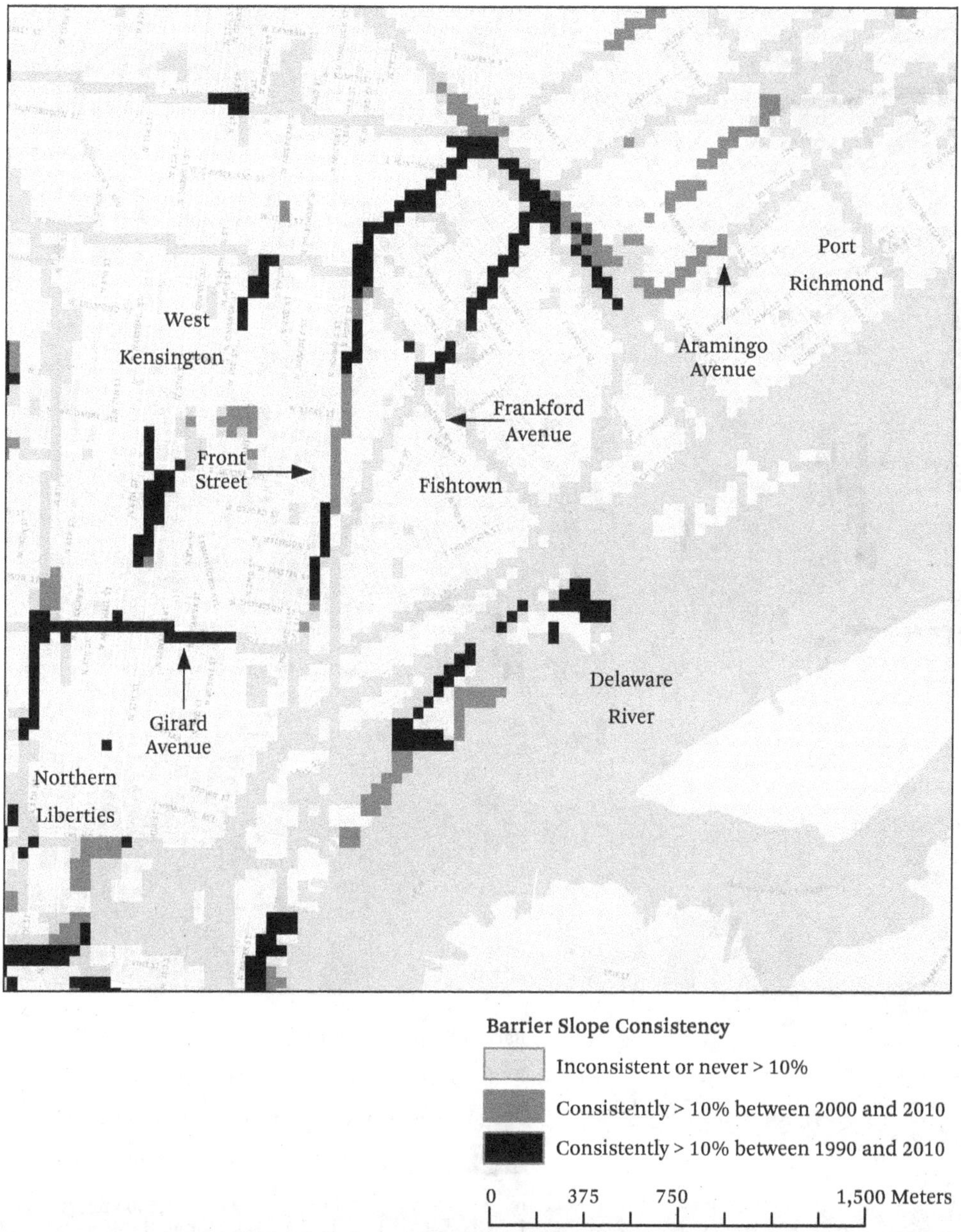

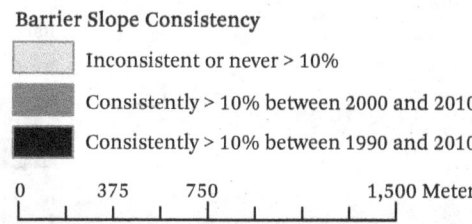

Source: Author's calculations based on U.S. Census Bureau 2011.
Note: Neighborhoods defined by one-thousand meter radius.

are divides not between black and white but instead between white and Hispanic. In figure 8, then, none of the barriers discussed earlier are consistent. Instead, the bulk of the slope consistency between black and nonblack areas are to the west, particularly defined by commuter railroad tracks that isolate black neighborhoods from areas experiencing Hispanic immigration and infusion of capital, and from the neighborhoods around Temple University, which are undergoing substantial improvement due to efforts by the university. The black population in that section of North Philadelphia is missing the redevelopment of

Figure 8. Racial Slopes, Fishtown, Port Richmond, and Kensington Neighborhoods, Black-Nonblack

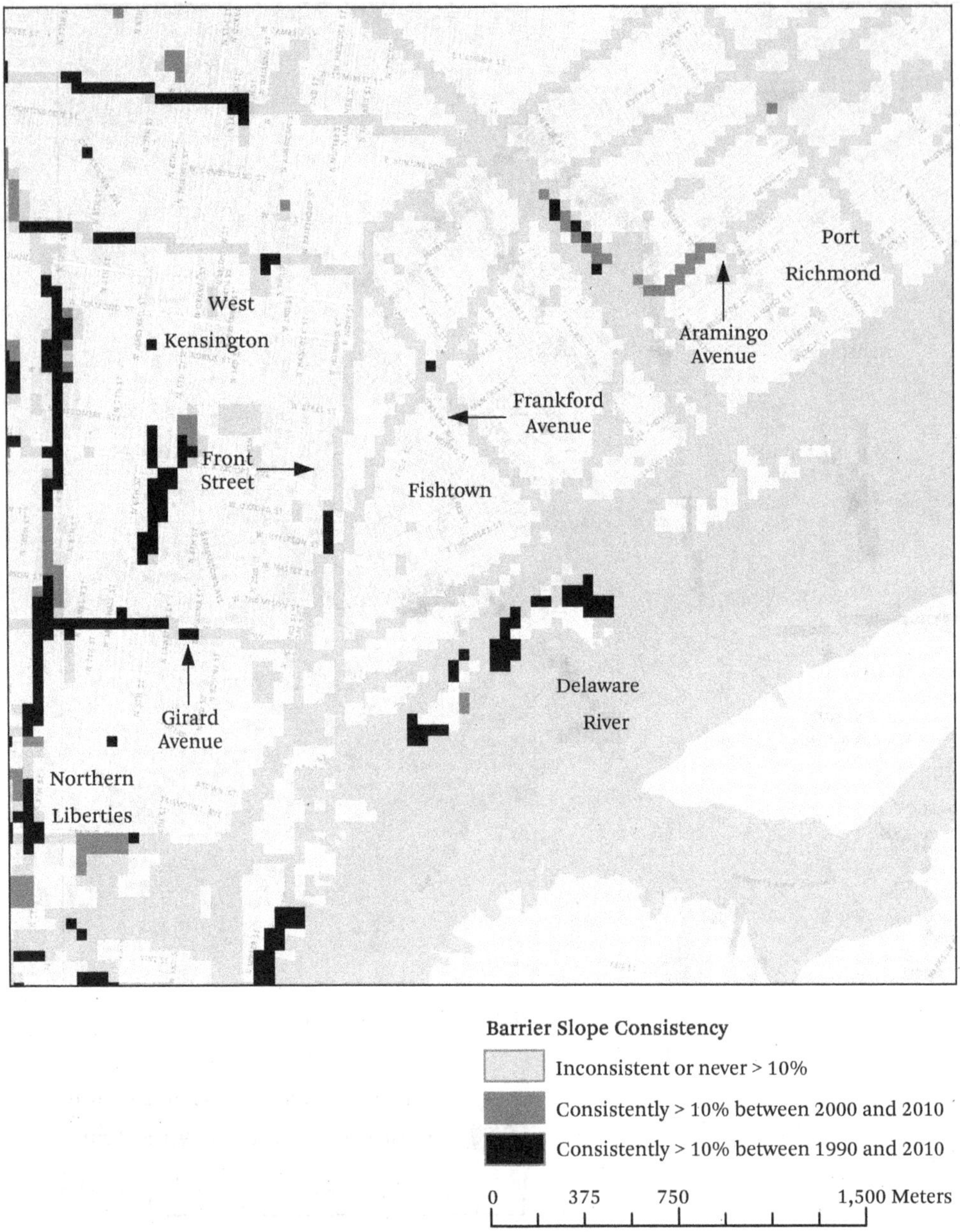

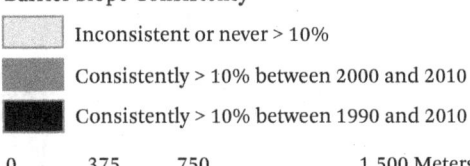

Source: Author's calculations based on U.S. Census Bureau 2011.
Note: Neighborhoods defined by one-thousand meter radius.

North Philadelphia in two directions. To the west, railroad tracks divide it from the reinvestment spurred by Temple, and though the gentrification of Fishtown may spread west into Kensington, that area is now primarily Hispanic.

DISCUSSION

Albert Hunter's (1982) work on symbolic communities points to a potential explanation for why certain barriers are consistent racial boundaries. Hunter argues that physical barriers made it easier for residents of Chicago to identify the boundaries of their smaller community. Those areas without clear physical boundaries may also lack the social cohesion and identity to create behavioral differences or symbolic meanings to specific roads, which may lead to the types of contested boundaries that are associated with conflict (Legewie and Schaeffer 2016). In Philadelphia, neighborhoods' ethnic identities, their physical barriers, and cultural identities in the 1960s and 1970s may help explain why those areas avoided the racial turnover other similar neighborhoods experienced, at least partially given the history of racial violence in those neighborhoods that linger today (Wolfinger 2007; Countryman 2005; Lin 1993).

Good fences may make good neighbors, but, as the case study of Philadelphia racial segregation shows, good neighborhood fences are created by perceptions of "bad" neighbors and have long-lasting shadows that extend beyond racial segregation, and have shaped the location of gentrification, commercial investment, and population growth in the city. Racial residential segregation boundaries orient and abet other inequalities by reifying differences between otherwise similar urban spaces. Recently, Point Breeze has become a focal point of intracommunity debate (as well as vandalism and accusations of racism) as the extensive gentrification that began in the early 2000s to its north and east has only now begun to make much delayed inroads into the neighborhood (Zuylen-Wood 2013). West Mount Airy is now struggling to ensure that affordable housing can stem a slide toward racial segregation caused by economic inequality. Fishtown is in the midst of a commercial and residential boom but continues to be a white enclave with few signs of diversification; neighboring Kensington remains largely untouched by the wave of investment and revitalization occurring to its south and west that is anchored in Fishtown. Where the general story in Philadelphia is one of racial turnover in neighborhoods that occurs without being shaped by sharp and persistent boundaries, much like Robert Sampson (2012) shows in Chicago, the legacy of ghettoization adjacent to "defended neighborhoods" (Suttles 1972) of the mid-twentieth century lasts into the twenty-first century.

More broadly, racial residential segregation can be thought of as built on two related but separate geographic processes: clustering within a neighborhood and defining that area's boundaries. Similarly, Galster's original theory of neighborhood as externality space considers externality spaces "from the perspective of a particular individual" (1986, 247), but also asserts that the boundaries of that space are critical to identifying and measuring externality spaces. This article presents a novel way of studying and measuring externality spaces that can identify locations for potential targeted policy interventions. From an exploratory analysis of Philadelphia's racial boundaries as an example of an externality space, I argue that white collective action during black in-migration may explain the location of persistent barriers. Future research should test this hypothesis in other cities and expand to other externalities such as income inequality.

Although this article presents an innovative quantitative methodology to analyze the spatial pattern of racial boundaries, it has limitations. First, the census definitions of major roads may be inaccurate and can miss roads with important local meanings. For example, Washington Avenue is a four-lane road that local residents consider to be a dividing line between neighborhoods. However, it is defined as a tertiary street by the census. Had Washington Avenue been identified as a major road like other roads of its size, the black neighborhood of Point Breeze would likely have been surrounded by steep racial boundaries in all four directions. This article also treats all possible boundary raster cells as equally difficult to cross even though the analysis shows that not all barriers are equally important racial boundaries. Future research should study which types of boundaries are more difficult to cross and test whether incorporating different friction values leads to substantively different results. Finally, many barriers are located near each other; for example, major roads lie on both sides of the Schuylkill River and thus may lower the average impact of barriers on racial slopes incorrectly. In that case, the roads would be the racial boundaries, even though it is the existence of the river that both divides the neighborhoods on each side and led to the construction of roads at that location.

Grannis (2009) shows that small interventions such as changed traffic patterns and improved signage can also change the social dynamics in and around major roads. That small shifts in the role of physical barriers can have dramatic impact on the local spatial opportunity structure is a valuable rejoinder to a sociology that has long treated the neighborhood—and, by extensions, neighborhood boundaries—as relatively static. Neighborhood shapes and racial boundaries change over time and that change should be considered more frequently and in a more dynamic way than traditional sociological methods provide (Bader 2010). Those few locations that have consistent barriers could be recast as locations rife with opportunity for shared use across racial and economic boundaries. Future research should use this method for comparison of urban areas to determine whether Philadelphia's demographics and urban layout contribute to the number and locations of persistent racial boundaries. It may be that these boundaries are greater in cities with a different history of white responses to nonwhite in-migration, more sprawl, or a newer, more car-oriented transportation system with greater reliance on large highways or roads such as Los Angeles or Houston.

Socially, having identifiable markers of neighborhood boundaries can help a "symbolic community" cohere and be maintained (Hunter 1982). Michele Lamont (1992, 2000) shows how people from different social classes find moral and symbolic value in their class status; individuals justify their social class by making negative moral judgments about those with objectively "better" or "worse" social class status. Similarly, being able to identify a neighborhood as predominantly black or Latino makes individuals judge its desirability more harshly (Krysan and Farley 2002; Krysan, Farley, and Couper 2008). That effect may be enhanced for neighborhoods with physical barriers. Easily identifiable boundaries mean that the neighborhood is easily defined as well, a useful step before imbuing a space with social and moral valuations. Barriers make it possible to easily and quickly identify "good" or "bad" areas, areas where some are "insiders" or "outsiders"[3] and thus become a "defended community" (Suttles 1972). Further, a physical barrier can also impede interaction and allow for mythmaking about people from "the other side of the tracks."

Spatial analysis in the social sciences has primarily focused on the experiences within a single spatial unit. Spatial inequality operates not only by clustering individuals together into one spatial opportunity structure, it is also driven by how groups divide a social space into separate components of that structure (Galster and Sharkey, this volume). This article offers a way to systematically identify how two or more spatial attributes of that structure interact by identifying externality boundaries and the consistency of those boundaries over time without relying on traditional a priori definitions of neighborhoods that introduce unknown error into the analysis. The physical geography of a given space and the collective efforts of residents to define neighborhoods as racially inclusive or exclusive cumulatively created contours of the spatial opportunity structure of Philadelphia's neighborhoods that last for generations.

Such contours of the spatial opportunity structure likely are a reality in all metro areas. Robert Moses's infamous decision to build the Cross-Bronx Expressway directly through the Bronx left a legacy of decay in the South Bronx is but the most famous example of the impact of physical boundaries on urban development patterns. That example is of a newly constructed highway and the use of eminent domain (for another, of how even proposing similar projects can affect investment patterns, see Hunter 2013). This article shows that long-lasting racial boundaries can and do emerge more organically as well. As the Philadelphia case demonstrates, local response to efforts to integrate continue to shape where racial segregation boundaries exist for generations without government involvement.

---

3. A parallel logic exists in how cities are divided into different *gang turfs* defined by their barriers and many gangs are named after major roads or barriers that they claim as part of their turf.

Although this article focuses on racial residential segregation, the methodology introduced here can be used to study other spatial structure or process that involves an interaction between two variables. For example, access to major roads or mass transit may benefit residents who use that transportation to expand their daily activity space to access more distant job markets or educational opportunities. Barriers-based analyses can also explore how land use is associated with differences in crime spillover across neighborhood boundaries, or which local housing submarket values shift in tandem or separately. More broadly, this article is an example of why scholars of spatial inequality and policymakers can and should focus not only on how and where the urban spatial opportunity structure operates by clustering individuals together, but also on how and where divisions within that structure emerge and persist.

REFERENCES

Ananat, Elizabeth Oltmans. 2011. "The Wrong Side(s) of the Tracks: The Causal Effects of Racial Segregation on Urban Poverty and Inequality." *American Economic Journal: Applied Economics* 3(2): 34–66.

Anderson, Elijah 2011. *The Cosmopolitan Canopy: Race and Civility in Everyday Life*. New York: W. W. Norton.

Bader, Michael. 2010. "Evolution of Racial and Ethnic Segregation: Pace and Place of Neighborhood Change." Unpublished paper. American University, Washington, D.C.

Bailey, Trevor, and Tony Gattrell. 1995. *Interactive Spatial Data Analysis*. Harlow, Essex, UK: Prentice Hall.

Brubaker, Rogers. 2002. "Ethnicity Without Groups." *European Journal of Sociology* 43(2): 163–85.

Charles, Camille Zubrinsky. 2003. "The Dynamics of Racial Residential Segregation." *Annual Review of Sociology* 29(1): 167–207.

———. 2006. *Won't You Be My Neighbor? Race, Class, and Residence in Los Angeles*. New York: Russell Sage Foundation.

Countryman, Matthew. 2005. *Up South: Civil Rights and Black Power in Philadelphia*. Philadelphia: University of Pennsylvania Press.

Crowder, Kyle, and Scott J. South. 2011. "Spatial and Temporal Dimensions of Neighborhood Effects on High School Graduation." *Social Science Research* 40(1): 87–106.

Davis, Mike. 1992. *City of Quartz*. New York: Vintage Books.

Deener, Andrew. 2012. *Venice: A Contested Bohemia in Los Angeles*. Chicago: University of Chicago Press.

Downey, Liam. 2006. "Using Geographic Information Systems to Reconceptualize Spatial Relationships and Ecological Context." *American Journal of Sociology* 112(2): 567–612.

Du Bois, W. E. B. 1996. *The Philadelphia Negro: A Social Study*. Reprint. Philadelphia: University of Pennsylvania Press. First published 1899.

Durlauf, Steven. 2004. "Neighborhood Effects." In *Handbook of Regional and Urban Economics*, vol. 4, edited by J. Vernon Henderson and Jacques-François Thisse. Amsterdam: Elsevier.

Ferman, Barbara, Theresa Singleton, and Don DeMarco. 1998. "West Mount Airy, Philadelphia." *CityScape: A Journal of Policy Development and Research* 4(2): 29–59.

Galster, George. 1986. "What Is Neighborhood? An Externality Space Approach." *International Journal of Urban and Regional Research* 10(2): 243–61.

———. 2001. "On the Nature of Neighborhood." *Urban Studies* 38(12): 2111–24.

———. 2008. "Quantifying the Effect of Neighbourhood on Individuals: Challenges, Alternative Approaches, and Promising Directions." *Schmollers Jahrbuch* 128(1): 7–48.

Galster, George, and Patrick Sharkey. 2017. "Spatial Foundations of Inequality: A Conceptual Model and Empirical Overview." *RSF: Russell Sage Foundation Journal of the Social Sciences* 3(2): 1–33. doi: 10.7758/RSF.3.2.01.

Grannis, Rick. 2005. "T-Communities: Pedestrian Street Networks and Residential Segregation in Chicago, Los Angeles, and New York." *City and Community* 4(3) 295–321.

———. 2009. *From the Ground Up: Translating Geography into Community Through Neighbor Networks*. Princeton, N.J.: Princeton University Press.

Grengs, Joe. 2007. "Reevaluating Poverty Concentration with Spatial Analysis: Detroit in the 1990s." *Urban Geography* 28(4): 340–60.

Harvey, David. 2000. *Spaces of Hope*. Berkeley: University of California Press.

Hunter, Albert. 1982. *Symbolic Communities*, 2nd ed. Chicago: University of Chicago Press.

Hunter, Marcus Anthony. 2013. *Black Citymakers: How the Philadelphia Negro Changed Urban America*. New York: Oxford University Press.

Hwang, Jackelyn. 2015. "The Social Construction of a Gentrifying Neighborhood: Reifying and Redefining Identity and Boundaries in Inequality." *Urban Affairs Review* March: 1–31. doi: 10.1177/1078087415570643.

Hyra, Derek, Gregory Squires, Robert Renner, and David Kirk. 2013. "Metropolitan Segregation and the Subprime Lending Crisis." *Housing Policy Debate* 23(1): 177–98.

Jacobs, Jane. 1961. *The Death and Life of Great American Cities*. New York: Random House.

Kramer, Rory. 2012. "What Is on the Other Side of the Tracks? A Spatial Examination of Neighborhood Boundaries and Segregation." PhD diss., University of Pennsylvania.

Krysan, Maria, and Reynolds Farley. 2002. "The Residential Preferences of Blacks: Do They Explain Persistent Segregation?" *Social Forces* 80(3): 937–80.

Krysan, Maria, Reynolds Farley, and Mick P. Couper. 2008. "In the Eye of the Beholder: Racial Beliefs and Residential Segregation." *Du Bois Review* 5(1): 5–26.

Lamont, Michelle. 1992. *Money, Morals, and Manners: The Culture of the French and American Upper-Middle Class*. Chicago: University of Chicago Press.

——— 2000.*The Dignity of Working Men: Morality and the Boundaries of Race, Class, and Immigration*. New York: Russell Sage Foundation.

Lee, Barrett, Sean Reardon, Glenn Firebaugh, Chad Farrell, Stephen Matthews, and David O'Sullivan. 2008. "Beyond the Census Tract: Patterns and Determinants of Racial Segregation at Multiple Geographic Scales." *American Sociological Review* 73(5): 766–91.

Legewie, Joscha, and Merlin Schaeffer. 2016. "Contested Boundaries: Explaining Where Ethno-Racial Diversity Provokes Neighborhood Conflict." *American Journal of Sociology* 122(5): 125–61.

Leventhal, Tama, and Jeanne Brooks-Gunn. 2000. "The Neighborhoods They Live in: The Effect of Neighborhood Residence on Child and Adolescent Outcomes." *Psychological Bulletin* 126(2): 309–37.

Lin, Jennifer. 1993. "In Kensington, Two Groups Live So Close, Yet So Far Away." *Philadelphia Inquirer*, August 8, 1993. Accessed January 14, 2015. http://articles.philly.com/1993-08-08/news/25967781_1_spray-painted-windows-police-and-clergy.

Logan, John, and Charles Zhang. 2010. "Global Neighborhoods: New Pathways to Diversity and Separation." *American Journal of Sociology* 115(4): 1069–109.

———. 2011. "Global Neighborhoods: New Evidence from Census 2010." US2010 Project. New York: Russell Sage Foundation.

Martin, Deborah G. 2003. "Enacting Neighborhood." *Urban Geography* 24(5): 361–85.

Massey, Douglas, and Nancy Denton. 1993. *American Apartheid*. Cambridge, Mass.: Harvard University Press.

Morenoff, Jeffrey. 2003. "Neighborhood Mechanisms and the Spatial Dynamics of Birth Weight." *American Journal of Sociology* 108(5): 976–1017.

Morris, Aldon. 2015. *The Scholar Denied: W. E. B. Du Bois and the Birth of Modern Sociology*. Cambridge, Mass.: Harvard University Press.

Openshaw, Stan, and Peter Taylor. 1979. "A Million or so Correlation Coefficients: Three Experiments on the Modifiable Areal Unit Problem." In *Statistical Applications for the Spatial Sciences*, edited by Neil Wrigley. London: Pion.

Owens, Ann. 2017. "Racial Residential Segregation of School-Age Children and Adults and the Role of Schooling as a Segregating Force." *RSF: Russell Sage Foundation Journal of the Social Sciences* 3(2): 63–80. doi: 10.7758/RSF.3.2.03.

Perkiss, Abigail. 2014. *Making Good Neighbors: Civil Rights, Liberalism, and Integration in Postwar Philadelphia*. Ithaca, N.Y.: Cornell University Press.

Peterson, Ruth, and Laurie Krivo. 2010. *Divergent Social Worlds: Neighborhood Crime and Racial-Spatial Divide*. New York: Russell Sage Foundation.

Reardon, Sean, and Kendra Bischoff. 2011. "Growth in the Residential Segregation of Families by Income, 1970–2009." US2010 Project. New York: Russell Sage Foundation.

Roberto, Elizabeth. 2015. "Spatial Boundaries and the Local Context of Residential Segregation." *Cornell University Library*. Accessed July 25, 2016. http://arxiv.org/abs/1509.02574.

Rothwell, Jonathan, and Douglas Massey. 2009.

"The Effect of Density Zoning on Racial Segregation in U.S. Urban Areas." *Urban Affairs Review* 44(6): 779–806.

Rugh, Jacob, and Douglas Massey. 2010. "Racial Segregation and the American Foreclosure Crisis." *American Sociological Review* 75(5): 629–51.

Sampson, Robert. 2012. *Great American City*. Chicago: University of Chicago Press.

Sampson, Robert, Patrick Sharkey, and Stephen Raudenbush. 2008. "Durable Effects of Concentrated Disadvantage on Verbal Ability Among African-American Children." *Proceedings of the National Academy of Sciences* 105(3): 845–52.

Sharkey, Patrick. 2014. *Stuck in Place: Urban Neighborhoods and the End of Progress Toward Racial Inequality*. Chicago: University of Chicago Press.

Smith, Sandy. 2014. "Philly Neighborhood Focuses on Schools as Key to Diversity." *Next City*. Accessed June 9, 2015. http://nextcity.org/daily/entry/philadelphia-diversity-mt-airy-schools.

Suttles, Gerald. 1972. *The Social Construction of Communities*. Chicago: University of Chicago Press.

U.S. Census Bureau. 2011. "2010 Census Summary File 1." Washington: Government Printing Office.

Wimmer, Andreas. 2009. "Herder's Heritage and the Boundary-Making Approach: Studying Ethnicity in Immigrant Societies" *Sociological Theory* 27(3): 244–70.

Wodtke, Geoffrey, David Harding, and Felix Elwert. 2011. "Neighborhood Effects in Temporal Perspective: the Impact of Long-Term Exposure to Concentrated Disadvantage on High School Graduation." *American Sociological Review* 76(5): 713–36.

Wolfinger, James. 2007. *Philadelphia Divided: Race and Politics in the City of Brotherly Love*. Chapel Hill: University of North Carolina Press.

Zuylen-Wood, Simon van. 2013. "Philadelphia Is Ori Feibush's World, We Just Live in It." *Philadelphia Magazine*. Accessed June 12, 2015. http://www.phillymag.com/articles/philadelphia-ori-feibushs-world-live/.

Urban Income Inequality and the Great Recession in Sunbelt Form: Disentangling Individual and Neighborhood-Level Change in Los Angeles

ROBERT J. SAMPSON, JARED N. SCHACHNER, AND ROBERT D. MARE

New social transformations within and beyond the cities of classic urban studies challenge prevailing accounts of spatial inequality. This paper pivots from the Rust Belt to the Sunbelt accordingly, disentangling persistence and change in neighborhood median income and concentrated income extremes in Los Angeles County. We first examine patterns of change over two decades starting in 1990 for all Los Angeles neighborhoods. We then analyze an original longitudinal study of approximately six hundred Angelenos from 2000 to 2013, assessing the degree to which contextual changes in neighborhood income arise from neighborhood-level mobility or individual residential mobility. Overall we find deep and persistent inequality among both neighborhoods and individuals. Contrary to prior research, we also find that residential mobility does not materially alter neighborhood economic conditions for most race, ethnic, and income groups. Our analyses lay the groundwork for a multilevel theoretical framework capable of explaining spatial inequality across cities and historical eras.

Keywords: income inequality, neighborhoods, residential mobility, Los Angeles

In the public imagination, the idea of the inner city appears suspended in a stylized time and place. Images of urban poverty, racially segregated housing projects, drug dealers, violence, and crumbling housing in places like Newark, Baltimore, the South Bronx, Detroit, and Chicago from the late 1960s to the early 2000s still resonate in the media, brought home dramatically in the television series *The Wire* and, more recently, in high-profile coverage of riots in Baltimore (Shane 2015). Scholars have likewise focused intently on the "urban crisis"; foundational research on urban poverty and inequality in the latter half of the twentieth century is dominated by social upheavals in the cities of the North and Midwest (for example, Sugrue 1996; Wilson 1987; Liebow 1967; Suttles 1968; Stack 1974).[1]

Robert J. Sampson is Henry Ford II Professor of the Social Sciences at Harvard University. **Jared N. Schachner** is a PhD candidate in sociology and social policy at Harvard University. **Robert D. Mare** is Distinguished Professor of Sociology at the University of California, Los Angeles.

© 2017 Russell Sage Foundation. Sampson, Robert J., Jared N. Schachner, and Robert D. Mare. 2017. "Urban Income Inequality and the Great Recession in Sunbelt Form: Disentangling Individual and Neighborhood-Level Change in Los Angeles." *RSF: The Russell Sage Foundation Journal of the Social Sciences* 3(2): 102–28. DOI: 10.7758/RSF.3.2.05. Originally presented at the Russell Sage Foundation Conference "The Spatial Foundations of Inequality" on February 12, 2015. We thank the RSF conference participants, special volume editors, and anonymous reviewers for helpful comments on a prior draft. This article was supported in part by a grant from the Hymen Milgrom Supporting Organization. Direct correspondence to Robert J. Sampson at rsampson@wjh.harvard.edu, Department of Sociology, Harvard University, William James Hall, 33 Kirkland St., Cambridge, MA 02138; Jared N. Schachner at jschachner@fas.harvard.edu, Department of Sociology, Harvard University, William James Hall, 33 Kirkland St., Cambridge, MA 02138; and Robert D. Mare at mare@ucla.edu, Department of Sociology, UCLA, Haines Hall, 375 Portola Plaza, Los Angeles, CA 90095.

1. Interestingly, the same can be said of classic studies of the ghetto in the prewar era (for example, Drake and Cayton 1945; Du Bois 1899; Zorbaugh 1929).

The location and theoretical assumptions of the urban poverty paradigm of the late twentieth century can nonetheless be challenged on at least three major fronts. One challenge comes in the form of new social transformations and crises that the cities of classic studies have undergone. Deindustrialization, the Great Migration, violence, the growth of concentrated poverty among African Americans and population loss defined an earlier era, but many American cities in the early twenty-first century have witnessed increases in population, concentrated affluence, gentrification, and the black middle class; declines in violence; rapid immigration from around the world; the Great Recession; and rising income inequality. Referencing one of the biggest changes in American cities, the historian Michael Katz has gone as far as to argue that the explosion of immigration has "irrevocably smashed the black/white frame" (2012, 100).

A second challenge follows from the first. If the Great Migration from the South to the North was the demographic force of its day, international migration and internal U.S. migration away from the North and Midwest have spawned rapid growth and diverse settlements in the Sunbelt that look and feel very different from the places made famous by the Chicago School of urban sociology. Even the epithet of Chicago as America's second city holds no more; Los Angeles (L.A.) is now the second most populous city in the country and one of the most diverse in the world. Recognizing this demographic and structural shift, inequality scholarship has itself increasingly migrated south and west, exemplified by the Multi-City Studies of Urban Inequality that included Los Angeles and Atlanta (Bobo et al. 2002; O'Connor, Tilly, and Bobo 2001) and a growing body of research on Los Angeles (for example, Halle 2003; Halle and Beveridge 2013; Hipp et al. 2012; Charles 2009). These and other studies have examined the concentration of poverty and processes of racial segregation in nontraditional urban forms.[2] Although much progress has been made, research on spatial inequality in the Sunbelt, in general—and Los Angeles, in particular—trails its predecessors in scope.

The third and perhaps largest challenge is analytic—isolating the mechanisms of urban change and understanding whether and how new social transformations have reshaped the fundamental spatial structure of earlier urban inequality. Whether the focus is on the ends of the income distribution or the loss of middle-class and mixed-income neighborhoods, changes in the spatial and socioeconomic distribution of populations in urban areas reflect a complex mixture of changes in income distributions of individuals and households, patterns of socioeconomic mobility, the residential choices of individuals, and the rise and fall of neighborhoods. The problem deepens when we consider that these components of change reflect both long-term trends, such as the drift to higher levels of income inequality in the United States and large-scale immigration over the past few decades, and shorter-term shocks, such as the financial crises and the subsequent Great Recession during the past decade. Although these sources and components of change are well recognized as general principles, how they fit together analytically and their relative importance have been understudied. In a seeming paradox, moreover, the fact of social change does not necessarily imply the overthrow of old urban hierarchies. Robert J. Sampson (2012) and Sampson, Robert D. Mare, and Kristin L. Perkins (2015) show that, at least in Chicago, changes in neighborhood inequality across recent decades were strongly shaped by historical neighborhood inequalities. As a

---

2. A detailed review is beyond the scope of this paper, but a related challenge rests on the idea that cities such as Los Angeles are so different in urban form that they demand a new paradigm. In the late twentieth century, this notion gave rise to the L.A. School—a group led mainly by geographers and cultural theorists who emphasized how forces such as postmodern culture, technology, and urban sprawl had "decentered" the city and elided neighborhood boundaries. Even though these claims have been contested (Abbott 2002) and proponents admit to the lack of a unified theoretical perspective or clear hypotheses (Dear 2001, 2002), the importance of urban scholars turning their attention to cities of the future, of which Los Angeles is a microcosm, if not the claimed paradigmatic metropolis, is hard to deny.

general theoretical matter, questions of persistence and change in income segregation, especially whether changes in income segregation map onto the "old inequality" in the nation's centers of growth and immigrant diversity, are central to our understanding of the spatial foundations of inequality.

This paper addresses these challenges by presenting a multilevel framework on the spatial and temporal dynamics of neighborhood income inequality in Los Angeles County from 2000 to 2013. A test bed for the future of American urban areas, Los Angeles County is the nation's most populous and arguably most ethnically diverse; immigrants from around the world account for a third of its over ten million residents. The region also reflects the car-dominated suburban sprawl typical of Sunbelt cities. Our analysis is based on an original longitudinal study with three waves of data that provide theoretically motivated measures at the individual and neighborhood levels, before and after the Great Recession. Specifically, we combine two waves of data from the Los Angeles Family and Neighborhood Survey (L.A.FANS) with a new follow-up study, providing longitudinal data on the residential mobility of families and individuals in Los Angeles County from 2000 to 2013. By integrating these data with the decennial census and American Community Survey for 1990, 2000, and 2008 to 2012, we reveal the distributions of neighborhood income extremes (poverty and affluence) and of mixed middle-income neighborhoods and develop an analytical model that disentangles stability and change in neighborhood income status. We also assess whether changes in exposure to different income levels are induced by individual mobility (residential and socioeconomic) or neighborhood-level change, and how trajectories of change in neighborhood income status vary by race, ethnic, and income groups, as well as before and after the Great Recession. This simultaneous exploration of neighborhood-level and individual-level spatial inequality patterns in L.A. during the early twenty-first century provides a novel analytic framework that reshapes prevailing understandings of urban social processes generated primarily from studies conducted within northeastern and midwestern cities. Moreover, our analysis raises additional questions—and proposes a corresponding set of hypotheses—that lay the groundwork for a multilevel framework capable of illuminating the particular mechanisms responsible for the persistence of, and variation in, spatial inequality's structure across cities and historical eras.

SPATIAL DYNAMICS IN THE AGE OF INCOME EXTREMES

The rising concentration of income at the very top of the distribution has generated considerable attention among scholars and the public at large. It is well known, for example, that the top 1 percent of earners account for an increasing share of all income (Piketty 2014). Although not with the same visibility, neighborhood-level inequality has come under scrutiny as well. Whereas William Julius Wilson emphasized the growth of concentrated poverty (1987), the simultaneous concentration of affluence gives meaning to what Douglas Massey calls the "age of extremes" in income segregation (1996). It is not that Wilson's focus is no longer relevant; rather, middle-income neighborhoods appear to be declining (Booza, Cutsinger, and Galster 2006), and both concentrated poverty and concentrated affluence in neighborhoods are on the rise (Reardon and Bischoff 2011).

Yet systematic empirical research on the dynamics of mixed-income neighborhoods is relatively rare and the studies that do exist are typically based on northeastern or midwestern cities (Joseph and Chaskin 2012; Chaskin and Joseph 2015). Moreover, the bulk of research and commentary on income mixing and concentrated poverty has focused on the effects of neighborhoods on individual outcomes, leaving aside mechanisms of persistence and change in income segregation and income mixing. A key theoretical question at the individual level is whether change is induced by sorting across neighborhoods (movers) or change within neighborhoods around those individuals who do not move (stayers). This distinction is crucial to understanding mechanisms of change (Sampson and Sharkey 2008). As also noted by Xavier de Souza Briggs and his colleagues (2009) and by Sampson, Mare, and Perkins (2015), residential mobility can sustain or undermine mixed-income neighborhoods and determine exposure to concentrated poverty or affluence.

We overcome these limitations by integrating individual and aggregate change, proposing a series of theoretically motivated questions on neighborhood-level and individual-level mobility, defined both by neighborhood income levels and the degree to which neighborhoods contain mixed-income populations. Our first set of analyses begins at the neighborhood level. We examine the patterns of stability and change in Los Angeles County neighborhoods, focusing specifically on the distributions of neighborhood income levels and income mixing. The thesis of enduring neighborhood effects predicts that neighborhoods are quite durable in their economic status, especially at the top and bottom, and as a result will largely retain their relative positions (Sampson 2012). Existing research is less clear on predictions about the stability of income mixing in middle-class neighborhoods, although recent research from Chicago (Sampson, Mare, and Perkins 2015) finds that mixed-income neighborhoods are rather fluid over time. In a city such as Los Angeles, which has less racial segregation and arguably weaker neighborhood boundaries than Chicago or other older industrial cities, it is reasonable to predict that mixed-income neighborhoods are even more changeable. We assess this prediction by evaluating the degree to which mixed middle-income neighborhoods are stable over time (see Galster, Booza, and Cutsinger 2008). Put differently, are mixed-income neighborhoods in Los Angeles transitory states that neighborhoods pass through as they move from concentrated affluence to concentrated poverty, or the reverse? In addressing this set of questions, we examine whether patterns of neighborhood mobility were similar throughout the 1990 to 2013 period or whether they differ between the relatively prosperous 1990s and the Great Recession era, and how patterns of neighborhood mobility for Los Angeles differ from the patterns for all American cities and traditional cities like Chicago (Williams, Galster, and Verma 2013).

The second and major focus of our paper is on persistence and change across neighborhood types for individuals in Los Angeles County from the late 1990s to 2013. Here we exploit fine-grained data from a new follow-up to L.A.FANS that permit us to answer the following questions motivated by prior theory and research: Do individuals tend to remain within their neighborhood income stratum, with regard to both level of income and degree of income mixing, or is there substantial upward and downward mobility? Do these patterns of change among individuals vary between the relatively prosperous late 1990s and early 2000s and the deep recession of the late 2000s? To what degree are patterns of change brought about by the residential mobility of individuals or the mobility of neighborhoods? For example, to what extent are changes induced by individuals staying put while their neighborhoods change around them rather than by individuals moving neighborhoods? Another kind of individual mobility is socioeconomic: to what degree are patterns of individuals' residential mobility across neighborhood types due to changes in their socioeconomic or family conditions? Posing these questions with our data allows us to assess the relative merits of competing hypotheses—upward mobility in income or education counteracts income inequality's spatial structure, or reinforces and exacerbates inequality's already strong hold.

In conducting our analysis, we are guided by theory and evidence on the link between the spatial foundations of income inequality and racial stratification. A long-standing finding in the United States is that black disadvantage relative to whites is sustained in large part by the connection of concentrated poverty and segregation (Massey and Eggers 1990; Sharkey 2013). At least in Chicago, the black-white frame of whites at the top and blacks at the bottom (and Latinos in between) is replicated even as people move to new neighborhoods (Sampson and Sharkey 2008). But little is known about how the individual-level neighborhood income status trajectories of Latinos, Asians, and immigrants compare to those of African Americans in a rapidly growing and diverse metropolis such as Los Angeles. A reshuffled hierarchy of race-ethnicity, or perhaps something more like a jumble among nonwhite groups, might be expected by scholars such as Michael Katz (2012) and Michael Dear (2002). By contrast, the literature on enduring neighborhood effects and racial segregation argues that residential selection patterns are part of the process of inequality reproduction, leading to the general prediction that the relative positions of race and ethnic groups by neighborhood income status will be largely persistent over time (Sampson 2012). We assess these hypotheses for whites, blacks, Latinos, and Asian Americans, adjusting for immigrant status (first, second, and third generation). We also account for other possible confounding factors highlighted in prior studies, such as changes in homeownership, family size, and marital status. Finally, we place special emphasis on patterns of change in the first part of the 2000s, when the economy was robust relative to the Great Recession, leveraging the fact that our second wave of data collection concluded just before the economy imploded in 2008 and our third wave of data collection was carried out between 2011 and 2013.

STUDY DESIGN

The larger project in which this study is embedded is the Mixed Income Project (MIP), which was designed, in part, to allow detailed examination of neighborhood context, residential mobility, and mixed-income housing in Los Angeles and Chicago. The two anchor studies for the MIP are the Project on Human Development in Chicago Neighborhoods (PHDCN) and the Los Angeles Family and Neighborhood Survey (L.A.FANS). The PHDCN and L.A.FANS are widely recognized for rich longitudinal data on neighborhoods and on educational, health, and behavioral outcomes, especially for children and adolescents in PHDCN and adults in L.A.FANS. The MIP design allows us to study the dynamics of income environments in a newer Southwest city fundamentally different in urban form and composition than the older Rust Belt urban context exemplified by Chicago.

L.A.FANS is a multilevel longitudinal study of children, families, and communities in Los Angeles County originally conducted under the direction of Anne Pebley of UCLA and Narayan Sastry at the University of Michigan with the sponsorship of the RAND Corporation (Sastry et al. 2006). Wave 1 of the survey was collected in 2000 and 2001 and consisted of a probability sample of sixty-five neighborhoods (census tracts) within L.A. County and—within neighborhoods—a sample of blocks within tracts, a sample of households within blocks, and a sample of individuals within households. Neighborhoods were stratified by poverty status: very poor (highest decile of percent poverty distribution), poor (next three deciles of the percent poverty distribution), and nonpoor.[3] Households with children (persons under eighteen) were oversampled and constitute 70 percent of the sample. From sampled households, the survey interviewed one randomly selected adult and one randomly selected child, the primary caregiver of the child (who might or might not be the same person as the randomly selected adult), and a randomly selected sibling. Within childless households, one member was selected as respondent, denoted as the randomly selected adult. Of the 4,110 households selected for the L.A.FANS sample, 3,085 households residing in sixty-five census tracts ultimately completed rosters in wave 1. Of the 3,085 randomly selected adults within these households, 2,620 (85 percent) completed an adult interview. The unweighted wave 1 adult sample was 25 percent white, 56 percent Latino, 9 percent black, and 7 percent Asian American.

Between 2006 and 2008 (wave 2), interviewers from RTI International attempted to reinterview the same respondents if they still lived in Los Angeles County. Ultimately, wave 2 interviews were conducted with 1,218 of the eligible 1,992 randomly selected adults who

---

3. From this grouping, twenty very poor, twenty poor, and twenty-five nonpoor tracts were selected. Subject to stratification, tracts were selected proportional to their population size. Within tracts, blocks were selected proportional to their population sizes. The survey consisted of 439 sampled blocks and an average of 6.6 inhabited blocks per tract. An equal number of households—fifty—were targeted in each tract.

completed a wave 1 interview (61 percent).[4] Extensive interview information was collected from these respondents to complement the detailed battery of items from wave 1, including a retrospective log of everywhere they had lived over the interim years. More than 90 percent of wave 2 interviews were completed before the economic crash of September 2008.

The MIP follow-up study (wave 3) attempted to locate and reinterview a random probability sample of approximately 1,500 participants (randomly selected adults, primary caregivers, and children) from the earlier L.A.FANS. The Los Angeles field operation first assigned selected respondents to a telephone survey center for interviews. Cases that were not interviewed by telephone were transferred to experienced field interviewers in the Los Angeles area. The final response rate was 75 percent of eligible participants, for a combined sample of 1,032. Given the approximately half-dozen years that lapsed since last contact at wave 2, the final yield results compare well with other research on contemporary urban settings.

Our main analytic focus is neighborhood change over the course of the study, which, as we argue, is brought about in part by residential mobility behavior. Because of this focus, we examine the neighborhood income trajectories of adults (with and without children), leading to an analytic file of 612 randomly selected MIP respondents who were adults (eighteen and older) during the initial L.A.FANS wave 1 interview and who were confirmed as living within L.A. County during their wave 2 and MIP interviews.[5] We then integrate tract-level U.S. census data from 2000 and American Community Survey (ACS) data from 2005 to 2009 and 2008 to 2012.[6] With this strategy, we match census data to the year of L.A.FANS and MIP data collection—Census 2000 for wave 1, ACS 2005–2009 for wave 2, and the ACS 2008–2012 for wave 3.

MEASURES

Our primary neighborhood outcome is *median family income* measured in year 1999 dollars.[7] Median family income provides a summary indicator of neighborhood quality and resource potential with a simple metric. We thus define median income quintiles for census tracts within Los Angeles County based on all U.S. census tracts within counties that are at least partly within a metropolitan statistical area (MSA),[8] excluding Puerto Rico and tracts with fewer than fifty families, at four points in time:

---

4. Among the 3,085 randomly selected adults from wave 1, 2,766 were released for wave 2; the remaining 319 cases were not released primarily because no individual interviews were completed within their households. An additional 145 of released cases were later deemed ineligible due to death, incarceration, institutionalization, physical or mental incapacity, or language barriers. Of the remaining 2,621 released cases, 2,109 still lived within Los Angeles County and 1,992 of these had completed a wave 1 interview.

5. We thus set aside dependent children under eighteen (N=300) at baseline. We also set aside new entrants from the refresher sample (N=89) and cases with missing or incorrect geocoding information or insufficient information to generate attrition weights (N=31). Future papers will focus on child mobility (through moves with and without their parents) and how refresher cases differ from baseline.

6. Given that census tracts are redrawn every decade by the Census Bureau, tracking neighborhood change over a ten-plus-year timeframe requires preserving a time-invariant set of tract boundaries. To this end, we use the 2000 census tract boundaries for our analyses, given that this is when the L.A.FANS survey began. To translate the ACS 2008–2012 neighborhood-level data, which applies 2010 tract boundaries, into estimates for the 2000 tract boundaries, we use the Backwards Longitudinal Tract Data Base's interpolation code (Logan, Xu, and Stults 2014). For analyses that relied on the 1990 census, we use the Neighborhood Change Database from GeoLytics to create estimates for 2000 boundaries (Tatian 2003).

7. We use 1999 dollars, the year the 2000 Census uses to calculate median family income.

8. We base our median family income quintiles on national MSA census tracts (excluding Puerto Rico and tracts with family populations below fifty)—rather than all census tracts (which would include rural areas)—because they constitute a more accurate basis of comparison for Los Angeles County, which is particularly urbanized. This national standard enables us to make direct comparisons of neighborhood-level trends in Los Angeles

Census 1990, Census 2000, ACS 2005–2009, and ACS 2008–2012. This approach enables us to track L.A. neighborhood trajectories relative to each other and relative to the national distribution simultaneously.

To meet our goal of studying income mixing in addition to income levels, we measure the degree of mutual exposure of lower- and higher-income persons within a census tract. Following Massey (2001), we define the *Index of Concentration at the Extremes*:

$$\text{ICE} = \frac{A_i - P_i}{T_i},$$

where A is the number of affluent residents in neighborhood i, P is the number of poor residents, and T is the total number of residents. ICE can range from –1 (all residents are poor) to 1 (all residents are affluent). Greater income mixing, in the form of a more even balance of the poor and affluent, typically in middle-class areas, is centered at zero. To determine cutoffs for classifying families as affluent or poor, we use the national upper- and lower-income quintiles of family income, respectively, constructing an ICE score for each census tract in our analytic sample at four points in time: Census 1990, Census 2000, ACS 2005–2009, and ACS 2008–2012.[9]

For each of these two dimensions of neighborhood income, we construct mobility tables for both neighborhoods and individuals. We measure neighborhood transitions across nationally determined median family income and ICE categories between Census 1990 and Census 2000 and between Census 2000 and ACS 2008–2012. These analyses illuminate the distribution of L.A. neighborhoods before and during the period in which the L.A.FANS and MIP surveys were fielded. At the individual level, we construct mobility tables for changes in median family income and ICE of respondents' neighborhoods between Census 2000 and ACS 2008–2012, aligned with L.A.FANS wave 1 and the MIP survey (wave 3). Our focus on quintiles comports with prior research on income mobility at the individual level (Chetty et al. 2014) and neighborhood level (Sampson, Mare, and Perkins 2015).

Our demographic measures consist of the respondent's *age*, *sex*, and *race-ethnicity*. The latter is coded with indicator variables signifying whether the respondent is white (the reference group), black, Latino (or Hispanic), Asian–Pacific Islander, or a member of another racial or ethnic group (for example, Native American, multiracial). The respondent's *immigrant generation* consists of indicator variables denoting one's status as first-generation immigrant (born outside the United States), second-generation (mother born outside the United States), or third-generation or higher (reference group). Length of residence is defined as the *duration of residence at the respondent's wave 1 location* in years.

Our time-varying covariates track key changes in respondents' household structure and socioeconomic status (SES), as well as residential location, at each wave of the survey. We measure the *employment status* of the respondent with a binary indicator (working or not working) and the respondent's *total household income*, including earned income, asset income, and transfers, using five indicator variables that indicate whether the total income is below $14,000; $14,000 to 24,999; $25,000 to 39,999; $40,000 to 74,999; or $75,000 and above, all in constant 1999 dollars. *Educational attainment* is a time-varying metric that consists of five binary variables indicating completion of primary school or less (Grade 6 or lower—the reference group), some high school short of

---

County and other urban contexts, like Chicago. However, the tract quintiles for Los Angeles County and the United States are similar, ensuring comparable substantive results in our analysis. For example, the lowest quintile in 1990 for median income is <$24,422 in L.A. and <$25,863 in urban areas nationally; in 2008–2012, the highest quintile is $97,927+ in L.A. and $93,981+ nationally. Note that quintiles are calculated based on nominal dollars.

9. ICE is robust to extremely high (and low) incomes within the top (and bottom) fifths of the family income distribution, whereas other plausible measures—including the Gini index of income inequality and the interquartile range for each tract—are not (for additional detail on our rationale and validation evidence for ICE, see Sampson, Mare, and Perkins 2015).

twelfth grade, twelfth grade or a high school degree, some college (including vocational school and A.A. degrees), or a B.A. and above. Additional time-varying measures of household structure–SES include *homeownership*; the *total number of children* residing in the household; and the respondent's *marital status*, which consists of indicator variables denoting whether the respondent is not married and not cohabiting (the reference group), married and cohabiting with spouse or partner, or cohabiting with a nonspouse.

To glean the impact of *mobility* on neighborhood outcomes, we include binary variables indicating whether the respondent stayed within the same tract (the reference group) or moved across tracts between waves 1 and 2 and between waves 2 and 3. To discern whether a core-periphery mobility pattern obtains, we also use a binary indicator variable to indicate *residence within central Los Angeles* or outside this area (the reference group) at each wave of the survey, along with indicators for whether the respondent moved from within central L.A. to another region of the county between waves 1 and 2 and between waves 2 and 3.[10]

We address missing data through two strategies: attrition weights and imputation. To adjust for any bias produced by panel attrition, we model the probability that individuals exited the survey at each wave and then weight all individual-level data based on the product of the inverse probability of attrition between waves 1 and 2 and waves 2 and 3, as well as sampling weights designed to adjust for the original sampling design of L.A.FANS, which stratified on neighborhood poverty status and household structure (the presence of children).[11] Fortunately, aside from attrition, missing data on key variables among adult MIP respondents is relatively infrequent (<5 percent). Of these variables, only one contains a concerning rate of missing data: total household income at wave 3 (16 percent). We therefore impute missing values of this variable by using our key covariates to generate predicted wave 3 household income levels. This approach assumes that the data are missing at random, conditional on observed covariates in the imputation model (Norholdt 1998; for details on the imputation of income and assets for waves 1 and 2, see Peterson et. al. 2012).[12] Weighted prevalence data on neighborhood outcomes and individual covariates are presented in table 1.

NEIGHBORHOOD-LEVEL TRANSITIONS

We begin with basic but important questions about the temporal nature of neighborhood-level income inequality. Table 2 reveals a strong pattern of persistence at the extremes of neighborhood median income in the 1990s. Indeed, 70 percent of affluent (top fifth) neighborhoods and a staggering 97 percent of poor (lowest fifth) neighborhoods remained in the same category across the decade. Considerably

10. We assign the central L.A. residence indicator variable based on a schematic map produced by the City of Los Angeles defining eight economic regions of Los Angeles County that are also widely recognized among area residents: Central Los Angeles, San Fernando Valley, San Gabriel Valley, Gateway Cities, South Bay, Westside Cities, Santa Clarita Valley, and Antelope Valley. According to this map, Central Los Angeles spans roughly from La Brea Avenue to the west, the 101 freeway to the east, the Hollywood Hills to the north, and Slauson Avenue to the south. At each wave, we use respondents' municipality and zip code to designate whether they resided within or outside of these boundaries.

11. To account for attrition between waves 2 and 3, we estimate a logit model of the probability of attrition at wave 3, based on respondents' race-ethnicity, age, immigrant generation, wave 1 household income, and wave 1 neighborhood income composition. We then calculate the inverse probability of each subject's response and standardize by the mean to generate final attrition weights. We multiply the stratification weights and attrition weights for waves 1 and 2 and waves 2 and 3 to produce the final weight (for further description of the construction of wave 2 attrition weights, see Peterson et al. 2012, 43–46; Sastry and Pebley 2010).

12. The imputation model for wave 3 total household income includes all time-varying covariates examined in this paper, in addition to age, sex, race-ethnicity, and immigrant generation. After removing negative predicted values, we replace all missing wave 3 total household income values with the values predicted by the imputation model. This approach reduces the rate of missing data on wave 3 total household income from 16 to 4 percent.

Table 1. Descriptive Statistics

Variable	Mean	SD	Minimum	Maximum
Outcome				
Neighborhood median income, in 1999 dollars (wave 3)	51,742	26,807	7,623	169,975
Index of concentrated extremes (wave 3)	0.06	0.31	−0.73	0.76
Demographics				
Age	41.3	14.4	18	82
Sex, 1 = female	0.54	0.50	0	1
Race-ethnicity				
White	0.38	0.49	0	1
Latino	0.38	0.49	0	1
African American	0.05	0.21	0	1
Asian or Pacific Islander	0.16	0.36	0	1
Other	0.03	0.18	0	1
Immigrant generation				
First generation	0.49	0.50	0	1
Second generation	0.07	0.25	0	1
Third generation or higher	0.44	0.50	0	1
Household structure-SES				
Total household income, in 1999 dollars				
Below $14,000	0.17	0.38	0	1
$14,000 to 24,999	0.19	0.39	0	1
$25,000 to 39,999	0.16	0.37	0	1
$40,000 to 74,999	0.26	0.44	0	1
$75,000 or more	0.21	0.41	0	1
Unemployment, 1 = unemployed	0.31	0.46	0	1
Respondent's education:				
Primary school or less	0.10	0.29	0	1
Some high school	0.13	0.34	0	1
Completed twelfth grade	0.21	0.41	0	1
Some college (includes A.A.)	0.27	0.44	0	1
B.A. or above	0.30	0.46	0	1
Homeownership, 1 = homeowner	0.49	0.50	0	1
Marital status				
Not married and not cohabiting	0.38	0.49	0	1
Married and with spouse/partner	0.55	0.50	0	1
Cohabiting with non-spouse	0.06	0.24	0	1
Number of children in household	1.11	1.36	0	7
Residential mobility				
Length of residence at wave 1 (years)	7.92	8.51	0	44
Mobility between waves 1 and 2, 1=moved	0.39	0.49	0	1
Mobility between waves 2 and 3, 1=moved	0.26	0.44	0	1

Source: Authors' calculations using L.A.FANS-MIP Longitudinal Study, decennial census, and ACS data.
Note: L.A.FANS-MIP Longitudinal Study, adult respondents (N=612; weighted). Means for time-invariant variables are at wave 1 unless otherwise indicated.

Table 2. Neighborhood-Level Transitions in Median Family Income, 1990 to 2000

	1990 Median Family Income Quintiles					
	1	2	3	4	5	Total
2000 Income Quintiles						
1	445	185	31	0	0	661
	96.74	53.01	9.87	0.00	0.00	32.77
2	14	147	148	44	0	353
	3.04	42.12	47.13	12.54	0.00	17.50
3	1	15	115	153	31	315
	0.22	4.30	36.62	43.59	5.71	15.62
4	0	1	19	134	132	286
	0.00	0.29	6.05	38.18	24.31	14.18
5	0	1	1	20	380	402
	0.00	0.29	0.32	5.70	69.98	19.93
Total	460	349	314	351	543	2,017
	100	100	100	100	100	100

Source: Authors' calculations using L.A.FANS-MIP Longitudinal Study, decennial census, and ACS data.
Note: Cell entries are the number of tracts with family populations 50 and above and column percent, respectively. Tract N=2,024 in 1990, 2,027 in 2000, and 2,031 in 2008–2012.

higher levels of fluidity mark the middle of the distribution, but this change is due almost entirely to declines in neighborhood affluence relative to the national distribution. More than 50 percent of neighborhoods in quintile categories two through four dropped to a lower category; about 6 percent or fewer ascended to a higher category. These trends are most accentuated in the case of the middle fifth of income (category three), where nearly 60 percent of neighborhoods deteriorated in their relative positions, and a nontrivial 10 percent fell two groups lower. By the end of the decade, a material downward shift in the distribution of Los Angeles neighborhoods relative to the national distribution occurred; more than 30 percent fell within the bottom fifth of affluence. This shift, combined with high rates of persistence at the top of distribution, contributed to a "hollowing out" of the middle insofar as only 47 percent of Los Angeles neighborhoods remained within the three middle categories of the national distribution by 2000 (see also Booza, Cutsinger, and Galster 2006).

The second decade, shown in table 3—from 2000 to 2008–2012—again reveals persistence at the extremes, but this time, it is the affluent neighborhoods that are most durable; almost 90 percent of affluent neighborhoods remain so, versus nearly 70 percent of poor neighborhoods. Moreover, whereas the 1990s were marked by fluidity and backsliding for income groups two through four, in the subsequent period we see increased stability and a higher rate of upgrading despite the intervening recession. Persistence increases from approximately 40 percent for neighborhoods in the three middle-income fifths during the 1990s to about 50 to 60 percent during the 2000s. As in the earlier period, fluidity is highest among the middle-fifth of income—the only category in which fewer than half of neighborhoods preserve their relative position across the timeframe. But in contrast to the prior decade, the neighborhood fluidity that exists is largely a product of relative upgrading rather than downgrading. Within each of the middle intervals, for example, nearly twice as many neighborhoods increase their quintile-based position (24 to 39 percent) as decrease (8 to 16 percent). This material recovery in relative affluence reduces the skew in the neighborhood distribution toward the very bottom of the national distribution and restores the proportion

Table 3. Neighborhood-Level Transitions in Median Family Income, 2000 to 2008–2012

	2000 Median Family Income Quintiles					
	1	2	3	4	5	Total
2008–2012 Income Quintiles						
1	457	29	1	1	0	488
	69.24	8.22	0.32	0.35	0.00	24.12
2	189	186	50	1	0	426
	28.64	52.69	15.87	0.35	0.00	21.06
3	11	111	152	42	2	318
	1.67	31.44	48.25	14.63	0.49	15.72
4	1	24	95	173	50	343
	0.15	6.80	30.16	60.28	12.25	16.96
5	2	3	17	70	356	448
	0.30	0.85	5.40	24.39	87.25	22.15
Total	660	353	315	287	408	2,023
	100	100	100	100	100	100

Source: Authors' calculations using L.A.FANS-MIP Longitudinal Study, decennial census, and ACS data.
Note: Cell entries are the number of tracts with family populations 50 and above and column percent, respectively. Tract N=2,024 in 1990, 2,027 in 2000, and 2,031 in 2008–2012.

of L.A. neighborhoods falling within the middle three-fifths of the national distribution. Interestingly, however, the proportion of neighborhoods falling within the middle-income fifth remains unchanged at 16 percent despite considerable flux in the particular neighborhoods in the middle-income category.

Shifting our neighborhood-level metric from median family income to ICE generates virtually identical results across both periods (data not shown). Transition matrices based on ICE quintiles confirm very high levels of durability at the extremes, with 96 percent of the poorest neighborhoods remaining in the bottom fifth of the distribution and 69 percent of the richest neighborhoods remaining at the top over the 1990s; in the 2000s, these rates are 72 percent and 87 percent, respectively. Also, like median income, mixed middle-income neighborhoods (the middle fifth) based on the ICE metric are the least likely to preserve their quintile-based position over time.

Whether the neighborhood-level metric employed is median family income or ICE, the patterns we have found in Los Angeles largely mirror trends in Chicago and the nation as a whole. Namely, despite some evidence of neighborhood downgrading (the 1990s) and upgrading (the 2000s), "stickiness" is the general rule, particularly at the extremes of the distribution (see also Sampson, Mare, and Perkins 2015). Surprisingly, these inertial tendencies are even stronger in Los Angeles than elsewhere. For example, whereas approximately 65 percent of Chicago neighborhoods in both the bottom and the top fifths remained in place between 1990 and 2005–2009, the proportion remaining stable in Los Angeles reaches 97 percent among lowest-income neighborhoods between 1990 and 2000 and 87 percent at the top between 2000 and 2008–2012. Even within the middle three income groupings, persistence rates tend to be higher among Los Angeles neighborhoods than they are among Chicago neighborhoods.[13]

13. Of course, conclusions about relative stability depend in part on poverty definitions. Nationally, neighborhoods with 40 percent+ poverty rates were about as likely to stay stable, increase their poverty rate 5+ points, or decrease 5+ points during the 1980s (Galster et al. 2003).

However, the similarities between neighborhood conditions in Los Angeles and other major American cities, such as Chicago, should not be overstated. Los Angeles stands out for its large Latino—and increasingly Asian—populations, fueled by foreign immigration. Moreover, its economic base and pattern of deindustrialization are distinct, as reflected in the aerospace manufacturing decline of the 1990s, for example. Additionally, the distinction between the core city and suburbs is less relevant in L.A. than in other cities, particularly when it comes to education. The Los Angeles Unified School District covers the city of Los Angeles plus thirty-one smaller municipalities and unincorporated areas of the county. Moving out of the city is thus less relevant for obtaining a different quality of schooling than in cities like Chicago.

Los Angeles neighborhoods also stand out in their trends, deteriorating relative to the national income distribution in the 1990s before recovering during the 2000s. Paul Jargowsky (2003) offers three possible explanations for the anomalous downgrading of L.A. neighborhoods over the course of the 1990s: escalating racial tensions fomented by the Rodney King verdict in 1992 and the O. J. Simpson trial in 1995 accelerated middle-class flight from central L.A.; massive flows of immigration from Latin American countries, particularly Mexico, substantially increased L.A.'s number of low-income residents; and the early 1990s recession severely affected Southern California and the Internet-fueled economic recovery buoyed L.A. less than other metropolitan areas in the United States. To assess these explanations, we compare compositional and economic county-level trends in Los Angeles and Chicago, using Census 1990, Census 2000, and ACS 2008–2012 data. If either the first or the second hypotheses were true, we would expect to see a larger decrease in the Los Angeles white population and a larger increase in its Hispanic population than in Chicago during the 1990s. Although the L.A. white population declined slightly more steeply than Chicago's over this timeframe—18 percent versus 12 percent—Chicago's staggering 54 percent Hispanic growth rate was twice that of Los Angeles. Compositional factors alone do not appear to drive the divergence in L.A. neighborhood trajectories from the national trend line.

Our analysis supports the economic explanation instead. During the 1990s, average household income in L.A. climbed an anemic 1 percent compared to Chicago's robust 14 percent growth. Income trends are also consistent with L.A.'s neighborhood recovery in the subsequent decade. Between 2000 and 2008–2012, average household incomes in L.A. declined by approximately 4 percent—far less precipitously than Chicago's 9 percent. In short, the distinct income trajectories across cities provides the most plausible account for why L.A. neighborhoods lost so much ground in the 1990s but then recovered relative to the national distribution during the 2000s.[14]

INDIVIDUAL-LEVEL TRANSITIONS

We now shift our primary unit of analysis from the neighborhood to the individual but retain our analytic focus on the nature of change. Tables 4 and 5 show the transition matrices of individual exposure to neighborhood income environments over thirteen years (2000 to 2013)

---

14. We also compare the race-ethnic composition of high-income and low-income neighborhoods across the two cities. In both Los Angeles and Chicago, minorities constitute approximately 95 percent of low-income neighborhoods based on the ACS 2008–2012 survey. But in Chicago, blacks comprise over 65 percent of low-income neighborhood residents, whereas in Los Angeles, Hispanics predominate with more than 70 percent of residents in the least affluent communities. The remainder of minority residents is roughly split between blacks and Asians who constitute 10 and 9 percent of low-income neighborhood residents, respectively; in Chicago, this remainder is dominated by Hispanics, at 25 percent, followed by Asians, a mere 2 percent. Divergence is diminished at the top. In both Los Angeles and Chicago, white residents constitute a majority of high-income neighborhood residents (61 and 76 percent, respectively) followed by a roughly even split of Asians and Hispanics and then blacks. The key difference is that Asians and Hispanics together make up nearly twice the share of residents in affluent L.A. neighborhoods as they do in socioeconomically similar Chicago neighborhoods—31 percent to 16 percent. Blacks, on the other hand, make up a mere 4 percent of high-income neighborhood residents in L.A. and 6 percent in Chicago.

Table 4. Individual-Level Transitions, Median Family Income

	Wave 1 Median Family Income Quintiles					
	1	2	3	4	5	Total
Wave 3 Income Quintiles						
1	82	13	0	2	0	97
	40.77	15.54	0.23	5.49	0.00	15.89
2	82	40	47	10	4	184
	41.03	48.55	34.65	24.50	2.84	30.00
3	19	28	44	1	12	104
	9.24	33.97	32.79	3.14	7.85	16.99
4	11	2	38	17	21	88
	5.63	1.94	27.91	39.80	13.57	14.39
5	7	0	6	11	115	139
	3.32	0.00	4.42	27.06	75.74	22.73
Total	201	81	136	42	152	612
	100	100	100	100	100	100

Source: Authors' calculations using L.A.FANS-MIP Longitudinal Study, decennial census, and ACS data.
Note: Los Angeles adult sample (N=612 individuals, 2000 to 2013). Cell entries are the weighted number of cases and column percent, respectively.

in our L.A.FANS-MIP sample of adults.[15] Table 4 reveals that over 75 percent of individuals who resided in the most affluent neighborhoods at baseline preserve their neighborhood position thirteen years later, versus an average of about 40 percent among respondents who resided within the least affluent neighborhood stratum at wave 1. If we consider the bottom two-fifths as lower-income brackets, nearly 80 percent of adults who started in these lower two groups remain there over the course of the study. Respondents residing in a middle-income neighborhood at wave 1 have the lowest likelihood of remaining in the same type of neighborhood by wave 3: only 33 percent of respondents who started the panel in this stratum remain there by wave 3. This share of respondents constitutes a mere 7 percent of the entire sample, versus 68 percent that did not reside in a middle-income neighborhood at wave 1 or wave 3. The balance, nearly 25 percent of the sample, transitions into or out of middle-income neighborhoods between 2000 and 2013. Despite the vast differences in urban structure, L.A.'s patterns largely mirror those found in Chicago (Sampson, Mare, and Perkins 2015), confirming fluidity in individuals' exposure to mixed middle-income neighborhoods.

Employing ICE as our neighborhood-level outcome of interest (table 5) reveals broadly similar trends but with some twists. Some 66 percent of Angelenos in the top neighborhood quintile are estimated to preserve their position based on ICE, versus 76 percent based on median family income. For residents who began the panel in neighborhoods constituting the middle three categories of ICE, the rate of persistence averages nearly 50 percent, versus an average of approximately 40 percent produced by the median family income matrix. Divergent estimates of temporal rigidity are most pronounced across metrics for those who lived in the least affluent neighborhoods at the beginning of the panel. Whereas the median family income matrix suggests that about 40 percent of respondents remain stuck in the lowest income neighborhoods between waves 1 and 3, the ICE matrix produces a proportion of 60 percent, an estimate closely aligned with

---

15. Data are weighted to correct for stratified sample design and potential attrition bias over the course of the follow-up.

Table 5. Individual-Level Transitions, ICE

	Wave 1 ICE Quintiles					
	1	2	3	4	5	Total
Wave 3 ICE Quintiles						
1	112	13	1	2	0	128
	59.98	12.02	1.36	3.04	0.00	21.00
2	38	73	29	11	9	160
	20.17	65.50	33.50	14.85	6.08	26.18
3	23	20	33	10	3	88
	12.11	17.51	37.89	13.75	2.07	14.44
4	12	2	23	32	40	109
	6.48	2.04	26.35	42.48	26.25	17.84
5	2	3	1	20	100	126
	1.26	2.94	0.91	25.89	65.60	20.55
Total	186	112	86	76	152	612
	100	100	100	100	100	100

Source: Authors' calculations using L.A.FANS-MIP Longitudinal Study, decennial census, and ACS data.
Note: Los Angeles adult sample (N=612 individuals, 2000 to 2013). Cell entries are the weighted number of cases and column percent, respectively.

the Chicago panel data (Sampson, Mare, and Perkins 2015). Estimated trajectories for those who started in mixed middle-income neighborhoods are more congruent across the two neighborhood-level metrics. Both matrices reveal that respondents residing in a middle-income neighborhood at wave 1 have the lowest likelihood of remaining in the same type of neighborhood by wave 3 (38 percent for ICE). Overall, then, the ICE and median family income analyses provide a broadly similar portrait of individual pathways.

RESIDENTIAL MOBILITY AND THE GREAT RECESSION

To what degree are the patterns of change in tables 4 and 5 brought about by the residential mobility of individuals or the mobility of neighborhoods? What is the role of the Great Recession? To answer these questions we estimate an unconditional multilevel model where median neighborhood income varies simultaneously over time t (waves 1 through 3 from 2000 to the 2011–2013 follow-up) and between individuals (i):

$$MEDIAN\ INCOME_{ti} = \beta_{00} + r_{0i} + e_{ti}, \quad (1)$$

where e_{ti} is the within-person or change error term and r_{0i} is the person-specific error term.

Our data reveal that the intercept, β_{00}, reflecting neighborhood median income in 2000, is $49,446 in 1999 dollars. For an identical model predicting ICE, the intercept hovers near the middle of the distribution as expected, at –0.04. But by far the greatest variation in median income status is between people rather than over time—80 percent and 20 percent, respectively. For ICE, the corresponding values are 82 percent and 18 percent. Interestingly, when we add a parameter for time (coded 0, 1, and 2) we find that change in median income for the sample as a whole is statistically no different than zero. For ICE, a modest trend is indicated by a significant effect of time, with an increment to ICE of 0.03 at each wave. These patterns are somewhat surprising given neighborhood income changes that might be expected to be induced by the Great Recession, but stable differences among individuals are the main story so far.[16]

---

16. The reliability coefficients that reflect the precision of our estimates to detect differences between individuals in neighborhood income status are also very high, at 0.81 for median income and 0.83 for ICE.

To disentangle residential mobility and temporal change pre- and postrecession we redefine equation (1) by introducing our moving indicators by wave along with an interaction of time with moving and estimate the initial mixed-effects model for individual i at time t:

$$MEDIAN\ INCOME_{ti} = \beta_{00} + \beta_{10}*Time_{ti} \\ + \beta_{20}*Mover_{ti} + \beta_{30}*Time\_X\_Mover_{ti} \\ + r_{0i} + e_{ti}, \quad (2)$$

where e_{ti} is the within-person or change error term and r_{0i} is the person-specific error term. We repeat the same model for the ICE measure. In this basic model, the coefficient for time (0.03) is significant ($p < 0.05$) for ICE, but not for median income; moreover, the coefficients for mover and the interaction of moving with time do not approach significance for either outcome of interest. Unlike in Chicago, where moving is associated with income gains (Sampson and Sharkey 2008), moving tracts in Los Angeles does not translate into systematic improvements or declines in neighborhood status, at least for the overall sample. Other differences are that white stayers at later waves reside in higher-income neighborhoods at baseline than movers, and that the level of moving is lower in Los Angeles in the second follow-up—39 percent of adults moved neighborhoods from waves 1 to 2 and 26 percent moved from waves 2 to 3, versus 35 percent and 36 percent in Chicago, respectively, for the adult caretakers.[17] Also, the last wave in the Los Angeles data corresponds to the Great Recession and we know that residential mobility declined nationally as a result of the downturn.

One plausible reason for the null pattern of neighborhood income change produced by moving is the distinct nature of Los Angeles's urban form, which is dominated by a sprawling structure with little in the way of American cities' typical core-periphery distinction other than perhaps the central L.A. or downtown sector versus the rest of the county. We thus examine whether any gains to moving were independently associated with moving out of central L.A. Although central L.A. has lower incomes overall, no significant relationship exists for either median income or ICE in a model specification similar to that described where we add an interaction of moving out of central L.A. with time. Probing further, we examine residential mobility over time within each of the eight metropolitan regions that carry distinct ecological and economic meaning (see note 10). Persistence or "pull" among movers is considerable in all sectors except central L.A. Among movers between waves 1 and 2, for example, more than 75 percent stayed within their communities of origin. From waves 2 to 3, all communities except central L.A. retained the majority of their residents as well, albeit at a slightly lower rate. Still, in some cases, retention was effectively complete, as in the San Fernando Valley and the more affluent Westside Cities, where 97 and 91 percent of between-neighborhood movers did not stray from their communities, respectively. Although central L.A. lost respondents at each follow-up, out-movers did not end up in higher-income neighborhoods overall, and they constitute just 1 percent of the sample.

Another possibility is that the consequences of moving differ by racial and ethnic groups. To test this hypothesis, we expand equation (2) to allow both time and moving by time interaction terms to vary by race and ethnicity. The data are weighted to reflect population estimates and adjusted for age, sex, and immigrant generation. But here too little if any broad pattern is evident, as shown in figures 1 and 2, which present neighborhood income trajectories by race and moving status, respectively. Median income shows little temporal trend—particularly among nonmovers—but does show a strong hierarchy of racial stratification. Throughout figure 1, white stayers preserve their place high atop the racial hierarchy, followed by Asians, and finally Latinos and blacks. The latter two groups are virtually indistinguishable from each other.

Among movers (figure 2), a similar story emerges with one modest divergence: Asians

---

17. The reliability of the change parameter alone is near zero for median income, but the interaction of time and moving is modestly reliable when the time parameter is fixed (0.30). For ICE, the reliability to detect change is a similar 0.31 with or without interactions with moving.

Figure 1. Median Family Income by Race-Ethnicity and Residential Mobility, Stayers

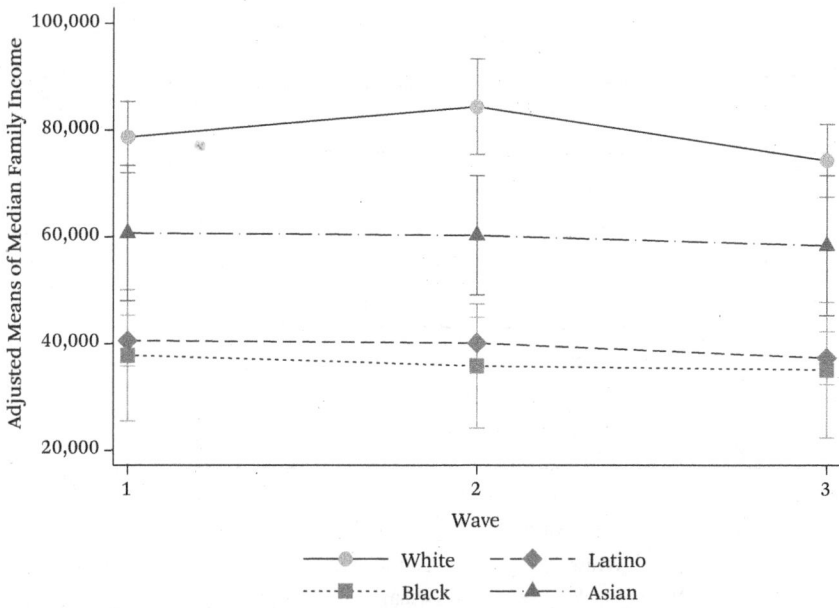

Source: Authors' calculations using L.A.FANS-MIP Longitudinal Study, decennial census, and ACS data.
Note: Weighted and adjusted for age, sex, and immigrant generation; trajectories shown with 95 percent confidence intervals; median family income is in 1999 dollars.

Figure 2. Median Family Income by Race-Ethnicity and Residential Mobility, Movers

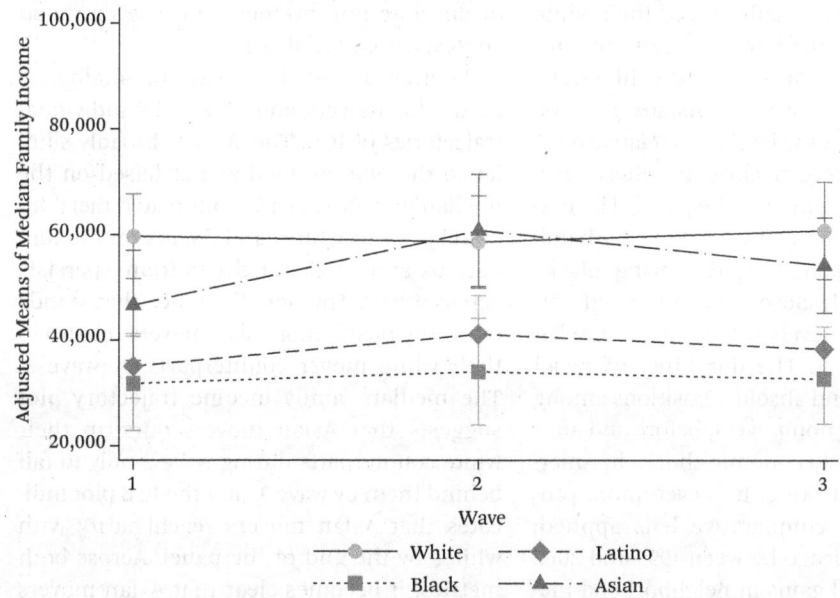

Source: Authors' calculations using L.A.FANS-MIP Longitudinal Study, decennial census, and ACS data.
Note: Weighted and adjusted for age, sex, and immigrant generation; trajectories shown with 95 percent confidence intervals; median family income is in 1999 dollars.

Figure 3. ICE by Race-Ethnicity and Residential Mobility, Stayers

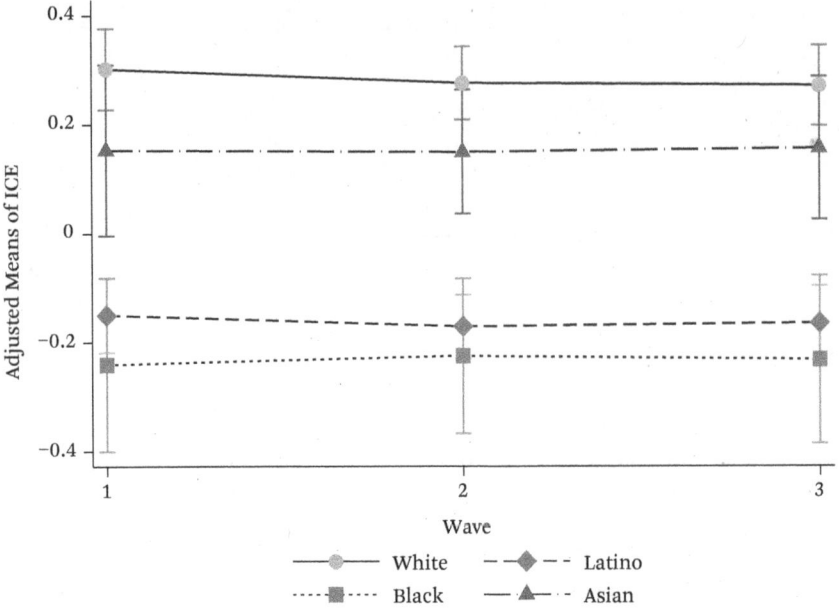

Source: Authors' calculations using L.A.FANS-MIP Longitudinal Study, decennial census, and ACS data.
Note: Weighted and adjusted for age, sex, and immigrant generation; trajectories shown with 95 percent confidence intervals.

in wave 2. Immediately before the Great Recession, Asian movers briefly exceed their white counterparts in neighborhood attainment. However, this disruption in the hierarchy proves fleeting; by wave 3, Asians movers' neighborhood income levels and relative position to whites return close to where they started at the beginning of the panel. The bottom of the racial hierarchy, on the other hand, remains fairly stable. Despite moving, blacks and Latinos barely close the gap in neighborhood attainment levels with white and Asian movers by wave 3. The durability of racial groups' relative and absolute positions among both movers and nonmovers, before and after one of the greatest economic shocks in American history, is striking. It is even more pronounced with a comparative lens applied; panel data in Chicago between 1995 and 2002 reveal substantial gains in neighborhood median family income among white, black, and Latino movers alike—with particularly steep inclines experienced by Latinos (Sampson and Sharkey 2008). In Los Angeles, mobility does not appear to translate into sustained relative or absolute improvements in neighborhood context across racial groups.

Figures 3 and 4 display an analogous model for movers and stayers by individual trajectories of ICE. The story is broadly similar to the one outlined earlier based on the median income metric. A bifurcated racial hierarchy—with whites and Asians on top and Latinos and blacks at the bottom—persists across waves. The one difference that stands out is the position of Asian movers relative to their white mover counterparts by wave 3. The median family income trajectory plot suggests that Asian movers outstrip their white counterparts during wave 2 only to fall behind them by wave 3, and the ICE plot indicates that Asian movers reach parity with whites by the end of the panel. Across both metrics, it becomes clear that Asian movers make substantial relative and absolute gains by wave 2; the question is whether those gains are preserved by wave 3. Latino movers, for their part, achieve modest absolute and rela-

Figure 4. ICE by Race-Ethnicity and Residential Mobility, Movers

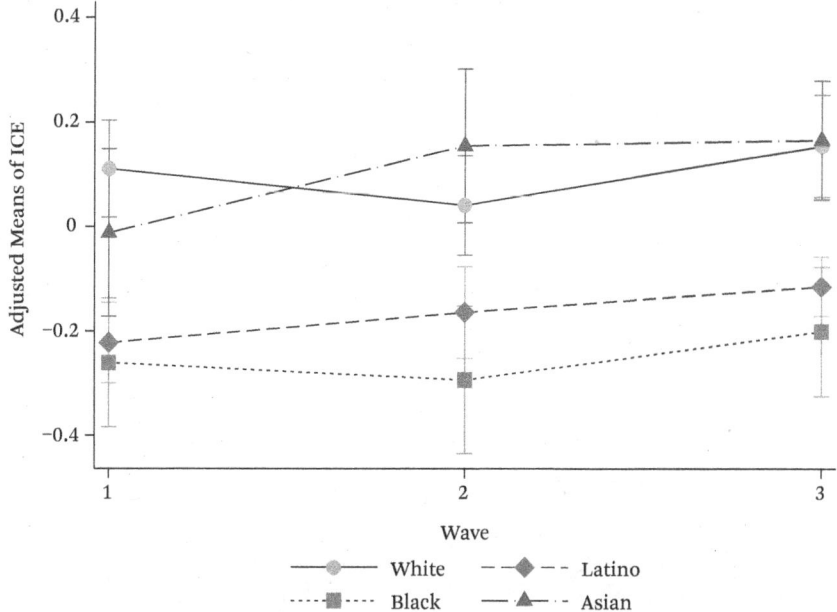

Source: Authors' calculations using L.A.FANS-MIP Longitudinal Study, decennial census, and ACS data.
Note: Weighted and adjusted for age, sex, and immigrant generation; trajectories shown with 95 percent confidence intervals.

tive gains across the panel, and blacks make nearly none.

Given the large and heterogeneous Latino population in Los Angeles, we examine two additional specifications of the models underlying figures 1 through 4—one that stratifies Latinos by immigrant generation and another by residence in an ethnic enclave at baseline.[18] These models confirm that the same overall racial hierarchy holds with only slight modifications. Among stayers and movers, Latinos with non-enclave origins exceed their enclave counterparts in terms of neighborhood median income and ICE throughout the entire panel, though the gap closes slightly over time. In each version of these models, whites and Asians preserve a sizable advantage over both enclave and non-enclave Latinos.

Figures 5 and 6, moreover, show that individual income groups—like racial groups—fol-

---

18. A large body of literature on immigration has debated whether ethnic immigrant enclaves serve as temporary way stations for Latinos and Asians en route to upward neighborhood mobility or as persistently disadvantaged communities that suppress residents' neighborhood attainment trajectories over time. Defining Latin American immigrant enclaves based on the similarity of each census tract's proportional representation of a given country-of-origin group with that of surrounding tracts and on the group's mean proportional representation of the overall metropolitan region, Richard Alba and his colleagues (2014) offer evidence in support of the latter view. To evaluate these claims, we use the simpler double-share criterion, whereby a tract is deemed an ethnic enclave if the proportion of residents reporting a given country of heritage is twice that of the overall proportion reporting the same heritage in Los Angeles County in the 2000 census (for a description, see Logan, Alba, and Zhang 2002; Alba, Logan, and Crowder 1997). A minimum threshold of 10 percent is applied for all heritage nationalities other than Mexicans (whose threshold is 64 percent—twice the share of L.A. County residents reporting Mexican heritage), given that no other national heritage encompasses a substantial share of the L.A. County population. Our ethnic enclave analysis largely confirms the Alba and colleague findings (2014).

Figure 5. Median Family Income by Baseline Income Quintiles and Residential Mobility, Stayers

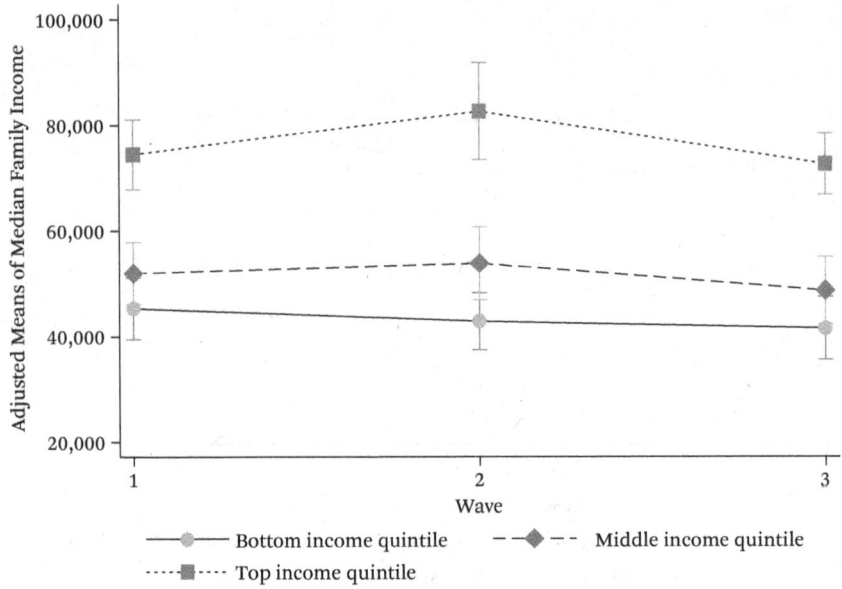

Source: Authors' calculations using L.A.FANS-MIP Longitudinal Study, decennial census, and ACS data.
Note: Weighted and adjusted for age, sex, immigrant generation, and race-ethnicity; trajectories shown with 95 percent confidence intervals; median family income is in 1999 dollars.

Figure 6. Median Family Income by Baseline Income Quintiles and Residential Mobility, Movers

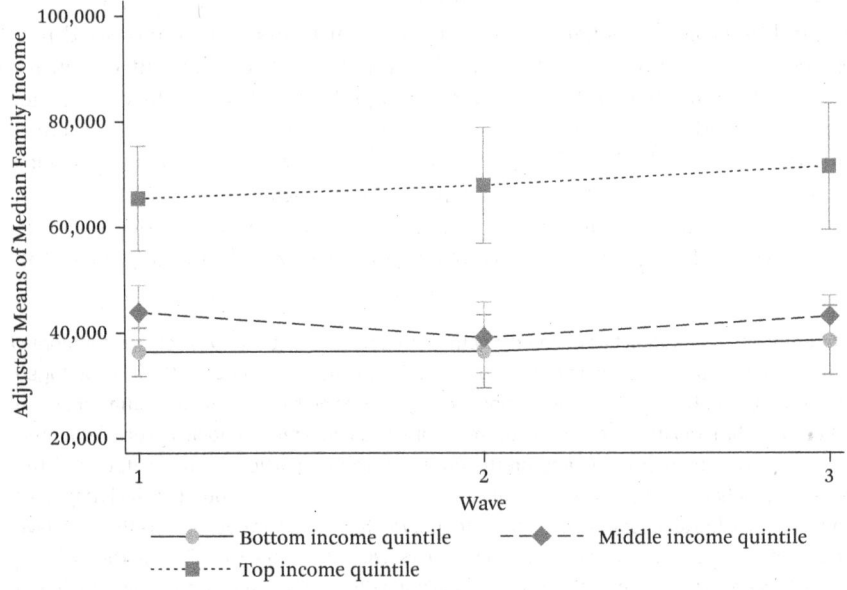

Source: Authors' calculations using L.A.FANS-MIP Longitudinal Study, decennial census, and ACS data.
Note: Weighted and adjusted for age, sex, immigrant generation, and race-ethnicity; trajectories shown with 95 percent confidence intervals; median family income is in 1999 dollars.

low a durable hierarchy across the length of the panel. Among stayers and movers alike, respondents who begin the panel within the top income group maintain a substantial advantage thirteen years later over those who start within the middle and bottom fifths. For stayers, no meaningful temporal trend is apparent; for movers, neighborhood income modestly increases between waves 1 and 3 from the top and bottom income groups. However, even among movers, the size of the neighborhood income gap between the rich and the rest barely budges, reinforcing the persistent dominance of affluent Angelenos in the neighborhood hierarchy.

INDIVIDUAL DIFFERENCES, SOCIAL MOBILITY, AND LIFE-COURSE CHANGE

The results to this point do not account for differences among our respondents in resources such as education, employment, and homeownership or for family factors, such as marital status (for example, married, single, cohabitating) or the number of children in the household. In addition, our models do not disentangle social mobility or individual change from stable between-person differences—the heart of the final analytic question of this paper. To what degree are patterns of individuals' residential mobility across neighborhood types due to changes in their socioeconomic or family conditions? To answer this question, we estimate multilevel models that separate individual change and between-individual differences in the following characteristics—income, education, number of children, marital status, employment, and homeownership. In addition to the race-ethnicity terms of interest we also adjust for length of residence in the neighborhood at baseline, age, sex, and immigrant generation. The models, an extension of equation (2), are estimated in a mixed-effects or hierarchical regression of median income and ICE that center time-varying covariates at their person means.

These models generate a large number of coefficients beyond the charge of this paper, so we focus on whether the fundamental patterns observed so far with respect to residential mobility and race-ethnicity and income groups are robust. Major patterns can be visualized by presenting the trajectories of income status change resulting from the multivariate results for the groups of interest. Figures 7 through 10 present the conditional trajectories of nonmovers and movers stratified by race-ethnicity and income group, respectively. Among nonmovers (figure 7), we see that accounting for a host of time-varying and time-invariant covariates compresses the distribution and clusters all minority groups together at the bottom: white dominance of the racial-income hierarchy proves remarkably stable over time.

A somewhat distinct story emerges among movers in figure 8, where we see a subtle shift in the race-based spatial hierarchy. Asian movers reach near parity with whites by wave 2 and largely preserve this position into wave 3, and Latino movers also close their neighborhood attainment gap with whites by wave 3. Stratifying Latinos by immigrant generation reveals that third-generation Latinos are driving the white-Latino gap reduction; in this mover model, they fall between whites and Asians at the top of the hierarchy throughout the panel, and first-generation Latinos follow a pattern similar to that of blacks, who remain at the bottom of the hierarchy. Grouping Latinos by ethnic enclave residence at baseline and controlling for immigrant generation, we again see a modest disadvantage associated with enclaves that diminishes over time. However, regardless of enclave status, Latino movers remain below whites and Asians and above blacks through most of the panel.

Among income groups in figures 9 and 10, the fully adjusted results look quite similar to the unadjusted—in particular, those at the top are seemingly impervious to change. The absolute dollar gaps also remain very large—at the end of our study approximately $20,000 separates blacks from whites in neighborhood median income, and over $30,000 separates the top and bottom income fifths despite individual differences, life-course change, and the Great Recession.

Most of the explanatory work is driven by stable differences among individuals rather than life-course change—a notable finding, especially in light of the Great Recession. Respondents' demographic characteristics, such as race, and mean SES-household structure

Figure 7. Median Family Income by Race-Ethnicity and Residential Mobility, Stayers

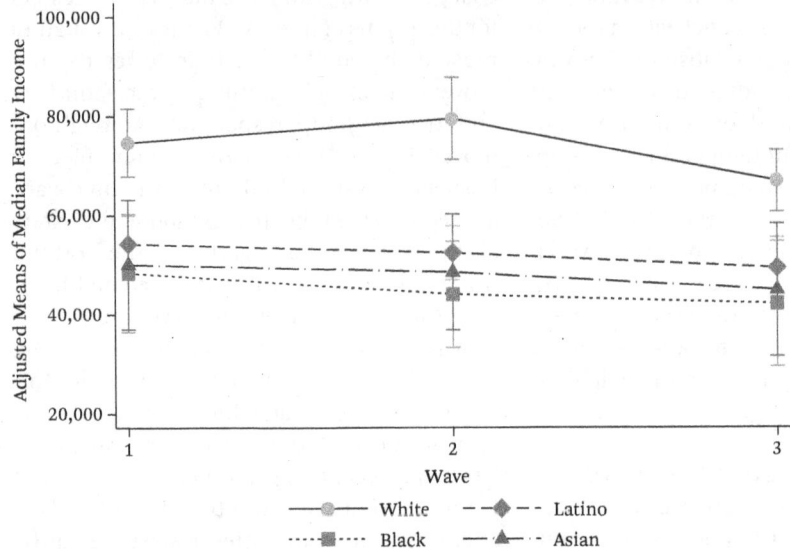

Source: Authors' calculations using L.A.FANS-MIP Longitudinal Study, decennial census, and ACS data.
Note: Weighted and adjusted for age, sex, immigrant generation, and length of residence at wave 1, and both change and person-levels of education, family income, homeownership, employment status, marital status, and number of children in the household; trajectories shown with 95 percent confidence intervals; median family income is in 1999 dollars.

Figure 8. Median Family Income by Race-Ethnicity and Residential Mobility, Movers

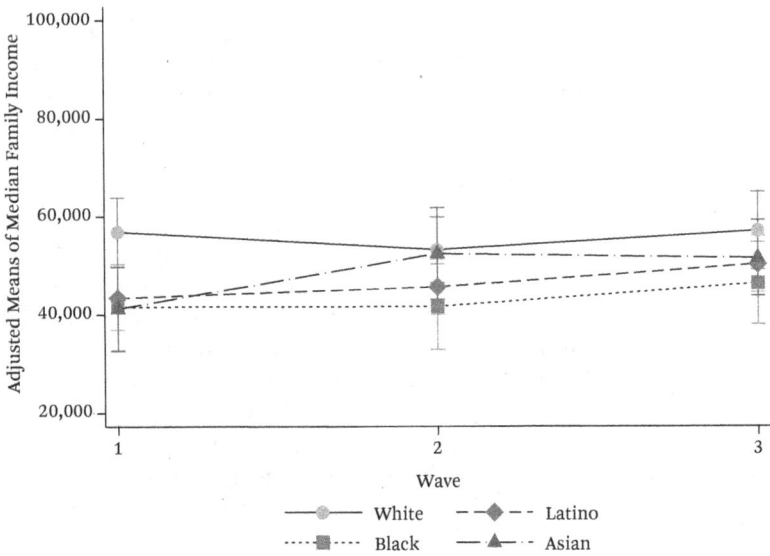

Source: Authors' calculations using L.A.FANS-MIP Longitudinal Study, decennial census, and ACS data.
Note: Weighted and adjusted for age, sex, immigrant generation, and length of residence at wave 1, and both change and person-levels of education, family income, homeownership, employment status, marital status, and number of children in the household; trajectories shown with 95 percent confidence intervals; median family income is in 1999 dollars.

Figure 9. Median Family Income by Time-Varying Income Quintiles and Residential Mobility, Stayers

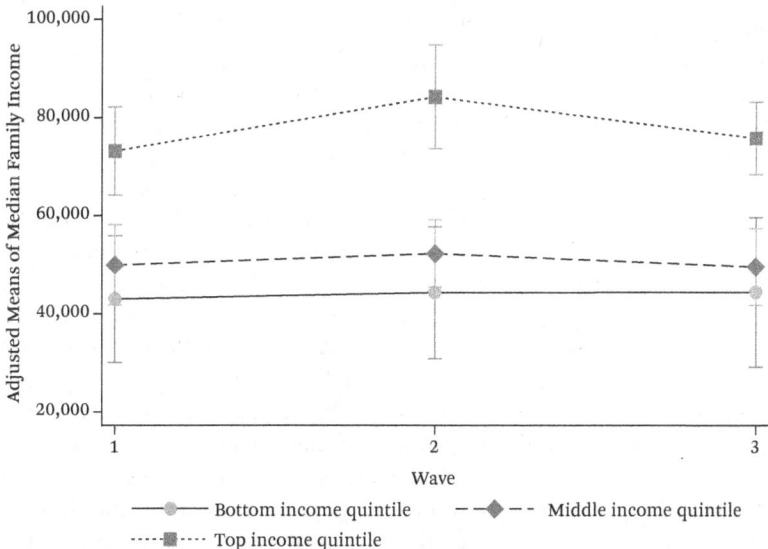

Source: Authors' calculations using L.A.FANS-MIP Longitudinal Study, decennial census, and ACS data.
Note: Weighted and adjusted for age, sex, immigrant generation, race-ethnicity, and length of residence at wave 1, and both change and person-levels of education, family income, homeownership, employment status, marital status, and number of children in the household; trajectories shown with 95 percent confidence intervals; median family income is in 1999 dollars.

Figure 10. Median Family Income by Time-Varying Income Quintiles and Residential Mobility, Movers

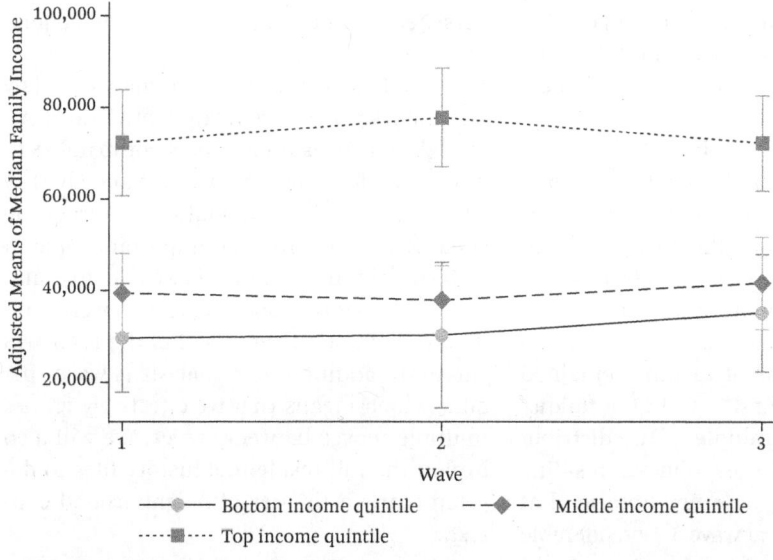

Source: Authors' calculations using L.A.FANS-MIP Longitudinal Study, decennial census, and ACS data.
Note: Weighted and adjusted for age, sex, immigrant generation, race-ethnicity, and length of residence at wave 1, and both change and person-levels of education, family income, homeownership, employment status, marital status, and number of children in the household; trajectories shown with 95 percent confidence intervals; median family income is in 1999 dollars.

profile over the course of the panel (between-person differences)—particularly with regard to income and education—account for most of the variation in neighborhood income status. Change in SES-household structure across waves (individual change) boost neighborhood income gains mainly for respondents who transition from single to married.

DISCUSSION

The persistence of spatial inequality in Los Angeles is revealed both across neighborhoods and in the lives of individuals over a period of rapid social change that included the disruption of the Great Recession. An overwhelming 97 percent of Los Angeles neighborhoods in the bottom income fifth in 1990 remained there ten years later. At the other end, and after the recession, 87 percent of the highest income neighborhoods in 2000 retained their status ten years later (2008–2012). Downward neighborhood mobility from the top was thus quite rare, as was neighborhood upgrading from the bottom fifth; the tendency was for low-income neighborhoods to remain "stuck in place" (Sharkey 2013). Where change does preside is in the middle of the distribution. Mixed middle-income neighborhoods were both less prevalent and more unstable; Los Angeles experienced a hollowing out of the middle of the distribution in the 1990s followed by a modest recovery in the 2000s.

Relative persistence is likewise the dominant pattern in our longitudinal individual-level analysis of contextual mobility. Notably, more than 75 percent of individuals who lived in the most affluent neighborhoods at wave 1 preserved their neighborhood position thirteen years later, and nearly 80 percent of adults in the lower two-fifths of income remained there over the course of the study. But fluidity again prevails in the middle of the distribution; only 33 percent of respondents residing in a mixed middle-income neighborhood at wave 1 remained there at wave 3. Considerable movement in and out of neighborhoods near the middle of the distribution was common. These patterns comport with those found in Chicago, confirming persistence at the extremes and fluidity in mixed-income neighborhoods and underscoring the significant challenges that mixed-income policies face in American cities (Sampson, Mare, and Perkins 2015).

Contrary to prior research, however, we find that neighborhood change in income is not materially influenced by residential mobility for most groups and that, with few exceptions, change around stayers and change induced by moving across neighborhoods are not fundamentally different by race, ethnic, and income groups. Even pre- and postrecession patterns are similar: despite an expected dip in neighborhood income status following the 2008 crash, it is not large, and most groups follow a similar trajectory. Importantly, though, these trajectories unfold at dramatically different levels: the hierarchy of difference between race and income groups at the individual level is largely invariant over time and across residential mobility groups (figures 1 through 10). This conclusion is robust to adjustments for age cohort and both time-variant and time-invariant differences in factors such as income, marital status, homeownership, children, and education. Social mobility and within-individual changes are present in the lives of our respondents, of course, but our results demonstrate that individual changes make little dent in the persistence of neighborhood income inequality.

Nevertheless, questions left unanswered by our analysis deserve further attention. Although our focus on adults is comparable to prior work (for example, Sampson and Sharkey 2008), the transition to adulthood during the Great Recession era is an important topic in its own right. In future work, we plan to examine the subset of respondents who were children or adolescents at wave 1 of the L.A.FANS survey. In addition, our analysis is wave specific, which means that we effectively ignore multiple moves between waves. We will also exploit the full residential history files to develop yearly estimates of neighborhood context.

Certain empirical questions within our current framework are also left open. Although our evaluation of geographic variation in neighborhood distributions supports the general thesis of durable urban inequality (Sampson 2012; Sharkey 2013), Los Angeles neighborhood conditions and trajectories of change diverge from those of Chicago and the nation at large. Curiously, Los Angeles neighborhoods tended to backslide in the purportedly prosperous 1990s and recover in the economically volatile 2000s (see tables 2 and 3). Moreover, neighborhood-level inequality decreased in the latter period, despite the well-documented rise in inequality at the top end of the income distribution (Reardon and Bischoff 2011). Although we believe that local economic conditions appear to be the most likely explanation for the countercyclical nature of L.A.'s neighborhood trajectories, further work is required. A longitudinal, multilevel analysis of census data with city- and neighborhood-level indicators of race-ethnic composition and segregation, economic conditions and workforce composition, and housing markets could illuminate what macro-level and city-level factors shape neighborhood-level conditions and changes in those conditions over time. Urban scholars should also examine whether salient ecological factors at the city and neighborhood levels vary based on the particular historical era in question.

At the individual level, we have seen considerable fluidity in the middle of the distribution. What factors are driving moves into and out of neighborhoods at various points in the income distribution—particularly mixed-income neighborhoods? How and why these changes come about deserves further inquiry, as does a closer look at patterns of residential mobility within and between regions of Los Angeles, where the distinction between central city and suburbs is less salient than in Chicago (Sampson and Sharkey 2008). To this end, we plan to analyze the fine-grained residential history files of L.A.FANS respondents within a discrete choice framework of neighborhood selection, revealing how individual- and household-level characteristics (such as race-ethnicity, SES, family structure) interact with various features of potential destination neighborhoods (such as income levels, race-ethnic compositions, housing costs, crime rates, school quality, distance from amenities) to produce mobility outcomes (Quillian 2015; Bruch and Mare 2012). This discrete choice analysis, as well as the multilevel historical comparative analysis described earlier, constitute natural extensions of the current study and promise to further illuminate the particular processes that reproduce spatial inequality across cities and across historical eras.

CONCLUSION

Taken as a whole, our empirical results are clear: residential income inequality is alive and well in Los Angeles. At first glance, poor L.A. neighborhoods look nothing like the images that dominate the urban classics and popular media accounts. Outsiders are also known to remark that the slums in L.A. and other western cities do not physically resemble those in cities such as Chicago or Baltimore, especially public housing projects. This is undeniable—Los Angeles poverty is low rise and suburban. But the concentration of poverty and affluence is nonetheless deeply rooted and highly persistent in L.A. despite radical differences in urban form.

Indeed, an unexpected finding of our study is that the spatial foundations of income inequality in Los Angeles are in some respects stronger than in traditional cities such as Chicago, at both the neighborhood level and at the individual level, and especially at the top. The contextual advantage of the affluent and whites, in particular, is virtually unaffected by residential and social mobility, individual differences, and changing life circumstances including the Great Recession. To be sure, inequality is manifested distinctly in Los Angeles. Unlike results derived from Chicago, we have seen in Los Angeles that the mover-stayer distinction is weaker and that within-region circulation is considerable but that a noticeable core-periphery distinction with respect to basic patterns is not. Moreover, Latinos are not that different from blacks in Los Angeles; both groups experience more or less stable levels of exposure to lower neighborhood income over time compared with whites. In Chicago, African Americans are decidedly worse off than Latinos. Katz (2012) asserts that the black-white frame is breaking down, but it still holds for minorities overall. In Los Angeles, the main story is one of white spatial advantage over Asians, blacks, and Latinos.

We are left, then, with the conclusion that though the spatial foundations and dynamics of income inequality in Los Angeles take on distinct manifestations, the underlying or latent structure is disturbingly familiar and rigid. That the persistence of advantage and disadvantage over time finds fertile soil in the sprawling metropolis of Los Angeles suggests that the mechanisms driving the "old inequality" may be even more durable than commonly thought.

REFERENCES

Abbott, Andrew. 2002. "Los Angeles and the Chicago School: A Comment on Michael Dear." *City and Community* 1(1): 33–38.

Alba, Richard, Glenn Deane, Nancy Denton, Ilir Disha, Brian McKenzie, and Jeffrey Napierela. 2014. "The Role of Immigrant Enclaves for Latino Residential Inequalities." *Journal of Ethnic and Migration Studies* 40(1): 1–20.

Alba, Richard D., John R. Logan, and Kyle Crowder. 1997. "White Neighborhoods and Assimilation: The Greater New York Region, 1980–1990." *Social Forces* 75(3): 883–909.

Bobo, Lawrence D., Melvin L. Oliver, James H. Johnson, and Abel Valenzua, eds. 2002. *Prismatic Metropolis: Inequality in Los Angeles*. New York: Russell Sage Foundation.

Booza, Jason, Jackie Cutsinger, and George Galster. 2006. "Where Did They Go? The Decline of Middle-Income Neighborhoods in Metropolitan America." Washington, D.C.: Brookings Institution.

Briggs, Xavier de Souza, Greg Duncan, Kathryn Edin, Mark Joseph, Robert D. Mare, John Mollenkopf, Mary Pattillo, Lincoln Quillian, Robert J. Sampson, Claudia Solari, Laura Tach, and Sudhir Venkatesh. 2009. "Research Designs for the Study of Mixed-Income Housing." Report to the John D. and Catherine T. MacArthur Foundation. Los Angeles: California Center for Population Research.

Bruch, Elizabeth E., and Robert D. Mare. 2012. "Methodological Issues in the Analysis of Residential Preferences and Residential Mobility." *Sociological Methodology* 42(1): 103–54.

Charles, Camille Zubrinsky. 2009. *Won't You Be My Neighbor? Race, Class, and Residence in Los Angeles*. New York: Russell Sage Foundation.

Chaskin, Robert J., and Mark L. Joseph. 2015. *Integrating the Inner City: The Promise and Perils of Mixed-Income Public Housing Transformations*. Chicago: University of Chicago Press.

Chetty, Raj, Nathaniel Hendren, Patrick Kline, and Emmanuel Saez. 2014. "Where is the Land of Opportunity? The Geography of Intergenerational Mobility in the United States." *Quarterly Journal of Economics* 129(4): 1553–623.

Dear, Michael, ed. 2001. *From Chicago to L.A.: Making Sense of Urban Theory*. Beverly Hills, Calif.: Sage Publications.

———. 2002. "Los Angeles and the Chicago School: Invitation to a Debate." *City and Community* 1(1): 5–32.

Drake, St. Clair, and Horace R. Cayton. 1945. *Black Metropolis: A Study of Negro Life in a Northern City*. Chicago: University of Chicago Press.

Du Bois, W. E. B. 1899. *The Philadelphia Negro: A Social Study*. Philadelphia: University of Pennsylvania Press.

Galster, George C., Jason Booza, and Jackie Cutsinger. 2008. "Income Diversity Within Neighborhoods and Very Low-Income Families." *Cityscape* 10(2): 219–62.

Galster, George C., Roberto G. Quercia, Alvaro Cortes, and Ron Malega. 2003. "The Fortunes of Poor Neighborhoods." *Urban Affairs Review* 39(2): 205–27.

Halle, David, ed. 2003. *New York and Los Angeles: Politics, Society, and Culture: A Comparative View*. Chicago: University of Chicago Press.

Halle, David, and Andrew A. Beveridge, eds. 2013. *New York and Los Angeles: The Uncertain Future*. New York: Oxford University Press.

Hipp, John R., Victoria Basolo, Marlon Boarnet, and Doug Houston. 2012. "Metropolitan Futures Initiative." School of Social Ecology. Irvine: University of California. Accessed December 1, 2014. http://mfi.soceco.uci.edu.

Jargowsky, Paul A. 2003. "Stunning Progress, Hidden Problems: The Dramatic Decline of Concentrated Poverty in the 1990s." Washington, D.C.: Brookings Institution.

Joseph, Mark L., and Robert J. Chaskin. 2012. "Mixed-Income Developments and Low Rates of Return: Insights from Relocated Public Housing Residents in Chicago." *Housing Policy Debate* 22(3): 377–405.

Katz, Michael B. 2012. *Why Don't American Cities*

Burn? Philadelphia: University of Pennsylvania Press.

Liebow, Elliott. 1967. *Tally's Corner: A Study of Negro Streetcorner Men.* Boston, Mass.: Little, Brown.

Logan, John R., Richard D. Alba, and Wenquan Zhang. 2002. "Immigrant Enclaves and Ethnic Communities in New York and Los Angeles." *American Sociological Review* 67(2): 299–322.

Logan, John R., Zengwang Xu, and Brian Stults. 2014. "Interpolating U.S. Decennial Census Tract Data from as Early as 1970 to 2010: A Longitudinal Tract Database." *Professional Geographer* 66(3): 412–20.

Massey, Douglas S. 1996. "The Age of Extremes: Concentrated Affluence and Poverty in the Twenty-First Century." *Demography* 33(4): 395–412.

———. 2001. "The Prodigal Paradigm Returns: Ecology Comes Back to Sociology." In *Does It Take a Village? Community Effects on Children, Adolescents, and Families*, edited by Alan Booth and Ann Crouter. Mahwah, N.J.: Lawrence Erlbaum Associates.

Massey, Douglas S., and Mitchell L. Eggers. 1990. "The Ecology of Inequality: Minorities and the Concentration of Poverty, 1970–1980." *American Journal of Sociology* 95(5): 1153–88.

Norholdt, Eric S. 1998. "Imputation: Methods, Simulation Experiments, and Practical Examples." *International Statistics Review* 66(2): 157–80.

O'Connor, Alice, Chris Tilly, and Lawrence Bobo. 2001. *Urban Inequality: Evidence from Four Cities.* New York: Russell Sage Foundation.

Peterson, Christine E., Anne R. Pebley, Narayan Sastry, Karen Yuhas, Bonnie Ghosh-Dastidar, Ann C. Haas, Jesse Gregory, and Marianne P. Bitler. 2012. "The Los Angeles Family and Neighborhood Survey, Wave 2: User's Guide and Codebook." Working Paper no. WR-240/20-L.A.FANS. Santa Monica, Calif.: RAND Corporation. Accessed December 1, 2014. http://www.rand.org/pubs/working_papers/WR240z20.html.

Piketty, Thomas. 2014. *Capital in the Twenty-First Century.* Cambridge, Mass.: Harvard University Press.

Quillian, Lincoln. 2015. "A Comparison of Traditional and Discrete-Choice Approaches to the Analysis of Residential Mobility and Locational Attainment." *Annals of the American Academy of Political and Social Science* 660(1): 240–60.

Reardon, Sean F., and Kendra Bischoff. 2011. "Income Inequality and Income Segregation." *American Journal of Sociology* 116(4): 1092–53.

Sampson, Robert J. 2012. *Great American City: Chicago and the Enduring Neighborhood Effect.* Chicago: University of Chicago Press.

Sampson, Robert J., Robert D. Mare, and Kristin L. Perkins. 2015. "Achieving the Middle Ground in an Age of Concentrated Extremes: Mixed Middle-Income Neighborhoods and Emerging Adulthood." *Annals of the American Academy of Political and Social Science* 660(1): 156–74.

Sampson, Robert J., and Patrick T. Sharkey. 2008. "Neighborhood Selection and the Social Reproduction of Concentrated Racial Inequality." *Demography* 45(1): 1–29.

Sastry, Narayan, Bonnie Ghosh-Dastidar, John Adams, and Anne R. Pebley. 2006. "The Design of a Multilevel Survey of Children, Families, and Communities: The Los Angeles Family and Neighborhood Survey." *Social Science Research* 35(4): 1000–24.

Sastry, Narayan, and Anne R. Pebley. 2010. "Family and Neighborhood Sources of Socioeconomic Inequality in Children's Achievement." *Demography* 47(3): 777–800.

Shane, Scott. 2015. "Baltimore Riots Are Another Scar on a City Long Battered by Neglect." *New York Times*, April 29, 2015, p. A1. Accessed May 15, 2015. http://www.nytimes.com/2015/04/29/us/baltimore-riots-are-another-scar-on-a-city-battered-by-neglect.html.

Sharkey, Patrick T. 2013. *Stuck in Place: Urban Neighborhoods and the End of Progress Toward Racial Equality.* Chicago: University of Chicago Press.

Stack, Carol. 1974. *All Our Kin: Strategies for Survival in a Black Community.* New York: Harper and Row.

Sugrue, Thomas. 1996. *The Origins of the Urban Crisis: Race and Inequality in Post-War Detroit.* Princeton, N.J.: Princeton University Press.

Suttles, Gerald D. 1968. *The Social Order of the Slum: Ethnicity and Territory in the Inner City.* Chicago: University of Chicago Press.

Tatian, Peter A. 2003. "Neighborhood Change Database (NCDB) 1970–2000 Tract Data: Data Users Guide." Washington, D.C.: Urban Institute. Accessed December 1, 2014. http://www.geolytics.com/pdf/NCDB-LF-Data-Users-Guide.pdf.

Williams, Sonya, George Galster, and Nandita Verma. 2013. "The Disparate Neighborhood Impacts of the Great Recession: Evidence from Chicago." *Urban Geography* 34(6): 737–63.

Wilson, William Julius. 1987. *The Truly Disadvantaged: The Inner City, the Underclass, and Public Policy*. Chicago: University of Chicago Press.

Zorbaugh, Henry. 1929. *The Gold Coast and the Slum: A Sociological Study of Chicago's Near North Side*. Chicago: University of Chicago Press.

From Bad to Worse: How Changing Inequality in Nearby Areas Impacts Local Crime

JOHN R. HIPP AND CHARIS E. KUBRIN

Recognition is growing that criminogenic neighborhood effects may not end at the borders of local communities, that neighborhoods are located relative to one another in ways that shape local crime rates. Inspired by this insight, this research explores the changing spatial distribution of race and income around a location and determines how such changes are associated with crime patterns and trends in neighborhoods in Los Angeles. We examine how changes from 2000 to 2010 in the income composition, racial composition, and intersection of these two constructs are linked with changes in levels of crime across local areas. We find that neighborhoods experiencing greater increases in spatial inequality in a broader area (two and a half miles around the neighborhood) experience greater increases in crime levels in the focal area over the decade, and that this pattern is strongest for neighborhoods simultaneously experiencing increasing average household income or increasing inequality. We also find that neighborhoods simultaneously experiencing increases in inequality and racial-ethnic heterogeneity experience increases in crime.

Keywords: neighborhoods, crime, egohoods, spatial effects, inequality

Most neighborhood crime studies focus on the effects of community-level conditions on crime within the communities where these conditions exist. For the most part, this literature has been silent about the possibility that community-to-community effects may not be bound by geographic proximity, that what occurs in neighborhoods may be affected by conditions external to them (Mears and Bhati 2006, 510). For some, this is problematic given that "many intervention efforts have failed because they did not adequately address the pressures toward crime in the community that derive from forces external to the community in the wider social structure" (Morenoff, Sampson, and Raudenbush 2001, 552).

More recently, however, researchers are recognizing the importance of studying communities as part of a broader social context. Along these lines, researchers examine spillover effects of violence leading, for example, to similar rates of violence among geographically contiguous communities (for example, Morenoff, Sampson, and Raudenbush 2001; Raleigh and Galster 2014). Other researchers consider the displacement of crime from one area to another due to an intervention targeting a specific area (for example, Weisburd and McEwen 1998). And still other researchers determine

---

John R. Hipp is professor in the Department of Criminology, Law, and Society and the Department of Sociology at the University of California, Irvine. **Charis E. Kubrin** is professor in the Department of Criminology, Law, and Society and the Department of Sociology at the University of California, Irvine.

© 2017 Russell Sage Foundation. Hipp, John R., and Charis E. Kubrin. 2017. "From Bad to Worse: How Changing Inequality in Nearby Areas Impacts Local Crime." *RSF: The Russell Sage Foundation Journal of the Social Sciences* 3(2): 129–51. DOI: 10.7758/RSF.3.2.06. This research is supported in part by NIJ grant 2012-R2-CX-0010. We thank George Galster and Nicholas Branic for comments on an earlier draft of this paper. Direct correspondence to: John R. Hipp at john.hipp@UCI.edu, Department of Criminology, Law, and Society, University of California, Irvine, 3311 Social Ecology II, Irvine, CA 92697; and Charis E. Kubrin at ckubrin@uci.edu, Department of Criminology, Law, and Society, University of California, Irvine, Social Ecology II, Room 3379, Irvine, CA 92697.

whether crime "hot spots" have spillover effects, with violence diffusing from these areas to geographically proximate communities (for example, Sherman, Gartin, and Buerger 1989). These are all excellent developments in the quest to identify and model "unbounded community effects" (Mears and Bhati 2006, 511), yet this literature does not sufficiently consider whether local area social conditions, particularly racial composition and income inequality, influence violence in spatially neighboring communities. That is, rather than simply asking whether crime in nearby areas impacts crime in a specific neighborhood (Hipp 2007; Morenoff, Sampson, and Raudenbush 2001), we can ask whether the sociodemographic characteristics of nearby areas impact the level of crime in a neighborhood (Kubrin and Hipp 2014; Peterson and Krivo 2010).

This general gap in scholarship has some notable exceptions. Recent research by Daniel Mears and Avinash Bhati (2006), Ruth Peterson and Lauren Krivo (2010), Patrick Sharkey (2014), and Elizabeth Griffiths (2013), for example, considers how spatial inequality plays an important role for social change in neighborhoods. In all of these studies, researchers find that, in varying ways, some neighborhoods experience a significant "spatial disadvantage," which may have serious implications for their crime rates (Sharkey 2014, 909).

In this study, we build on the growing literature by taking up recent calls to "consider the ways in which individual neighborhoods are embedded within highly stratified urban landscapes that may influence the risks and opportunities to which individuals are exposed throughout different stages of the life course" (Sharkey 2014, 937). In particular, we examine the relationship between the changing racial and income composition of the neighborhood, and nearby areas, and changes in neighborhood crime rates. The study is conducted on neighborhoods in the city of Los Angeles from 2000 to 2010. We make several innovative contributions to the literature.

Our first contribution is to move beyond administrative units for defining neighborhoods and instead use egohoods, as recently introduced by John Hipp and Adam Boessen (2013). Egohoods are overlapping concentric circles that surround each block in the city. The egohood approach builds on insights from the mental mapping literature, the social networks literature, the daily activities pattern literature, and the travel to crime literature. Egohoods are conceptualized as waves washing across the surface of cities, as opposed to independent units with non-overlapping boundaries. These spatially overlapping units more appropriately capture the true amount of social interaction between residents of various groups.

A second innovation is that whereas the growing body of spatial neighborhood research has focused on the relationship between nearby disadvantage and neighborhood crime (primarily based on socioeconomic measures but sometimes on the share of minorities in a neighborhood), we construct and use measures of income distribution (inequality) and racial-ethnic heterogeneity. We employ these measures to assess the relationship between inequality and heterogeneity in the neighborhood, and nearby, with crime rates.

Third, a limitation of existing literature on the relationship between spatial inequality and crime is the frequent use of cross-sectional analyses and the treatment of this relationship as static. We argue instead that it is necessary to explore this potentially dynamic relationship with longitudinal data to better understand how spatial inequality and crime are related. A novel contribution, therefore, is to use longitudinal data and models to explore the consequences of changes in neighborhood characteristics for changing levels of crime.

Finally, an important consideration is the potential limitation of focusing on inequality solely within a neighborhood and a small surrounding area. Rather, the level of inequality in a much broader area may also have important consequences. Given evidence in the literature that higher levels of inequality in larger units such as cities affect crime in those units (see, for example, Blau and Blau 1982; Messner and Golden 1992), a natural question is whether inequality at larger scales will impact crime levels in local neighborhoods. Our innovation is to explore this possibility by focusing on whether any change in inequality in a broader area surrounding an egohood is associated with the change in crime in the egohood itself.

NEIGHBORHOODS, SPATIAL INEQUALITY, AND CRIME

Scholars working within the social disorganization theory framework often focus exclusively on the impact of structural conditions on crime within neighborhoods. In line with this approach, neighborhoods with higher levels of economic disadvantage, residential instability, and racial-ethnic heterogeneity are posited to have more social disorganization and hence more crime. Although this research has provided considerable insights, a limitation is that it often neglects conditions in nearby areas. Given the well-documented finding that offenders travel distances to crime that frequently exceed the typical size of the neighborhoods used in such studies (for example, Rossmo 2000), this approach likely overlooks an important component of the social processes generating crime in neighborhoods by failing to account for conditions in nearby areas. Fortunately, researchers are increasingly recognizing the importance of taking into account the effect of nearby areas (Mast and Wilson 2013; Mears and Bhati 2006; Popkin et al. 2012).

Despite this recent push to consider spatial areas surrounding neighborhoods, research rarely considers the presence of spatial inequality. We define *spatial inequality* as inequality that exists across areas without specific boundaries. *Inequality* more generally is a concept that fundamentally refers to a specific unit, for example, the level of inequality for a city, a county, or a country. Alternatively, spatial inequality refers to the case where units are more difficult, or even impossible, to explicitly define. Spatial inequality, then, refers to inequality that occurs not in previously defined non-overlapping units (for example, cities or counties) but rather across overlapping units based on some distance from a neighborhood. Although some researchers measure the level of inequality in neighborhoods (Crutchfield 1989; Hipp 2007; Hipp and Yates 2011; Messner and Tardiff 1986), the boundaries of neighborhoods themselves are quite contested and uncertain. Thus, if the scale at which the social process of inequality affects levels of crime is not consistent with the boundaries of certain units such as neighborhoods or cities, then measuring the level of inequality contained in various subareas of a city—spatial inequality—is critical. This is generally known as the modifiable areal unit problem (Openshaw and Taylor 1979).

Only a handful of studies have begun to address the issue of how the spatial pattern of concentrated disadvantage across the landscape might be important; nonetheless, these studies have not explicitly measured *inequality*. For example, Sharkey (2014) descriptively explores the spatial patterning of economic disadvantage by the racial composition of neighborhoods. Using national data from the 1970–2000 Censuses, Sharkey integrates spatially lagged measures of neighborhood characteristics into an analysis of neighborhood inequality (measured at the census tract level) to produce a more comprehensive picture of the residential environments surrounding different racial and ethnic groups, including their neighborhoods as well as those that border them. He notes a distinct spatial pattern in which black middle-class neighborhoods were more likely to be located near poorer neighborhoods than were white middle-class neighborhoods. Although his study does not focus on the consequences of these spatial patterns for neighborhood crime rates, it does highlight the importance of such patterns.

In another set of studies, Peterson and Krivo (2009, 2010) explore the spatial patterning of neighborhoods, measured as tracts, based on racial composition and concentrated disadvantage using data from the National Neighborhood Crime Study. In their study of neighborhoods in ninety-one U.S. cities at one point in time, the authors (2010) evaluate whether the character of neighboring areas—reflected by levels of disadvantage, residential instability, immigration, community investments, and white residents—accounts for differentials in crime over and above differences produced by the internal character of neighborhoods. Although they do not measure inequality per se, they do find that the level of economic disadvantage in nearby areas was positively related to crime levels in the focal neighborhood. Moreover, they find that while white neighborhoods benefit from the dual privileges of low internal disadvantage and embeddedness within a context of other white and advantaged areas, African American and Latino neighborhoods suffer a double jeopardy—they are at risk of greater violence stemming from their own internal, often highly disadvantaged, character and they bear the brunt of isolation from violence-reducing structures and processes because they are surrounded by disadvantaged areas (2010, 104).

Finally, Mears and Bhati (2006) examine whether resource deprivation (measured using an index combining the percentage of families with children headed by females, percentage of the resident population below the poverty level, unemployment rate, median household income, and median family income) contributes not only to local area violence but also to violence in geographically contiguous (and to noncontiguous but socially similar) communities in Chicago. Despite their focus on the spatial and social patterning of disadvantage, they did not measure inequality. Still, Mears and Bhati find that higher resource deprivation is associated with higher homicide rates, regardless of spatial location. Collectively, these studies push our thinking regarding the importance of concentrated disadvantage in nearby areas but what remains necessary is to explicitly consider the relationship between spatial *inequality* and crime—the focus of the current research.

Theoretical and Methodological Challenges

Despite the relative lack of research, theoretical reasons why spatial inequality may have important consequences for neighborhood crime exist. In social disorganization theory, for example, economic differences between residents are expected to reduce social interactions and subsequent levels of informal social control (Hipp 2007; Kubrin and Weitzer 2003). In routine activities theory and its geographic expression in crime pattern theory, to the extent that the wealthy represent more attractive targets and the poor are more likely to be offenders due to limited economic resources, the close proximity of these groups—which reflects spatial inequality—is expected to generate more crime (Rountree and Land 1996; Smith, Frazee, and Davison 2000). Finally, relative deprivation theory posits that economic inequality entails conflict of interest over the distribution of resources, which spells a potential for violence (Blau and Blau 1982). Inequality can lead members of the disadvantaged group to feel deprived and therefore they are more likely to respond by committing crime (Agnew 1999; Messner and Golden 1992; Taylor and Covington 1988).

Despite these theoretical arguments, empirical support in the literature documenting this relationship is relatively scant. This is likely due to methodological limitations of existing research rather than to a failing of these theories. As Hipp and Boessen (2013) explain, a feature of nearly all constructed neighborhoods in existing research is defining neighborhood boundaries such that they yield similarity within the neighborhood and generate difference across neighborhoods. This approach has strong implications for assessing the impact of spatial inequality; effectively, the boundaries of such neighborhoods attempt to remove all inequality within neighborhoods. The consequence is that studies of neighborhood inequality and crime often find a minimal relationship given that most of the spatial inequality in the larger area has been defined away (Crutchfield 1989; Messner and Tardiff 1986).

Hipp and Boessen (2013) suggest two possible solutions. One is to explicitly model spatial inequality across units such as census tracts. This approach at least attempts to recapture some of the spatial inequality that was systematically removed in defining neighborhoods. A second, and better, solution Hipp and Boessen ultimately implemented is to use a definition of neighborhoods that does not rely on non-overlapping boundaries—an approach they term *egohoods*. This approach considers egohoods to be centered on a block and to include some area surrounding the block to capture the activity patterns of residents. The result is that egohoods are overlapping "waves washing across the surface of cities" (Hipp and Boessen 2013, 287). An egohood takes a block as the center point and then incorporates all other blocks within a particular-sized buffer to be part of it.

Egohoods are distinct from other approaches that might appear the same at first blush. For example, some research has measured levels of inequality in existing units as well as in nearby units (Raleigh and Galster 2014). However, such approaches still measure inequality based on non-overlapping units that are typically predefined (by the U.S. Census) and therefore treat the units as being appropriate for measuring inequality. The egohood approach differs in that it combines small discrete units (blocks) into larger units, and then computes the level of inequality in these larger, overlapping units. Another strategy that appears similar to the egohoods approach is what Hipp and Boessen (2013) refer to as the individual social environment (ISE) perspective. In the ISE approach, the focus is on how some environment measured as the buffer around a person's residence affects the individual. This approach is common in the public health literature (Brownson et al. 2009) and is explored using data in a Scandinavian context (Andersson and Musterd 2010). This approach also underlies the segregation measures that Sean Reardon and his colleagues developed (2008). The egohoods approach differs in that it does not posit that this surrounding area acts on the block at the center of the buffer as is done in the ISE approach, but rather that the entire buffer operates as an ecological unit of interest.

Hipp and Boessen (2013) show that employing egohoods as the unit of analysis resulted in a model that better predicts the location of crime than a model using non-overlapping units such as tracts did. Particularly notable is their finding that the relationship between inequality and crime was extremely strong in the egohoods approach, but nonexistent when using census tracts, highlighting the methodological limitation of prior research using traditional units to test this relationship. They also show that the ISE approach found essentially no such effect of inequality. Hipp and Boessen also discover that the racial-ethnic heterogeneity-crime relationship was often stronger when employing egohoods as the unit of analysis. Indeed, heterogeneity is conceptually similar in key ways to inequality; to the extent that neighborhoods are defined based on racial homogeneity, then such neighborhoods artificially understate the racial heterogeneity across the social environment. Egohoods appropriately capture this heterogeneity and therefore are better able to detect the possible relationship with crime rates.

Although Hipp and Boessen (2013) compare results using egohoods with different sized buffers, it was beyond the scope of their study to explore whether inequality levels in the area *surrounding* the egohood had any additional impact on crime rates within the egohood, something we address in the current study. Such spatial inequality can be conceptualized in different ways. One approach compares the average socioeconomic status (SES) in the egohood to that in the surrounding area, allowing one to test whether the difference in the average SES in the two locations has an impact on crime levels in the egohood. This approach, however, ignores the level of inequality within the egohood or in the surrounding area. Therefore, a second approach tests whether inequality in the surrounding area impacts crime in the egohood and a variant of this approach considers whether this nearby inequality is accentuated when inequality is high within the egohood itself.

Another important extension for exploring the spatial inequality-crime relationship is to move beyond static, cross-sectional approaches and instead to focus on change in neighborhoods. Given that theories such as defended neighborhoods theory (Grattet 2009; Green, Strolovitch, and Wong 1998) argue it is the change in neighborhood composition that has critical consequences for crime, cross-sectional models assuming a system in equilibrium are unable to capture such dynamic processes. Likewise, whereas relative deprivation theory (Agnew 1999; Hipp 2007; Messner and Golden 1992; Taylor and Covington 1988) focuses on how perceptions of inequality may lead to a sense of injustice and hence more crime, it may be that changes in inequality levels are particularly salient to residents and, therefore, may have the strongest impact on changes in crime levels. Longitudinal data that explicitly measure such changes are needed to assess this claim.

Beyond changes in inequality is the likely importance that changes in the racial-ethnic composition have for crime. Occasional research has explored the relationship between racial-ethnic change and neighborhood crime (Green, Strolovitch, and Wong 1998; Kubrin 2000), but next to no studies have considered whether the spatial patterning of this racial change is consequential. In particular, it may be that racial-ethnic churning, when accompanied by increasing inequality, has a particularly pronounced relationship with changes in crime. This may occur because simultaneous changes in the racial composition as well as the economic distribution may be perceived as a strong threat to the stability of the neighborhood, resulting in more pronounced withdrawal from the neighborhood and hence lowered collective efficacy. We explore this possible interaction effect in the analyses.

Broader Spatial Impact

We have so far considered only that neighborhood inequality and inequality of nearby areas might affect neighborhood crime levels. Yet spatial inequality may play out on a larger geographic scale with consequences for neighborhood crime. Given theories focusing on the consequences of inequality at larger scales, this is certainly a plausible suggestion.

Various theories posit why spatial inequality at a larger scale might impact levels of crime. We highlight two broad perspectives. First, higher levels of inequality in a larger community reduce the level of social capital among residents, resulting in residents who are less willing to provide resources to more disadvantaged neighborhoods that would allow them to address crime problems (Putnam 1995). A consequence is that this broader scale inequality would generate higher crime levels in neighborhoods. We might also expect this spatial inequality to result in higher crime rates in lower-income neighborhoods, given their inability to obtain resources to combat crime and disorder from the broader community.

A second possible mechanism is that higher levels of inequality across a broader spatial area create a sense of injustice among some residents, the result of which would be more offenders in the environment (Blau and Blau 1982). Relative deprivation theory posits that feelings of injustice can result from inequality, but defining the appropriate reference group, especially geographically, is particularly challenging (Hipp 2007). It may be that the level of inequality within a neighborhood, or nearby, is not the proper scale at which such feelings of injustice are engendered if residents take into account inequality at a larger spatial scale. If such perceived injustice indeed creates more offenders, and offenders have specific spatial patterns in where they offend as evidenced in the journey to crime literature (Rossmo 2000), then we would expect to see higher levels of crime in egohoods. That is, residents may perceive this spatial inequality as structural inequality that reduces their opportunities and therefore, be less willing to pursue educational opportunities that could enable employment in high-quality mainstream jobs. To the extent that a lack of quality employment changes the calculus of residents in choosing between employment in the mainstream economy and crime (Bushway 2011), this would indeed result in more offenders.

Notably, nearly all studies exploring inequality at larger scales also have measured crime rates at similarly large geographic scales (for example, Blau and Blau 1982; Harer and Steffensmeier 1992; Messner and Golden 1992). Thus, researchers have typically failed to explore whether inequality at a larger scale has consequences for crime levels in certain types of neighborhoods within the larger area. We might expect, for example, that the most vulnerable areas—those that are more structurally disadvantaged and socially disorganized—are more likely to be negatively affected by greater inequality in the broader spatial area around them, in large part because these areas lack the internal dynamics to combat crime. This implies an interaction effect, which we assess in the analyses.

Another limitation of this literature is that studies typically use politically determined units of analysis (such as cities, counties, and so on). In relatively dense urban areas, it is questionable whether city boundaries provide a substantively important break in the social environment between cities (for a more complete discussion of this issue, see Hipp and Roussell 2013). If, in fact, social interactions among residents—as well as offenders—transgress city boundaries, then analyses that assume these boundaries capture substantively important units may impose incorrect assumptions. This issue is similar to the earlier discussion of the problem with defining neighborhoods. One solution is consistent with the egohoods approach and uses boundaries around various neighborhood units, but with a much larger-sized buffer (Hipp and Roussell 2013). Although Hipp and Aaron Roussell (2013) suggest drawing large-scale buffers around each neighborhood in a community, they lack the fine-grained crime data we use in this study to explore whether this larger-scale spatial inequality is related to crime in the local neighborhood.

It also may be that changes in spatial inequality in the broader area have important consequences. As inequality increases at the larger spatial scale, the impact the increase has on residents' perceptions may be particularly strong, reducing their sense of social capital as well as their sense of "being in it together." Despite these theoretical possibilities, we are aware of no studies that explore this question.

Before turning to a description of our data and methods, we consider a complication—that crime itself can play a role in neighborhood change. It can do so because crime induces residential mobility in general, induces disproportionate residential mobility by higher income residents, and induces disproportionate residential mobility by white residents. Regarding general mobility, a burgeoning literature shows that crime can lead to residential mobility (Dugan 1999; Xie and McDowall 2008). Neighborhood studies have also detected this pattern. Census tracts in Chicago with high numbers of homicides experienced population losses over time (Morenoff, Sampson, and Raudenbush 2001), and a study of neighborhoods across thirteen cities found that higher levels of crime led to population loss and increased vacancies ten years later (Hipp 2010a). Regarding disproportionate mobility based on economic resources, studies find that crime in neighborhoods can lead to disproportionate mobility based on economic resources, which will lead to lower average income and lower home values in these neighborhoods. For example, neighborhoods with higher rates of crime have lower home values (Buck and Hakim 1989; Schwartz, Susin, and Voicu 2003; Thaler 1978), and neighborhoods experiencing increasing levels of crime also experience decreasing relative home values (Hipp, Tita, and Greenbaum 2009; Tita, Petras, and Greenbaum 2006). Evidence also suggests disproportionate mobility by race-ethnicity of residents. To the extent that racial-ethnic minorities have limited access to certain neighborhoods, they may be less able to leave a neighborhood with more crime and more likely to enter one. For example, evidence shows that black homeowners are more likely to enter more disadvantaged neighborhoods independent of their socioeconomic resources (Deng, Ross, and Wachter 2003). Studies also find that such disproportionate mobility by minorities is related to victimization experiences for residents on a block (Xie and McDowall 2010), the perception of crime among residents on a block (Hipp 2010b), and levels of violence in the broader neighborhood (Hipp 2011). Longitudinal studies of neighborhoods in Chicago find that higher delinquency rates were associated with more nonwhites at the next time point (Bursik 1986), and that increasing homicide rates were associated with more black residents ten years later (Morenoff and Sampson 1997). Finally, a study of neighborhoods across thirteen cities likewise indicates that higher levels of violence were associated with higher proportions of African Americans ten years later (Hipp 2010a). This literature suggests that certain neighborhood structural characteristics may be endogenous to crime. Specifically, residential instability, poverty, and the presence of racial-ethnic minorities are all potentially affected by levels of neighborhood crime.

Yet we argue that the pattern is more complicated when considering distributional measures such as economic inequality and racial-ethnic heterogeneity. If anything, we would expect these measures to decrease in neighborhoods with more crime. That is, if higher income residents are more likely to leave a neighborhood because of its higher crime rates, then the neighborhood will not only become poorer over time but will have lower levels of inequality (given that mostly low-income residents remain in the neighborhood). The logic is the same for racial-ethnic heterogeneity: to the extent that white households are disproportionately leaving a neighborhood, it will transition into a neighborhood with more racial-ethnic minorities but less racial-ethnic heterogeneity. Given that our analytic technique is descriptive, we do not attempt to disentangle these relationships by using instrumental variables. We merely raise these points to highlight that we are particularly unlikely to detect a positive relationship between the change in inequality in a neighborhood and the change in crime given these previously observed mobility patterns. Furthermore, it is particularly difficult to predict how crime in local neighborhoods might systematically affect the level of inequality in broader area. Nonetheless, our analytic strategy is one simply trying to describe these patterns.

DATA AND METHODS

Our study area is the city of Los Angeles, an ideal location given levels of racial and ethnic heterogeneity and large disparities in income levels. This study site allows us to explore the patterns of spatial inequality in a city whose sprawling suburban growth is representative of newer Sunbelt cities that have blossomed since the end of World War II in the United States.

Data

Crime data come from the Los Angeles city police department. The dependent variables are created from crime reports officially coded and reported by the police department. We classified crime events into five Uniform Crime Report crime types: aggravated assault, robbery, burglary, motor vehicle theft, and larceny. We averaged these measures over three years at the beginning (2000–2002) and the end (2009–2011) to minimize yearly fluctuations. Given that we know the actual location of all crime events, we were able to aggregate this information into egohoods. We do not compute these measures as crime rates because doing so would generate missing values for observations with no population. We instead residualize these results by directly including population in the models.

Unit of Analysis: Egohoods, and Surrounding Area

The notion of egohoods, first introduced by Hipp and Boessen (2013), begins by identifying each block in the city and drawing a buffer around each individual block. This buffer represents the egohood for a particular block and includes all blocks whose centroids are contained in this buffer. Thus, whereas the U.S. Census uses tracts, block groups, and blocks—all of which are based on a common population size—egohoods are based on a common area size. For this study, we used a buffer of one-quarter mile given Hipp and Boessen found that this sized egohood often revealed a relatively stronger relationship with crime relative to larger buffers. We also, however, take into account the area surrounding the egohood. For variables that the census aggregates to blocks, it is straightforward to sum all of the blocks within an egohood to compute the measures. The city of Los Angeles includes 29,157 egohoods, one for each block.

A novel contribution of the present study is not only to compute egohoods, but also to compute information on the area surrounding these egohoods. Conceptually, these areas can be thought of as donuts; where the egohood captures a particular sized area around a block (quarter-mile buffers in this study), we also measure the next quarter mile radius around the egohood as a spatial area of interest (the donut).

Constructing the Measures

The covariates in the models come from data collected by the 2000 U.S. Census, the 2007–2011 American Community Survey five-year estimates, and the Southern California Association of Governments, which contains land use data. We aggregate the data to egohoods at the beginning and end time points, and then compute difference variables for all variables described in this section.

We capture change in the economic environment of the egohood with two measures: average household income and household income inequality. To construct the average income measure, at each time point we first assign household incomes to the midpoint of their reported range (the census only reports household incomes in particular ranges), and compute the average income for residents from this information.[1] We then compute the difference in this measure over the two time points. Household income inequality is measured as the standard deviation (SD) of the logged household income. We compute the midpoints of the income bins, log transform these values, multiply them by the number of observations in each bin, compute the mean logged household income, and determine the standard deviation of income based on these values. We then calculate the difference in this measure at the two time points.

A challenge for constructing the inequality measures is that the census data regarding income is aggregated to block groups. Where Hipp and Boessen (2013) use a population-weighted approach to apportion such data to blocks, we use a more principled imputation approach for our inequality measures. Our approach exploits the fact that the census provides information on the income distribution by racial-ethnic group in each block group and provides information on the composition of racial-ethnic groups in each block. To get the representation (R) of group g of G groups in a particular block, we compute the proportion of group members in the block group who live in a particular block:

$$R_g = g_b / g_g, \qquad (1)$$

where g_b is the population of group g in the block (b) of 1 to G groups and g_g is the population of group g in the block group (g). To obtain an estimate of the number of persons for an income category (IC) in the block (b) in a particular income category q of Q categories provided by the census for group A, we multiply the number of persons in a bin for the block group (g) by the group representation (R) in the block:

$$IC_{qb} = IC_{qg} * R_g. \qquad (2)$$

After computing equation (2) for each of the G groups, we generate estimates of the number of persons in each income category for each of the groups in the blocks. These can be used to aggregate the information of all blocks in the egohood and then to compute inequality measures by racial group. We use this information for each of the separate groups and sum them together within each block, and then sum them over all the blocks in the egohood to compute the overall level of inequality in the egohood (as the standard deviation).

To capture the possible disruptive effects of a lack of oversight from single-parent households, we construct a measure of the change in the percentage of single-parent households. Although researchers often combine this measure into a scale of concentrated disadvantage that might include average income, we keep these two measures separate to assess their independent relationship with changing crime rates. The correlation between these measures for our change variables is not as high as for cross-sectional measures: these change variables are correlated at –0.60 in egohoods and –0.68 in the surrounding area. With our large sample, we are able to empirically distinguish between these two relationships.

We measure the changing racial-ethnic composition of the egohood using three approaches: the percentage in various racial-ethnic categories; racial-ethnic heterogeneity; and racial-ethnic churning (Pastor, Sadd, and Hipp 2001). The change in the racial-ethnic composition is captured by measures of the change in the percentage African American, Latino, and Asian (with percentage white and other race as the reference category). We measure racial-ethnic heterogeneity with the Herfindahl index of the same five racial-ethnic groups at each time point, and then compute the difference over the two time points. We measure ethnic churning of the same five groups as

$$EC_k = \sqrt{\sum_1^J (G_{jt} - G_{jt-1})^2}, \qquad (3)$$

where G represents the proportion of the population of ethnic group j out of J ethnic groups at time t (2010) and time t-1 (2000) in egohood k. This yields a measure of the degree of racial-ethnic transformation that occurred in the tract during the decade (this is a sum of squares

---

1. For the highest range, we assigned the value as being 25 percent greater than the bottom value in the range.

of differences and we take the square root to return it approximately to the original metric) (Hipp and Lakon 2010). If racial-ethnic composition does not change, it will have a value of zero.

These measures are conceptually different in how they represent change in the racial-ethnic composition of an egohood. The parameters for the composition measures are capturing the change in crime given a change in the composition of a particular group; thus, the coefficient for the change in percentage black shows the change in crime when a neighborhood experiences an increase in the percentage black and an equal decrease in the percentage white or other race (given that this is the reference category). This parameterization implies that a similar increase in the percentage white or other race along with a decrease in the percentage black will have an opposite relationship with the crime rate. As such, it presumes that something about the specific group moving in will be related to the crime rate. In contrast, the ethnic churning measure posits that *any* change in the racial-ethnic composition of an egohood will have an equal relationship with the change in crime. Thus, for example, a neighborhood that experiences a 10 percentage point increase in any group will experience the same change in crime regardless of which group is moving in. This implies that something about change in the racial composition in and of itself is related to crime rates; indeed, such churning may reduce collective efficacy and therefore result in more crime (Sampson, Raudenbush, and Earls 1997). Finally, the parameter for the change in racial-ethnic heterogeneity implies that change in the racial-ethnic composition will have a distinctly different relationship with crime when heterogeneity is increasing in the egohood than when it is decreasing. For example, a 10 percentage point increase in blacks in a neighborhood that is 30 percent black and 70 percent white will result in an increase in the level of heterogeneity but the same 10 percentage point increase in blacks in a neighborhood that is 70 percent black and 30 percent white will result in a decrease in the level of heterogeneity. This parameterization tests whether these types of change have differential associations with the change in crime.

To minimize the possibility of obtaining spurious results, we include several additional measures that may be related to the change in crime in egohoods. Given prior work suggesting that home owners are more willing to provide social control capability, we include a measure of the change in the percentage owners in the egohood. Evidence indicates that vacant units can be crime generators (Kubrin and Hipp 2014; Rice and Smith 2002; Smith, Frazee, and Davison 2000) and we therefore construct a measure of the change in the percentage vacant units. Life-course literature suggests that the ages sixteen to twenty-nine are the prime ages of offenders. We therefore construct a measure of the change in the percentage ages sixteen to twenty-nine in the egohood. To capture the presence of nearby persons, we include a measure of the change in population in the egohood (given the constant areal size of egohoods, this is effectively a measure of population density).

Because certain land use types can be crime generators (Kubrin and Hipp 2014; Stucky and Ottensmann 2009), we construct measures of the change in the percentage of land area that is one of six types of land use: office, industrial, retail, residential, vacant, and other (such as parking lots, parks, cemeteries, and so on).

We also construct similar measures for the quarter-mile area surrounding each egohood by computing similar measures in half-mile egohoods and then subtracting the quarter-mile egohood values. Finally, we compute measures of the socioeconomic status of the broader area by computing the average income and inequality in a 2.5-mile egohood of the block. This broader area captures a much larger context. For example, whereas the average population for a quarter-mile egohood in the study area is 2,130 persons and for a half-mile egohood is 8,814 persons, it is just under 200,000 for a 2.5-mile egohood.[2] Thus, these measures are indeed capturing a quite broad

---

2. We do not subtract the characteristics of the half-mile buffer within this larger 2.5-mile buffer, given that it is a relatively small proportion of the total area. Indeed, the half-mile buffer is less than 5 percent of the 2.5-mile buffer.

Table 1. Summary Statistics

	Mean	SD	Mean	SD
Crime in egohood				
Aggravated assault	-37.04	46.73		
Robbery	-7.34	19.18		
Burglary	-10.66	21.26		
Motor vehicle theft	-16.69	24.60		
Larceny	-60.13	96.97		
Demographics	Egohood		Surrounding area	
Income inequality	-0.01	0.14	-0.01	0.10
Average household income	0.25	0.37	0.27	0.25
Racial-ethnic heterogeneity	0.01	0.08	0.01	0.06
Ethnic churning	0.13	0.11	0.11	0.08
Percent black	-1.42	5.46	-1.52	4.03
Percent Asian	0.91	4.82	1.05	2.74
Percent Latino	2.51	8.66	2.38	6.32
Percent vacant units	1.60	5.71	1.74	3.53
Percent owners	-0.58	8.52	-0.51	5.56
Percent single-parent households	-3.75	4.44	-4.03	3.75
Percent age sixteen to twenty-nine	0.42	5.00	0.26	2.91
Population	-0.08	0.92	129.98	919.66
Land use				
Percent office land use	0.03	0.07		
Percent industrial land use	-0.01	0.08		
Percent retail land use	0.04	0.10		
Percent residential land use	-0.23	0.25		
Percent vacant lots	-0.01	0.06		
Change in surrounding 2.5 mile area				
Average income	0.29	0.06		
Inequality	-0.01	0.03		

Source: Authors' compilation.
Note: Variables measured in quarter mile egohoods, and surrounding quarter mile. All measures capture change from 2000 to 2010.

context. The summary statistics for the variables used in the analyses are presented in table 1.

Methods

The outcome measures represent the change in the number of crime events between the first and last time points. Given that they can have negative values, it is not feasible to estimate the models as negative binomial regression models. We instead estimate linear regression models. The first set includes the main effects of our variables of interest. The second set assesses whether the relationships between changing inequality and changing crime rates are moderated by certain characteristics. We test several moderating relationships. First, we create a multiplicative measure of inequality in the egohood and inequality in the surrounding area to determine whether this spatial patterning moderates the results. Second, we assess whether changing inequality and racial-ethnic heterogeneity operate in tandem by constructing multiplicative measures of inequality and racial-ethnic heterogeneity in the egohood, and in the surrounding quarter mile. Third, we examine whether the relationship of the change in inequality in the egohood or sur-

Table 2. Models Predicting Change in Crime from 2000 to 2010

	Aggravated Assault	Robbery	Burglary	Motor Vehicle Theft	Larceny
Egohood					
Income inequality	-1.727	-2.0269*	0.529	-0.3744	-10.762**
	-0.9	-2.22	0.52	-0.33	-2.66
Average household income	-5.3143**	-1.6426**	-1.5822**	-0.4878	-2.4146
	-6.22	-4.03	-3.53	-0.97	-1.34
Ethnic churning	48.7338**	3.6324**	-1.2155	7.0134**	-19.221**
	18.2	2.85	-0.86	4.45	-3.41
Racial-ethnic heterogeneity	21.1866**	1.6426	1.2246	0.7025	28.586**
	5.79	0.94	0.64	0.33	3.71
Percent black	0.5178**	0.0882**	-0.1069**	-0.2733**	-0.3483*
	7.8	2.79	-3.07	-6.99	-2.49
Percent Asian	-0.4172**	0.1176**	0.0759*	-0.0748*	0.8814**
	-6.92	4.09	2.4	-2.11	6.94
Percent Latino	-0.1094**	0.094**	0.0905**	0.0151	0.8703**
	-2.81	5.07	4.43	0.66	10.62
Percent vacant units	0.1475**	0.0368†	0.0537*	-0.2131**	-0.0581
	3.52	1.84	2.44	-8.64	-0.66
Percent owners	0.166**	-0.0169	-0.0093	-0.0148	-0.0196
	6.03	-1.29	-0.64	-0.91	-0.34
Percent single-parent households	1.4449**	0.2892**	0.2875**	0.5845**	1.3074**
	23.7	9.96	8.98	16.29	10.19
Percent age sixteen to twenty-nine	0.0385	-0.1677**	-0.0021	0.1112**	-1.4748**
	0.77	-7.06	-0.08	3.79	-14.05
Population	-0.1872	-0.189	-0.5672**	0.0934	-4.066**
	-0.67	-1.42	-3.86	0.57	-6.89
Surrounding area					
Income inequality	-7.3686*	-27.626**	-11.269**	-3.9366*	-79.234**
	-2.23	-17.55	-6.49	-2.02	-11.39
Average household income	-24.007**	-21.8518**	-11.443**	-9.2061**	-74.521**
	-11.51	-21.99	-10.44	-7.49	-16.96
Ethnic churning	14.311**	2.8835	-0.1141	0.3097	-70.385**
	2.94	1.24	-0.04	0.11	-6.87
Racial-ethnic heterogeneity	52.7358**	10.2722**	23.5257**	23.137**	87.831**
	10.49	4.29	8.91	7.82	8.3
Percent black	1.2583**	-0.2155**	-0.4967**	-0.7538**	-1.0095**
	13.09	-4.71	-9.84	-13.32	-4.99
Percent Asian	-1.7226**	-0.1766**	-0.4532**	-1.2743**	-1.5517**
	-16.52	-3.56	-8.28	-20.76	-7.07
Percent Latino	-0.03	0.227**	0.3609**	-0.0341	2.0017**
	-0.5	7.95	11.47	-0.97	15.86
Percent vacant units	0.3049**	-0.3347**	-0.0237	-0.7551**	-1.4952**
	3.96	-9.12	-0.59	-16.65	-9.22
Percent owners	0.2609**	-0.1353**	-0.1346**	0.1399**	-0.7203**
	5.61	-6.11	-5.51	5.11	-7.36
Percent single-parent households	1.4801**	0.0903*	0.1372**	1.166**	1.8981**
	16.66	2.13	2.94	22.28	10.14

Table 2. (*cont.*)

	Aggravated Assault	Robbery	Burglary	Motor Vehicle Theft	Larceny
Percent age sixteen to twenty-nine	-0.2898**	-0.5461**	0.0537	-0.0944†	-1.7571**
	-3.11	-12.31	1.1	-1.72	-8.96
Population	-0.002**	-0.0021**	-0.0028**	0.0012**	-0.0134**
	-7.75	-16.72	-20.46	7.87	-24.27
Land use in egohood					
Percent office land use	-11.531**	2.3166	-15.565**	-38.826**	-100**
	-3.47	1.46	-8.92	-19.84	-14.82
Percent industrial land use	-40.167**	-15.5464**	-17.858**	-14.617**	-99.697**
	-14.29	-11.61	-12.1	-8.83	-16.84
Percent retail land use	-47.429**	-30.327**	-30.425**	-27.565**	-170**
	-21.24	-28.52	-25.95	-20.97	-35.2
Percent residential land use	-36.636**	-3.0648**	-9.468**	5.9359**	-54.025**
	-34.53	-6.06	-16.99	9.5	-24.18
Percent vacant lots	-28.765**	-6.6386**	-7.6593**	-15.325**	-69.341**
	-8.11	-3.93	-4.11	-7.34	-9.29
Broader 2.5 area					
Average income	-58.228**	-19.7598**	-33.234**	-53.411**	-110**
	-10.62	-7.57	-11.55	-16.55	-9.4
Inequality	309.698**	71.861**	37.3361**	47.226**	331.58**
	28.61	13.94	6.57	7.41	14.55
Intercept	-8.0763**	6.2898**	2.1292*	12.199**	6.0332†
	-5.01	8.2	2.52	12.86	1.78

Source: Authors' compilation.
Notes: T-values below coefficient estimates. Linear binomial regression models. N=29,157 egohoods. All measures capture change from 2000 to 2010.
†$p < .05$ (one-tail test); *$p < .05$ (two-tail test); **$p < .01$ (two-tail test)

rounding area is moderated by the level of inequality in the broader 2.5-mile egohood by constructing multiplicative interactions. Finally, we examine whether the level of inequality within 2.5 miles has the strongest impact on low-income egohoods by constructing a multiplicative interaction. By constructing difference variables, our fixed-effects models eliminate the influence of time-invariant unobserved characteristics of blocks and egohoods. They do not, however, remove the possibility of endogeneity. For this reason, we treat these results as descriptive of these inequality patterns.

RESULTS

The models assess the relationship between the change in our inequality measures and the change in crime over the decade. Turning first to the relationship with changing average income, we detect a relatively strong relationship in the egohood but an even stronger relationship for the surrounding buffer (see table 2). Egohoods experiencing an increase in average household income simultaneously experience decreases in aggravated assaults, robberies, and burglaries over the decade, controlling for the other measures in the models. A 1 SD increase in average household income is associated with between 0.027 and 0.042 SD decreases in these crime types. This could alternatively reflect a feedback effect of crime onto the level of income in the neighborhood. There is also a spatial pattern, given that egohoods surrounded by areas with falling average household incomes also experience an increase in all crime types during the decade. This is a strong relationship, and much stronger than that of income change within the egohood itself, because a 1 SD increase in average income in the surrounding area is associated with anywhere between 0.095 SD fewer motor vehicle thefts to 0.29 SD fewer robberies. Note the additional relationship with the increasing presence of single-parent households, even after accounting for the change in the average income, because egohoods experiencing an increase in single-parent households also experience sharp increases for all crime types during the decade (between 0.06 and 0.137 SDs). An additional spatial pattern is evident, because egohoods experiencing an increase in single-parent households in the surrounding area experience sharp increases in aggravated assaults and motor vehicle thefts as well as an increase in the other crime types.

The relationship between increasing inequality in the egohood and crime rates is modest. Egohoods with increasing inequality experience significantly decreasing robbery and larceny rates during the decade, holding constant the other measures. Furthermore, increasing inequality in the surrounding area has a negative relationship with these crime types, which is opposite expectations.

Whereas no evidence indicates that increasing inequality in the egohood or surrounding quarter mile is associated with higher levels of crime in an egohood, the economic conditions of the even broader 2.5-mile surrounding area have a quite strong association. An egohood with a 1 SD increase in inequality in the surrounding 2.5-mile area is associated with anywhere from a 0.046 SD increase in burglaries to a 0.174 SD increase in aggravated assaults. Likewise, an egohood with a 1 SD increase in average income in the surrounding 2.5-mile area will experience, on average, anywhere from 0.062 SD fewer robberies to 0.131 SD fewer motor vehicle thefts. These associations are quite strong, suggesting that accounting for this broader context is imperative.

The findings also reveal that changes in the racial-ethnic composition of the egohood are related to changes in the crime rate. However, the pattern differs across crime types and measures of racial change. For example, the relationship with ethnic churning is quite strong for aggravated assaults, even after controlling for changes in specific groups or changes in the level of racial-ethnic heterogeneity. A 1 SD increase in ethnic churning in an egohood is associated with a 0.111 SD increase in aggravated assaults, a 0.02 SD increase in robberies, and a 0.03 SD increase in motor vehicle thefts. Yet such neighborhoods also experience a 0.02 SD decrease in larcenies, holding constant the other measures. The actual change in the racial-ethnic composition matters: neighborhoods that experience an increase in percentage black and a simultaneous decrease in percentage white or other race are more likely to experience an increase in violent crime but a decrease in property crime. Again, this relationship with violence could also reflect disproportionate mobility out of the neighborhood by white residents. And neighborhoods that experience an increase in percentage Latino and a simultaneous decrease in percentage white or other race are more likely to experience increases in robberies, burglaries, and larcenies, which may also reflect, at least to some extent, disproportionate mobility. Finally, a neighborhood experiencing a 1 SD increase in racial-ethnic heterogeneity experiences, on average, a 0.037 SD increase in aggravated assault and 0.024 SD increase in larcenies. It is hard to explain this relationship in terms of disproportionate mobility given that prior evidence would imply that higher levels of crime would reduce levels of heterogeneity, at least in the long-term.

The change in the racial-ethnic composition of the surrounding area also appears related to crime levels. On the one hand, increasing ethnic churning in the surrounding area is associated with modest increases in aggravated assaults, but decreases in larcenies (and no change in the other crime types). On the other hand, increasing racial-ethnic heterogeneity in the surrounding area is associated with greater increases in all crime types in the egohood. A 1 SD increase in nearby racial-ethnic heterogeneity is associated with anywhere from a 0.034 SD increase in robberies to a 0.073 SD increase in aggravated assaults. Changes in the actual composition of the racial groups nearby have differential relationships: whereas increases in the percentage Latino nearby (compared to percentage white and other) are associated with greater increases in three of the crime types, increases in the percentage Asian nearby (compared with percentage white and other) are actually associated with greater decreases in all crime types. Likewise, increases in percentage black nearby (versus percentage white and other) are associated with greater decreases in all crime types (except aggravated assault), controlling for the other measures in the models.

Moderating Relationships with Inequality

We next explore whether the relationship between changes in inequality and crime rates in an egohood is moderated by the characteristics of the surrounding quarter mile area. The results for the models that include these interactions are shown in table 3. We find that the relationship between increasing inequality in the egohood and crime rates is attenuated when there are greater increases in inequality in the nearby area for robberies and larcenies. Figure 1 plots this relationship for changes in the robbery rate for egohoods with low, average, and high changes in inequality in the egohood or the nearby area (1 SD below the mean, the mean, and 1 SD above the mean, respectively). Egohoods with greater decreases in nearby inequality have the largest increases in robbery rates, as evidenced by the top line in this figure. Moreover, these egohoods will experience an even larger increase in robberies if they themselves are experiencing increasing inequality. In contrast, an egohood experiencing increasing inequality but that is surrounded by areas with increasing inequality is more likely to experience decreases in robberies (as shown in the bottom line in this figure). The plot for the larceny model looked similar (not shown).

When plotting the interactions between individual egohoods and the greater area (2.5 miles), we find that the broader context has a much stronger relationship with changes in crime rates than does the nearby context. For example, figure 2 demonstrates that the positive relationship with increasing inequality in the surrounding 2.5 miles dwarfs the relationship of changing inequality in the egohood itself (that is, the gap between the lines is much greater than is the difference in the steepness of the slopes). Nonetheless, when egohoods experience an increase in inequality, aggravated assault increases more, on average, when inequality is increasing in the surrounding 2.5-mile area. The pattern is similar when plotting the relationship for robberies or burglaries (not shown).

We next assess whether changing inequality has different associations with crime rates when it is accompanied by changing racial-ethnic heterogeneity. We find consistent evidence that all crime types increase more in egohoods that are simultaneously experiencing larger increases in inequality and racial-ethnic heterogeneity. For example, figure 3 illustrates that whereas the relationship between increasing racial-ethnic heterogeneity in the egohood and burglary rates is relatively flat in egohoods experiencing decreasing inequality, egohoods that are simultaneously experiencing increases in racial-ethnic heterogeneity and inequality experience the sharpest increases in burglary. The pattern for motor vehicle theft is similar (not shown). In the aggravated assault model, figure 4 shows that the largest increases were also found in egohoods experiencing a simultaneous increase in inequality and racial-ethnic heterogeneity, but egohoods experiencing increasing inequality simultaneously with decreasing racial-ethnic heterogeneity experienced the largest decreases in aggravated assault. The pattern for larceny, and to a lesser extent robbery, looks similar (not shown).

Finally, we assess whether low-income egohoods within areas of increasing spatial inequality experience the largest crime increases. The detected pattern was the opposite: egohoods with increasing average household income experience the largest crime increases when they are experiencing larger increases in inequality in the surrounding 2.5 miles. This relationship was robust for all crime types except motor vehicle theft. The plot for aggravated assault is shown in figure 5 and demonstrates that aggravated assault is highest in egohoods surrounded by increasing spatial inequality (the top line in the graph), but that it is higher if the egohood is experiencing increasing income (the right side) rather than

Table 3. Interaction Models Predicting Change in Crime from 2000 to 2010

	Aggravated Assault	Robbery	Burglary	Motor Vehicle Theft	Larceny
Egohood					
Income inequality	1.7359	−0.744	1.4826	−0.905	−5.7898
	0.88	−0.8	1.43	−0.78	−1.39
Average household income	−1.8525*	−0.8918*	−0.6437	−0.2903	−0.6738
	−2.06	−2.1	−1.37	−0.55	−0.36
Racial-ethnic heterogeneity	28.6037**	2.8244	1.692	1.8876	30.171**
	7.82	1.64	0.88	0.88	3.93
Surrounding area					
Income inequality	−7.9605*	−30.0706**	−12.464**	−4.4887*	−87.563**
	−2.32	−18.59	−6.95	−2.23	−12.17
Average household income	−25.417**	−22.3602**	−12.077**	−9.6117**	−77.211**
	−12.05	−22.45	−10.94	−7.76	−17.42
Racial-ethnic heterogeneity	50.9482**	11.6738**	23.9835**	22.478**	82.625**
	10.17	4.93	9.15	7.64	7.85
Broader 2.5 mile area					
Average income	−65.503**	−22.9498**	−34.765**	−52.934**	−110**
	−11.91	−8.83	−12.07	−16.38	−9.45
Inequality	188.462**	27.7296**	7.519	47.356**	312.38**
	14.44	4.5	1.1	6.18	11.39
Interactions					
Egohood inequality X nearby inequality	−16.069	−110**	−43.529**	42.273**	−210**
	−1.22	−17.9	−6.29	5.44	−7.67
Egohood inequality X racial heterogeneity	68.9863**	24.1965**	21.5654**	30.155**	72.08*
	4.51	3.35	2.7	3.36	2.24
Nearby inequality X racial heterogeneity	−64.677†	31.3009†	−2.0426	18.238	30.288
	−1.86	1.9	−0.11	0.89	0.41
Egohood inequality X inequality in surrounding 2.5 miles	103.707	118.819**	141.447**	−17.881	1300**
	1.45	3.52	3.78	−0.43	8.8
Nearby inequality X inequality in surrounding 2.5 miles	−600**	180.392**	−61.056	−290**	32.078
	−5.38	3.4	−1.04	−4.4	0.14
Egohood income X inequality in surrounding 2.5 miles	502.119**	183.44**	129.822**	5.7793	145.19*
	16.95	13.11	8.37	0.33	2.33
Intercept	−0.594	8.2372**	2.7041**	12.61**	1.1996
	−0.37	10.94	3.24	13.46	0.36

Source: Authors' compilation.
Note: T-values below coefficient estimates. Linear regression models. N=29,157 egohoods. Models include all control variables listed in table 2. All measures capture change from 2000 to 2010.
†$p < .05$ (one-tail test); *$p < .05$ (two-tail test); **$p < .01$ (two tail test)

Figure 1. Effect of Changing Egohood and Nearby Inequality on Change in Robberies

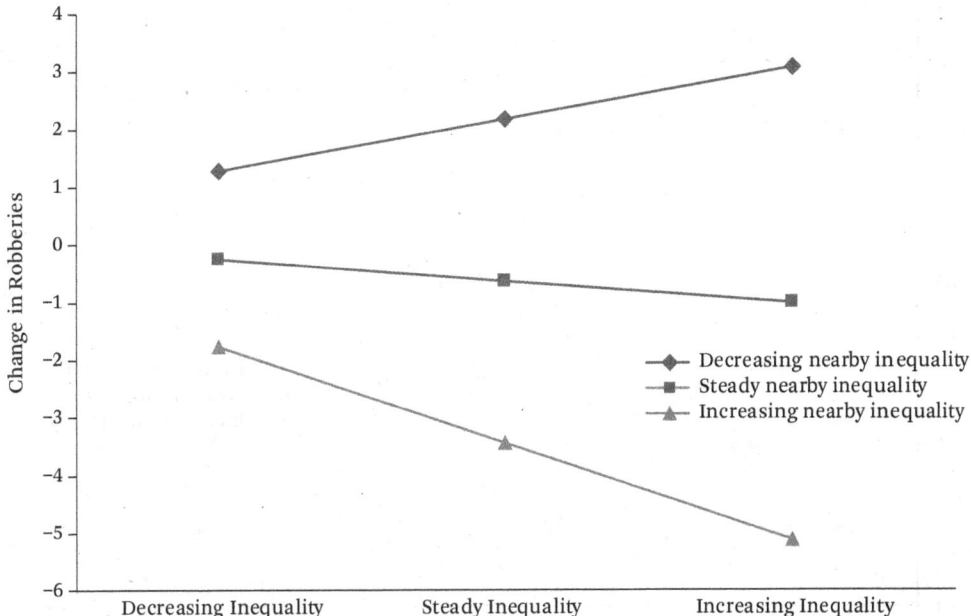

Source: Authors' compilation.

Figure 2. Effect of Changing Inequality in Egohood and Within 2.5 Miles on Change in Aggravated Assaults

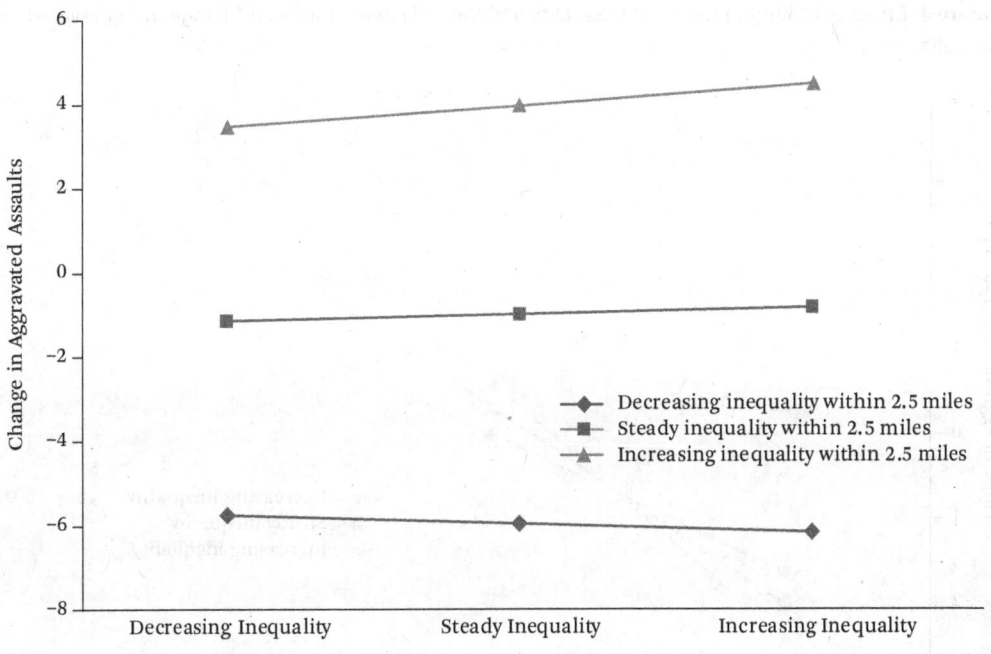

Source: Authors' compilation.

Figure 3. Effect of Changing Egohood Inequality and Racial Heterogeneity on Changing Burglaries

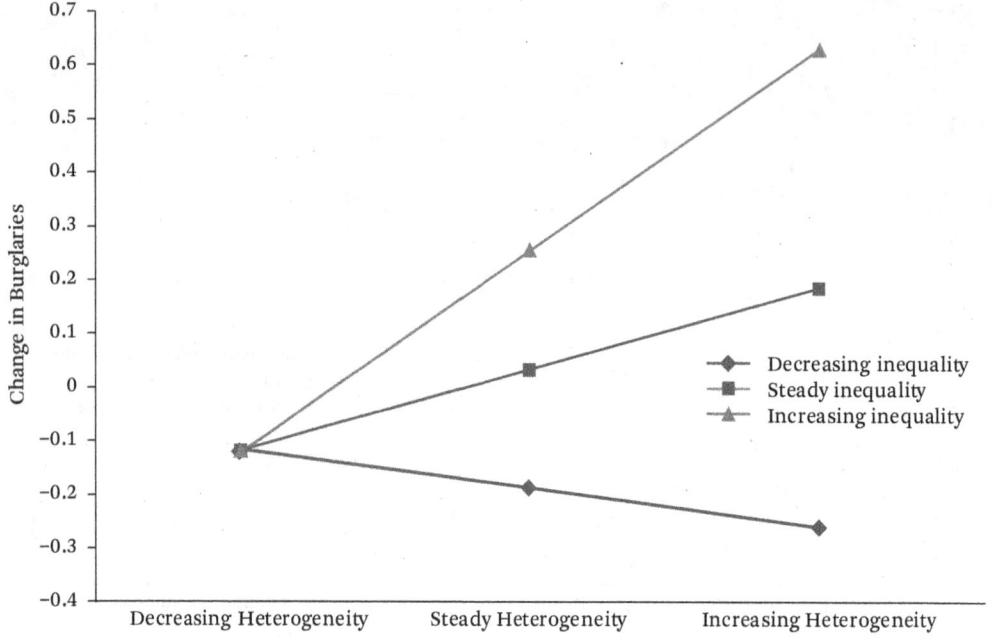

Source: Authors' compilation.

Figure 4. Effect of Changing Egohood Inequality and Racial Heterogeneity on Change in Aggravated Assaults

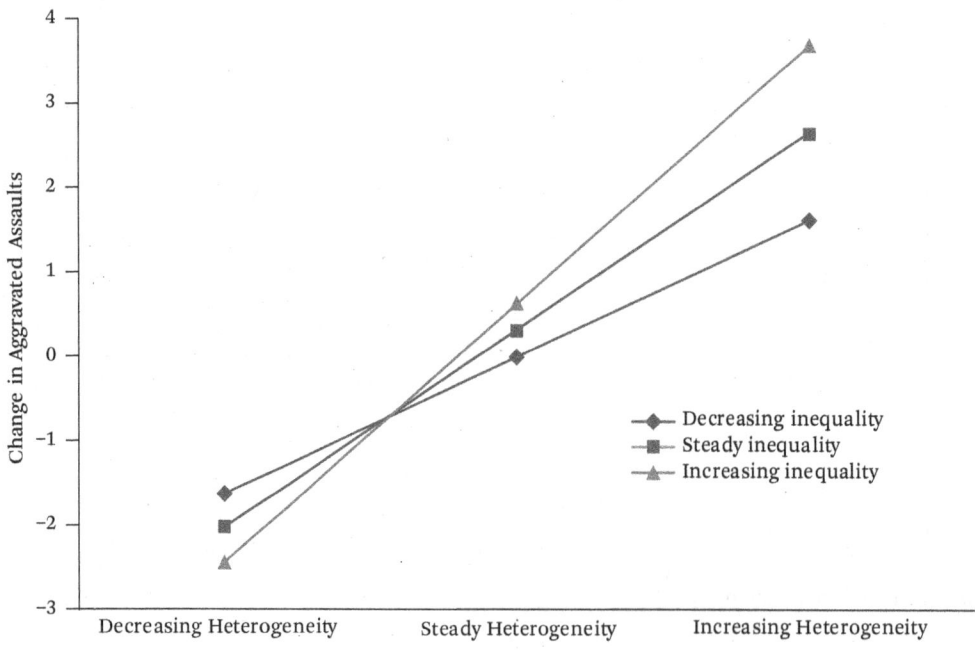

Source: Authors' compilation.

Figure 5. Effect of Changing Income in Egohood and Inequality Within 2.5 Miles on Change in Aggravated Assaults

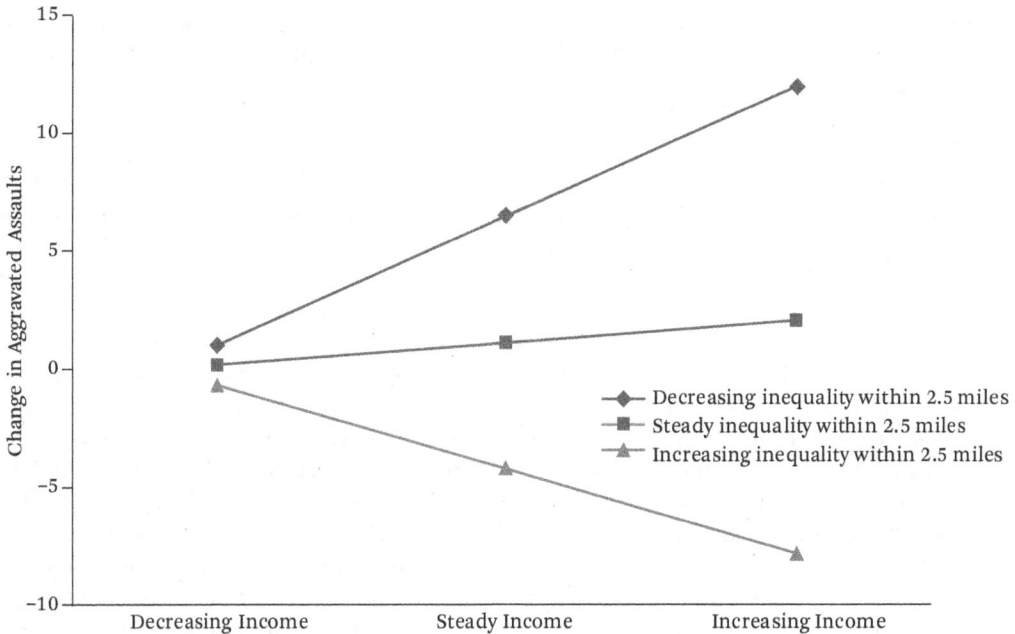

Source: Authors' compilation.

decreasing income (the left side). The pattern is similar for robbery, burglary, and larceny (not shown).

CONCLUSION

We explore the relationship between spatial inequality and neighborhood crime rates using several innovations to the literature. Our study emphasizes the importance of considering the spatial distribution of inequality rather than focusing only on inequality within specific geographic units. We also take a longitudinal approach by explicitly examining the change in Los Angeles neighborhoods over ten years. In using the spatially overlapping approach of egohoods to measure neighborhoods, we find that changing levels of inequality in the broader 2.5-mile area are related to increasing levels of nearly all crime types in the egohood. Thus, we find that conceptualizing spatial inequality on various spatial scales is important. We summarize the key findings.

Racial-ethnic change in the egohood, and the surrounding area, had a strong association with how crime changed in the egohood. We explore racial-ethnic change using three approaches: change for specific groups, change of any type, and change that increases heterogeneity. The most robust relationships are for changing heterogeneity, given that egohoods that experienced increasing racial-ethnic heterogeneity in them, or in the surrounding area, experienced consistent increases in crime over the decade. An important implication of this pattern is that it is less likely that crime could actually induce racial-ethnic heterogeneity. Whereas existing literature has shown that crime can, at least to some extent, increase the racial minority composition of a neighborhood, there is no reason to expect it to increase heterogeneity. In fact, heterogeneity will increase in the earliest stages of in-movement of a group but will decrease in the latter stages. Thus, our modeling strategy captures general racial turnover (churning) and increases of specific groups, and these showed weaker associations with changes in crime. Instead, the change in heterogeneity is most strongly related to increases in crime, which is consistent with social disorganization theory (Kubrin 2000; Sampson and Groves 1989).

Another key finding is that egohoods with greater increases in inequality experienced larger increases in crime when that change was accompanied by increasing racial-ethnic heterogeneity. The results here suggest a dynamic process in which increasing levels of spatial inequality and racial-ethnic heterogeneity in the egohood are associated with increases in all crime types. Although we posited that increasing inequality in the area immediately surrounding an egohood would be associated with increased crime, this is not the case. Egohoods in which the immediate surrounding area was undergoing decreasing inequality experienced greater increases in robbery and larceny, but this relationship was particularly pronounced if the level of inequality in the egohood itself was increasing. Thus, we find no evidence that increasing nearby inequality was associated with increased levels of crime, at least when measuring *nearby* relatively proximately.

A particularly important finding of the present study, however, is that changing spatial inequality in a broader area (2.5 miles around the egohood) demonstrated a notable relationship with the change in the level of crime in the egohood—something that prior scholarship has not explored. We find that increasing levels of inequality in a 2.5-mile area surrounding an egohood was associated with increasing crime levels, even when accounting for the change in the level of inequality in the egohood itself as well as the quarter-mile buffer around the egohood. Whereas prior research has assessed the relationship between levels of inequality and crime as measured in larger units such as cities or counties, it has not assessed whether this inequality has consequences for specific neighborhoods within these larger units. The evidence here suggests that *even within a particular city*, the change in the level of inequality in such broader areas is associated with higher crime rates in specific egohoods within that city.

Prior research, however, has rarely considered the possible role of spatial inequality in the macro context for higher levels of crime in the micro context. Existing neighborhood-level theories can possibly account for the relationship of inequality at a smaller scale through offender behavior as posited by opportunity theories, or reduced social interaction as posited by social disorganization theory, but these theories are unable to account for the relationship we detect for macro spatial inequality and crime. We identify two theories that posit mechanisms by which inequality at the larger macro context would affect crime. In the first, Putnam (1995) suggests that higher levels of inequality in the larger community reduce the level of social capital among residents and as a consequence, residents are less willing to provide resources to more disadvantaged neighborhoods that would allow them to address crime problems. However, for these larger areas with increasing spatial inequality, egohoods with greater increases in income had larger crime increases than egohoods with lower increases in income, in direct contrast to this prediction. This result would be consistent with a relative deprivation argument (Merton 1968) or a crime opportunity argument (Brantingham and Brantingham 1984), because neighborhoods with increasing income surrounded by inequality in the broader area might be particularly attractive targets. Future research would need to explore the possible mechanisms to determine why this pattern is observed.

A second possibility is that higher levels of inequality can create a sense of injustice among some residents and result in more offenders in the environment (Blau and Blau 1982). This increase in offenders combined with their spatial patterns as discussed in the journey to crime literature (Rossmo 2000), implies that we would expect to see higher levels of crime in egohoods. This is precisely what was observed here. That higher levels of crime were observed in egohoods with increasing income that were surrounded by increasing spatial inequality may indicate that such neighborhoods are more attractive targets. These results highlight the challenge of understanding the impact of spatial inequality for various processes: spatial inequality at larger scales may result in consequences for units of much smaller scale within these larger units. We posit that residents who perceive more spatial inequality may view this as structural inequality that reduces their opportunities. If so, such spatial inequality may reduce the perceived effectiveness of pursuing educational opportunities that can enable employment in high-quality mainstream jobs. One consequence is that researchers might detect that broader spatial inequality will affect educational achievement of adolescents beyond any neighborhood effects. We are unable to say what mechanisms were at work in our study; these should be explored in future research.

Although this study provides novel insights by exploring questions using an innovative approach, we nonetheless acknowledge some limitations. First, data were constrained to a single city. Although other research has similarly been limited to exploring processes within a single city, generalizing these results too broadly is a concern. Second, we explore the relationships of changes in spatial inequality for particular spatial scales, which are necessarily chosen somewhat arbitrarily. We thus cannot be certain that these are the proper geographic scales for capturing spatial inequality processes, and future work no doubt should explore other spatial scales. Third, as noted, we do not explore the possible mechanisms that might explain these relationships, leaving us in the dark about why such relationships exist. That task, too, is left for future researchers.

In conclusion, this study extends the literature on the relationship between spatial inequality and crime. That we find such a robust relationship between the change in the level of inequality in the broader 2.5-mile area and the change in crime in the egohood itself is a strong indicator that researchers need to carefully explore such spatial processes. And while a body of literature in criminology explores the relationship between structural characteristics and crime in smaller geographic units, finding notable relationships (see, for example, Weisburd, Groff, and Yang 2012), our results emphasize that much broader geographic scales cannot be ignored. Although the characteristics of a 2.5-mile buffer with nearly two hundred thousand people might, at first glance, appear far too distal to be related to crime in a quarter-mile egohood, findings from this study reveal that how inequality changes in this broader context in fact is quite notably related to the change in local crime.

REFERENCES

Agnew, Robert. 1999. "A General Strain Theory of Community Differences in Crime Rates." *Journal of Research in Crime and Delinquency* 36(2): 123–55.

Andersson, Roger, and Sako Musterd. 2010. "What Scale Matters? Exploring the Relationships Between Individuals' Social Position, Neighbourhood Context and the Scale of Neighbourhood." *Geografiska Annaler: Series B, Human Geography* 92(1): 23–43.

Blau, Judith R., and Peter M. Blau. 1982. "The Cost of Inequality: Metropolitan Structure and Violent Crime." *American Sociological Review* 47(1): 114–29.

Brantingham, Paul J., and Patricia L. Brantingham. 1984. *Patterns in Crime*. New York: Macmillan.

Brownson, Ross C., Christine M. Hoehner, Kristen Day, Ann Forsyth, and James F. Sallis. 2009. "Measuring the Built Environment for Physical Activity: State of the Science." *American Journal of Preventive Medicine* 36(4): S99–123.

Buck, Andrew J., and Simon Hakim. 1989. "Does Crime Affect Property Values?" *Canadian Appraiser* 33(1): 23–27.

Bursik, Robert J. 1986. "Delinquency Rates as Sources of Ecological Change." In *The Social Ecology*, edited by James M. Byrne and Robert J. Sampson. New York: Springer-Verlag.

Bushway, Shawn D. 2011. "Labor Markets and Crime." In *Crime and Public Policy*, edited by James Q. Wilson and Joan Petersilia. New York: Oxford University Press.

Crutchfield, Robert D. 1989. "Labor Stratification and Violent Crime." *Social Forces* 68(2): 489–512.

Deng, Yongheng, Stephen L. Ross, and Susan M. Wachter. 2003. "Racial Differences in Homeownership: The Effect of Residential Location." *Regional Science and Urban Economics* 33(5): 517–56.

Dugan, Laura. 1999. "The Effect of Criminal Victimization on a Household's Moving Decision." *Criminology* 37(4): 903–30.

Grattet, Ryken. 2009. "The Urban Ecology of Bias Crime: A Study of Disorganized and Defended Neighborhoods." *Social Problems* 56(1): 132–50.

Green, Donald P., Dara Z. Strolovitch, and Janelle S. Wong. 1998. "Defended Neighborhoods, Integration, and Racially Motivated Crime." *American Journal of Sociology* 104(2): 372–403.

Griffiths, Elizabeth. 2013. "Race, Space, and the Spread of Violence Across the City." *Social Problems* 60(4): 491–512.

Harer, Miles D., and Darrell Steffensmeier. 1992. "The Differing Effects of Economic Inequality on Black and White Rates of Violence." *Social Forces* 70(4): 1035–54.

Hipp, John R. 2007. "Income Inequality, Race, and Place: Does the Distribution of Race and Class Within Neighborhoods Affect Crime Rates?" *Criminology* 45(3): 665–97.

———. 2010a. "A Dynamic View of Neighborhoods: The Reciprocal Relationship Between Crime and Neighborhood Structural Characteristics." *Social Problems* 57(2): 205–30.

———. 2010b. "The Role of Crime in Housing Unit Racial-Ethnic Transition." *Criminology* 48(3): 683–723.

———. 2011. "Violent Crime, Mobility Decisions, and Neighborhood Racial-Ethnic Transition." *Social Problems* 58(3): 410–32.

Hipp, John R., and Adam Boessen. 2013. "Egohoods as Waves Washing Across the City: A New Measure of 'Neighborhoods.'" *Criminology* 51(2): 287–327.

Hipp, John R., and Cynthia M. Lakon. 2010. "Social Disparities in Health: Disproportionate Toxicity Proximity in Minority Communities over a Decade." *Health & Place* 16(4): 674–83.

Hipp, John R., and Aaron Roussell. 2013. "Micro- and Macro-environment Population and the Consequences for Crime Rates." *Social Forces* 92(2): 563–95.

Hipp, John R., George E. Tita, and Robert T. Greenbaum. 2009. "Drive-Bys and Trade-Ups: The Impact of Crime on Residential Mobility Patterns in Los Angeles." *Social Forces* 87(4): 1777–812.

Hipp, John R., and Daniel K. Yates. 2011. "Ghettos, Thresholds, and Crime: Does Concentrated Poverty Really Have an Accelerating Increasing Effect on Crime?" *Criminology* 49(4): 955–90.

Kubrin, Charis E. 2000. "Racial Heterogeneity and Crime: Measuring Static and Dynamic Effects." *Research in Community Sociology* 10: 189–219.

Kubrin, Charis E., and John R. Hipp. 2014. "Do Fringe Banks Create Fringe Neighborhoods? Examining the Spatial Relationship Between Fringe Banking and Neighborhood Crime Rates." *Justice Quarterly* 33(3): 755–84.

Kubrin, Charis E., and Ronald Weitzer. 2003. "New Directions in Social Disorganization Theory." *Journal of Research in Crime and Delinquency* 40(4): 374–402.

Mast, Brent D., and Ronald E. Wilson. 2013. "Housing Choice Vouchers and Crime in Charlotte, NC." *Housing Policy Debate* 23(3): 559–96.

Mears, Daniel P., and Avinash S. Bhati. 2006. "No Community Is an Island: The Effects of Resource Deprivation on Urban Violence in Spatially and Socially Proximate Communities." *Criminology* 44(3): 509–48.

Merton, Robert K. 1968. *Social Theory and Social Structure*. New York: The Free Press.

Messner, Steven F., and Reid M. Golden. 1992. "Racial Inequality and Racially Disaggregated Homicide Rates: An Assessment of Alternative Theoretical Explanations." *Criminology* 30(3): 421–47.

Messner, Steven F., and Kenneth Tardiff. 1986. "Economic Inequality and Levels of Homicide: An Analysis of Urban Neighborhoods." *Criminology* 24(2): 297–317.

Morenoff, Jeffrey D., and Robert J. Sampson. 1997. "Violent Crime and the Spatial Dynamics of Neighborhood Transition: Chicago, 1970–1990." *Social Forces* 76(1): 31–64.

Morenoff, Jeffrey D., Robert J. Sampson, and Stephen W. Raudenbush. 2001. "Neighborhood Inequality, Collective Efficacy, and the Spatial Dynamics of Urban Violence." *Criminology* 39(3): 517–59.

Openshaw, Stan, and Peter J. Taylor. 1979. "A Million or so Correlation Coefficients: Three Experiments on the Modifiable Areal Unit Problem." In *Statistical Applications in the Spatial Sciences*, edited by Neil Wrigley. London: Pion.

Pastor, Manuel, Jr., Jim Sadd, and John Hipp. 2001. "Which Came First? Toxic Facilities, Minority Move-in, and Environmental Justice." *Journal of Urban Affairs* 23(1): 1–21.

Peterson, Ruth D., and Lauren J. Krivo. 2009. "Segregated Spatial Locations, Race-Ethnic Composition, and Neighborhood Violent Crime." *The Annals of the American Academy of Political and Social Science* 623(1): 93–107.

———. 2010. *Divergent Social Worlds: Neighborhood Crime and the Racial-Spatial Divide*. New York: Russell Sage Foundation.

Popkin, Susan J., Michael J. Rich, Leah Hendey, Chris Hayes, Joe Parilla, and George C. Galster. 2012.

"Public Housing Transformation and Crime: Making the Case for Responsible Relocation." *Cityscape* 14(3): 137–60.

Putnam, Robert D. 1995. "Bowling Alone: America's Declining Social Capital." *Journal of Democracy* 6(1): 65–78.

Raleigh, Erica, and George Galster. 2014. "Neighborhood Disinvestment, Abandonment, and Crime Dynamics." *Journal of Urban Affairs* 37(4): 367–96.

Reardon, Sean F., Stephen A. Matthews, David O'Sullivan, Barrett A. Lee, Glenn Firebaugh, Chad R. Farrell, and K. Bischoff. 2008. "The Geographical Scale of Metropolitan Racial Segregation." *Demography* 45(3): 489–514.

Rice, Kennon J., and William R. Smith. 2002. "Socioecological Models of Automotive Theft: Integrating Routine Activity and Social Disorganization Approaches." *Journal of Research in Crime and Delinquency* 39(3): 304–36.

Rossmo, D. Kim. 2000. *Geographic Profiling*. Boca Raton, Fl.: CRC Press.

Rountree, Pamela Wilcox, and Kenneth C. Land. 1996. "Burglary Victimization, Perceptions of Crime Risk, and Routine Activities: A Multilevel Analysis Across Seattle Neighborhoods and Census Tracts." *Journal of Research in Crime and Delinquency* 33(2): 147–80.

Sampson, Robert J., and W. Byron Groves. 1989. "Community Structure and Crime: Testing Social-Disorganization Theory." *American Journal of Sociology* 94(4): 774–802.

Sampson, Robert J., Stephen W. Raudenbush, and Felton Earls. 1997. "Neighborhoods and Violent Crime: A Multilevel Study of Collective Efficacy." *Science* 277(5328): 918–24.

Schwartz, Amy Ellen, Scott Susin, and Ioan Voicu. 2003. "Has Falling Crime Driven New York City's Real Estate Boom?" *Journal of Housing Research* 14(1): 1–35.

Sharkey, Patrick. 2014. "Spatial Segmentation and the Black Middle Class." *American Journal of Sociology* 119(4): 903–54.

Sherman, Lawrence W., Patrick R. Gartin, and Michael E. Buerger. 1989. "Hot Spots of Predatory Crime: Routine Activities and the Criminology of Place." *Criminology* 27(1): 27–55.

Smith, William R., Sharon Glave Frazee, and Elizabeth L. Davison. 2000. "Furthering the Integration of Routine Activity and Social Disorganization Theories: Small Units of Analysis and the Study of Street Robbery as a Diffusion Process." *Criminology* 38(2): 489–523.

Stucky, Thomas D., and John R. Ottensmann. 2009. "Land Use and Violent Crime." *Criminology* 47(4): 1223–64.

Taylor, Ralph B., and Jeanette Covington. 1988. "Neighborhood Changes in Ecology and Violence." *Criminology* 26(4): 553–89.

Thaler, Richard. 1978. "A Note on the Value of Crime Control: Evidence from the Property Market." *Journal of Urban Economics* 5(1): 137–45.

Tita, George E., Tricia L. Petras, and Robert T. Greenbaum. 2006. "Crime and Residential Choice: A Neighborhood Level Analysis of the Impact of Crime on Housing Prices." *Journal of Quantitative Criminology* 22(December): 299–317.

Weisburd, David, Elizabeth Groff, and Sue-Ming Yang. 2012. *The Criminology of Place*. New York: Oxford.

Weisburd, David, and Tom McEwen. 1998. "Crime Mapping and Crime Prevention." In *Crime Prevention Studies*, vol. 8, edited by Ronald V. Clarke. Monsey, N.Y.: Criminal Justice Press.

Xie, Min, and David McDowall. 2008. "Escaping Crime: The Effects of Direct and Indirect Victimization on Moving." *Criminology* 46(4): 809–40.

———. 2010. "The Reproduction of Racial Inequality: How Crime Affects Housing Turnover." *Criminology* 48(4): 865–96.

Segregation as a Source of Contextual Advantage: A Formal Theory with Application to American Cities

LINCOLN QUILLIAN

A frequently cited model of why segregation contributes to inequality is that segregation increases the level of contextual advantage of advantaged segregated groups and the level of contextual disadvantage of disadvantaged segregated groups. This paper provides a formal demographic model of this process. The model begins with two groups that differ along a dimension of average advantage and disadvantage, for instance, two racial groups that differ in their poverty rates. The model illustrates how the contextual advantages and disadvantages from segregation are affected by a series of demographic conditions: group relative size, group advantage-disadvantage rates, group effects on advantage-disadvantage rates of nongroup neighbors, and advantage-disadvantage effects on group contact. The paper outlines a series of eleven conclusions from the theoretical model and applies the theoretical model to understanding racial segregation effects on racial group neighborhood poverty contact in American cities.

Keywords: segregation, neighborhoods, racial inequality, poverty

Segregation has long been thought to contribute to inequality, especially racial inequality. Although a variety of explanations are typically offered for why segregation may contribute to inequality, the most common in contemporary discussions is that segregation is associated with affluent contexts for whites and impoverished contexts for nonwhites. The explanation is the primary one offered by two of the most prominent social scientists who emphasize the importance of racial segregation in producing racial inequality, Douglas Massey and Gary Orfield.[1]

Douglas Massey, for instance, argues that, as segregation increases, "the average residential environment of whites improves and the average residential environment of blacks deteriorates" (1990, 333). This occurs because segregation separates affluent and poor racial groups into different neighborhoods, producing racial inequality in neighborhood conditions. Massey then goes on to argue that these concentrations of neighborhood poverty are a key to the existence of an "urban underclass" and to racial inequality more generally.

Gary Orfield has made parallel arguments as applied to schools. Indeed, the main reason we should be concerned with segregation by race, he says, is because "segregation by race is systematically linked to other forms of segregation, including segregation by socioeconomic status, by residential location, and in-

---

Lincoln Quillian is professor of sociology at Northwestern University and chair of the Institute for Policy Research's Program on Urban Policy and Community Development.

© 2017 Russell Sage Foundation. Quillian, Lincoln. 2017. "Segregation as a Source of Contextual Advantage: A Formal Theory with Application to American Cities." *RSF: The Russell Sage Foundation Journal of the Social Sciences* 3(2): 152–69. DOI: 10.7758/RSF.3.2.07. Direct correspondence to: Lincoln Quillian at l-quillian@northwestern.edu, Department of Sociology, Northwestern University, 1810 Chicago Avenue, Evanston, IL 60208.

1. This point is not entirely original to Massey and Orfield. Their work extends previous scholarship, most notably Kenneth Clark (1989).

creasingly by language" (Orfield and Lee 2005, 14). He argues that segregation by race is primarily of concern exactly because it creates high-poverty schools for many minority students and high-poverty school environments are not conducive to learning.

The basic argument both these scholars make is that segregation produces neighborhoods and schools that are either predominately white and low poverty or predominately nonwhite and high poverty. In general, their logic suggests that as segregation increases, members of advantaged segregated groups increasingly experience high rates of advantaged persons in their contexts, and that members of disadvantaged groups experience high rates of disadvantaged persons. To the extent that experiencing contexts with advantaged members is itself a source of advantage and that experiencing contexts with disadvantaged members is itself a source of disadvantage—as a large body of research suggests[2]—segregation then increases the on-average contextual advantage of the advantaged and the contextual disadvantage of the disadvantaged. Correspondingly, several studies note the large gap in the affluence of neighborhoods and related social contexts experienced by whites, blacks, and Latinos and argue that this is an important factor contributing to persistent racial inequality (see, for example, Pattillo 1999; Logan 2011; Sharkey 2013).

Does racial segregation always increase the concentration of poverty for members of disadvantaged racial groups and affluence for advantaged racial groups? Both Massey and Orfield suggest that it does, as a necessity of the mathematical demography of the combination of segregation and racial disparities in poverty. Neither, however, develop a formal model of this process or make the mathematical demography explicit.

Yet an increase in segregation need not increase the contextual advantage of advantaged groups and the contextual disadvantage of disadvantaged groups in all situations, nor need a decrease in segregation decrease it. A prominent example of how racial desegregation can fail to reduce a disadvantaged group's level of contextual disadvantage is William Julius Wilson's (1987) black middle-class outmigration thesis. Wilson claims that declines in residential segregation in the 1960s and 1970s were a process by which affluent blacks moved out of poor black neighborhoods leaving poorer blacks behind (see Wilson 1987, 55–58). As a result, middle-class blacks gained white neighbors—thus making this a migration flow that reduced racial segregation—and poor blacks lost middle-class black neighbors. Overall, Wilson's suggestion is that *average* black neighborhood income showed little improvement in the wake of black middle-class migration into white neighborhoods.

In this article, I consider conditions under which segregation acts more as Massey and Orfield suggest than as Wilson suggests. In effect, this analysis produces a set of scope conditions under which Massey and Orfield's theories operate. The contribution is in developing a broader understanding of the complex factors that determine how the spatial arrangement of segregation contributes to group contextual advantage or disadvantage. The analysis clarifies spatial factors that amplify or dampen the effects of segregation on contextual advantage and contextual disadvantage via spatial arrangement. Finally, it assess the extent to which these conditions hold in contemporary U.S. metropolitan areas, and thus helps clarify the role of segregation in producing unequal neighborhood poverty rates among persons of different racial and ethnic backgrounds.

A FORMAL MODEL OF SEGREGATION AND CONTEXT

Both Massey and Orfield's descriptions suggest the concentration of disadvantage in the

---

2. If affluent neighborhoods tend to have low crime and good neighborhood schools, and high-poverty neighborhoods high crime and bad neighborhood schools—as much research indicates (Coleman 1966; Peterson and Krivo 2010)—then crime and poor neighborhood schools are then also concentrated in nonwhite neighborhoods by segregation. Likewise, an increasingly convincing body of knowledge finds that neighborhood poverty is associated with long-term disadvantages for disadvantaged children that profoundly reduce their chance of upward social mobility (Wodtke, Harding, and Elwert 2011; Chetty et al. 2014; Chetty, Hendren, and Katz 2015).

neighborhoods of blacks and Hispanics is a necessary result of the mathematical demography of segregation combined with racial inequality. Neither, however, actually develops an explicit model of this process. The closest effort is a simulation model Massey developed, first published as an article in the *American Journal of Sociology* (1990) that later became chapter 5 in Massey and Nancy Denton's seminal *American Apartheid* (1993).

Massey begins with a hypothetical city with black and white residents (only) and studies changes in poverty contact as the level of segregation changes. In his hypothetical city, the black poverty rate is 20 percent and the white rate is 10 percent. He shows that as segregation between blacks and whites is increased, holding other conditions constant, the average neighborhood poverty of whites decreases and of blacks increases. In a second simulation, he adds income segregation within race, showing that as segregation of whites from blacks increases in the presence of income segregation, neighborhood poverty contact for black poor residents increases even more sharply.

Massey's simulations illustrate how segregation combined with racial disparities in poverty rates produce racial inequalities in neighborhood environments. But his simulation imposes several conditions that receive little direct attention in his discussion. For instance, the simulation sets the size of the two racial groups in his hypothetical city to be equal, does not allow income to affect cross-race contact, and does not allow race to affect the income level of other-race neighbors. It is unclear how the logic of segregation concentrating poverty might be changed if these circumstances are changed.

Wilson's black middle-class outmigration thesis implies a different relationship between segregation and contextual advantage and disadvantage. In his account in *The Truly Disadvantaged*, the migration of middle-class blacks out of black central-city neighborhoods in the 1960s and 1970s resulted in decreased neighborhood poverty for middle-class blacks and increased neighborhood poverty for poor blacks (Wilson 1987, 53–57). Wilson is less clear about where middle-class blacks migrated to, but he suggests the suburbs, including some into white neighborhoods. In his account, racial desegregation of residence did not decrease black neighborhood poverty but instead increased it for poor blacks and reduced it for middle-class blacks.[3]

A key difference between Massey's account of the effect of segregation and Wilson's of black middle-class outmigration is that in Massey's account desegregation occurs across all income levels, whereas in Wilson's only middle-class blacks see an increase in white neighbors.[4] This contrast suggests a broader point: income gradients in a process of segregation or desegregation are important to how segregation affects contextual inequality. An income gradient is an income-selective pattern of cross-race contact, such as high-income African Americans having more white neighbors than low-income African Americans do. If the income gradient to segregation is strong, Massey and Orfield's basic arguments about how segregation contributes to contextual inequality may not operate.

To get more precise about the conditions under which segregation concentrates or deconcentrates poverty, I develop a formal model. This model provides a precise description of how this process occurs and details related spatial conditions that can increase or weaken the effects of segregation on concentrating advantage and disadvantage. Effectively, it can be viewed as formalizing and generalizing Massey's theory, which suggested mathematical necessity, but without developing the math.

The decomposition discussed here is closely related to a decomposition model developed

---

3. Wilson does not use the term *desegregation* in discussing black middle-class outmigration, but middle-class black migration into white neighborhoods is a process that must contribute to racial desegregation.

4. Massey's argument is buttressed by the findings of Denton and Massey (1989) that in the 1970s middle-class blacks were not much less segregated from whites than low-income blacks. More recent evidence suggests middle-class blacks are significantly more likely to live in nonblack neighborhoods than poorer blacks (Sharkey 2014).

and applied to understand poverty concentration (Quillian 2012). The model examines the outcome of poverty concentration by group, or the extent to which poor members of a racial group tend to have poor neighbors. By contrast, in the analysis in this manuscript, average poverty concentration is considered for all members of a racial or ethnic group. The model then examines how segregation affects contextual advantage or disadvantage on average for the segregated groups.

Spatial Arrangement and Substantive Segregation Effects

In examining the effects of segregation on concentrating poverty, Massey's simulations focus purely on the mathematical effect of spatial rearrangement of population when segregation is increased. Other conditions, such as group size and poverty rates, are held fixed as segregation is changed. Yet as many scholars argue—including Massey—segregation has important substantive effects on populations beyond its mechanical spatial effect on neighborhood poverty. A reduction in segregation would increase the disadvantaged group's access to better labor markets and schools, which would decrease the disadvantaged group's poverty rate (see, for instance, Massey and Denton 1993, chapter 6; Quillian 2014).

Following Massey's simulations, the model I develop examines spatial arrangement effects of segregation only, omitting substantive effects. The spatial arrangement effect can be estimated precisely once the dynamics of the system are understood: they are a mathematical function of patterns of cross-group contact, as Massey and Orfield suggest. By contrast, substantive effects depend on a behavioral model with attendant uncertainties; in the literature of substantive segregation effects, estimates vary substantially. Also, spatial rearrangement effects on neighborhood poverty rates are immediate, whereas much of the behavioral effect occurs in a longer time scale gradually after segregation changes. For simplicity, in what follows I refer to spatial rearrangement effects simply as *segregation effects*. This omits potentially important but distinct substantive effects, which are not a focus of this article.

A Formal Population Model

The formal model considers segregation of a social group, the *group*, from the rest of the population, the *nongroup*. In the most common application, the group would be a racial or ethnic group.

In the model, aside from their group membership, individuals are either advantaged or disadvantaged. Although the dimension of advantage and disadvantage can be based on anything defined for individuals and distinct from the social groups, income is the typical dimension. Advantage or disadvantage are defined for individuals, but rates of advantage and disadvantage differ across groups. Advantaged groups are groups with low rates of individual disadvantage (and high rates of advantage); disadvantaged groups have high rates of individual disadvantage (and low rates of advantage).

In this analysis, the disadvantaged members of each group are operationalized as poor (income below the government poverty line) and the advantaged individuals as nonpoor (income above the poverty line). The group we focus on are denoted g in our models, and the poverty rate of group g is Pov_g. Everyone not in the focal group is in the nongroup, denoted ng. The poverty rate of the nongroup is Pov_{ng}. If the focal group is disadvantaged, $Pov_g > Pov_{ng}$. If the focal group is advantaged, $Pov_g < Pov_{ng}$. The most obvious application is to racial groups. In the United States, blacks or Hispanics would typically be disadvantaged groups and whites an advantaged group.

Consider the average contact that members of the group and the nongroup have with poor and nonpoor persons in a social context. This context could be a neighborhood, a school, a social network, or some other setting. For the ith context (neighborhood) denote the number of poor persons (both group and nongroup) in the context as p_i, the total number of persons in the context as t_i, and the number of group members in the context as g_i. Denote the total number of persons in the group summed across all contexts (all neighborhoods) with G. The average context of group poor persons with poor persons in their social context can be denoted using the P^* index of contact popularized by Stanley Lieberson (1988):

$$_gP_g^* = \sum_i \left(\frac{g_i}{G}\right)\left(\frac{p_i}{t_i}\right).$$

This measure can be interpreted as the average percentage poor (disadvantaged) in the contexts of members of the group. Segregation will be measured with a standardized index related to indexes of contact, the variance ratio index of segregation, as discussed further.

The theory that segregation increases contextual disadvantage for disadvantaged groups or advantage for advantaged groups effectively proposes that as segregation between disadvantaged group g and others who are not in group g (ng) increases, $_gP^*_p$ increases. If group g is advantaged, then $_gP^*_p$ will decrease with segregation, reflecting declining contextual advantage with segregation for an advantaged group.

To formalize this relationship, we need to incorporate how segregation affects the average contact with contextual poverty of the poor and nonpoor. The additive decomposability of P^* indexes is useful in this regard. Average contact with poor in the social context is the sum of contact with poor of the disadvantaged group and contact with poor of who are not members of the group; although members of the nongroup have a lower poverty rate than members of the disadvantaged group, some members of the nongroup are poor:

$$_gP^*_p = {_gP^*_{gp}} + {_gP^*_{ngp}}.$$

This formula includes two measures that are closely related to segregation: contact of group members with their own racial or ethnic group and with persons not of their own race or ethnic group. Segregation, however, is generally defined based on contact with all members of each group, not just their poor members. We want to introduce segregation overall to this equation but still get to a formulation with components that are substantively interpretable. To do so, first I manipulate the formula to include terms for own-group and other-group contact:

$$_gP^*_p = {_gP^*_g}\left(\frac{_gP^*_{gp}}{_gP^*_g}\right) + {_gP^*_{ng}}\left(\frac{_gP^*_{ngp}}{_gP^*_{ng}}\right).$$

We can improve the interpretation of the ratios in parentheses by norming them by the poverty rate of each group:

$$_gP^*_p = {_gP^*_g}\left(\frac{\frac{_gP^*_{gp}}{_gP^*_g}}{Pov_g}\right)Pov_g + {_gP^*_{ng}}\left(\frac{\frac{_gP^*_{ngp}}{_gP^*_{ng}}}{Pov_{ng}}\right)Pov_{ng}. \quad (1)$$

The two components in the large brackets capture what we might think of as group membership effects on contact with poor persons of their own group (left term) and poor persons of the nongroup (right term). These ratios will be greater than 1 if members of the group have disproportionate contact with *disadvantaged* members of their own group (left term) or disproportionate contact with nongroup persons who are disadvantaged (right term), disproportionate being defined relative to their group's or the nongroup's poverty rate. If they are more likely to be in contact with nonpoor member of their own group (left term) or the nongroup (right term), these ratios will be less than one.

We can relate these terms mathematically to segregation by using the variance ratio index of segregation, a measure of segregation that is in the same family of measures as the exposure indexes. The variance ratio index is a well-established measure that fits key criteria desired in a segregation index (see James and Taeuber 1985).[5] Like the index of dissimilarity, the variance ratio index varies from 0 (no segregation between groups) to 1 (perfect segregation). Also like dissimilarity, the variance ratio is a measure of evenness of distribution of one

5. The variance ratio index is defined as

$$V_{(g)(ng)} = \sum_i \frac{t_i\left(\frac{g_i}{t_i} - \pi\right)^2}{T\pi(1-\pi)},$$

where g_i denotes the population of the racial group in the ith tract, t_i is the total number of persons in the ith tract, T is the total population of the metropolitan area for which the measure is calculated, and π is the group proportion of the population in the metropolitan area.

group against the other (see Massey and Denton 1988).

The variance ratio index of segregation is related to the P^* contact index between group members and nonmembers by the relation:

$$_gP^*_{ng} = p_{ng}(1 - V_{(g)(ng)}), \quad (2)$$

where p_{ng} is the proportion of the population nongroup and $V_{(g)(ng)}$ is the variance ratio index of segregation between the group and the nongroup. Applying this relation to equation (1) we get:

$$_gP^*_p = (1 - p_{ng}(1 - V_{(g)(ng)}))\left(\frac{\frac{_gP^*_{gp}}{_gP^*_g}}{Pov_g}\right)Pov_g$$

$$+ p_{ng}(1 - V_{(g)(ng)})\left(\frac{\frac{_gP^*_{ngp}}{_gP^*_{ng}}}{Pov_{ng}}\right)Pov_{ng}. \quad (3)$$

This last formula, (3), allows us to understand group neighborhood poverty contact in social context as a function of segregation (V) between the two groups and a series of other conditions: group poverty rates (Pov_g and Pov_{ng}), group relative size (p_{ng}), and the two ratios shown in the big parentheses.

The ratios in the two large parentheses in (3) each have an interpretable meaning. They indicate relative contact of group members with, first, poor group members and, second, poor persons not in the group. Denote these terms $GxGP$ and $GxNGP$:

$$GxGP = \frac{\frac{_gP^*_{gp}}{_gP^*_g}}{Pov_g}$$

$$GxNGP = \frac{\frac{_gP^*_{ngp}}{_gP^*_{ng}}}{Pov_{ng}}.$$

Rewriting (3) with these terms we get the following:

$$_gP^*_p = (1 - p_{ng}(1 - V_{(g)(ng)}))(GxGP)Pov_g$$
$$+ p_{ng}(1 - V_{(g)(ng)})(GxNGP)Pov_{ng}. \quad (4)$$

This formula is the same as (3) but $GxGP$ and $GxNGP$ replace the corresponding terms. Each term has an interpretable meaning. The formula in (4) is a decomposition of group contact with poor into a series of components.

These components represent:

1. Segregation of the group from the nongroup ($V_{(g)(ng)}$).
2. Relative group size, indicated here by percentage nongroup (p_{ng}).
3. The poverty rate of the group (Pov_g).
4. The poverty rate of the nongroup (Pov_{ng}).
5. The ratio ($GxGP$), indicating group members have disproportionately high or low contact with poor members of their own group. A ratio greater than one suggests disproportionate contact of the group with poor own-group members, a ratio less than one suggests disproportionate contact with nonpoor group members. This captures a poverty status effect on own-group contact.
6. The ratio ($GxNGP$), indicating group members have disproportionate contact with poor persons not in their group. A ratio greater than one suggests disproportional contact of the group with poor nongroup persons. This captures a group effect on the income level of nongroup persons in contact with group members.

Note that equation (4) includes no error term: it is a decomposition, not a statistical model. We can *perfectly* predict the average neighborhood poverty rate of a group in any city or other area for which these components are known. The equation in a sense defines the mathematically necessary accounting relationships that Massey and Orfield's discussions suggest underlie the process they observe.

One factor is not included in these components: a measure of within-group segregation between the poor and nonpoor. This is because within-group poverty status segregation shifts poverty contact between the poor and nonpoor of a group, but does not change average poverty contact across an entire group, which is the outcome of this analysis.

The components each represent different spatial conditions that we can manipulate to predict poverty contact of a group under hypothetical changes in some of these conditions. Some combinations of component spatial conditions are not possible—a topic I lack space to explore in detail here—but these combinations can be avoided by focusing on small changes from observed values.

What does this imply about segregation? Equation (4) shows substantial interaction—multiplication—between different factors in predicting the outcome. Terms that multiply together with segregation condition its effect, or increase or decrease the importance of segregation for increasing a group's contact with poverty. To clarify, we can multiply out (4) and group terms interacting with segregation, which produces

$$_gP^*_p = (GxGP)Pov_g + p_{ng}[(GxNGP)Pov_{ng} \\ -(GxGP)Pov_g] + p_{ng}V_{(g)(ng)}[(GxGP)Pov_g \\ -(GxNGP)Pov_{ng}]. \quad (5)$$

The term on the second line of (5) shows components that multiply with segregation. This term is the key to understanding effects that alter the spatial rearrangement effect of segregation on group poverty concentration. Segregation matters for poverty concentration, but its effect in producing contextual advantage or disadvantage depends on several other factors represented in this model.

This formula implies that if the other components of the formula are held constant, then the effect of segregation is linear, and the slope of segregation is as follows:

$$Slope\ of\ V_{(g)(ng)} = p_{ng}[(GxGP)Pov_g \\ -(GxNGP)Pov_{ng}]. \quad (6)$$

One possible application of this is to calculate the components and calculate the slope of segregation in a particular situation. For instance, using values computed for African Americans in Milwaukee from the 2007–2011 American Community Survey:

$$Slope\ of\ V_{(g)(ng)} = 0.835[(1.042)0.363 \\ -(1.899)0.095 = 0.165.$$

This gives an implied slope of segregation on poverty contact for blacks in Milwaukee of 0.165, holding other conditions constant, which is a large slope relative to most other segregation effects in American cities, as discussed further.

Equation (6) suggests several conclusions about segregation and poverty contact across racial groups:

- Conclusion 1: Under regular conditions, segregation will tend to increase the average advantage of the contexts of the advantaged segregated group and increase the average disadvantage of contexts of the disadvantaged segregated group.

I will delay my discussion of regular conditions, but to preview, as long as the subtraction in the middle of (6) is positive and group g is a disadvantaged group, segregation will build contextual advantage and disadvantage as Massey suggests.

- Conclusion 2: All else equal, the strength of effect of segregation in increasing average contextual advantage or disadvantage for a group is proportional to the difference in the level of advantage or disadvantage between the group and persons in other groups.

Segregation does not matter for group contextual advantage if the group and nongroup have the same level of advantage or disadvantage. In equation (6), this is evident from how the group poverty rate and the nongroup rate subtract.

Past accounts get this point partially incorrect by focusing on only the poverty rate of the disadvantaged group alone. In particular, Massey and Mitchell Eggers (1990) emphasize that there should be an interaction between segregation and nonwhite group poverty rates in predicting group neighborhood poverty contact. But, in fact, the interaction should be between segregation and the difference in poverty rates between the group and everyone not in that group, not the group poverty rate.

- Conclusion 3: All else equal, the strength of the segregation effect on contextual disadvantage of a group is increased if the group members in contact with their own group are more often individually disadvantaged.

In the model, the ratio ($GxGP$) indicates how much more likely disadvantaged group members are to be in contact with their own group (g) than all group members. A ratio larger than one indicates disadvantaged persons have more own-group neighbors than the average for their group. If black middle-class migration has occurred, resulting in affluent blacks living in mostly nonblack neighborhoods and poorer blacks living in black neighborhoods, we would expect a ratio significantly above one for blacks.

A sharp own-group income gradient to segregation—in which group members who are advantaged have fewer own-group neighbors than disadvantaged group members—tends to increase the effect of the level of segregation on creating contextual disadvantage for disadvantaged groups (relative to the same level of segregation with a less-sharp income gradient to segregation) because as segregation increases in the presence of a sharp income gradient to segregation, the poorer members of the group are sorted into poor own-group neighborhoods, concentrating their contact among group members and reducing contact of nongroup members with group poverty.

In Wilson's account of black middle-class outmigration, black racial segregation decreased and the income gradient to black segregation increased. He suggests that these two changes roughly offset each other, producing no major change in average black poverty contact. As he emphasizes, however, this increased average poverty concentration for poor blacks while decreasing it for middle-class blacks.

- Conclusion 4: The strength of the segregation effect on contextual disadvantage for a group is decreased if the nongroup members in contact with group members are disproportionately likely to be disadvantaged.

Conclusion 4 is based on the ($GxNGP$) term in equation (6). To the extent that nongroup members in contact with group members are more likely to be disadvantaged, segregation effects are weakened because as segregation declines, group members trade disadvantaged own-group members for disadvantaged other-group members. This condition is indicated by ratios of ($GxNGP$) substantially above one.

- Conclusion 5: The segregation effect on the focal group's neighborhood poverty contact will be larger if a group is small in relative size.

Segregation changes more strongly influence contextual disadvantage (or advantage) when group size is relatively small. Group relative size is inversely related to the percentage nongroup, shown as P_{ng} in the slope formula of equation (6).

If a group is relatively small in size, then a change in the standardized segregation index will have more effect on contact than if a group is large. A group that is only 10 percent of the local population, for instance, will generally have many more nongroup neighbors as segregation declines and they are spread out over the metropolitan neighborhoods that are mostly composed of other-group members. By contrast, if a group is relatively large then a change in segregation will have much weaker effect on who they are in contact with. A group that is 80 percent of the population of an area will only have a moderate increase in other-group neighbors with substantially lower segregation.

- Conclusion 6 (regularity conditions for conclusion 1): For a disadvantaged group g, if ($GxGP$)Pov_g > ($GxNGP$)Pov_{ng} segregation will increase contextual disadvantage as suggested by the Massey model. For an advantaged group g, if ($GxGP$)Pov_g < ($GxNGP$)Pov_{ng} segregation will increase contextual advantage as suggested by the Massey model.

This condition comes straight from the slope formula for segregation of equation (6).

Figure 1. Metropolitan Neighborhood Poverty Contact, 2007–2011, Whites

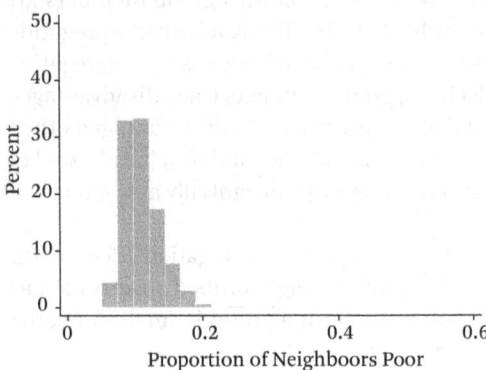

Source: American Community Survey 2007–2011 (Minnesota Population Center 2011).

Figure 2. Metropolitan Neighborhood Poverty Contact, 2007–2011, Blacks

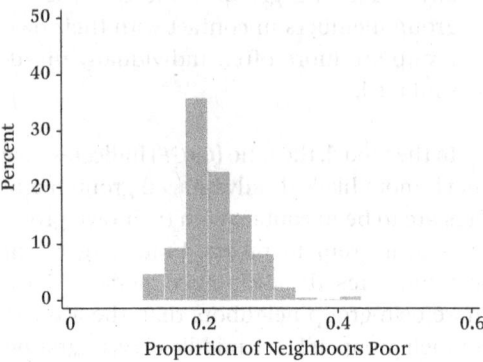

Source: American Community Survey 2007–2011 (Minnesota Population Center 2011).

APPLICATION

We can examine the parts of this model to assess how segregation contributes to contextual advantage or disadvantage through spatial rearrangement in a particular situation. My application of this model is to segregation between residential neighborhoods and racial groups in American cities from 2007 to 2011.

The groups in the analysis are non-Hispanic whites, blacks, and Hispanics.[6] For this analysis, I define disadvantaged as poor and advantaged as nonpoor. Poverty is defined as living in a family with income below the official U.S. government poverty threshold.

I calculate the basic elements of the decomposition using data from the American Community Survey from 2007 to 2011. I use the version of the data from the National Historical Geographic Information System (Minnesota Population Center 2011). The context I use here is the neighborhood, census tracts serving as the usual proxy. Only metropolitan areas with at least twenty thousand persons in the group are used for calculating statistics by group, because segregation measures are often thought to have little meaning when groups are very small in size.

Figure 3. Metropolitan Neighborhood Poverty Contact, 2007–2011, Hispanics

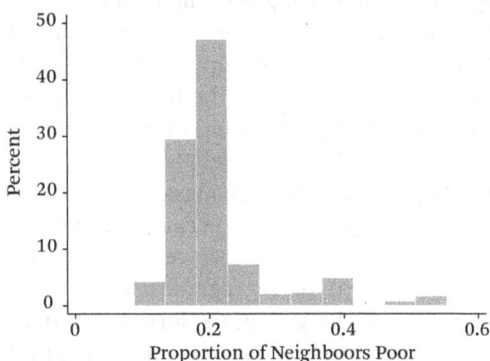

Source: American Community Survey 2007–2011 (Minnesota Population Center 2011).

As discussed, the outcome variable is average group member contact with poor in their census tracts, $_g P^*_p$, where the groups are the three racial-ethnic groups. This measure is equivalent to average neighborhood poverty rate among persons of each racial-ethnic group. Calculated separately for each metropolitan area with at least twenty thousand

---

6. Non-Hispanic whites are persons who identify themselves as white (alone, selecting no other-race category) on the census race question and indicate they are not of Hispanic origin. Blacks are respondents who identify as black alone on the race question, including black Hispanics. The category Hispanic includes everyone who indicates Hispanic origin. The black and Hispanic categories overlap somewhat. Poverty counts in the American Community Survey are not provided separately for non-Hispanic blacks.

Table 1. Neighborhood Poverty Contact Decomposition, Metropolitan Means

Variable	White	Black	Hispanic
Outcome: share poor neighbors in tract of average group resident ($_gP^*_p$)	0.108 (0.029)	0.215 (0.049)	0.212 (0.081)
Segregation group/not group ($V_{(g)(ng)}$)	0.270 (0.119)	0.357 (0.144)	0.219 (0.104)
Group poverty rate (Pov_g)	0.090 (0.027)	0.247 (0.060)	0.243 (0.077)
Nongroup poverty rate (Pov_{ng})	0.237 (0.056)	0.113 (0.035)	0.132 (0.082)
Percentage not group (p_{ng})	0.335 (0.162)	0.799 (0.098)	0.627 (0.251)
GxGP: own-group disproportionality in neighbors of group poor ($gp \to g$)	0.930 (0.036)	1.093 (0.060)	1.123 (0.080)
GxNGP: poverty disproportionality in other-race neighbors of group ($g \to ngp$)	0.830 (0.096)	1.449 (0.264)	1.230 (0.188)
N (metropolitan areas)	380	175	184

Source: American Community Survey 2007–2011, NHGIS version (Minnesota Population Center 2011).
Note: Means calculated with weights for MSA population of indicated group. Metropolitan areas with twenty thousand or more group members are included. Standard deviations in parentheses.

members of each group, the metropolitan $_gP^*_p$ figures are shown as histograms in figures 1 through 3. As we can see, blacks and Hispanics have significantly higher rates of neighborhood poverty contact than whites, a result also noted by John Logan (2011) and others.

I calculate the components of the decomposition formula (5) from tract data for each metropolitan area. Means of components at the metropolitan level by race and ethnic group are shown in table 1.

For *GPxG*, the ratios above one for blacks and Hispanics indicate that poor blacks and Hispanics have more black or Hispanic neighbors than nonpoor blacks or Hispanics. But these ratios are not very far above 1, indicating that the disparity is not very large. The white ratio below 1 indicates that, on average, poor whites have fewer white neighbors than nonpoor whites.

For *GxNGP*, the ratios for blacks and Hispanics deviate further from one, averaging 1.449 for blacks and 1.230 for Hispanics. What this suggests is that the other-race neighbors of blacks and Hispanics tend to have significantly higher poverty rates than the other-race average. This is highlighted in Quillian (2012): disproportionate poverty of the nongroup neighbors of blacks and Hispanics contributes importantly to high neighborhood poverty contact for these groups.

The Role of Segregation in Racial Disparities in Neighborhood Poverty Contact

The decomposition model developed earlier validates the intuition of Massey (1990) that segregation concentrates poverty, but also demonstrates that this effect depends on a set of other spatial conditions.

The first question I consider is whether the correct conditions hold for segregation to increase contextual advantage for whites and contextual disadvantage for blacks and Hispanics. To address this question, I calculate the slope of the segregation effect on contextual disadvantage for whites, blacks, and Hispanics for each metropolitan area from equation (6). This leads to a distribution of slopes for each group across metropolitan areas. For a 1 unit change in segregation, holding other conditions present in the decomposition constant, the slope is the indicated change in average neighborhood poverty for the group.

Table 2 shows means of the slopes by group, and figures 4 through 6 show histograms of the

Table 2. Metropolitan Segregation Slopes

All Variables at Original Values	Whites	Blacks	Hispanics
Mean	−0.034	0.086	0.075
	(0.014)	(0.051)	(0.049)
GxGP = 1 for all metro areas			
Mean	−0.032	0.067	0.054
	(0.013)	(0.042)	(0.033)
GxNGP = 1 for all metro areas			
Mean	−0.048	0.125	0.093
	(0.022)	(0.054)	(0.061)
N (metropolitan areas)	380	175	184

Source: American Community Survey 2007–2011, NHGIS version (Minnesota Population Center 2011).
Note: Means calculated with weights for group metropolitan population. Only MSAs with at least twenty thousand group members are included. Standard deviations in parentheses.

slopes over metropolitan areas for each group. For whites, almost all of the slopes are negative, indicating that contextual disadvantage goes down as segregation goes up. Their contextual advantage increases with segregation, indicated here by a decline in their average neighborhood poverty rate as segregation increases. Of 379 metropolitan areas (with at least twenty thousand non-Hispanic white residents), all but one have negative slopes; the exception is Honolulu.

For blacks and Hispanics almost all slopes of segregation on neighborhood poverty contact are positive. For blacks, the slope is negative rounded to two decimal places for only three of 175 metropolitan areas; for Hispanics, the slope is positive for all metropolitan areas.[7] A marginal change in segregation, keeping other spatial conditions constant, increases neighborhood poverty rates for blacks and Hispanics in almost every American metropolitan area. This leads to a further conclusion.

- Conclusion 7: In almost all American metropolitan areas, an increase in segregation, holding other conditions in the decomposition constant, would decrease white neighborhood poverty contact and increases black and Latino poverty contact. The con-

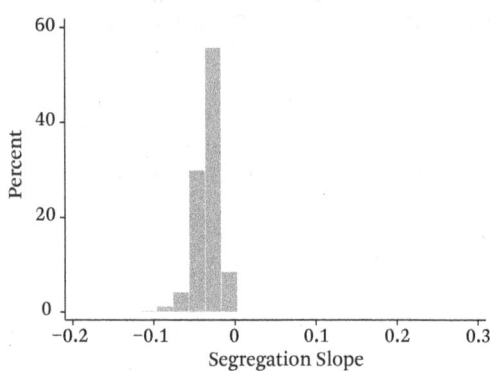

Figure 4. Slope of Segregation on Neighborhood Poverty, 2007–2011, Whites

Source: American Community Survey 2007–2011, NHGIS version (Minnesota Population Center 2011).

ditions for segregation to build contextual advantage via spatial rearrangement among advantaged racial groups and contextual disadvantage for disadvantaged groups hold for residential segregation in almost all American metropolitan areas.

A fixed change in segregation in general has a bigger effect on increasing neighborhood poverty for black and Hispanics than decreas-

---

7. The metropolitan areas with negative black slopes are Springfield, Massachusetts; El Paso, Texas; East Stroudsburg, Pennsylvania; and New York City. These slopes are relatively very small, and the slope for New York is nearly zero (−0.005).

Figure 5. Slope of Segregation on Neighborhood Poverty, 2007–2011, Blacks

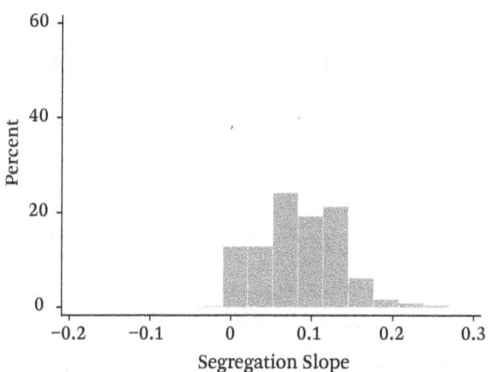

Source: American Community Survey 2007–2011, NHGIS version (Minnesota Population Center 2011).

Figure 6. Slope of Segregation on Neighborhood Poverty, 2007–2011, Hispanics

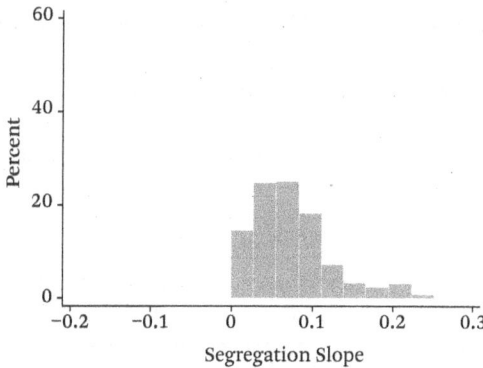

Source: American Community Survey 2007–2011, NHGIS version (Minnesota Population Center 2011).

ing neighborhood poverty for whites. As shown in figures 4 through 6, the negative slopes for whites are generally smaller in magnitude than the positive slopes for blacks and Hispanics. On average, the effect are two to two and a half times larger at increasing black and Hispanic neighborhood poverty rates than at decreasing white neighborhood poverty rates.

This is mostly a result of differences in group size (see conclusion 5). Because whites are a larger share of the population of their metropolitan areas, desegregation increases average neighborhood poverty contact only a little because other groups are too small to boost the white neighborhood poverty rate very much. By contrast, blacks and Hispanics are usually smaller shares of their metropolitan areas, with the result that decreases in segregation produce a larger percentage of nongroup members in their neighborhoods. This is another conclusion.

- Conclusion 8: An increase in segregation, holding other conditions constant, would cause black and Hispanic neighborhood poverty rates to increase more than white rates drop, which largely reflects effects of group size.

A final area of investigation of the slopes relates to conclusions 3 and 4. Conclusion 3 is that segregation effects will tend to be stronger if poor group members have disproportionately more own-group neighbors. Conclusion 4 is that segregation effects will tend to be weaker if a group has disproportionately poor nongroup neighbors.

Table 2 addresses the question of how important in practice these conditions are for segregation effects. In the group decomposition model, I force the situation of no income gradient to own-race neighborhood residence: poor and nonpoor are then treated as equally likely to have own-race neighbors. As expected, this results in weaker segregation effects—the means of the slopes are closer to zero. Although the effects do get smaller, the changes are not especially large. This is not too surprising given that on average the $GxGP$ term is close to one.

The nongroup decomposition model forces the condition that other-race neighbors have poverty rates equal to the other-race average. It shows that this condition makes a significant difference. The slopes increase in magnitude by 25 percent (Hispanics) to about 45 percent (blacks) relative to the base slopes. This yields a further conclusion.

- Conclusion 9: Neighborhood segregation effects in U.S. metropolitan areas are partially suppressed because the other-race neighbors of disadvantaged group members tend to be disproportionately poor.

Table 3. Changes in Neighborhood Poverty Contact with Segregation Decrease

Metropolitan Averages	Whites	Blacks	Hispanics
Estimated effect 25 percent reduction in segregation	0.002	−0.008	−0.004
	(0.001)	(0.006)	(0.003)
Effect as percentage change from base $_gP^*_p$	2.5%	−3.4%	−2.2%
	(1.5)	(2.2)	(1.2)
Effect as percentage change toward racial equality in neighborhood poverty contact	9.0%	9.8%	9.6%
	(6.0)	(5.3)	(9.6)
N (metropolitan areas)	380	175	184

Source: American Community Survey 2007–2011, NHGIS version (Minnesota Population Center 2011).
Note: Means calculated with weights for group metropolitan population. Only MSAs with at least twenty thousand group members are included. Standard deviations in parentheses.

As segregation declines, blacks or Hispanics often trade own-race neighbors for poor other-race neighbors, weakening the reduction in contextual disadvantage with declines in segregation from other groups.

Spatial Arrangement Effects of Segregation on Contextual Advantage

How much of contextual advantage for whites, and disadvantage for blacks and Latinos, can be attributed to the spatial arrangement effect of segregation? I address this question initially by simulating a 25 percent reduction in racial segregation while holding other conditions constant based on the decomposition model. This is assuming segregation declines, but spatial patterns of how income influences cross-race contact, group relative size, and group poverty rates are unchanged by this migration.

In holding poverty rates constant, these estimates omit substantive effects. Empirical studies suggest a decline in segregation would also tend to reduce the poverty rate of the disadvantaged group, although this effect may tend to lag a change in segregation. In the spirit of the Massey (1990) simulation, I focus only on estimating the effect from spatial rearrangement with declining segregation.

The effect of a 25 percent reduction in residential segregation is estimated for all metropolitan areas by using the slope formula to estimate the change in neighborhood poverty for each group with a 25 percent segregation reduction, holding all other components of the decomposition constant. Metropolitan mean effects from this procedure are shown in table 3. Table 3 also shows effects scaled two other ways: as the percentage change in average neighborhood poverty contact relative to the metropolitan base level, and as a percentage change in average neighborhood poverty contact relative to the rate that would prevail if there was no racial inequality in poverty contact. Racial equality in neighborhood poverty contact is the situation in which each racial group on average lives in a neighborhood with the average metropolitan poverty rate.

The results show effects in the expected direction. For blacks the average slope is −0.008, which corresponds to an average change in poverty contact from base of −3.4 percent. This is a reduction in racial neighborhood inequality of 9.8 percent.[8] For Hispanics the change is −0.004, or an average change from base of −2.2 percent, which is a 9.6 percent reduction in racial neighborhood inequality in poverty contact. A 25 percent decrease in segregation then moves the black and Hispanic rate about 10 percent of the way toward the level that would hold if there were racial equality in poverty contact. As conclusion 9 states, a 25 percent reduction does not produce more change, in part be-

---

8. The reduction in racial neighborhood inequality percentage is the change in poverty contact divided by the difference between group poverty contact and group poverty contact if all groups experienced equal neighborhood poverty (in which case all groups would experience the average metropolitan poverty rate).

Table 4. Estimates of Change in Poverty Contact with 25 Percent Decrease in Segregation

Metropolitan Area	Change	% Change from Base	% Reduction in Group Inequality
Whites			
1 Pine Bluff, AR	0.009	5.9	14.8
2 Albany, GA	0.009	5.4	10.8
3 Monroe, LA	0.009	5.9	12.6
4 Memphis, TN-MS-AR	0.008	7.2	11.9
5 Montgomery, AL	0.007	6.1	13.8
6 Jackson, MS	0.007	5.9	11.0
7 Yakima, WA	0.007	4.2	12.3
8 Brownsville-Harlingen, TX	0.007	2.4	10.1
9 Yuma, AZ	0.007	4.3	12.3
10 Macon, GA	0.006	4.3	10.1
Blacks			
1 Niles-Benton Harbor, MI	−0.029	−8.1	15.2
2 Milwaukee-Waukesha, WI	−0.024	−7.8	14.1
3 Monroe, LA	−0.023	−6.5	17.7
4 Peoria, IL	−0.022	−7.4	12.2
5 St. Louis, MO-IL	−0.019	−8.1	16.5
6 Saginaw, MI	−0.019	−5.0	10.0
7 Detroit-Warren-Dearborn, MI	−0.019	−6.3	13.4
8 Cleveland-Elyria, OH	−0.018	−6.4	13.2
9 Chicago-Naperville-Elgin, IL	−0.018	−7.3	15.3
10 Cincinnati, OH-KY-IN	−0.017	−7.1	14.4
Hispanics			
1 Reading, PA	−0.024	−7.4	12.4
2 Springfield, MA	−0.020	−6.5	13.4
3 Allentown-Bethlehem-Easton, PA	−0.014	−6.0	11.1
4 Hartford, CT	−0.012	−5.4	9.8
5 Lancaster, PA	−0.011	−5.5	10.5
6 Philadelphia-Camden, PA-NJ	−0.011	−4.8	10.1
7 Worcester, MA-CT	−0.011	−5.1	9.7
8 Kennewick-Richland, WA	−0.011	−4.7	13.9
9 Providence-Warwick, RI-MA	−0.010	−4.2	8.3
10 New Haven-Milford, CT	−0.010	−4.5	9.6

Source: American Community Survey 2007–2011, NHGIS version (Minnesota Population Center 2011).
Note: For metropolitan areas with at least twenty thousand persons in the indicated group. Changes are holding other decomposition elements constant. Reduction in group inequality is equal to change/ (base-(total metropolitan poverty rate)).

cause of the disproportionate poverty of the other-race neighbors of blacks and Hispanics.

These are metropolitan averages and hide considerable heterogeneity in the effects. Table 4 shows the effects of segregation on poverty concentration from this procedure for cities in which these effects tend to be largest. Some metropolitan areas have conditions that produce larger segregation effects. In these metropolitan areas, effects are significantly larger, changing average poverty contact by 3 percent to 8 percent from base, which produces reductions of racial inequality in neighborhood poverty rates of 7 percent to 15 percent.

- Conclusion 10: A 25 percent decrease in racial segregation, holding other factors constant, produces reductions in racial inequality in neighborhood poverty of 9 to 10 percent from base due to change in spatial arrangement. The effects are not larger because of the effects of other spatial conditions like the segregation of blacks and Hispanics from more affluent other-race neighbors.

The cities for which segregation effects are largest, shown in table 4, are also worth attention. The largest white contextual advantage effects from segregation are typically found in cities in the South and Texas border cities. These areas tend to have high nonwhite poverty rates and large shares of their population nonwhite. Segregation under these conditions especially shields whites from neighborhood poverty.

Black neighborhood poverty rates are most elevated by segregation in former industrial cities, disproportionately in the Midwest, such as Milwaukee, Detroit, Cleveland, Chicago, and Cincinnati. Two primary reasons explain this phenomenon. First, these cities tend to have the highest black-nonblack segregation scores—giving them large changes corresponding to a 25 percent decrease. Second, these cities tend to have high black poverty rates and low to moderate nonblack poverty rates.

Hispanic neighborhood poverty rates tend to be most sensitive to change in segregation in several northeastern cities. These tend to be areas with relatively small Hispanic populations and high poverty rates for their Hispanic residents.

- Conclusion 11: The neighborhood poverty reduction to whites from segregation, holding other conditions constant, tend to be largest in midwestern, southern, and Texas border cities. The neighborhood poverty increase for blacks from an increase in segregation tends to be largest in midwestern cities. The neighborhood poverty increase for Hispanics from an increase in segregation tends to be largest in northeastern cities.

Effects from Eliminating Racial Segregation

Finally, I consider a last counterfactual to assess segregation effects: estimated levels of poverty contact if racial segregation was in fact zero (no racial segregation at all). In this circumstance, every tract has the same percentage of each group.

This is an extremely strong counterfactual. With zero racial segregation, many of the other parameters in the model are also necessarily zero (or one in cases where that indicates no effect). For instance, the average poverty rate of other-race neighbors for any racial group must be the same as the nongroup average in this circumstance, implicitly forcing $GxGP$ to be one.

I calculate the effect on group poverty rates from a change to zero segregation by taking the metropolitan poverty rate overall (across all groups), and then the difference between each group's actual metropolitan neighborhood poverty rate and this rate. In complete racial integration, each groups' poverty contact is equal to the overall metropolitan poverty rate.

The corresponding averages are shown in table 5. These effects are much larger than those in table 3. We might expect them to be four times as large as the estimates in table 3—because table 3 was based on a 25 percent reduction—but because this zeros out related conditions (there can be no tendency of blacks to have poorer nonblack neighbors than whites on average when integration is perfect) these effects are significantly larger. White contact with neighborhood poverty increases by 28 percent in this scenario, black poverty contact decreases by 34 percent, and Hispanic contact decreases by 21 percent.

- Conclusion 12: Without racial segregation there would be no metropolitan differences in neighborhood poverty exposure across racial groups, which correspond to increases (whites) or decreases (blacks, Latinos) of 20 to 34 percent in average neighborhood poverty contact, holding group poverty rates constant.

Table 5. Contributions of Segregation to Neighborhood Poverty Contact, Metropolitan Averages

	Whites	Blacks	Hispanics
Estimated total effect of segregation (100%)	0.028	−0.075	−0.041
	(0.016)	(0.035)	(0.026)
Effect as percentage change from base $_gP^*_p$	28.3	−33.8	−21.2
	(18.8)	(11.1)	(12.1)
N (metropolitan areas)	380	175	184

Source: American Community Survey 2007–2011, NHGIS version (Minnesota Population Center 2011).
Note: Means calculated with weights for group metropolitan population. Only MSAs with at least twenty thousand group members are included. Standard deviations in parentheses.

CONCLUSION

By separating groups with unequal poverty rates into different contexts, segregation builds contextual advantage for advantaged groups and disadvantage for disadvantaged groups. This basic point is illustrated famously in Massey's (1990) simulations. Massey's model, however, does not include other spatial conditions regarding group poverty rates and spatial patterns through which income is related to cross-race contact that can alter or, if strong enough, invert Massey's predicted segregation effects.

The model developed here provides a more detailed specification of Massey's simulation model, showing multiple factors interact with segregation in determining contextual advantage and disadvantage levels experienced by segregated groups. The extent to which a change in the level of segregation contributes to contextual advantage and disadvantage depends on several other conditions, notably group relative size, effects of individual advantage or disadvantage of group members on group contact, and the advantage/disadvantage level of the nongroup members whom group members are in contact.

In the spirit of Massey's (1990) simulations, the estimates here only capture the spatial arrangement effects of segregation. Because a reduction in segregation would in the long term probably reduce black and Latino poverty rates, the overall effect of a long-term reduction in segregation is underestimated in these results. Nevertheless, the spatial arrangement effect is basic to understanding segregation effects on the social contexts of segregated groups, and can be understood with greater precision than substantive effects.

A potential application of the model is to understand how and why race group neighborhood poverty changes as migration and other processes shift group spatial patterns. A change in group neighborhood poverty between decades, for instance, could be decomposed into how different parts of the decomposition have changed, providing a deeper understanding of the changing spatial position of race and income groups that shift group neighborhood poverty.

In the case of American cities, I find that the conditions for segregation to contribute to a reduction in white neighborhood poverty rates and an increase in black and Latino poverty rates hold for almost all metropolitan areas. This analysis verifies Massey's broad account of segregation's role in accounting for racial disparities in neighborhood poverty contact in American cities, even without accounting for substantive ways that segregation feeds back to increase the poverty rates of disadvantage groups.

We might expect from Massey's original model that a decrease in segregation would produce a nearly one-for-one proportionate decrease in black and Latino neighborhood poverty, together with a proportionate increase in white neighborhood poverty, which in fact specifications in Massey's test of these ideas imply (Massey and Eggers 1990). The model reveals instead that the average marginal effect of segregation on racial disparities in neighborhood poverty rates, holding other conditions constant, are smaller than directly proportionate. A 25 percent decrease in segregation produces on average about a 10 percent decrease in neighborhood poverty inequality for blacks and Latinos. This is primarily because the other-race neighbors of blacks and Hispanics are significantly poorer than the nonblack and non-Hispanic average, and this reduces the effect of marginal changes in segregation on poverty contact. These results imply that the trend of gradually declining racial segregation in American metropolitan areas (Logan and Stults 2011) will then not reduce poverty as much in black and Latino environments as a straight application of Massey's simulation would suggest.

Such an outcome suggests that policies to reduce racial segregation with the goal of reducing concentrations of poverty in black and Latino neighborhoods need to attend to the income character of desegregation. If only higher-income blacks and Latinos enter whiter environments, reduction in neighborhood poverty among blacks and Latinos overall may not follow. Likewise, if the white neighbors of blacks and Latinos have high poverty rates, then the poverty deconcentrating effect of a reduction in segregation is reduced. By contrast, desegregation and neighborhood poverty deconcentration are increased when lower-income blacks and Latinos move into nonpoor white neighborhoods, suggesting that siting of public housing and assistance for voucher holders to enter white low-poverty neighborhoods can have especially strong effects of reducing racial segregation and racial inequality in neighborhood poverty contact.

If we consider the strong counterfactual of no racial segregation, racial segregation effects on poverty concentration through spatial arrangement are quite large for most American cities. Although this is a strong counterfactual—it is difficult to imagine what American metropolitan areas would be like without any racial segregation—it also illustrates the important way that neighborhood racial residential segregation is a critical condition to produce unequal neighborhood income conditions across racial and ethnic groups.

REFERENCES

Chetty, Raj, Nathaniel Hendren, and Lawrence F. Katz. 2015. "The Effects of Exposure to Better Neighborhoods on Children: New Evidence from the Moving to Opportunity Experiment." *NBER* working paper no. 21156. Cambridge, Mass.: National Bureau of Economic Research. Accessed July 1, 2016. http://www.nber.org/papers/w21156.

Chetty, Raj, Nathaniel Hendren, Patrick Kline, and Emmanuel Saez. 2014. "Where Is the Land of Opportunity? The Geography of Intergenerational Mobility in the United States." *Quarterly Journal of Economics* 129(4): 1553–623. doi:10.1093/qje/qju022.

Clark, Kenneth B. 1989. *Dark Ghetto: Dilemmas of Social Power*, 2nd ed. Middletown, Conn: Wesleyan University Press.

Coleman, James Samuel. 1966. *Equality of Educational Opportunity*. Washington: U.S. Department of Health, Education, and Welfare.

Denton, Nancy, and Douglas S. Massey. 1989. "Residential Segregation of Blacks, Hispanics, and Asians by Socioeconomic Status and Generation." *Social Science Quarterly* 69(2): 797–817.

James, David R., and Karl E. Taeuber. 1985. "Measures of Segregation." In *Sociological Methodology 1985*, edited by Nancy B. Tuma. San Francisco: Jossey-Bass.

Lieberson, Stanley. 1980. *A Piece of the Pie: Black and White Immigrants Since 1880*. Berkeley: University of California Press.

Logan, John R. 2011. "Separate and Unequal: The Neighborhood Gap for Blacks, Hispanics, and Asians in Metropolitan America." *US2010 Project* report. Providence, R.I.: Brown University. Accessed July 1, 2016. http://www.s4.brown.edu/us2010/Data/Report/report0727.pdf.

Logan, John R., and Brian Stults. 2011. "The Persistence of Segregation in the Metropolis: New Findings from the 2010 Census." *Project US2010* census brief. Providence, R.I.: Brown University. Accessed April 1, 2016. http://www.s4.brown.edu/us2010.

Massey, Douglas S. 1990. "American Apartheid: Segregation and the Making of the Underclass." *American Journal of Sociology* 96(2): 329–57.

Massey, Douglas S., and Nancy A. Denton. 1988. "The Dimensions of Residential Segregation." *Social Forces* 67(2): 281–315.

———. 1993. *American Apartheid: Segregation and*

the Making of the Underclass. Cambridge, Mass.: Harvard University Press.

Massey, Douglas S., and Mitchell L. Eggers. 1990. "The Ecology of Inequality: Minorities and the Concentration of Poverty, 1970–1980." *American Journal of Sociology* 95(5): 1153–88.

Minnesota Population Center. 2011. National Historical Geographic Information System: version 2.0. Minneapolis: University of Minnesota.

Orfield, Gary, and Chungmei Lee. 2005. "Why Segregation Matters: Poverty and Educational Inequality." Cambridge, Mass.: The Civil Rights Project of Harvard University.

Pattillo, Mary. 1999. *Black Picket Fences: Privilege and Peril Among the Black Middle Class*. Chicago: University of Chicago Press.

Peterson, Ruth D., and Lauren J. Krivo. 2010. *Divergent Social Worlds: Neighborhood Crime and the Racial-Spatial Divide*. New York: Russell Sage Foundation.

Quillian, Lincoln. 2012. "Segregation and Poverty Concentration: The Role of Three Segregations." *American Sociological Review* 77(3): 354–79.

———. 2014. "Does Segregation Create Winners and Losers? Residential Segregation and Inequality in Educational Attainment." *Social Problems* 61(3): 402–26.

Sharkey, Patrick. 2013. *Stuck in Place: Urban Neighborhoods and the End of Progress Toward Racial Equality*. Chicago: University of Chicago Press.

———. 2014. "Spatial Segmentation and the Black Middle Class." *American Journal of Sociology* 119(4): 903–54.

Wilson, William Julius. 1987. *The Truly Disadvantaged: The Inner City, the Underclass, and Public Policy*. Chicago: University of Chicago Press.

Wodtke, Geoffrey T., David J. Harding, and Felix Elwert. 2011. "Neighborhood Effects in Temporal Perspective: The Impact of Long-Term Exposure to Concentrated Disadvantage on High School Graduation." *American Sociological Review* 76(5): 713–36.

How Living in the 'Hood Affects Risky Behaviors Among Latino and African American Youth

ANNA MARIA SANTIAGO, EUN LYE LEE,
JESSICA L. LUCERO, AND REBECCA WIERSMA

Using data from a natural experiment in Denver, we investigate whether the initiation of running away from home, aggressive or violent behavior, and marijuana use during adolescence are statistically related to the neighborhood contexts in which low-income Latino and African American youth were raised. Our analysis is based on retrospective child, caregiver, household, and neighborhood data for a sample of approximately 850 Latino and African American youth whose families were quasi-randomly assigned to public housing operated by the Denver (CO) Housing Authority during part of their childhood. We used Cox PH models and accelerated failure time models to estimate ethnic differentials in the hazards and timing of initiation of these risky behaviors during adolescence. We found that multiple dimensions of neighborhood context—especially safety, ethnic and nativity composition, and socioeconomic status—strongly and robustly predicted initiation of running away, aggressive or violence behavior, and marijuana use during adolescence.

Keywords: risky behaviors, neighborhood effects, natural experiments, Cox PH models, accelerated failure time (AFT) models

The last decade has seen a marked upsurge in the fraction of low-income families of color residing in neighborhoods with poverty rates exceeding 40 percent (Bischoff and Reardon 2013; Jargowsky 2013). Although the facts of this growing spatial inequality are indisputable, the potential consequences are very much a point of contention. Despite a rapidly expanding social scientific literature focusing on the role of neighborhood contexts on child and adolescent outcomes emerging over the past twenty years (for recent comprehensive reviews

---

Anna Maria Santiago is professor at the School of Social Work at Michigan State University. Eun Lye Lee is postdoctoral scholar at the Prevention Research Center for Healthy Neighborhoods at Case Western Reserve University. Jessica L. Lucero is assistant professor in the Department of Sociology, Social Work, and Anthropology at Utah State University. Rebecca Wiersma is Oakland MSW Field Coordinator at the School of Social Work at Michigan State University.

© 2017 Russell Sage Foundation. Santiago, Anna Maria, Eun Lye Lee, Jessica L. Lucero, and Rebecca Wiersma. 2017. "How Living in the 'Hood Affects Risky Behaviors Among Latino and African American Youth." *RSF: The Russell Sage Foundation Journal of the Social Sciences* 3(2): 170–209. DOI: 10.7758/RSF.3.2.08. This research was supported by NICHD grant 5R01 HD47786–2, and grants from the MacArthur Foundation, the W. K. Kellogg Foundation, the Annie E. Casey Foundation, and the U.S. Department of Housing and Urban Development. The views represented in this paper do not necessarily reflect the views of these sponsors. The authors also gratefully acknowledge the programming assistance of Dr. Albert Anderson and the research assistance of Kristen Berg, Ana Sanroman, Gabriela Sehinkman, Tanisha Tate, and Leigh Taylor. Direct correspondence to: Anna Maria Santiago at santia63@msu.edu, Michigan State University, School of Social Work, 655 Auditorium Road, Baker Hall 124, East Lansing, MI 48823; Eun Lye Lee at eunlye.lee@case.edu, Case Western Reserve University, School of Medicine, Prevention Research Center for Healthy Neighborhoods, Cleveland, OH 44106; Jessica L. Lucero at jessica.lucero@usu.edu, Utah State University, Department of Sociology, Social Work, and Anthropology, 0730 Old Main Hill, Logan, UT 84322; and Rebecca Wiersma at wiersma3@msu.edu, Michigan State University, School of Social Work, 655 Auditorium Road, Baker Hall 206, East Lansing, MI 48823.

of this literature, see Galster 2008; Leventhal, Dupéré, and Brooks-Gunn 2009; Zimmerman and Messner 2010; Chilenski 2011; Karriker-Jaffe 2011; Foster and Brooks-Gunn 2012; Jackson, Denny, and Ameratunga 2014; and Oakes et al. 2015), numerous questions remain as to the magnitude, mechanisms, and contingent natures of such effects and the extent to which these effects shape the short- and long-term opportunities available to children.

In this paper, we assess the effects on low-income, minority youth of early and sustained residence in different kinds of neighborhoods on their involvement in risky behaviors during adolescence. Specifically, we investigate whether running away from home, using aggressive or violent behavior, or marijuana use was statistically related to a wide variety of conditions in the neighborhoods in which the youth were raised. To answer these questions, we use administrative and survey data from Latino and African American current and former public housing tenants who were exposed to a naturally occurring experiment in Denver, Colorado, and whose children resided in public housing for substantial periods during childhood. Our survey of caregivers provides retrospective information on a battery of youth outcomes, child, caregiver and household characteristics, and perceived neighborhood contexts. Administrative data provide us with a rich array of neighborhood environmental contexts.

Our paper introduces several methodological innovations to the study of spatial inequality. First, we use a natural experiment using quasi-random allocation to subsidized public housing units in Denver to assess neighborhood effects on low-income Latino and African American children. We rigorously test the degree to which this initial assignment process mimicked a random process and determine through a series of balancing tests and Monte Carlo simulations that this indeed was the case. Therefore, the natural experiment in our study likely removes the correlation between any remaining unobservable parental characteristics that potentially affect both the location initially assigned by the City and County of Denver Housing Authority (DHA) and subsequent initiation of child risky behaviors that may follow from this location. The potential for selection biases to reappear grows, however, as time passes since initial assignment. Therefore, we use instrumental variable estimates of neighborhood environment for those locations where families moved after initial assignment to assess the robustness of our results.

Our work advances the literature on neighborhood effects on children's risky behavioral outcomes in three ways. First, because the primary caregivers of sampled children were quasi-randomly assigned to neighborhoods when they first entered the public housing program, the challenge of parental geographic selection bias has been substantially overcome. Second, we evaluate an unprecedented variety of measures of neighborhood environmental contexts measured at different spatial scales. Third, in contrast to previous studies that have focused primarily on the experiences of low-income, African American children, we examine differences in these effects for Latino children as well.

THEORETICAL AND EMPIRICAL LITERATURE REVIEW

Since the late 1980s, interest in the investigation of neighborhood effects on child and youth outcomes has revived among social scientists (Wilson 1987; Billy, Brewster, and Grady 1994; Leventhal and Brooks-Gunn 2000; Zimmerman and Messner 2010; Jackson, Denny, and Ameratunga 2014). This wave of neighborhood effects research has been motivated by a growing recognition of the complex, multisystem constellation of risk factors that increases the vulnerability of children (Werner and Smith 1982; Rutter 1989; Sameroff et al. 1993; Foster and Brooks-Gunn 2012; Gilliard-Matthews et al. 2015). Underlying the study of neighborhood developmental contexts is the assumption that children and youth who face a multitude of adverse conditions and risk factors in their neighborhoods tend to have poorer outcomes as well as constrained access to opportunities across childhood and into adulthood (Coulton and Korbin 2007). Yet, scholarship to date has not conclusively ascertained whether any bona fide causal connection exists between neighborhood and child outcomes and, if so, what the underlying causal mechanism is. In the next section, we provide an overview of the theoretical literature that examines how neighborhoods might influence youth risky behaviors and assess the extant empirical literature testing these purported associations.

How Neighborhoods Might Influence Child and Adolescent Risky Behaviors

The theoretical framework that underlies much of the existing literature is Bronfenbrenner's ecological systems model of human development, which postulates that children's developmental outcomes are shaped by the proximal (for example, family) as well as distal (for example, neighborhood) contexts in which children live and interact (for example, Bronfenbrenner and Morris 1998). Ecological systems theory argues that neighborhood may influence children's behavior through an array of causal mechanisms operating through social, institutional, or biological processes (see Duncan, Connell, and Klebanov 1997; Gephart 1997; Leventhal and Brooks-Gunn 2000; Sampson 2001; Sampson, Morenoff, and Gannon-Rowley 2002; Leventhal, Dupéré, and Brooks-Gunn 2009; Harding et al. 2010; Galster 2012; Foster and Brooks-Gunn 2012; and Oakes et al. 2015). The potential mechanisms relevant for risky behaviors include peer influences, socialization and social control, exposure to violence and social disorder, and local institutional resources. Because these mechanisms are well documented in the literature, we describe them only briefly.

Peer Influences

Youth may develop and modify attitudes, values, behaviors and expectations about running away, use of aggressive or violent behavior, or marijuana use as a result of interactions with similarly aged neighborhood peers as well as peer pressure (Case and Katz 1991). These peer effects may be transmitted among youth through peer interaction and social learning (Crane 1991; South, Baumer, and Lutz 2003).

Socialization and Social Control

Youths' attitudes, values, behaviors and expectations about the use of aggressive or violent behavior and marijuana drug use may be shaped by neighborhood adult role models and norms enforced by the community or local culture (Wilson 1987; Sampson 2001; Burlew et al. 2009; Foster and Brooks-Gunn 2012).

Exposure to Violence and Social Disorder

Exposure to neighborhood violence may lead to early initiation of risky behaviors as a way of coping with the heightened levels of stress associated with such exposure (Lambert et al. 2004; Tyler and Bersani 2008; Copeland-Linder et al. 2010; Farrell et al. 2010; Furr-Holden et al. 2011; Jennings et al. 2011; Sampson, Sharkey, and Raudenbush 2008; Sanbonmatsu et al. 2011; Fagan, Wright, and Pinchevsky 2015).

Local Institutional Resources

Public and private institutions controlling services and facilities for children (for example, medical facilities, parks, recreational centers, counseling or mentoring centers) vary in their quantity and quality on the basis of neighborhood context, thereby affecting access to safe, supervised activities for children and youth differently (Leventhal and Brooks-Gunn 2000; Leventhal, Dupéré, and Brooks-Gunn 2009; Foster and Brooks-Gunn 2012).

Although evidence supports several of the identified neighborhood effect mechanisms, the specific causal mechanisms that reputedly produce these behavioral outcomes remain poorly understood. No consensus has been reached on which mechanism or mechanisms are the primary pathway or pathways associated with specific behavioral outcomes, which remains a critical realm of future research (Galster 2012; Oakes et al. 2015).

Prior Evidence on Neighborhood Attributes and Child and Adolescent Risky Behaviors

Neighborhood Concentrated Disadvantage

A series of comprehensive reviews of observational studies on neighborhood effects and child and adolescent well-being (see Leventhal and Brooks-Gunn, 2000; Galster 2008; Leventhal, Dupéré, and Brooks-Gunn 2009; Sanbonmatsu et al. 2011; and Foster and Brooks-Gunn 2012) underscore the persistent negative influence of living in socioeconomically disadvantaged neighborhoods on child and adolescent behavioral outcomes. Across these studies, neighborhood concentrated disadvantage was defined and operationalized using some derivative of a composite measure of tract-level census data including poverty rates, female headship or single parent households, percent African American, and various ratios depicting the relative share of children residing in two-parent families. Citing work spanning several decades of research using data ranging from national longitudinal studies (for example, PSID, NLSY) or case studies in multiple metropolitan areas (for example, LAFANS, PHDCN, Moving to Opportunity), the aforementioned authors report that aggressive, violent or criminal behavior, risky sexual behavior, and externalizing behaviors during adolescence were strongly associated with increasing levels of socioeconomic disadvantage in the neighborhoods in which these youths resided. Further, these youth are more likely to encounter difficulties in adulthood such as unemployment, substance abuse, and mental health disorders (Kellam et al. 2008; Poduska et al. 2008). However, this purported association between neighborhood disadvantage and marijuana use has not proven as straightforward: some studies (for example, Fite et al. 2009; Mennis and Mason 2012) have reported early initiation of marijuana use in more disadvantaged neighborhoods while others have reported the inverse (Boardman 2001; Bolland et al. 2007; Ford and Beverage 2006; Hoffman 2002; Snedker, Herting, and Walton 2009) or no relationship (Allison et al. 1999) at all.

Exposure to Violence
Exposure to high levels of crime and violence has been found in observational studies to further exacerbate behavioral problems during adolescence. Kimberly Tyler and Bianca Bersani (2008) find that early exposure to gun shots, bullying, and residential break-ins, significantly increased the likelihood of running away during mid-adolescence. Dana Haynie and colleagues (2009) find that exposure to neighborhood violence increased the risk of youth running away from home, dropping out of school, teen childbearing, attempting suicide, and having juvenile or criminal justice involvement. Further, increased actual or perceived levels of neighborhood violence were associated with higher levels of physical aggression and violent behavior among youth (Vanfossen et al. 2010; Brook et al. 2011; Foster and Brooks-Gunn 2012). A recent study by Abigail Fagan, Emily Wright, and Gillian Pinchevsky (2015) reports higher marijuana use among youth who experienced violence victimization.

Experimental Evidence
The causal interpretation of these neighborhood-behavioral outcome relationships measured in these observational studies is subject to many methodological challenges, however, perhaps the most daunting one being geographic selection bias (Galster 2008). A consensus has developed that studies based on random-assignment experiments or natural quasi-experiments that mimic the random assignment of households to neighborhoods are the strongest designs to estimate unbiased neighborhood effects and to generate reliable causal inferences (Leventhal and Brooks-Gunn 2000; Leventhal, Dupéré, and Brooks-Gunn 2009; Oakes et al. 2015).

The only extant example of either of these random or quasi-random neighborhood assignment approaches relevant to child and adolescent risky behaviors is the well-known Moving to Opportunity (MTO) demonstration (Gennetian, Sanbonmatsu, and Ludwig 2011; Sanbonmatsu et al. 2011). Early findings suggested substantial reductions on girls' rates of risky behaviors and boys' drug use attributed to residence in lower-poverty neighborhoods (see Gennetian, Sanbonmatsu, and Ludwig 2011; Goering and Feins 2003). However, after initial declines in risky behavior, boys living in lower-poverty neighborhoods four to seven years after their first move were more likely to reengage in risky behavior (see Sanbonmatsu et al. 2011). By the end of the demonstration project, girls assigned to low-poverty neighborhoods were less likely to have serious behavioral problems. Group differences on more serious antisocial, problem or criminal behavior were not significant (Sanbonmatsu et al. 2011).

As provocative as these findings are, because of methodological and operational shortcomings, they do not settle unambiguously all questions about neighborhood impacts on children's initiation of risky behavior (see extensive discussion in Sampson 2008). First, MTO randomly assigned participants to one of three comparison groups but not to their specific initial or subsequent neighborhoods, thereby enabling potential self-selection of neighborhood characteristics by anyone in the study. Second, after the first year of residence in a low-poverty location, households in the treatment group were free to move to different, higher-poverty neighborhoods if they desired; as Tom Kingsley and Kathryn Pettit (2007) note, 85 percent did so. As a result, relatively few MTO treatment group households experienced sustained exposure to low-poverty neighborhoods. Third, the low-poverty neighborhoods where treatment group households lived typically had inferior public services, limited access to transportation and jobs, and primarily racial or ethnic minority residents (Sampson 2008). Fourth, the separable impacts of different aspects of the residential environment cannot be ascertained given the "bundled" nature of the "treatment" being applied in MTO.

Thus, the existing literature has not provided definitive evidence about the potential behavioral benefits to low-income Latino and African American youth from sustained residence in more-advantaged, safer and opportunity-rich neighborhoods. Our study hopes to contribute clarification by leveraging a natural experiment related to the DHA.

DATA

The Denver Child Study derives its study population from a natural experiment involving the Denver Housing Authority's conventional and dispersed housing programs. Since 1969, the DHA has operated a dispersed housing program providing approximately 1,500 low-income families with opportunities to live in scattered-site, single-family and small-scale, multifamily units in addition to approximately three thousand units of conventional public housing. Unlike the conventional developments, which tend to be located in less-advantaged neighborhoods, dispersed housing units are found in approximately 60 percent of all neighborhoods throughout the city and county of Denver. From 1987 onward, eligible applicants who came to the top of the common DHA wait list were offered vacant housing units in either conventional or dispersed programs appropriate for their family size and gender of children. Applicants who did not accept their initial offer received a second offer for the next similarly sized unit that became available. Applicants who did not accept this second offer were dropped to the bottom of the wait list, creating a wait of a year or more (see Santiago et al. 2014). Although nearly nine out of ten applicants accepted their first or second offers and three-quarters of all DHA applicants accepted housing units in their initially assigned neighborhoods, a nontrivial number of applicants did not, which prompted us to assess the DHA initial assignment process more closely.

We conducted an array of statistical balancing tests to ascertain the extent to which applicants were quasi-randomly assigned neighborhood characteristics through the DHA housing allocation process (for details, see appendix A). Findings demonstrate that the process mimicked random assignment but with one notable exception. African American households in DHA, regardless of their size, tended to be concentrated in areas with higher percentages of African Americans. Although we cannot ascertain whether this pattern was the result of any systematic actions by the DHA or geographic self-selection by African American applicants, the outcome was inconsistent with quasi-random assignment of this neighborhood characteristic. To address this inconsistency, our statistical analyses are stratified by ethnicity and results involving neighborhood racial mix should be interpreted with caution.

Of course, bias can arise after initial assignment due to potential selection on unobservables that affect who stays and who leaves their original DHA dwellings.[1] To avoid such bias, we use instrumental variables (IV) for neighborhood characteristics. We are therefore con-

---

1. In the analyses reported here, between 62 and 67 percent of study youth were residing in the neighborhood originally assigned by DHA.

fident that the relationships we observe between neighborhood characteristics and youth behaviors can be interpreted in causal terms rather than in relation to parental geographic selection.

Another important feature of our natural experiment in Denver is the comparatively long exposures children in DHA households had to their assigned neighborhoods. Our sample had a six-year mean (five-year median) DHA residential duration, approximately twice as long as reported for the MTO experimental group (mean = 2.7 years; median = 3.3 years). Previous studies underscore the importance of accounting for the duration of neighborhood exposure to estimate the true effects that neighborhoods have on youth outcomes (Wodtke, Hardling, and Elwert 2011; Crowder and South 2011; Chetty, Hendren, and Katz 2015).

Although this is a case study from a single metropolitan area, we believe that our findings can be generalized to other low-income, Latino and African American families who apply for and remain on the waiting list long enough to obtain public housing. It may not be fully generalizable to the population of minority families who obtain subsidized rental housing, and certainly may not be to the larger population of minority families who qualify for housing assistance. Nevertheless, it is similar to—yet considerably more general than—the populations forming the samples for the MTO-based scholarship noted earlier.

Denver Child Study Retrospective Survey and Analysis Sample
At the core of the Denver Child Study was a retrospective survey administered to current and former DHA residents identified as primary caregivers whose families entered DHA during the period between January 1, 1987, and December 31, 2005; had resided in DHA for a minimum of two years; had at least one child under eighteen when they moved into DHA; and were of Latino or African American ethnic origin.[2] Attempts to recruit subjects for the study were made by mail and phone, in both English and Spanish when appropriate. Surveys were administered by phone or in person between April 2006 and February 2008 to all eligible caregivers with valid contact information (N=1,334). A total of 710 caregivers and their 1,702 children met all of the eligibility criteria for the study, yielding a final response rate of 53 percent. Caregivers were asked about their children's physical and mental health, education, exposure to violence, risky behaviors, employment, and marriage and childbearing. Additionally, residential histories from birth through age eighteen or age of time of the survey (if younger than eighteen) were compiled for all eligible children in the household. Finally, respondents were asked to provide extensive details about all of the neighborhoods in which the children lived during childhood and about the characteristics of all members of the household corresponding to each place of residence.

Because the outcomes of interest for this study are running away from home, use of aggressive or violent behavior, or marijuana use during adolescence (between ages eight and eighteen), the final analysis sample from the Denver Child Study includes only youth who were at least eight years old at the time of the survey; were randomly assigned to a DHA neighborhood prior to onset of the specific outcomes of interest; resided in DHA for a minimum of two years; and had complete information for all variables used in our analytical models. These criteria resulted in analysis samples of 855 for running away from home, 782 for aggressive or violent behavior, and 742 for marijuana use.

Youth, Caregiver, and Household Characteristics
Our analytical models control for an array of youth, caregiver, and household characteristics associated with the initiation of running away from home, use of aggressive or violent behavior, or marijuana use during adolescence (see table 1). In addition to controlling for gender and ethnicity, the analytical models control for caregiver age, immigrant status, disability status, educational attainment, and earnings with

---

2. A nontrivial number of youth in our study were raised by grandparents or other family members. Therefore, we have opted to refer to the adult respondents in our study as caregivers rather than parents.

Table 1. Descriptive Characteristics of Youth, Caregivers, Households, and Neighborhoods

Predictor Measures	Run Away from Home (N=855) Mean	SD	Use of Aggressive or Violent Behavior (N=782) Mean	SD	Marijuana Use (N=742) Mean	SD	Denver, 2008 Mean	SD
Youth characteristics								
Gender and ethnicity of youth								
Latina female	0.28	0.45	0.29	0.45	0.28	0.45	—	—
Latino male	0.30	0.46	0.29	0.46	0.30	0.46	—	—
African American female	0.21	0.41	0.21	0.41	0.21	0.41	—	—
African American male	0.22	0.41	0.21	0.41	0.21	0.41	—	—
Caregiver and household characteristics								
Number of siblings in household					1.86	1.33	—	—
Caregiver age	40.80	9.35	40.99	9.40	40.87	9.20	—	—
Caregiver immigrant status (omitted=no)	0.17	0.38					—	—
Caregiver disability status (omitted=not disabled)			0.08	0.28			—	—
Caregiver educational attainment (omitted=no degree)								
High school diploma or higher			0.63	0.48	0.62	0.49	—	—
Caregiver earnings (in dollars)	12,200.90	13,205.47	11,733.30	12,643.74	11,892.60	12,654.68	—	—
Natural log of caregiver earnings (in dollars)	2.49	2.09	2.47	2.08	2.48	2.09	—	—
Caregiver available to monitor-supervise children FT-PT (omitted=not available)	0.48	0.50					—	—
Household stressor scale (range 0–5)	1.34	1.18			1.29	1.11	—	—
Total number of moves from birth to time of initiation					3.25	2.37	—	—
Neighborhood characteristics (all continuous variables reflect predicted values at age of initiation)								
Social vulnerability score (range 0–400)	119.90	28.72	122.40	30.98	119.80	29.40	96.73	42.01
Percentage African American residents	14.31	8.98	14.60	9.30	13.98	9.32	11.54	16.66
Occupational prestige score (range 0–100)	37.39	1.69	37.27	1.65	37.40	1.73	41.01	4.37
Percentage foreign-born residents	27.31	7.06	26.45	7.12	27.15	7.27	15.83	10.76
Violent crime rate per 1,000	10.91	3.48	11.31	3.73	10.94	3.49	5.62	6.69
Property crime rate per 1,000	49.82	13.30	53.31	15.17	49.33	13.62	46.76	43.59

Source: Authors' calculations.

Note: Denver 2008 data were derived from the Geolytics Neighborhood Change Database and Piton Foundation's Neighborhood Facts Database.

all time-varying characteristics measures at time of first offer or time of initiation of specified risky behavior depending on the analytical model discussed. Household indicators include measures controlling for the number of siblings in the household and number of residential moves through time of first offer or initation of risky behavior. In addition, we included a household economic stressors index of five items inquiring about difficulties faced by the household in terms of finances, employment, health insurance, unemployment or job loss, illness or injury, health and health insurance, utilities and housing. This index measures the magnitude of stressors facing the household during each year in a youth's life. Scores ranged from 0 to 5, with higher values indicating a higher degree of household stress. The Cronbach's alpha for this index was 0.52. For youth who did not engage in any risky behaviors, caregiver and household characteristics were measured at age of time-of-survey for youth under age eighteen or at age eighteen for youth who were eighteen or older (for additional details, see Santiago et al. 2014, chapter 3).

As shown in table 1, 49 percent of the sample youth were female and 58 percent were Latino. Approximately one out of every five youth were first- or second-generation immigrants. The primary caregiver was, on average, between forty and forty-one years old. One in ten caregivers was disabled. Approximately 63 percent had completed a high school diploma, post–high school technical certificate, or college degree. Caregiver earnings averaged $12,000 across the three analysis samples, ranging from $0 to $66,352. The typical youth had 1.9 siblings and had moved, on average, 3.3 times during childhood. Households experienced, on average, 1.3 economic stressors measured at time of initiation of the specific risky behavior.

Neighborhood Context Indicators
Residential history information obtained on the survey was verified for accuracy and then geo-coded using the U.S. Census Bureau's *American FactFinder*. We were able to link 92 percent of the residential locations identified by caregivers to a census tract which then permitted us to link these locations to a rich set of census and noncensus neighborhood indicators from two sources: U.S. Census and the Piton Foundation's Neighborhood Facts database. We used linear interpolation or extrapolation to derive annual estimates of neighborhood conditions for the period between 1970 and 2007 (see detailed discussion in Santiago et al. 2014, chapter 3, appendix B). Because we also asked the caregiver when (if ever) specific outcomes occurred during childhood, we were able to use this timing information to temporally match outcomes with corresponding neighborhood indicators.

In this paper, census indicators for neighborhood ethnic composition (percentage foreign born and African American) and socioeconomic status (social vulnerability index and occupational prestige) were derived from the Neighborhood Change Data Base (a Geolytics proprietary product). Our composite measure of neighborhood disadvantage, which we call our social vulnerability index, was estimated using principal components analysis that across the 1970 to 2000 censuses consistently produced a single component composed of the roughly equally weighted sum of census tract percentages of poor, unemployed, renters, and female household heads. Index scores range from 0 to 400 and the Cronbach's alpha for this index was 0.910.

We compute an occupational prestige score based on the 1989 General Social Survey prestige score by occupation (Davis et al. 1991) weighted by the observed proportional distribution of occupations of employees in the census tract. This scale has a minimum possible score of 29.44 (when all employees are laborers) and a maximum possible score of 62.24 (when all employees are in managerial-professional occupations).

We obtain two indicators of exposure to neighborhood violence (violent crime rate and property crime rate per one thousand population) from the Piton Foundation's Neighborhood Facts Database. This database provides small area, annual estimates for a wide array of noncensus demographic, health, and criminal justice indicators for the neighborhoods that comprise the city and county of Denver. Piton data are aggregated to seventy-seven named community areas consisting of two census tracts, on average.

To get a sense of the places where our sample youth resided, we present descriptive statistics in the bottom panel of table 1. Variation is substantial around the means, indicating that the youth we analyze lived in a wide array of neighborhoods across the city and county of Denver. Nonetheless, DHA youth were also living in neighborhoods that were less diverse and advantaged relative to the typical youth living in Denver as a whole. The typical youth in our DHA analysis samples resided in a neighborhood that was approximately 27 percent foreign born, 14 percent African American, had relatively low levels of occupational prestige (mean=37) suggesting an occupational mix that was laborer intensive, and experienced moderate levels of social vulnerability (mean=123) suggesting some level of concentrated disadvantage. In contrast, the typical Denver resident lived in a neighborhood that was 16 percent foreign born, 12 percent African American, higher levels of occupational prestige (mean=41), and levels of social vulnerability that were 22 percent lower. Further, these youth resided in neighborhoods that had, on average, violent crime rates that were nearly twice the average for Denver as a whole (10.9 versus 5.6 per 1,000, respectively) and property crime rates that were about 5 percent higher (49.8 versus 46.8 per 1,000, respectively).

Youths' Risky Behavioral Outcome Measures

Caregivers in the Denver Child Study were asked about a variety of behavioral issues affecting children who were age eight or older at the time of the survey, for example, "Has your child ever (insert run away from home, used aggressive or violent behavior, used marijuana)? ... If so, how old was your child when this first occurred?" The dependent variables of interest here are whether a child had initiated one or more of three risky behaviors between the ages of eight and eighteen: ran away from home, used aggressive or violent behavior, or used marijuana. We used the responses to these questions to estimate the prevalence of adolescent runaway, aggressive or violent behavior, and marijuana use as well as to determine the average age of initiation into each of these risky behaviors. We recognize the potential shortcomings of these behavioral indicators. First, they are subject to recall error by the caregiver survey respondent, though we intentionally chose outcomes for which this likely would be minimal. Second, they are based on caregiver perceptions of the behaviors. Although caregivers may have firsthand knowledge or child reports as the basis of these perceptions, their perceptions may not always be accurate, because children may deliberately hide some of these behaviors from them. Third, they are subject to caregivers' willingness to reveal socially sensitive behaviors of their children to the interviewer. Although all three concerns likely create considerable noise in our dependent variables, we assume no systematic pattern in these errors related to neighborhood indicators. Given the concerns about caregiver self-reports of these behaviors, however, we also report the prevalence rates and ages of initiation from the following sources: the National Longitudinal Survey of Youth 1997 (NLSY97) for running away (Pergamit 2010); the Project on Human Development and Chicago Neighborhoods data for aggressive and violent behavior (Molnar et al. 2008); and Colorado data from the National Survey on Drug Use and Health survey for marijuana use (Substance Abuse and Mental Health Services Administration 2013).

As shown in table 2, caregivers reported that approximately 7 percent of their children ran away from home during adolescence; the average age at time of first occurrence was 14.6 years. Nearly one in five (18 percent) youth used aggressive or violent behavior with the average age of initiation at 12.2 years. About one in ten using marijuana; the average age of initiation was 15.8 years. The prevalence rates for running away from home derived from NLSY97 data were similar: 7.8 percent but occurring at slightly younger ages (see table 2). Given considerable variation in the ways in which aggression and violent behavior are measured, there was no single source that provided comparable statistics for the prevalence of such behavior during adolescence. However, estimates from Beth Molnar and her colleagues (2008) provide some parameters from which to gauge our findings: approximately 14 percent of Chicago youth were identified as engaging in aggressive

Table 2. Prevalence and Age of Initiation of Risky Behaviors During Adolescence

Risky Behavior	Contemporaneous Neighborhood Models		First Offered Neighborhood Models		Instrumental Variable Neighborhood Models		Denver or U.S Rates[a]
	Mean	SD	Mean	SD	Mean	SD	
Running away from home							
Ever ran away from home							
Full sample	0.065	0.248	0.066	0.249	0.063	0.243	0.1
Latinos	0.063	0.249	0.067	0.251	0.063	0.243	
African Americans	0.064	0.246	0.065	0.248	0.064	0.245	
Age when first ran away from home							
Full sample	14.62	1.525	14.92	1.614	14.59	1.524	13.0
Latinos	14.73	1.585	14.90	1.482	14.74	1.527	
African Americans	14.48	1.455	14.94	1.784	14.39	1.530	
Use of aggressive or violent behavior							
Ever used aggressive or violent behavior							
Full sample	0.172	0.378	0.178	0.382	0.182	0.386	0.138
Latinos	0.119	0.325	0.127	0.333	0.121	0.326	
African Americans	0.246	0.431	0.241	0.428	0.266	0.443	
Age of initiation of aggressive-violent behavior							
Full sample	12.24	2.757	12.21	2.795	12.09	2.736	12.0
Latinos	12.22	2.762	12.11	2.662	12.09	2.696	
African Americans	12.25	2.768	12.27	2.890	12.09	2.777	
Marijuana use							
Ever smoked marijuana							
Full sample	0.096	0.295	0.096	0.295	0.099	0.300	0.121
Latinos	0.094	0.292	0.094	0.293	0.097	0.297	
African Americans	0.098	0.298	0.098	0.298	0.103	0.305	
Age of initiation of marijuana use							
Full sample	15.83	1.648	15.90	1.687	15.84	1.736	13.9
Latinos	15.80	1.784	15.86	1.826	15.86	1.868	
African Americans	15.87	1.474	15.95	1.529	15.81	1.575	

Source: Authors' calculations.
Note: Prevalence and age of onset were based on caregiver restrospective reports of these behaviors for children age eight and older at the time of the Denver Child Study survey.
[a]Self-reported prevalence rates for aggressive behaviors were derived from the Project on Human Development in Chicago Neighborhoods (Molnar et al. 2008). Self-reported prevalence rates and age of onset for running away from home were estimated by Pergamit (2010) using data from the National Longitudinal Survey on Youth, 1997. Prevalence rates for marijuana use for Denver youth derived from Substance Abuse and Mental Health Services Adminstration (2013).

behavior with an average age of initiation at twelve years. Prevalence rates for adolescent marijuana use in Colorado were 12 percent; the average age of initiation was 13.9 years. Although prevalence rates and initiation ages were similar for running away from home and marijuana use between Latino and African American youth, the reported use of aggressive or violent behavior was more than twice as high for African American youth (25 percent) relative to Latino youth (12 percent) in the study, though the mean age of initiation was similar.

METHODS

We merged information regarding sampled households, caregivers, youth and their corresponding neighborhood environments to create a pseudo-longitudinal database in which the *child-year* becomes the unit of analysis. We used this database for modeling how the neighborhood to which a youth was exposed affected their hazard in engaging in our three risky behaviors during adolescence. The youth, caregiver, and household covariates served as controls.

Our analytical approach for causal identification exploits the DHA natural experiment that produces exogenous variation in neighborhood context. Specifically, we take three complementary approaches in measuring youths' neighborhood exposure. First, we measure all neighborhood indicators contemporaneously when the youth first engaged in the behavior, or at time-of-survey or age eighteen (whichever younger) if the youth never engaged in the behavior. This measure would be most appropriate if context generated behavioral effects occur fairly quickly and if any subsequent mobility patterns since initial DHA assignment were not substantially influenced by uncontrolled parental characteristics that also affected youths' behaviors. Second, we measure neighborhood as the indicators associated with the dwelling first offered to (not necessarily accepted by) the household. This measure would be most appropriate if context generated behavioral effects only after sustained, consistent exposure and change in context since initial assignment was minimal. Third, we measure neighborhood with instrumental variable (IV) estimates based purely on variables that were exogenous to all selection processes and were not themselves causally related to the risky behavior outcomes being analyzed (other than through their relationship to adolescent neighborhood context). This measure would be most appropriate if context generated behavioral effects through cumulative exposure but youth were exposed to temporally varying contexts due to residential mobility or in-place changes.

Our primary instrument was the corresponding set of neighborhood characteristics associated with the neighborhood *first offered* by DHA to the applicant. Our independent evaluation of DHA records shows that 75.5 percent accepted this first offered neighborhood from DHA.[3] We can safely assume that neighborhood characteristics first offered to applicants will be uncorrelated with their unobserved characteristics that might be associated both with whether they accept and remain in the offered neighborhood and economic outcomes for their children when they become young adults. Using similar logic, we specify as additional identifying instruments the calendar year when the DHA offer is first made. We emphasize that we only consider youths' initiation of running away from home, aggressive or violent behavior or marijuana use occurring after their families have been quasi-randomly assigned to a DHA public housing unit, thereby preserving the value of the natural experiment for drawing causal inferences.

The results of our first-stage ordinary least squares (OLS) regressions of contemporaneous adolescent neighborhood context variables on the above instruments (and all the covariates in our second-stage model) are presented in appendix B. Overall results are encouraging: the R-squares range from 0.18 to 0.29 and all chi-squares are highly significant. Characteristics of the neighborhood first offered by DHA proved to be strong instruments for their corresponding characteristics during our sampled young adults' adolescence. Covariates mea-

---

3. Although 69.5 percent accepted the originally offered DHA dwelling another 6 percent accepted the second unit in the same neighborhood as the first dwelling.

sured at time of first offer and the calendar year of offer were weaker instruments for neighborhood characteristics during adolescence.

Cox Proportional Hazard and Accelerated Failure Time Specifications

Our analytical approach models the timing of a particular risky behavioral outcome at time t for an individual ij with covariate vector χ using a Cox proportional hazards model:

$$\lambda(t|\chi_{ij}) = \lambda_0(t) \exp(\beta_1 \chi_{1ij} + \ldots + \beta_n \chi_{nij})$$
$$= \lambda_0(t) \exp(\chi_{ij} \beta)$$

where $\lambda(t|\chi_{ij})$ is the observed time of outcome (or the censoring time of age eighteen) for youth ij and $\lambda_0(t)$ is the baseline hazard. We then conducted a global chi-square test to ascertain whether the residuals of the Cox model violated the assumption of proportionality. If they did (as was the case of running away from home), we calculated accelerated failure time (AFT) models to estimate the extent to which the time to initiation of the risky behavior was accelerated or decelerated.[4] The AFT model is generally preferred to the Cox proportional hazard model with data that violate the assumptions of proportionality because it is more robust to omitted covariates and less sensitive to choice of probability distribution. In the AFT model, the outcome is the natural logarithm of the survival time t, which is expressed as a linear function of the covariates:

$$\ln(tij) = \chi_{ij} \beta + \varepsilon_{ij}$$

where all symbols are defined as before. In AFT models, a time ratio (TmR) greater than 1 means prolonged time to initiation while TmR < 1 means accelerated time to initiation of the risky behavior. Specifically, we use the frailties version of the AFT model to address the clustering of siblings within families.

We intentionally omit from our models any variables describing the youths' (parentally assessed) exposure to violence, fertility, educational performance, or other outcomes, inasmuch as these may themselves be affected by neighborhood environment. This way, we avoid over-controlling and thus minimizing the apparent influence of neighborhood on risky behavior. We can therefore interpret our models as akin to yielding reduced-form estimates of the degree to which neighborhood indicators correlate with running away from home, use of aggressive or violent behavior, or marijuana use through unspecified intervening causal pathways.

Given the potential of multicollinearity across our neighborhood variables, we conducted several sensitivity tests that resulted in the exclusion of any predictors with variance inflation factors (VIFs) exceeding 5.[5] Finally, to provide the most parsimonious model and avoid maximum likelihood algorithm convergence problems, we model only a subset of youth, caregiver and household control variables that proved predictive. We experimented with a much more expansive set of controls in preliminary runs that are available on request. Given the theoretical rationale for exploring ethnic heterogeneity in neighborhood effects (Crowder and South 2003; Galster and Santiago 2006; Galster, Andersson, and Musterd 2010; Bennett 2011; Galster 2012; Small and Feldman 2011; Francois, Overstreet, and Cunningham 2012; Sharkey and Faber 2014), and the issue related to nonrandom assignment of racial composition, we present stratifications of our analyses for Latino and African American youth.

RESULTS

Standardized hazard and time ratios and robust standard errors for our models predicting whether the youth ever ran away from home, used aggressive or violent behavior or used marijuana during adolescence are presented

---

4. We use Stata's STREG algorithm with a lognormal model for the AFT model; for estimating the parameters, we use maximum likelihood.

5. We use the conventions for the VIF cutoff point and decisions to remove violating predictors that Peter Rogerson describes (2001). There are two exceptions when theoretically important neighborhood indicators with VIFs exceeding 5 are retained in the models for running away and marijuana use: violent crime rates and social vulnerability. The VIFs for these two neighborhood indicators fall between 5 and 6. We conduct sensitivity analyses to assess the effects of including one or both of these indicators in our models and find no significant changes in the results.

Table 3. Standardized AFT Models Predicting Running Away from Home

Predictor Measures (All Continuous Variables Reflect Standardized Values Measured at Time of Initiation, First Offer or Predicted)	Neighborhood Characteristics First Occurrence			
	Latino		African American	
	TR	SE	TR	SE
Youth characteristics				
Gender and ethnicity of youth (omitted=African American male)				
Female (omitted=no)	0.937	(0.036)	1.059	(0.041)
Caregiver and household characteristics				
Caregiver age	1.265***	(0.051)	1.285***	(0.041)
Caregiver immigrant status (omitted=no)	1.032	(0.078)	1.875***	(0.263)
Caregiver educational attainment (omitted=no degree)				
High school diploma or higher	0.925	(0.049)	1.143*	(0.074)
Natural log of caregiver earnings (in dollars)	1.006	(0.055)	0.852**	(0.050)
Caregiver was available to monitor-supervise children FT-PT (omitted=not available)	0.951	(0.099)	0.717**	(0.085)
Neighborhood characteristics				
Social vulnerability score (range 0–400)	0.873	(0.075)	1.120*	(0.062)
Percentage African American residents	1.028	(0.048)	1.024	(0.024)
Occupational prestige score (range 0–100)	1.071	(0.053)	1.131***	(0.036)
Percentage foreign-born residents	1.045	(0.033)	1.089*	(0.040)
Violent crime rate per 1,000	1.286***	(0.096)	1.001	(0.041)
Property crime rate per 1,000	0.922*	(0.034)	0.960**	(0.015)
Number of observations	494		361	
Number of clusters	233		181	
Number of failures	31		23	
Time at risk	6,912		4,926	
Sigma	0.215		0.186	
Log-likelihood	−41.19		−28.53	
Chi²	90.01***		295.00***	

Source: Authors' calculations.
Note: Exponentiated coefficients. Robust standard errors in parentheses. Frailties models reflect adjustments for clustering by families.
* $p < 0.05$; ** $p < 0.01$; *** $p < 0.001$

in tables 3 through 5.[6] Each table compares estimated parameters across ethnic strata for three alternative specifications of neighborhood treatment: measured contemporaneously when the youth first engaged in the behavior or at time-of-survey or age eighteen (whichever was younger) if the youth never engaged in the behavior (model 1); at time of first offer (model 2), or cumulative exposure at time of initiation as reflected by our instrumental variables (model 3). Across all of the stratified models, overall model performance was acceptable as demonstrated by the log-likelihood values and statistically significant chi-square tests. Heterogeneity of estimated neighborhood effects depending on ethnicity is clear, as expected. Given concerns about potential selection bias, our discussion focuses on the re-

6. The interpretation is that a 1 standard deviation change in the predictor is associated with the increase/decrease in hazard equal to the estimated standardized hazard ratio given in the table. In the AFT models, the time

Neighborhood Characteristics								
First Offer				Instrumental Variables				
Latino		African American		Latino		African American		
TR	SE	TR	SE	TR	SE	TR	SE
0.921*	(0.032)	1.049	(0.039)	0.923*	(0.036)	1.064	(0.040)
1.205***	(0.048)	1.359***	(0.059)	1.228***	(0.048)	1.369***	(0.057)
0.971	(0.063)	2.008***	(0.278)	0.953	(0.059)	1.916***	(0.265)
0.923	(0.047)	1.063	(0.072)	0.917	(0.050)	1.099	(0.076)
0.967	(0.052)	0.914	(0.047)	0.958	(0.046)	0.912	(0.048)
0.907	(0.095)	0.801*	(0.070)	0.904	(0.090)	0.801*	(0.074)
0.994	(0.058)	1.081	(0.053)	1.194	(0.144)	1.230*	(0.108)
1.092*	(0.047)	0.996	(0.029)	1.092*	(0.042)	0.991	(0.028)
1.036	(0.031)	1.107**	(0.041)	1.058	(0.041)	1.115**	(0.047)
1.019	(0.030)	1.082	(0.045)	1.048	(0.038)	1.111*	(0.048)
0.946	(0.038)	0.964	(0.026)	0.853	(0.076)	0.884	(0.065)
1.051	(0.057)	1.074	(0.051)	0.973	(0.070)	1.024	(0.043)
494		361		494		361	
233		181		233		181	
31		23		31		23	
6912		4926		6912		4926	
0.223		0.18		0.213		0.18	
-50.42		-25.6		-47.46		-26.03	
81.43***		197.70***		85.25***		230.10***	

sults from our instrumental variable models. The magnitudes of the estimated neighborhood effects, however, do not differ substantially across the three models, especially when statistically significant parameters are compared. This suggests that the size of the neighborhood effects on outcomes investigated here are robust to alternative measures of a given indicator. Given space constraints, we discuss results for only neighborhood indicators, not covariates.

As shown in table 3, the risk of running away from home was prolonged by about 9 percent for Latino youth residing in neighborhoods with more African American residents and by about 11 percent for African American youth residing in neighborhoods with more foreign-born and higher occupational status

ratio refers to the acceleration or delay of risk. Also the AFT model conditions for clustering in families using frailties.

Table 4. Standardized Cox PH Models Predicting Hazard of Initiating Aggressive or Violent Behavior

	Neighborhood Characteristics			
	Initiation			
	Latino		African American	
Predictor Measures (All Continuous Variables Reflect Standardized Values Measured at Time of Initiation, First Offer or Predicted)	HR	SE	HR	SE
Youth characteristics				
Gender and ethnicity of youth (omitted=African American male)				
Female (omitted=no)	0.554*	(0.136)	0.752	(0.140)
First born in family (omitted=0)	0.681	(0.182)	0.389***	(0.088)
Caregiver and household characteristics				
Caregiver age	0.104***	(0.031)	0.115***	(0.030)
Caregiver disability status (omitted=not disabled)	1.526	(0.651)	4.916***	(1.920)
Caregiver educational attainment (omitted=no degree)				
High school diploma or higher	1.273	(0.326)	1.216	(0.375)
Natural log of caregiver earnings (in dollars)	1.121	(0.150)	1.118	(0.185)
Neighborhood characteristics				
Social vulnerability score (range 0–400)	0.337*	(0.178)	0.763	(0.150)
Percentage African American residents	0.839	(0.278)	1.101	(0.144)
Occupational prestige score (range 0–100)	0.557*	(0.159)	0.825	(0.134)
Percentage foreign-born residents	0.633*	(0.139)	0.673	(0.137)
Violent crime rate per 1,000	1.225	(0.661)	1.071	(0.133)
Property crime rate per 1,000	2.600***	(0.509)	1.320**	(0.139)
Number of observations	455		327	
Number of clusters	224		172	
Number of failures	55		87	
Time at risk	6,519		4,477	
Log-likelihood	−255.9		−388.6	
Chi^2	105.50***		151.30***	

Source: Authors' calculations.
Note: Exponentiated coefficients. Robust standard errors in parentheses.
* $p < 0.05$; ** $p < 0.01$; *** $p < 0.001$

neighbors, respectively. Perhaps counterintuitively, the risk of running away was delayed for African American youth in more disadvantaged neighborhoods: a 1 standard deviation higher social vulnerability score was associated with a 23 percent delay in running away during adolescence.

Several neighborhood characteristics were significant predictors of adolescent use of aggressive or violent behavior (see table 4). For African American youth, residence in neighborhoods with 1 standard deviation higher violent crime rates resulted in 2.1 times higher hazards of using aggressive or violent behavior. However, residence in neighborhoods with 1 standard deviation higher fractions of foreign-born residents or levels of social vulnerability reduced the hazards of initiating such behavior for African American youth by 42 and 52 percent, respectively. For Latino youth, a 1 stan-

	Neighborhood Characteristics							
	First Offer				Instrumental Variables			
	Latino		African American		Latino		African American	
	HR	SE	HR	SE	HR	SE	HR	SE
	0.524*	(0.137)	0.877	(0.162)	0.484**	(0.135)	0.812	(0.157)
	0.629	(0.181)	0.441***	(0.082)	0.631	(0.177)	0.449***	(0.082)
	0.115***	(0.040)	0.108***	(0.028)	0.101***	(0.038)	0.102***	(0.027)
	1.545	(0.740)	5.815***	(2.774)	1.745	(0.800)	4.077**	(2.008)
	1.293	(0.371)	1.268	(0.415)	1.464	(0.440)	1.165	(0.370)
	1.117	(0.150)	1.252	(0.237)	1.103	(0.153)	1.220	(0.225)
	1.023	(0.359)	1.088	(0.276)	0.401	(0.242)	0.481*	(0.157)
	0.475**	(0.136)	1.025	(0.147)	0.489*	(0.154)	1.015	(0.143)
	0.877	(0.219)	0.956	(0.155)	0.684	(0.225)	0.774	(0.138)
	0.954	(0.169)	0.672	(0.158)	0.847	(0.186)	0.576*	(0.153)
	1.854*	(0.536)	1.12	(0.134)	1.988	(1.172)	2.104*	(0.697)
	0.611	(0.241)	0.973	(0.221)	1.540	(0.739)	0.913	(0.281)
	455		327		455		327	
	224		172		224		172	
	55		87		55		87	
	6,519		4,477		6,519		4,477	
	−263.1		−393.4		−262.1		−393.6	
	83.54***		133.40***		92.31***		136.10***	

dard deviation higher fraction of African American neighbors was associated with a 52 percent reduction in the hazard of using aggressive or violent behavior during adolescence.

As shown in table 5, several neighborhood conditions increased the hazards of marijuana initiation. Most robustly, a 1 standard deviation higher violent crime rate was associated with an 81 percent lower hazard of marijuana use by Latino youth. For African American youth, residence in neighborhoods with higher fractions of immigrants reduced the hazard of marijuana use by 69 percent.

DISCUSSION

The results reported in this paper make it clear that several aspects of the neighborhood—safety, social status, and ethnicity-nativity—are statistically and substantively important predictors of risky adolescent behaviors. We

Table 5. Standardized Cox PH Models Predicting Hazard of Marijuana Use Initiation

	Neighborhood Characteristics			
	Initiation			
	Latino		African American	
Predictor Measures (All Continuous Variables Reflect Standardized Values Measured at Time of Initiation, First Offer or Predicted)	HR	SE	HR	SE
Youth characteristics				
Gender and ethnicity of youth (omitted=African American male)				
Female (omitted=no)	0.642	(0.220)	0.769	(0.282)
Caregiver and household characteristics				
Number of siblings in household	0.750	(0.165)	0.525*	(0.140)
Caregiver age	0.130***	(0.037)	0.194***	(0.052)
Caregiver educational attainment (omitted=no degree)				
High school diploma or higher	1.434	(0.514)	0.628	(0.376)
Natural log of caregiver earnings (in dollars)	1.197	(0.193)	0.908	(0.269)
Household stressor scale (0–5)	1.047	(0.159)	0.816	(0.160)
Number of moves from birth to onset	0.805	(0.110)	0.971	(0.152)
Neighborhood characteristics				
Social vulnerability score (range 0–400)	1.230	(0.641)	1.613	(1.000)
Percentage African American residents	1.280	(0.411)	1.428	(0.419)
Occupational prestige score (range 0–100)	0.649	(0.178)	1.031	(0.442)
Percentage foreign-born residents	0.725	(0.149)	0.715	(0.275)
Violent crime rate per 1,000	0.392	(0.204)	0.680	(0.419)
Property crime rate per 1,000	1.939*	(0.516)	1.109	(0.257)
Number of observations	432		310	
Number of clusters	215		162	
Number of failures	42		32	
Time at risk	6,179		4,392	
Log-likelihood	−186.7		−135.1	
Chi^2	80.38***		104.10***	

Source: Authors' calculations.
Note: Exponentiated coefficients. Robust standard errors in parentheses.
* $p < 0.05$; ** $p < 0.01$; *** $p < 0.001$

organize our discussion around these thematic categories of neighborhood context. Some of our results were unexpected and challenging to explain, although lack of empirical consensus around the determinants of youths' risky behaviors has long characterized this field of study (see Leventhal and Brooks-Gunn 2000; Foster and Brooks-Gunn 2012; Oakes et al. 2015).

Neighborhood Safety
The findings highlight the mixed roles of neighborhood safety on the hazards of engaging in risky behaviors during adolescence. Neighborhood violent crime rates exhibited a statistically significant and substantively large positive relationship with initiation of the use of aggressive or violent behavior among African American youth. Several underlying (not

Neighborhood Characteristics							
First Offer				Instrumental Variables			
Latino		African American		Latino		African American	
HR	SE	HR	SE	HR	SE	HR	SE
0.586	(0.214)	0.865	(0.299)	0.555	(0.204)	0.785	(0.296)
0.781	(0.118)	0.547**	(0.111)	0.768	(0.125)	0.543**	(0.110)
0.167***	(0.046)	0.166***	(0.064)	0.145***	(0.044)	0.127***	(0.056)
1.332	(0.491)	0.541	(0.279)	1.266	(0.493)	0.428	(0.232)
1.271	(0.221)	0.911	(0.221)	1.225	(0.229)	0.892	(0.229)
1.072	(0.171)	0.817	(0.183)	1.190	(0.193)	0.856	(0.204)
0.944	(0.158)	1.098	(0.207)	0.771	(0.159)	0.955	(0.198)
0.832	(0.405)	0.789	(0.384)	1.675	(1.360)	0.437	(0.390)
0.941	(0.233)	1.007	(0.190)	1.034	(0.248)	1.098	(0.164)
0.569	(0.173)	0.828	(0.344)	0.497	(0.208)	0.621	(0.267)
1.147	(0.245)	0.444	(0.212)	1.267	(0.471)	0.313**	(0.134)
0.795	(0.306)	1.103	(0.275)	0.191*	(0.152)	1.985	(1.616)
0.885	(0.359)	0.983	(0.191)	2.061	(0.939)	0.813	(0.239)
432		310		432		310	
215		162		215		162	
42		32		42		32	
6,179		4,392		6,179		4,392	
−189.8		−135.8		−187.4		−133.3	
68.19***		49.44***		63.1***		45.9***	

mutually exclusive) causal pathways are plausible here. In neighborhoods that have more violent crime there may be weaker collective social norms proscribing violence, more role models exhibiting violence, or higher incidences of youth being victimized by crimes, which creates psychological reactions leading to aggression.

Surprisingly. Latino youth living in places with more violent crime were, all else equal, less likely to use marijuana. Fear of violence in the wider geographic context may induce more caregiver or self-imposed restrictions on youths' movements outside the home or immediate environs (Byrnes, Miller, Chen, and Grube 2010). Such geographic restrictions in activity spaces could result in more intensive parental monitoring of behaviors that may reduce chances of youth initiating marijuana use.

Neighborhood Social Status

Our results indicate that neighborhoods inhabited by higher status residents were associated with delayed incidence of running away from home for low-income African American youth. We posit that neighborhoods of higher social status may be associated with several mechanisms that could produce the observed relationship, including collective socialization, role modeling, and collective efficacy and social control of public spaces that provide neighborhood youth with heightened sense of security and belonging.

Less intuitive is the negative relationship between neighborhood disadvantage and the initiation of risky behaviors such as running away or the use of aggressive or violent behavior by African American youth. Although this finding differs from several prior studies, others have reported that African American youth are less likely to engage in risky behaviors (for example, Allison et al. 1999; Bolland et al. 2007; Snedker, Herting, and Walton 2009)—observations that have been supported by national surveys on youth behaviors such as Monitoring the Future. The initiation of risky behaviors among African American youth in more disadvantaged neighborhoods may be mediated by the presence of family support networks or high-achieving friends within personal networks (Allison et al. 1999). Alternatively, low-income African American youth may weigh the costs associated with initiating risky behaviors, including being subject to heightened police scrutiny as well as the consequences of such behavior on current and future educational or employment outcomes. Further, it may be that neighborhood disadvantage may operate differently for adolescents or be more relevant to engaging in risky behaviors later during the life course. Indeed, Jason Boardman and his colleagues argue that it is "unlikely that neighborhood disadvantage operate in the same way for all subgroups of the population and for all health outcomes and behaviors" (2001, 163). Another potential explanation might revolve around the way we have measured neighborhood contexts: we have included many more neighborhood indicators (such as crime and occupational prestige) that enable us to unbundle the separate effect of a wider array of conditions found in vulnerable neighborhoods. Finally, we speculate that the observed relationship between neighborhood disadvantage and risky behaviors may have been produced by collective social norms involving the definition of the risky behaviors in question. If African American parents in socially vulnerable neighborhoods become less likely to define particular behaviors of their adolescents as running away, aggressive, or violent as a result of these norms, they will be less likely to report in our survey that their children have engaged in them. Put differently, this result may be an artifact of reporting created by a neighborhood effect.

Neighborhood Ethnic and Nativity Composition

Higher percentages of foreign-born neighbors substantially reduced the hazards of our low-income African American adolescents engaging in any of the three risky behaviors investigated. Additionally, relationships were significant between African American composition of the neighborhood's population and initiation of aggressive or violent behavior and running away during adolescence for Latino youth. We find that higher percentages of these groups in the neighborhood are associated with a lower likelihood of engaging in any of these risky behaviors.

We think our results are consistent with the notion that a dominant ethnic-nativity group in the neighborhood can play powerful normative, role modeling, and behavioral monitoring functions whose impacts extend to other youth beyond those in the given group. For example, groups with multigenerational households and extended family networks (more likely Latino and immigrant in Denver) may more heavily monitor the behavior of all children residing in the neighborhood. A dominant group of ethnic minority–immigrant neighbors may serve as adult role models and make resources available to all resident low-income children of color, thereby enhancing collective socialization in the neighborhood. Immigrant families who maintain values and behaviors from their countries of origin may experience reduced intergenerational conflict, which is often linked to initiation of adolescent risky behaviors. Further, these families may continue to enforce strong cultural proscriptions regarding such behaviors with their second-generation children. These children, in turn, may serve as agents of "positive behavioral contagion" for other neighboring peers, even when they are in different ethnic groups.

CONCLUSIONS, CAVEATS, AND FUTURE DIRECTIONS

Researchers have struggled with the daunting methodological challenges of obtaining unbiased estimates of the causal impact of neighborhood on adolescent risky behavioral outcomes, due primarily to incomplete controls for selection biases and little variation in the environments experienced by low-income, minority children over a sustained period. Moreover, previous research has not been able to examine how these neighborhood effects might vary for minority children who were not African American. An innovative public housing program instituted by the Denver Housing Authority provides a unique opportunity to explore both of these issues because the DHA housing allocation process mimics random assignment to a wide range of neighborhoods for Latino and African American families with children who apply for DHA housing. Moreover, families typically reside in DHA housing for nontrivial periods, thereby producing sustained exposure to context. We thus have an unusual opportunity to measure context-individual behavior associations that are plausibly produced by causal relationships.

We use Cox PH and accelerated failure time models, stratified by ethnicity, to estimate parameters. Three alternative measures of each of our neighborhood indicators provide robustness tests. We find that cumulative exposure to multiple dimensions of neighborhood context (especially safety, social status, and ethnicity-nativity) predict whether adolescents run away from home, use aggressive or violent behavior, or initiate marijuana use.

Although we think that our methodological approach offers important advances in providing convincing evidence of causal connections between residential context and behavioral outcomes, we acknowledge that our study has weaknesses. The first is that our measures of youth behaviors are retrospectively reported by caregivers. We recognize that this can yield both random errors associated with the timing of onset and may also introduce inaccuracies in reporting whether the behavior occurred, particularly when such behaviors are illegal. To the extent that these random recall or reporting errors crept into our data, they would push the neighborhood effect findings toward null. Second, we do not investigate the frequency of these behaviors, because this is not recorded in our survey. Third, we do not attempt to probe in this paper potential pathways through which neighborhood environment may affect adolescent behavior through intervening outcomes, especially as they might play out through exposure to violence or school performance. We will address this last shortcoming in future work. Fourth, Denver is not a representative metro area; in particular, it does not exhibit large areas of extreme deprivation, which some others do.

Finally, despite these caveats our results clearly suggest that policymakers should be cognizant of neighborhood as an important developmental context affecting the behavioral outcomes of low-income minority adolescents. Each of the risky behaviors we examine is clearly influenced by more than individual or family characteristics. Moreover, we know that these behaviors create severe and durable physical and mental health problems that, in turn, inhibit intellectual growth, academic performance, and—ultimately—economic opportunities during adulthood (Partnership for Maternal, Newborn and Child Health 2011). Thus, by powerfully influencing risky behaviors, neighborhood plays an important role in shaping future opportunities and outcomes.

The daunting policy challenge is creating and opening access to neighborhood environments that can be more developmentally friendly to all youth (Cook and Wing 2012). Our results imply that well-designed assisted housing programs (potentially involving both site-based and voucher-based subsidies) and community redevelopment programs have the potential to expand the access to places that enhance opportunities for disadvantaged youth. On the one hand, scattered-site public housing programs like the one operated by the Denver Housing Authority have opened access to good-quality housing in a wider range of neighborhood contexts for thousands of low-income youth and their families. Limits to the scope of assisted housing programs and rent subsidies, however, underscore the need to increase opportunity-rich neighborhoods for low-income families and their children through place-based neighborhood redevelopment and reinvestment. One recent example from the Denver context is the private-public partnership supporting the Mariposa redevelopment of the La Alma/Lincoln Park neighborhood. Replacing the South Lincoln Homes public housing development operated by the DHA, this project involved the creation of a multigenerational, mixed income neighborhood with new rental housing construction and neighborhood revitalization maximizing transit access, walkability and safety, healthy living, and economic sustainability. In addition to the nine hundred units of rental housing of varying sizes and prices that were built, neighborhood revitalization efforts included refurbishing local recreational facilities, parks, and the public library as well as the addition of public art, safe walking spaces, and community gardens. Workforce development activities have been targeted toward at-risk neighborhood youth and include vocational training for various careers in the arts industry as well as the culinary arts. All of these efforts are aligned with Patrick Sharkey's (2013) call for durable reinvestment in our most disadvantaged neighborhoods to stem the intergenerational transmission of neighborhood disadvantage.

APPENDIX A

Investigating Quasi-Random Assignment in our DHA Natural Experiment

Natural experiments have been advocated as a vehicle from which valid implications about causal neighborhood effects may be drawn (for example, Oakes 2004). One should have assurance, however, that they in fact produce a quasi-random assignment of households across space. Such would convincingly minimize geographic selection bias by rupturing the association between neighborhood characteristics and unobserved individual characteristics, both of which might be correlated with the outcome under investigation. This appendix uses our natural experiment involving public housing in Denver and investigates whether it produced an essentially quasi-random allocation of both observed and unobserved household characteristics across neighborhood characteristics.

Several investigations of neighborhood effects using natural experiments have probed the degree to which quasi-random assignment was achieved (Oreopoulos 2003; Edin, Fredricksson, and Åslund 2003; Jacob 2004; Lyle 2007; Damm 2009, 2014). Typically, the allocation processes in the natural experiments are described and probed in detail in an effort to uncover points at which nonrandom selections could occur. Regression analysis is then used in balancing tests to assess whether any nonzero relationships between observed individual characteristics and neighborhood characteristics signal nonrandom allocations. We use these strategies here and present another, original approach involving Monte Carlo simulation with typically unoserved individual characteristics.

Possibilities for Tenant Self-Selection and Staff Selection

First, we explore the possibility of selection arising because prospective tenants can potentially choose between two DHA units that may be located in quite different neighborhoods. Our independent evaluation of DHA records showed that 69.5 percent accepted their first offer from DHA, 18.8 percent accepted their second offer, 7.9 percent ended up rejecting both offers and taking a third offer later (after returning to the bottom of the wait list), and 3.8 percent rejected three or more offers before being placed. However, 75 percent accepted offers of units in the originally assigned neighborhood.

Perhaps more revealing is probing whether applicants ended up in neighborhoods they would have selected on their own. Before their initial assignment to a DHA dwelling, clients were asked by DHA whether they had any geographic location preferences. DHA administrative data show that 42.5 percent of the clients in our sample did not articulate any locational preference, approximately 33 percent expressed general geographical areas (such as southwest Denver), and the remaining 23.5 percent provided responses that ranged from specific addresses to specific DHA developments. To assess whether those who stated a preference were assigned to a housing unit in their specified area, we follow the following procedures. For those who specified a particular address, we check to see whether that address was the DHA unit to which the client was initially assigned. For those who specified a preference for a particular DHA development, we use the unit number reported by DHA (which has an abbreviation of the development embedded in it) to assess whether the initial DHA unit was in that development. For those who specified a preference for a particular neighborhood, we rely on our survey data to determine whether the original DHA unit was in the specified neighborhood. Last, initially assigned DHA units were mapped to identify where they were within the Denver metropolitan area for those who specified a preference for a particular area. Once these assessments are complete, we calculate frequencies and percentages for those who specified a geographic preference and got it to occupy (N=190; 25.8 percent) and those who specified a geographic preference but did not occupy a housing unit that met that preference (N=233; 31.7 percent).[7] Because we cannot ascertain the geographic location of all potential DHA unit vacancies that arose during the times that each client was assigned to their initial unit, we cannot perform any formal statistical tests to determine whether the frequencies we obtained for those who were assigned their expressed preference were any different than what would be expected by chance. Nevertheless, we are encouraged by the roughly equal percentages of those expressing a geographic preference granted and not granted, suggesting the equivalent of a coin toss by DHA staff in each case.

A second potential source of selection can arise from the actions of DHA staff members. If occupancy staff members have multiple vacancies to consider at one time, they may make dwelling offers on the basis of observable characteristics of the applicants at the top of the waiting list or by systematically granting particular geographic preferences of applicants based on their characteristics. Although we cannot fully ascertain the extent to which this may have occurred from the administrative data available to us, we also cannot discount this as a possibility. Indeed, evidence from our balancing tests indicates that DHA staff did make some systematic neighborhood allocations on the basis of ethnicity.

In sum, the DHA dwelling allocation process leaves room for selection. A nontrivial share of DHA applicants did not accept their first offer from DHA (30.5 percent) and ended up in a neighborhood they said they preferred (26 percent). It may also be that DHA staff practiced some selection in their dwelling offers, perhaps in response to expressed applicant preferences.

Relationships Between Individual and Neighborhood Characteristics

Even if some assignments to DHA developments or neighborhood were nonrandom, it would not necessarily follow that we would observe strong statistical relationships between observable DHA tenant characteristics and neighborhood characteristics. Thus, here we use a wide range of continuously measured neighborhood characteristics to probe their potential systematic covariation with characteristics of individual DHA families. Specifically, we use multivariate regression to estimate balancing tests of the statistical associations between twenty-seven individual household and eight characteristics of the neighborhoods first offered by DHA (see table A1). The latter include characteristics of census tracts' population and housing, including our social vulnerability index score, percentage (non-Latino) African American population, percentage foreign-born population, percentage homes built before 1940, occupational prestige score, and property and violent crime

---

7. There are no significant ethnic differences in these percentages.

rates (see text for details). These regressions control for tenant characteristics that DHA uses in their allocation process (that is, disability status and number of bedrooms for which the family qualifies) because of the distinctive geographic differences in locations of variously sized and ADA (Americans with Disabilities Act) disabled-accessible DHA dwellings. A quasi-random assignment would be reflected in coefficients approximating zero and an insignificant F test for the set of applicant characteristics that were reputedly not used in the DHA dwelling allocation process.

Results are shown in table A1. Overall, of the 208 regression coefficients of individual household characteristics, 185 (89 percent) yielded coefficients that were statistically insignificant using the conventional $p < 0.05$ level. The clear violation of quasi-randomness was the consistently strong significance of the ethnicity of the DHA tenant in predicting almost every feature of the offered neighborhood. As a result, all F tests on the set of non-allocation variables rejected the null hypothesis of uniformly zero coefficients in all neighborhood characteristics except the percentage of units built before 1940.

We think that this finding may be partly explicable on the grounds that African American applicants could have expressed preferences for DHA dwellings in neighborhoods with higher percentages of blacks and that these preferences were systematically granted by DHA staff members. At least three reasons are plausible for why African American applicants' expressed preferences could have yielded offers in neighborhoods with somewhat higher percentages of black residents. The first is the desire to maintain close ties to kin, friends, and ethnically distinctive institutions. For example, second-generation DHA applicants may have desired to return to the same neighborhoods they came from expressly to maintain close ties with networks providing bonding social capital. Second, black applicants may have perceived a more welcoming, familiar environment in neighborhoods with higher percentages of residents from their same ethnic group. The converse of the same point is that African American applicants may feel less comfortable or welcome in neighborhoods with higher percentages of Latino residents. Third, the relationship may be partially spurious because many of the neighborhoods with higher percentages of black residents are located along the major residential and commercial growth corridor of Denver, which stretches east-northeast from the former Stapleton Airport redevelopment toward the current airport. These areas are likely attractive for non-ethnic reasons. Many black DHA applicants likely had previously established intra-ethnic social networks in this corridor through which they learned about the attractive prospects for employment and quality of life there.[8]

We also believe, however, that some systematic assignments may have been made by DHA staff on the basis of tenant ethnicity rather than expressed preferences. We reestimated our balancing tests for various strata of tenants: those expressing a geographic preference and receiving it versus those expressing either no preference or a geographic preference and not receiving it; and those who accepted the first dwelling offered by DHA and those who did not. In all cases (except those who rejected the first offer), the strong correlation between African American tenants and neighborhood ethnic composition persisted. We have no information about why DHA staff members may have steered applicants to neighborhoods where their ethnic group was more concentrated, regardless of their expressed preferences, but we think the evidence persuasive.

Indeed, the central issue remains whether the DHA allocation process succeeded in eliminating the correlation between unobserved tenant–child caregiver characteristics and neighborhood characteristics. In this realm we think this was highly likely. Table A1 shows thirteen characteristics of caregivers that were virtually impossible to observe by DHA and by

---

8. Most of both African American and Latino study participants who expressed a geographic preference to DHA identified areas where their ethnic group was disproportionately represented, with the former focusing on the east and northeast parts of Denver and the latter on the west and southwest. Maps showing the ethnic residential geography of Denver are available from the authors.

most researchers using public-access observational data to investigate neighborhood effects; we demarcate these as "characteristics not observed by DHA." Only four of the associated 104 coefficients (4 percent) for this set of typically unobserved characteristics were significantly different from zero using conventional standards. The F tests on this subset of applicant characteristics could not reject the null hypothesis of their coefficients jointly equaling zero in all cases except one (occupational prestige).

Regardless of underlying cause, what does our finding of neighborhood ethnic composition nonrandom selection on the basis of tenant ethnicity imply for our analysis? Can we say that we have quasi-random assignment *conditional on ethnicity* of tenant? The answer is yes (see tables A2 and A3). We repeat our balancing tests for black and Latino tenants separately. For both strata, only 6 percent of the coefficients of individual household characteristics proved statistically significant at conventional levels, and only 4 percent of the unobserved characteristics did so, results easily due to chance. Moreover, for the majority of neighborhood characteristics in both strata, F tests fail to reject the null hypothesis of jointly zero coefficients of all individual tenant characteristics. For all neighborhood characteristics but one, F tests fail to reject the null of jointly zero coefficients of all unobserved individual characteristics.

We therefore conclude that this regression evidence suggests the DHA allocation process produced a quasi-random assignment across geography, with the exception of one characteristic observable by the DHA—ethnicity—that is easily controlled in our analyses. Even more importantly, we conclude that the DHA allocation process produced a quasi-random assignment across geography in terms of individual characteristics not observable by the DHA but observable to us from our survey. This gives us some confidence that any additional household characteristics we do not observe in our study are similarly quasi-randomly allocated across neighborhood characteristics. Our confidence is further bolstered by the Monte Carlo experiments.

Relationships Between Neighborhood and Typically Unobserved Individual Characteristics Using Monte Carlo Simulation

Here we present the results of a complementary test of the degree to which characteristics of caregivers in our sample that typically are not observed in neighborhood effect studies are correlated with characteristics of their neighborhoods at the time of initial assignment by DHA. The balancing test uses multiple regression to assess the partial correlations of individual caregiver characteristics with a given neighborhood characteristic, assuming that each of the former were relatively independent. By contrast, the complementary test described here takes as given the combination of caregiver characteristics, hypothetically allocates this bundle randomly across DHA locations in repeated Monte Carlo trials, estimates the hypothetical pairwise correlations (and standard errors) of the individual and neighborhood characteristics that result, and then compares the actual pairwise correlations to these randomly generated reference points to see whether they are similar.

The intuition guiding this procedure is as follows. An actual random assignment of DHA applicants to DHA dwellings will likely produce by chance a few nonzero pairwise correlations between DHA household characteristics and neighborhood characteristics. A Monte Carlo simulation repeating such random assignments will generate bootstrapped standard errors of correlations across all the permutations of these characteristics. If the actual correlations fall within the respective confidence intervals produced by the simulation, we will fail to reject the null hypothesis that the DHA assignment process yielded a quasi-random geographic assignment of households.

In particular, we implement this strategy as follows. We again consider the unobserved (by DHA and typically in other studies) characteristics of caregivers and census tracts noted earlier. For each of three family sizes of DHA tenants (less than two, two, or three or more children), we calculate the Pearsonian correlation between each pairwise combination of caregiver characteristics and neighborhood characteristics observed when the DHA first assigned our sample

(Text continues on page 200.)

Table A1. Relationships Between DHA Resident and Offered Neighborhood Characteristics

	Social Vulnerability		% Foreign Born		% African American	
	Coefficient	p value	Coefficient	p value	Coefficient	p value
Observed caregiver characteristics used for DHA assignment						
Disabled	-8.9432	0.2879	1.8565	0.1733	0.1377	0.9477
Number of bedrooms eligible for three	-19.4022**	0.0014	-0.0990	0.9193	2.2680	0.1322
Number of bedrooms eligible for four	15.9609	0.1682	1.6191	0.3879	1.4592	0.6133
Observed caregiver characteristics not used for DHA assignment						
Not married	-1.3525	0.8358	0.6148	0.5608	1.4662	0.3679
Employed at time of DHA move-in	8.1493	0.4798	0.1524	0.9350	-0.4196	0.8840
Hourly wage	-2.1139	0.0639	-0.1050	0.5694	0.2292	0.4200
Receiving welfare at time of DHA move-in	16.1895**	0.0086	-3.6024***	0.0003	-0.4651	0.7616
Receiving food stamps at time of DHA move-in	-4.0611	0.5216	1.4446	0.1596	1.1474	0.4679
Had a checking account at time of DHA move-in	-0.3302	0.9538	-1.2808	0.1660	2.6842	0.0596
Had health insurance at time of DHA move-in	-6.8130	0.2573	-0.1534	0.8749	-1.5845	0.2908
Born in United States	-10.0892	0.3024	1.0307	0.5153	2.0134	0.4092
Spanish language interview completed	-17.3190	0.2252	-0.4722	0.8382	-1.6530	0.6424
Age at time of DHA move-in	-0.6680*	0.0241	0.0304	0.5249	-0.0201	0.7853
African American	13.8708**	0.0096	-0.2804	0.7457	10.0679***	0.0000
High school diploma at time of DHA move-in	0.1608	0.9774	0.0647	0.9439	-0.4465	0.7525
Higher education at time of DHA move-in	2.0297	0.8172	3.3509*	0.0188	0.0542	0.9802
Caregiver-family characteristics not observed by DHA						
Had too little money for food at time at DHA move-in	4.4665	0.4307	0.0461	0.9599	0.6885	0.6262
Had difficulty paying all bills at time of DHA move-in	-9.1352	0.1041	1.5902	0.0808	-2.2443	0.1094
Frequency drinking alcohol since becoming a parent	-0.2056	0.9211	0.4408	0.1903	-0.9359	0.0712
Frequency smoking marijuana since becoming a parent	0.1440	0.9487	-0.1005	0.7818	0.5174	0.3545
Frequency using other drugs since becoming a parent	-3.1725	0.3556	-0.7525	0.1763	0.1114	0.8965
Ever seen psychiatrist	-2.7823	0.6292	-2.2937*	0.0142	-0.0092	0.9949
Ever lived in public housing	0.3805	0.5029	0.0174	0.8500	0.0176	0.9011
Ever lived in owner-occupied house	0.2882	0.4198	-0.0084	0.8840	0.1076	0.2273
Father always lived in household with child(ren)	-11.3981	0.1071	-0.7946	0.4876	-3.0255	0.0865
All children share same biological father	0.7790	0.8835	1.2157	0.1586	0.0422	0.9746
CESD depression scale	0.2289	0.4203	0.0591	0.1990	-0.0355	0.6159
Parenting efficacy scale	-0.9228	0.2546	0.1272	0.3323	-0.1625	0.4212
Parenting beliefs scale	0.3170	0.6536	0.1689	0.1403	-0.2279	0.1963
Constant	213.0636***	0.0000	10.5699*	0.0114	14.6348*	0.0228
R^2	0.1082		0.0884		0.1700	
F test	2.2845		1.8254		3.8565	
p value	0.0002		0.0058		0.0000	
F test'	2.2800		1.8300		3.8600	
p value	0.0002		0.0058		0.0000	
F test"	0.7100		1.4900		1.0900	
p value	0.7571		0.1157		0.3689	
N=576 households						

Source: Authors' calculations.

Notes: F test' based on variables listed as "observed caregiver characteristics not used for DHA assignment" and "caregiver-family characteristics not observed by DHA."

F test" based on variables listed as "caregiver-family characteristics not observed by DHA."

*$p < 0.05$; **$p < 0.01$; ***$p < 0.001$

% Units Built Pre-1940		% Moved Prior Year		Occup. Prestige		Property Crime Rate		Violent Crime Rate	
Coefficient	p value	Coefficient	p value	Coefficient	p value	Coefficient	p value	Coefficient	p value
4.3903	0.0840	0.4278	0.6824	0.1283	0.7557	−8.4113	0.2460	−1.4556	0.2425
0.3316	0.8554	−1.6398*	0.0291	0.2682	0.3645	−13.1295*	0.0118	−2.1009*	0.0189
−1.2345	0.7237	1.0968	0.4459	−1.4512*	0.0107	0.6564	0.9475	1.7253	0.3139
−0.4094	0.8353	−0.1515	0.8518	0.1831	0.5670	−4.8932	0.3842	−0.3378	0.7265
6.0388	0.0830	3.0050*	0.0364	−1.0377	0.0668	5.2182	0.5994	3.0159	0.0776
−0.5899	0.0865	−0.3527*	0.0130	0.2067***	0.0002	−1.2583	0.2001	−0.4303*	0.0109
1.5624	0.3996	1.5864*	0.0382	−0.8063**	0.0076	15.5302**	0.0035	1.8963*	0.0375
1.7102	0.3711	−1.3062	0.0976	0.0908	0.7699	−0.3177	0.9536	−0.2854	0.7608
0.7935	0.6447	−0.3739	0.5980	0.7627**	0.0066	2.9943	0.5424	0.4709	0.5770
2.4224	0.1820	−0.7024	0.3473	0.4972	0.0919	−1.4022	0.7866	−0.7122	0.4235
−1.3759	0.6409	−1.7854	0.1422	−0.2258	0.6376	−5.3223	0.5276	0.4458	0.7580
4.6304	0.2824	−1.8254	0.3037	0.4430	0.5265	0.3679	0.9761	−0.2764	0.8959
−0.0674	0.4497	−0.0774*	0.0355	0.0239	0.1000	−0.4737	0.0632	−0.0677	0.1221
2.8302	0.0792	1.5651*	0.0186	0.3148	0.2291	15.9971***	0.0005	4.6105***	0.0000
1.8915	0.2697	−0.0465	0.9475	−0.1961	0.4812	3.7359	0.4451	−1.3924	0.0978
−3.6308	0.1710	1.1814	0.2794	−0.3089	0.4732	−8.2299	0.2770	−0.8420	0.5172
1.3399	0.4333	1.1050	0.1171	−0.3799	0.1717	7.6855	0.1158	1.3214	0.1155
−0.3657	0.8291	0.5504	0.4304	0.6645*	0.0160	−12.3970*	0.0106	−1.5869	0.0565
0.0629	0.9200	−0.0063	0.9806	−0.1587	0.1193	−1.1144	0.5333	−0.2580	0.4012
−0.4993	0.4599	0.1089	0.6955	−0.1512	0.1686	−0.7121	0.7121	0.3598	0.2778
0.8451	0.4146	−0.6033	0.1577	−0.1098	0.5143	0.6483	0.8265	−0.3806	0.4538
0.0977	0.9552	−0.6641	0.3539	0.1966	0.4864	−4.2869	0.3879	−0.6084	0.4755
0.0078	0.9635	0.1167	0.0987	−0.0433	0.1204	0.2866	0.5581	0.0597	0.4775
−0.0844	0.4337	0.0296	0.5051	−0.0484**	0.0059	0.1539	0.6170	0.0563	0.2866
−1.3759	0.5187	−0.3611	0.6810	0.5513	0.1118	−10.6727	0.0800	−1.7662	0.0916
0.3819	0.8119	0.5339	0.4194	0.1225	0.6385	−4.9666	0.2786	−0.3739	0.6347
0.0758	0.3763	0.0200	0.5716	−0.0049	0.7247	0.0731	0.7650	0.0152	0.7167
0.3127	0.2008	−0.1729	0.0863	−0.0016	0.9681	−0.7727	0.2682	−0.0854	0.4759
−0.2344	0.2717	0.1033	0.2397	−0.0400	0.2485	−0.2944	0.6286	−0.0289	0.7822
26.4738***	0.0007	33.3296***	0.0000	35.1429***	0.0000	136.9434***	0.0000	18.5677***	0.0000
0.0524		0.0839		0.1732		0.1063		0.1298	
1.0417		1.7254		3.9446		2.2403		2.8073	
0.4079		0.0114		0.0000		0.0003		0.0000	
1.0400		1.7300		3.9400		2.2400		2.8100	
0.4079		0.0114		0.0000		0.0003		0.0000	
0.4300		1.1200		2.1900		1.1300		0.9500	
0.9592		0.3363		0.0091		0.3332		0.5014	

Table A2. Relationships Between DHA Resident and Offered Neighborhood Characteristics, African American Subsample

	Social Vulnerability		% Foreign Born		% African American	
	Coefficient	p value	Coefficient	p value	Coefficient	p value
Observed caregiver characteristics used for DHA assignment						
Disabled	-16.5307	0.1609	1.7151	0.3839	-2.1186	0.5886
Number of bedrooms eligible for three	-11.8797	0.1801	-2.2010	0.1378	4.7088	0.1107
Number of bedrooms eligible for four	33.7791*	0.0453	-2.3066	0.4120	-5.4033	0.3342
Observed caregiver characteristics not used for DHA assignment						
Not married	-8.5925	0.3960	-0.1345	0.9366	4.4906	0.1831
Employed at time of DHA move-in	2.6748	0.8768	-1.2746	0.6588	-0.2060	0.9714
Hourly wage	-2.4384	0.1391	0.0949	0.7301	0.4306	0.4317
Receiving welfare at time of DHA move-in	5.3271	0.5591	-2.8763	0.0602	-1.4139	0.6413
Receiving food stamps at time of DHA move-in	-4.1395	0.6610	1.6877	0.2856	1.9086	0.5436
Had a checking account at time of DHA move-in	-3.7498	0.6569	-1.6499	0.2433	3.4643	0.2183
Had health insurance at time of DHA move-in	-12.8891	0.1537	0.5803	0.7004	-4.1114	0.1714
Born in United States	-0.2532	0.9852	0.3277	0.8861	4.9926	0.2733
Age at time of DHA move-in	-0.7993	0.0689	0.0697	0.3416	0.1847	0.2057
High school diploma at time of DHA move-in	-11.3109	0.1598	1.9720	0.1429	-1.1034	0.6797
Higher education at time of DHA move-in	5.3309	0.6581	1.1702	0.5614	0.8062	0.8406
Caregiver-family characteristics not observed by DHA						
Had too little money for food at time at DHA move-in	-11.9466	0.1580	0.3821	0.7868	1.5327	0.5856
Had difficulty paying all bills at time of DHA move-in	2.7109	0.7388	2.4246	0.0756	-5.3046	0.0509
Frequency drinking alcohol since becoming a parent	-1.1718	0.6648	0.4032	0.3731	-1.2255	0.1741
Frequency smoking marijuana since becoming a parent	2.2313	0.4018	-0.0983	0.8252	0.9982	0.2601
Frequency using other drugs since becoming a parent	-4.5224	0.3164	-0.2199	0.7706	-0.0140	0.9925
Ever seen psychiatrist	-6.4189	0.4396	-2.2943	0.0994	0.6635	0.8102
Ever lived in public housing	-0.6897	0.4002	0.0045	0.9741	0.0398	0.8838
Ever lived in owner-occupied house	0.3988	0.4435	-0.0418	0.6308	0.1352	0.4349
Father always lived in household with child(ren)	-19.3218	0.0590	-0.3283	0.8473	-5.2695	0.1213
All children share same biological father	4.3872	0.5930	-0.1443	0.9163	-0.4311	0.8745
CESD depression scale	0.5852	0.1530	0.0092	0.8927	-0.0441	0.7458
Parenting efficacy scale	-0.3432	0.7795	0.0127	0.9507	-0.0666	0.8704
Parenting beliefs scale	0.7286	0.4546	0.1304	0.4238	-0.3802	0.2415
Constant	227.2691***	0.0000	13.1581*	0.0430	16.2848	0.2068
R^2	0.1610		0.0970		0.1273	
F test	1.6420		0.9186		1.2479	
p value	0.0281		0.5851		0.1932	
F test'	1.6400		0.9200		1.2500	
p value	0.0281		0.5851		0.1932	
F test"	1.0000		0.7200		0.9200	
p value	0.4526		0.7431		0.5358	

N=259 households

Source: Authors' calculations.

Notes: F test' based on variables listed as "observed caregiver characteristics not used for DHA assignment" and "caregiver-family characteristics not observed by DHA."

F test" based on variables listed as "caregiver-family characteristics not observed by DHA."

* $p < .05$; ** $p < 0.01$; *** $p < 0.001$

% Units Built Pre-1940		% Moved Prior Year		Occup. Prestige		Property Crime Rate		Violent Crime Rate	
Coefficient	p value	Coefficient	p value	Coefficient	p value	Coefficient	p value	Coefficient	p value
9.2370*	0.0204	0.6615	0.6353	0.5583	0.3872	-6.8709	0.5190	-2.0642	0.3339
-2.1949	0.4612	-1.3793	0.1890	0.4292	0.3766	-8.1380	0.3100	-2.1185	0.1875
-4.4109	0.4356	0.9076	0.6485	-1.7615	0.0568	17.6105	0.2475	0.3565	0.9068
2.1990	0.5185	-1.8143	0.1311	0.5301	0.3397	-7.1744	0.4336	0.9154	0.6179
3.7928	0.5138	4.5852*	0.0257	-1.8183	0.0556	-0.4107	0.9790	1.8034	0.5645
-0.1265	0.8192	-0.6079**	0.0020	0.3064***	0.0008	-1.3888	0.3513	-0.4763	0.1112
1.7583	0.5667	0.1676	0.8767	-0.5122	0.3061	4.9438	0.5493	1.2837	0.4378
0.6091	0.8479	-1.8380	0.1013	-0.2382	0.6455	0.8714	0.9188	-0.5976	0.7270
0.3710	0.8961	-1.8512	0.0652	0.6250	0.1778	8.7737	0.2515	0.8714	0.5694
2.0641	0.4965	-0.9200	0.3895	0.5108	0.3020	-10.7041	0.1904	-1.8074	0.2696
-4.6401	0.3140	-1.8607	0.2516	-0.9155	0.2230	1.0558	0.9320	0.7951	0.7486
-0.0278	0.8502	-0.1316*	0.0118	0.0277	0.2493	-0.8754*	0.0280	-0.0495	0.5334
1.3853	0.6083	-1.2263	0.1982	-0.1518	0.7303	-7.3303	0.3137	-2.3580	0.1064
-1.5219	0.7073	1.2532	0.3802	-0.4687	0.4782	-2.2067	0.8396	-0.9769	0.6548
5.5116	0.0534	-0.3139	0.7538	0.2650	0.5673	4.4287	0.5625	1.9245	0.2097
-5.3720	0.0506	1.6787	0.0825	0.2390	0.5921	-14.1381	0.0557	-2.5178	0.0888
0.7407	0.4161	-0.2733	0.3942	-0.0375	0.8001	-1.0472	0.6689	-0.5268	0.2834
-1.2626	0.1593	0.2061	0.5133	-0.2294	0.1167	0.1534	0.9492	0.4912	0.3091
0.4904	0.7466	-1.0601*	0.0482	-0.1561	0.5281	-0.2417	0.9528	-0.2171	0.7906
-0.4526	0.8713	-0.2568	0.7941	0.4580	0.3149	-14.5821	0.0532	-0.9572	0.5251
0.3042	0.2705	-0.0405	0.6763	-0.0123	0.7844	-0.4109	0.5796	0.1324	0.3735
0.0174	0.9209	-0.0094	0.8782	-0.0554	0.0530	0.3863	0.4121	0.1037	0.2724
-4.4309	0.1973	-2.6489*	0.0291	0.5213	0.3515	-16.7525	0.0704	-2.0959	0.2576
-0.8951	0.7459	1.3245	0.1740	0.3033	0.5005	-6.3351	0.3941	-0.4218	0.7768
0.0438	0.7504	0.0416	0.3906	-0.0029	0.8965	0.6094	0.1004	0.0436	0.5561
0.1668	0.6860	-0.2396	0.1001	0.0458	0.4963	-0.4324	0.6968	0.0431	0.8463
-0.1621	0.6210	0.0545	0.6366	0.0016	0.9763	-0.1240	0.8881	-0.1809	0.3063
30.7572*	0.0189	43.3677***	0.0000	33.6352***	0.0000	166.1123***	0.0000	24.5571***	0.0006
0.0794		0.1994		0.2185		0.1266		0.1034	
0.7376		2.1309		2.3920		1.2401		0.9866	
0.8257		0.0015		0.0003		0.1996		0.4883	
0.7400		2.1300		2.3900		1.2400		0.9900	
0.8257		0.0015		0.0003		0.1996		0.4883	
0.7900		1.6500		1.1100		1.2000		0.8000	
0.6677		0.0719		0.3521		0.2779		0.6576	

Table A3. Relationships Between DHA Resident and Offered Neighborhood Characteristics, Latino Subsample

	Social Vulnerability		% Foreign Born		% African American	
	Coefficient	p value	Coefficient	p value	Coefficient	p value
Observed caregiver characteristics used for DHA assignment						
Disabled	−5.8184	0.6414	1.8870	0.3460	2.3759	0.2451
Number of bedrooms eligible for three	−23.7068**	0.0064	1.5351	0.2677	0.2721	0.8472
Number of bedrooms eligible for four	5.9880	0.7173	3.7916	0.1531	8.5948**	0.0016
Observed caregiver characteristics not used for DHA assignment						
Not married	8.3353	0.3530	0.7505	0.6014	0.6258	0.6695
Employed at time of DHA move-in	12.3528	0.4530	0.1215	0.9632	0.7667	0.7756
Hourly wage	−1.7890	0.2826	−0.1919	0.4717	−0.0081	0.9762
Receiving welfare at time of DHA move-in	23.3654**	0.0079	−4.4738**	0.0015	1.6032	0.2626
Receiving food stamps at time of DHA move-in	−4.7942	0.5868	1.5199	0.2825	−0.1849	0.8980
Had a checking account at time of DHA move-in	4.7637	0.5540	−1.0435	0.4185	2.0107	0.1272
Had health insurance at time of DHA move-in	3.7506	0.6534	−0.7858	0.5570	−0.1573	0.9083
Born in United States	−18.9955	0.1855	1.5200	0.5079	−0.7684	0.7429
Spanish language interview completed	−19.6426	0.2604	−1.2195	0.6624	−3.5100	0.2188
Age at time of DHA move-in	−0.5477	0.1931	0.0054	0.9363	−0.1609*	0.0197
High school diploma at time of DHA move-in	10.4278	0.2031	−1.6450	0.2101	−0.4258	0.7503
Higher education at time of DHA move-in	−7.4198	0.5828	6.2377**	0.0042	−3.1085	0.1598
Caregiver-family characteristics not observed by DHA						
Had too little money for food at time at DHA move-in	12.7347	0.1120	0.1893	0.8825	0.1502	0.9085
Had difficulty paying all bills at time of DHA move-in	−16.6751*	0.0396	0.9923	0.4431	−0.2664	0.8400
Frequency drinking alcohol since becoming a parent	1.8991	0.5837	0.4648	0.4026	−0.6423	0.2573
Frequency smoking marijuana since becoming a parent	−2.3576	0.5878	−0.4499	0.5186	−0.0424	0.9524
Frequency using other drugs since becoming a parent	−2.7444	0.6290	−0.9057	0.3198	0.4718	0.6114
Ever seen psychiatrist	4.7386	0.5751	−2.6909*	0.0476	−1.8324	0.1854
Ever lived in public housing	0.9888	0.2345	0.0504	0.7051	−0.0614	0.6513
Ever lived in owner-occupied house	0.2867	0.5797	0.0139	0.8668	0.0311	0.7136
Father always lived in household with child(ren)	0.0185	0.9985	−1.5976	0.3229	−0.5927	0.7191
All children share same biological father	−2.5571	0.7245	2.1622	0.0636	0.2721	0.8185
CESD depression scale	−0.0785	0.8485	0.1210	0.0668	−0.0129	0.8481
Parenting efficacy scale	−1.1420	0.3084	0.1471	0.4127	−0.0854	0.6411
Parenting beliefs scale	−0.1294	0.9026	0.2155	0.2040	−0.0656	0.7042
Constant	205.1510***	0.0000	9.5790	0.0987	16.8546**	0.0046
R^2	0.1339		0.1379		0.0975	
F test	1.5906		1.6454		1.1113	
p value	0.0330		0.0241		0.3234	
F test'	1.5900		1.6500		1.1100	
p value	0.0330		0.0241		0.3234	
F test''	0.6700		1.2100		0.4000	
p value	0.7894		0.2682		0.9708	

N=317 households

Source: Author's calculations.

Notes: F test' based on variables listed as "observed caregiver characteristics not used for DHA assignment" and "caregiver-family characteristics not observed by DHA."

F test'' based on variables listed as "caregiver-family characteristics not observed by DHA."

*$p < 0.05$; **$p < 0.01$; ***$p < 0.001$

% Units Built Pre-1940		% Moved In Prior Year		Occup. Prestige		Property Crime Rate		Violent Crime Rate	
Coefficient	p value	Coefficient	p value	Coefficient	p value	Coefficient	p value	Coefficient	p value
-0.4502	0.8959	0.3339	0.8322	-0.0877	0.8768	-15.4185	0.1344	-1.6817	0.2737
1.7691	0.4571	-1.4448	0.1855	0.0855	0.8270	-18.9716**	0.0080	-2.3218*	0.0294
2.4442	0.5915	1.0476	0.6157	-1.2083	0.1075	-10.4417	0.4432	2.8824	0.1568
-2.4954	0.3126	1.2581	0.2667	-0.1352	0.7394	2.0173	0.7846	-0.7143	0.5170
9.6523*	0.0338	2.0870	0.3152	-0.2238	0.7640	8.3531	0.5375	3.0368	0.1338
-1.0810*	0.0188	-0.1988	0.3439	0.1120	0.1381	-1.0394	0.4479	-0.2946	0.1502
3.1000	0.1985	2.8812**	0.0094	-0.8794*	0.0271	23.9034**	0.0010	3.1783**	0.0033
2.4764	0.3082	-1.0096	0.3646	0.3401	0.3950	-0.0990	0.9891	-0.3682	0.7341
1.4939	0.5003	0.9920	0.3289	0.8271*	0.0239	3.1186	0.6378	0.4605	0.6415
1.5749	0.4935	0.0894	0.9324	0.2729	0.4708	9.1788	0.1824	0.0599	0.9534
1.6458	0.6765	-2.2479	0.2142	0.4653	0.4736	-12.3510	0.2953	-0.0525	0.9762
7.0191	0.1444	-2.0726	0.3465	0.8957	0.2573	0.3554	0.9802	0.1693	0.9370
-0.1163	0.3154	-0.0320	0.5460	0.0257	0.1770	-0.0884	0.7983	-0.0769	0.1372
2.8906	0.2001	1.2061	0.2433	-0.2556	0.4907	15.6148*	0.0210	-0.4633	0.6450
-8.4990*	0.0229	0.7687	0.6519	-0.2248	0.7133	-21.1616	0.0577	-2.0401	0.2195
-0.5290	0.8101	1.7401	0.0853	-0.7566*	0.0374	6.3155	0.3375	0.8047	0.4130
3.1297	0.1598	-0.0765	0.9401	1.0743**	0.0035	-11.1153	0.0951	-1.1199	0.2594
-0.8081	0.3972	0.5121	0.2420	-0.3138*	0.0463	0.7588	0.7902	0.1137	0.7894
0.8591	0.4733	-0.4362	0.4268	0.0401	0.8386	-2.4248	0.4983	-0.0385	0.9426
0.7204	0.6450	-0.0550	0.9388	-0.1094	0.6707	0.2264	0.9614	-0.4980	0.4757
0.4117	0.8596	-0.2186	0.8376	-0.1722	0.6529	8.9078	0.2010	-0.0299	0.9770
-0.2737	0.2320	0.2222*	0.0347	-0.0507	0.1786	0.5677	0.4067	-0.0328	0.7481
-0.1945	0.1730	0.0811	0.2149	-0.0451	0.0552	0.0272	0.9491	0.0157	0.8052
0.6157	0.8244	1.9359	0.1287	0.3687	0.4197	-2.4811	0.7649	-1.2950	0.2962
1.5011	0.4525	0.0742	0.9354	0.0577	0.8607	-4.5208	0.4492	-0.2585	0.7718
0.0993	0.3804	-0.0175	0.7360	-0.0064	0.7321	-0.5056	0.1356	-0.0018	0.9709
0.5229	0.0908	-0.1319	0.3512	-0.0274	0.5900	-0.6860	0.4571	-0.1351	0.3266
-0.3706	0.2038	0.1281	0.3376	-0.0877	0.0681	-0.5270	0.5451	0.0746	0.5661
25.3125*	0.0114	26.9287***	0.0000	36.4559***	0.0000	115.9573***	0.0001	16.5494***	0.0002
0.1104		0.0998		0.1744		0.1582		0.1173	
1.2760		1.1409		2.1728		1.9334		1.3669	
0.1649		0.2895		0.0008		0.0041		0.1077	
1.2800		1.1400		2.1700		1.9300		1.3700	
0.1649		0.2895		0.0008		0.0041		0.1077	
0.7600		1.0700		1.8400		0.6900		0.3700	
0.7023		0.3825		0.0367		0.7768		0.9790	

households to their DHA units. As a comparative benchmark for these correlations, we conduct Monte Carlo simulations in which each sample household was randomly assigned to one of the DHA units (for the appropriate family size) with its associated bundle of neighborhood characteristics that we observed for the year corresponding to when the initial assignment of household in our study actually occurred.[9] After all households were randomly assigned during each iteration, we calculate correlations for all pairwise combinations of caregiver and neighborhood characteristics. We use ten thousand repetitions of these simulations to produce distributions for all such pairwise correlations and their associated bootstrapped standard errors. This allows us to estimate: a 95 percent confidence interval for each correlation; and how many significantly different pairwise correlations among all the permutations would be expected by chance when produced by a random assignment process.

The results are presented in table A4. Caregiver characteristics are listed in rows and the three family-size strata in columns. The cells show for how many of the possible neighborhood characteristics the initial DHA assignment produced an actual correlation with the given caregiver characteristic that was significantly different from zero at the 5 percent level (two-tailed test); the actual correlation coefficient and the neighborhood characteristic involved are reported in these cases. The exhibit shows that for families with no or one child and families with two children, only eight (5 percent of possible correlations) were statistically different from zero; the corresponding figure for families with three or more children was twelve (8 percent of possible correlations). Our simulations show that in more than 98 percent and 95 percent of the cases, respectively, a larger number of statistically significant correlations were produced by random assignment. This strongly indicates that the relatively rare nonzero correlations we observe from initial DHA allocations of tenants to neighborhoods (table A1) are consistent with those that would have been generated by a process of random assignment. These results suggest that the DHA natural experiment likely removed the correlation between any unobserved caregiver characteristics (which we cannot control in our Denver study) that may potentially affect both initial DHA neighborhood characteristics and subsequent youth outcomes.

Conclusions

Natural experiments involving residential placements under the auspices of some public program offer potentially powerful vehicles for measuring neighborhood effects because they can rupture the association between unobserved characteristics of the individuals being studied and characteristics of their neighborhood. We investigate in this appendix the extent to which a natural experiment involving public housing in Denver offers such potential.

Our analysis of the Denver Housing Authority's dwelling allocation procedures reveals room for tenant self-selection or DHA staff selection to enter. We find that, *conditioned on ethnicity*, the DHA allocation process produced a quasi-random initial offer of neighborhood characteristics. The empirical implication is that our models estimating neighborhood effects using the current data must control for ethnicity to avoid geographic selection bias. We, in fact, do so in all analyses we conduct.

Even more importantly, two complementary analyses indicate that the DHA allocation process produced a quasi-random assignment across neighborhood conditions in terms of individual characteristics not observable by the DHA (but observable to us from our survey data). This gives us confidence that any additional household characteristics we do not observe in our study are similarly quasi-randomly allocated across neighborhood characteristics. In other words, we are confident that the DHA dwelling allocation process sufficiently limited the possibility that some characteristics of the caregiver we cannot observe are so strongly correlated with both youths' outcomes and the neighborhood in which they resided that it would confound our causal interpretation of neighborhood effects.

---

9. The programming and execution of these simulations was conducted by Dr. Albert Anderson of Public Data Queries Inc., whose contribution we gratefully acknowledge.

Table A4. Number of Statistically Significant Correlations Between Neighborhood Characteristics and Typically Unobserved Household Characteristics

Household Characteristic	Families with No or One Child	Families with Two Children	Families with Three or More Children
Ever not enough food for family while residing in this location	0	1 (%African American=.14)	0
Ever unable to pay all bills while residing in this location	2 (%foreign-born = .13; %vacant = −.16)	2 (%elem. school ed. = −.17; %vacant = −.14)	1 (%vacant = −.12)
Frequency of alcohol use since becoming a parent	2 (%unemployed = −.16; %owner =.13)	0	1 (%African American = −.09)
Frequency of marijuana use since becoming a parent	1 (%African American = .17)	0	0
Frequency of drug use since becoming a parent	1 (%African American = .13)	0	0
Ever seen psychologist, psychiatrist, or counselor	0	0	0
Did your parents ever live in public housing when you were growing up?	1 (%female heads = .22)	0	1 (%foreign born = −.18)
Did your parents ever own their home when you were growing up?	0	3 (%elem. school = .26; %college = −.26; %own = .20)	0
Born in United States	1 (%college = −.16;)	0	0
Primary language is Spanish	0	0	0
Father of child always lived at home while child growing up	0	0	5 (%female heads = −.11; %elementary school = −.10; %poor = −.10; %own = .09; %pre-1940 homes= −.12)
Parental depression (CESD) scale	0	1 (%Latino = .13)	2 (%elem. school = .13; %Latino=.13)
Parental self-efficacy scale	0	0	0
Parental beliefs & practices scale	0	1 (%Latino = −.21)	2 (%college = −.09; %African American = −.12)

Source: Authors' calculations based on Monte Carlo simulations of Denver Child Study survey data.

Note: Number of statistically significant household-neighborhood characteristic correlations actually observed are shown, with the corresponding neighborhood indicators and pairwise correlations shown parenthetically.

APPENDIX B

Table B1. First Stage Regression Results for Neighborhood Conditions at Time of First Occurrence of Running Away from Home

Dependent Variables: Neighborhood Conditions at Time of Initiation

Exogenous Predictors	Social Vulnerability		% African American		Occupational Prestige		% Foreign Born		Violent Crime Rate		Property Crime Rate	
	b	SE	b	SE	b	SE	b	SE	b	SE	b	SE
Covariates at time of first offer												
Female (omitted=male)	2.436	−2.901	1.028	−0.918	−0.398*	−0.189	0.732	−0.802	0.368	−0.364	1.418	−1.78
Number of siblings in household	−1.825	−2.427	0.655	−0.672	−0.053	−0.124	0.615	−0.51	−0.39	−0.289	−0.924	−1.132
Caregiver age	0.443	−0.464	−0.059	−0.079	−0.027	−0.02	−0.121	−0.078	0.072	−0.057	0.406*	−0.171
Caregiver has high school diploma or higher	−9.778	−5.179	2.541	−1.652	0.453	−0.317	−1.072	−1.281	−0.699	−0.628	−3.848	−2.632
Natural log of household income	−0.177	−0.586	0.005	−0.158	0.019	−0.034	0.058	−0.138	−0.031	−0.072	0.054	−0.274
Household economic stressor index	−2.676	−2.321	0.323	−0.713	0.162	−0.14	−0.588	−0.578	−0.289	−0.273	−1.089	−1.197
Number of moves from birth to time of first offer	1.805	−0.951	0.107	−0.269	−0.051	−0.064	−0.348	−0.289	0.069	−0.108	1.302*	−0.595
Timing of DHA first offer (omitted=pre–1990)												
Offer 1990–1991	−9.011	−9.793	−0.945	−3.372	0.441	−0.624	3.729	−2.547	−1.884	−1.327	−1.822	−6.813
Offer 1992–1993	−15.856	−11.03	−1.322	−3.914	0.457	−0.702	3.505	−3.504	−1.823	−1.455	−5.461	−5.801
Offer 1994–1995	8.487	−12.756	−1.28	−3.095	−0.273	−0.717	2.117	−2.562	1.051	−1.623	0.83	−5.034
Offer 1996–1997	21.49	−13.057	−1.366	−3.278	−0.537	−0.8	1.188	−3.021	2.507	−1.717	5.17	−5.786
Offer 1998–1999	13.548	−13.79	−1.697	−3.185	−0.831	−0.751	2.712	−2.988	1.963	−1.763	1.315	−5.664
Offer 2000–2001	9.67	−13.652	−3.13	−3.297	−0.809	−0.784	2.182	−2.922	1.719	−1.715	−0.305	−5.868
Offer 2002–2003	32.635*	−13.824	1.917	−3.568	−0.608	−0.788	−2.47	−3.35	3.562*	−1.811	6.928	−6.592
Offer 2004–2005	14.234	−21.581	−2.454	−3.78	0.631	−1.055	−1.014	−3.985	1.642	−2.487	8.381	−8.918
Neighborhood of first offer												
Social vulnerability score (range 0–100)	0.420***	−0.064	−0.008	−0.019	−0.006	−0.004	−0.004	−0.019	0.031***	−0.009	0.051	−0.037
Percentage African American residents	−24.318	−12.465	48.284***	−5.48	1.495	−1.114	4.548	−3.602	−2.639	−1.568	−13.574*	−6.636
Occupational prestige score (range 0–100)	−0.308	−1.466	0.158	−0.317	0.515***	−0.091	−0.413	−0.33	−0.163	−0.183	0.155	−0.618
Percentage foreign-born residents	−6.714	−44.858	6.707	−8.916	−0.14	−2.359	70.774***	−10.376	0.297	−5.338	−8.088	−18.045
Violent crime rate per 1,000	0.273	−0.315	−0.322*	−0.138	−0.005	−0.024	0.149	−0.094	0.159**	−0.055	0.072	−0.212
Property crime rate per 1,000	−0.032	−0.076	0.084***	−0.022	0.008	−0.004	−0.013	−0.018	0.001	−0.01	0.175***	−0.037
Constant	48.155	−60.604	−1.987	−12.688	20.376***	−3.652	31.329*	−13.606	7.151	−7.428	7.715	−24.902
Observations	1024		1025		1024		1025		927		927	
R^2	0.244		0.265		0.215		0.228		0.266		0.182	

Source: Authors' calculations.
Note: Standard errors in column 2 for each dependent variable.
All chi-square statistics are significant at the $p < 0.001$ level.
* $p < 0.05$; ** $p < 0.01$; *** $p < 0.001$

Table B2. First Stage Regression Results for Neighborhood Conditions at Time of Initiation of Aggressive or Violent Behaviors

Dependent Variables: Neighborhood Conditions at Time of Initiation

Exogenous Predictors	Social Vulnerability		% African American		Occupational Prestige		% Foreign Born		Violent Crime Rate		Property Crime Rate	
	b	SE	b	SE	b	SE	b	SE	b	SE	b	SE
Covariates at time of first offer												
Female (omitted=male)	-0.264	-3.424	0.703	-0.959	-0.473*	-0.206	1.582	-0.836	0.333	-0.445	-0.747	-2.047
Number of siblings in household	-0.681	-2.337	0.3	-0.68	-0.041	-0.121	0.526	-0.479	-0.045	-0.331	0.444	-1.336
Caregiver age	0.39	-0.47	-0.042	-0.079	-0.028	-0.021	-0.094	-0.078	0.06	-0.062	0.281	-0.181
Caregiver has high school diploma or higher	-8.281	-5.301	2.962	-1.73	0.341	-0.323	-0.908	-1.284	-0.522	-0.671	-2.991	-3.005
Natural log of household income	-0.125	-0.588	0.001	-0.167	0.018	-0.035	0.031	-0.136	-0.026	-0.073	0.06	-0.304
Household economic stressor index (range 0–5)	-0.792	-2.328	0.491	-0.718	0.035	-0.139	-0.426	-0.595	0.029	-0.284	0.07	-1.403
Number of moves from birth to time of first offer	1.905*	-0.946	0.264	-0.265	-0.031	-0.065	-0.478	-0.288	0.028	-0.119	1.468*	-0.626
Timing of DHA first offer (omitted=pre-1990)												
Offer 1990–1991	-10.459	-9.45	-1.347	-3.372	0.481	-0.607	4.151	-2.463	-2.682*	-1.284	-6.825	-6.957
Offer 1992–1993	-19.987	-10.926	-4.118	-3.949	0.339	-0.72	4.805	-3.86	-2.381	-1.609	-10.921	-6.221
Offer 1994–1995	7.609	-11.761	-1.665	-3.191	-0.279	-0.705	2.536	-2.553	0.053	-1.509	-0.892	-5.166
Offer 1996–1997	26.337*	-12.513	-1.983	-3.198	-0.95	-0.744	1.125	-2.995	1.65	-1.56	6.344	-6.798
Offer 1998–1999	17.215	-12.782	-2.334	-3.193	-0.744	-0.743	0.979	-2.92	1.378	-1.637	2.616	-5.956
Offer 2000–2001	13.524	-12.307	-4.174	-3.648	-0.827	-0.793	2.079	-2.998	0.639	-1.572	-2.659	-5.932
Offer 2002–2003	31.250*	-12.858	0.094	-3.71	-0.363	-0.786	-2.47	-3.409	2.257	-1.693	2.839	-6.775
Offer 2004–2005	8.12	-22.077	-1.189	-4.34	0.925	-1.125	-2.012	-4.437	0.511	-2.535	2.968	-9.674
Neighborhood of first offer												
Social vulnerability score (range 0–100)	0.462***	-0.072	-0.015	-0.023	-0.008	-0.005	-0.001	-0.021	0.034***	-0.01	0.014	-0.048
Percentage African American residents	-34.298***	-13.186	52.554***	-5.797	1.621	-1.257	4.449	-3.752	-3.474*	-1.713	-15.622	-8.096
Occupational prestige score (range 0–100)	-0.252	-1.411	0.142	-0.341	0.513***	-0.088	-0.428	-0.331	-0.085	-0.181	0.639	-0.657
Percentage foreign-born residents	-9.842	-43.459	15.732	-9.739	-0.215	-2.373	72.861***	-10.43	2.742	-5.255	2.522	-19.991
Violent crime rate per 1,000	0.454	-0.329	-0.308*	-0.139	-0.005	-0.026	0.154	-0.089	0.196***	-0.056	0.306	-0.245
Property crime rate per 1,000	-0.036	-0.101	0.094**	-0.029	0.009	-0.006	-0.024	-0.023	0.002	-0.013	0.246***	-0.06
Constant	39.002	-60.219	-3.238	-13.639	20.742***	-3.647	30.203*	-13.625	3.622	-7.733	-8.68	-27.214
Observations	915		916		915		916		834		834	
R^2	0.277		0.280		0.216		0.249		0.272		0.197	

Source: Authors' calculations.
Note: Standard errors in column 2 for each dependent variable.
All chi-square statistics are significant at the $p < 0.001$ level.
* $p < 0.05$; ** $p < 0.01$; *** $p < 0.001$

Table B3. First Stage Regression Results for Neighborhood Conditions at Time of Initiation of Marijuana Use

Dependent Variables: Neighborhood Conditions at Time of Initiation

Exogenous Predictors	Social Vulnerability		% African American		Occupational Prestige		% Foreign Born		Violent Crime Rate		Property Crime Rate	
	b	SE	b	SE	b	SE	b	SE	b	SE	b	SE
Covariates at time of first offer												
Female (omitted=male)	1.911	-3.395	1.031	-0.963	-0.473*	-0.219	1.265	-0.858	0.479	-0.418	0.724	-1.746
Number of siblings in household	-0.9	-2.554	0.8	-0.781	-0.053	-0.131	0.279	-0.537	-0.277	-0.304	-0.989	-1.268
Caregiver age	0.432	-0.489	-0.042	-0.08	-0.029	-0.022	-0.111	-0.081	0.059	-0.062	0.283	-0.167
Caregiver has high school diploma or higher	-10.869*	-5.212	2.831	-1.661	0.421	-0.324	-0.906	-1.295	-0.962	-0.624	-2.969	-2.701
Natural log of household income	-0.137	-0.593	-0.001	-0.167	0.016	-0.035	-0.035	-0.14	-0.037	-0.072	0.168	-0.294
Household economic stressor index (range 0–5)	-1.394	-2.374	0.339	-0.789	0.04	-0.143	-0.251	-0.6	-0.083	-0.28	-0.839	-1.271
Number of moves from birth to time of first offer	2.113*	-0.999	0.201	-0.286	-0.031	-0.065	-0.512	-0.297	0.106	-0.114	1.674**	-0.61
Timing of DHA first offer (omitted=pre-1990)												
Offer 1990–1991	-5.673	-10.032	-1.436	-3.742	0.181	-0.635	4.104	-2.61	-2.006	-1.269	-4.55	-6.31
Offer 1992–1993	-15.234	-11.167	-2.202	-4.178	0.363	-0.783	0.999	-3.459	-2.627	-1.461	-7.927	-6.474
Offer 1994–1995	9.1	-12.726	-1.196	-3.591	-0.466	-0.713	2.866	-2.597	0.893	-1.569	-0.708	-5.3
Offer 1996–1997	19.686	-12.641	-1.655	-3.608	-0.647	-0.772	1.51	-3.052	2.102	-1.628	4.443	-6.42
Offer 1998–1999	14.443	-13.545	-2.6	-3.516	-0.961	-0.754	2.849	-3.081	1.989	-1.689	0.771	-6.073
Offer 2000–2001	8.482	-13.025	-3.989	-3.656	-0.77	-0.797	2.454	-2.983	1.497	-1.592	-0.024	-5.976
Offer 2002–2003	30.830*	-13.733	0.116	-3.903	-0.782	-0.798	-1.599	-3.405	3.409	-1.756	6.61	-6.831
Offer 2004–2005	10.549	-22.158	-3.585	-4.149	0.459	-1.092	-1.239	-4.119	1.915	-2.511	9.546	-9.6
Neighborhood of first offer												
Social vulnerability score (range 0–100)	0.429***	-0.062	-0.008	-0.019	-0.004	-0.004	-0.003	-0.018	0.028***	-0.008	0.024	-0.052
Percentage African American residents	-22.649	-13.053	49.016***	-5.997	1.005	-1.264	4.688	-3.936	-1.899	-1.648	-7.241	-7.64
Occupational prestige score (range 0–100)	0.065	-1.365	0.328	-0.323	0.553***	-0.09	-0.507	-0.324	-0.188	-0.17	0.195	-0.602
Percentage foreign-born residents	14.076	-42.759	13.511	-9.327	-0.173	-2.4	68.874***	-10.23	0.716	-5.063	-3.769	-17.127
Violent crime rate per 1,000	0.298	-0.32	-0.197	-0.163	0	-0.024	0.139	-0.102	0.136**	-0.044	0.014	-0.204
Property crime rate per 1,000	-0.02	-0.074	0.081***	-0.022	0.008	-0.005	-0.026	-0.016	0.007	-0.009	0.220***	-0.063
Constant	24.999	-57.067	-11.51	-12.544	19.110***	-3.674	36.028**	-13.232	8.277	-7.065	7.992	-25.286
Observations	904		905		904		905		821		821	
R^2	0.257		0.294		0.232		0.25		0.272		0.223	

Source: Authors' calculations.
Note: Standard errors in column 2 for each dependent variable.
All chi-square statistics are significant at the $p < 0.001$ level.
* $p < 0.05$; ** $p < 0.01$; *** $p < 0.001$

REFERENCES

Allison, Kevin W., Isaiah Crawford, Peter E. Leone, Edison Trickett, Alina Perez-Febles, Linda M. Burton, and Ree Le Blanc. 1999. "Adolescent Substance Use: Preliminary Examinations of School and Neighborhood Context." *American Journal of Community Psychology* 27(2): 111–41.

Bennett, Pamela R. 2011. "The Relationship Between Neighborhood Racial Concentration and Verbal Ability: An Investigation Using the Institutional Resources Model." *Social Science Research* 40(4): 1124–41.

Billy, John O. G., Karin L. Brewster, and William R. Grady. 1994. "Contextual Effects on the Sexual Behavior of Adolescent Women." *Journal of Marriage and the Family* 56(2): 387–404.

Bischoff, Kendra, and Sean F. Reardon. 2013. "Residential Segregation by Income, 1970–2009." *US2010: Discover America in a New Century* working paper. New York: Russell Sage Foundation.

Boardman, Jason D., Brian Karl Finch, Christopher G. Ellison, David R. Williams, and James S. Jackson. 2001. "Neighborhood Disadvantage, Stress, and Drug Use Among Adults." *Journal of Health and Social Behavior* 42(2): 151–65.

Bolland, John M., Chalandra M. Bryant, Bradley E. Lian, Debra M. McCallum, Alexander T. Vazsonyi, and Joan M. Barth. 2007. "Development and Risk Behavior Among African American, Caucasian, and Mixed-Race Adolescents Living in High Poverty Inner-City Neighborhoods." *American Journal of Community Psychology* 40(3–4): 230–49.

Bronfenbrenner, Urie, and Pamela A. Morris. 1998. "The Ecology of Developmental Processes." In *Handbook of Child Psychology*, vol. 1: *Theoretical Models of Human Development*, 5th ed., edited by William Damon. Hoboken, N.J.: John Wiley & Sons.

Brook, David W., Judith S. Brook, Elizabeth Rubenstone, Chenshu Zhang, and Naomi S. Saar. 2011. "Developmental Associations Between Externalizing Behaviors, Peer Delinquency, Drug Use, Perceived Neighborhood Crime, and Violent Behavior in Urban Communities." *Aggressive Behavior* 37(4): 349–61.

Burlew, Ann Kathleen, Candace S. Johnson, Amanda M. Flowers, Bridgette J. Peteet, Kyna D. Griffith-Henry, and Natasha D. Buchanan. 2009. "Neighborhood Risk, Parental Supervision and the Onset of Substance Use Among African American Adolescents." *Journal of Child and Family Studies* 18(6): 680–89.

Byrnes, Hilary F., Brenda A. Miller, Meng-Jinn Chen, and Joel W. Grube. 2010. "The Roles of Mothers' Neighborhood Perceptions and Specific Monitoring Strategies in Youths' Problem Behavior." *Journal of Youth and Adolescence* 40(3): 347–60.

Case, Anne, and Lawrence Katz. 1991. "The Company You Keep: The Effects of Family and Neighborhood on Disadvantaged Youths." NBER working paper no. 3705. Cambridge, Mass.: National Bureau of Economic Research.

Chetty, Raj, Nathaniel Hendren, and Lawrence F. Katz. 2015. "The Effects of Exposure to Better Neighborhoods on Children: New Evidence from the Moving to Opportunity Experiment." NBER working paper no. 21156. Cambridge, Mass.: National Bureau of Economic Research.

Chilenski, Sarah M. 2011. "From the Macro to the Micro: A Geographic Examination of the Community Context and Early Adolescent Problem Behaviors." *American Journal of Community Psychology* 48(3-4): 352–64.

Cook, Thomas D., and Coady Wing. 2012. "Making MTO Health Results More Relevant to Current Housing Policy: Next Steps." *Cityscape: A Journal of Policy Development and Research* 14(2): 169–80.

Copeland-Linder, Nikeea, Sharon F. Lambert, Yi-Fu Chen, and Nicholas S. Ialongo. 2010. "Contextual Stress and Health Risk Behaviors Among African American Adolescents." *Journal of Youth and Adolescence* 40(2): 158–73.

Coulton, Claudia J., and Jill E. Korbin. 2007. "Indicators of Child Well-being through a Neighborhood Lens." *Social Indicators Research* 84(3): 349–61.

Crane, Jonathan. 1991. "The Epidemic Theory of Ghettos and Neighborhood Effects on Dropping Out and Teenage Childbearing." *American Journal of Sociology* 96(5): 1226–59.

Crowder, Kyle, and Scott J. South. 2003. "Neighborhood Distress and School Dropout: The Variable Significance of Community Context." *Social Science Research* 32(4): 659–98.

——. 2011. "Spatial and Temporal Dimensions of Neighborhood Effects on High School Graduation." *Social Science Research* 40(1): 87–106.

Damm, Anna P. 2009. "Ethnic Enclaves and Immigrant Labor Market Outcomes: Quasi-Experimental Evidence." *Journal of Labor Economics* 27(2), 281–314.

———. 2014. "Neighborhood Quality and Labor Market Outcomes: Evidence from a Quasi-Random Neighborhood Assignment of Immigrants." *Journal of Urban Economics* 79(1): 139–66.

Davis, James A., Tom W. Smith, Robert W. Hodge, Keiko Nakao, and Judith Treas. 1991. "Occupational Prestige Ratings from the 1989 General Social Survey." Chicago: National Opinion Research Center [producer]. Ann Arbor, Mich.: Inter-University Consortium for Political and Social Research [distributor]. http://doi.org/10.3886/ICPSR09593.v1 Dataset.

Duncan, Greg J., James P. Connell, and Pamela K. Klebanov. 1997. "Conceptual and Methodological Issues in Estimating Causal Effects of Neighborhoods and Family Conditions on Individual Development." In *Neighborhood Poverty*, vol. 1: *Context and Consequences for Children*, 5th ed., edited by Jeanne Brooks-Gunn, Greg J. Duncan, and J. Lawrence Aber. New York: Russell Sage Foundation.

Edin, Per-Anders, Peter Fredricksson, and Olof Åslund. 2003. "Ethnic Enclaves and the Economic Success of Immigrants: Evidence from a Natural Experiment." *Quarterly Journal of Economics* 113(3): 329–57.

Fagan, Abigail A., Emily M. Wright, and Gillian M. Pinchevsky. 2015. "Exposure to Violence, Substance Use, and Neighborhood Context." *Social Science Research* 49(January): 314–26.

Farrell, Albert D., Sally Mays, Amie Bettencourt, Elizabeth H. Erwin, Monique Vulin-Reynolds, and Kevin W. Allison. 2010. "Environmental Influences on Fighting Versus Nonviolent Behavior in Peer Situations: A Qualitative Study with Urban African American Adolescents." *American Journal of Community Psychology* 46(1–2): 19–35.

Fite, Paula J., Porche Wynn, John E. Lochman, and Karen C. Wells. 2009. "The Influence of Neighborhood Disadvantage and Perceived Disapproval on Early Substance Use Initiation." *Addictive Behaviors* 34(9): 769–71.

Ford, Julie M., and Andrew A. Beveridge. 2006. "Varieties of Substance Use and Visible Drug Problems: Individual and Neighborhood Factors." *Journal of Drug Issues* 36(2): 377–88.

Foster, Holly, and Jeanne Brooks-Gunn. 2012. "Neighborhood Influences on Antisocial Behavior during Childhood and Adolescence." In *Handbook of Life-Course Criminology: Emerging Trends and Directions for Future Research*, edited by Chris L. Gibson, and Marvin D. Krohn. New York: Springer Science + Business Media.

Francois, Samantha, Stacy Overstreet, and Michael Cunningham. 2012. "Where We Live: The Unexpected Influence of Urban Neighborhoods on the Academic Performance of African American Adolescents." *Youth & Society* 44(2): 307–28.

Furr-Holden, C. Debra M., Myong Hwa Lee, Adam J. Milam, Renee M. Johnson, Kwang-Sig Lee, and Nicholas S. Ialongo. 2011. "The Growth of Neighborhood Disorder and Marijuana Use Among Urban Adolescents: A Case for Policy and Environmental Interventions." *Journal of Studies on Alcohol and Drugs* 72(3): 371–79.

Galster, George C. 2008. "Quantifying the Effect of Neighbourhood on Individuals: Challenges, Alternative Approaches, and Promising Directions." *Journal of Applied Social Science Studies* 128(1): 7–48.

———. 2012. "The Mechanism(s) of Neighbourhood Effects: Theory, Evidence, and Policy Implications." In *Neighbourhood Effects Research: New Perspectives*, edited by Maarten van Ham, David Manley, Nick Bailey, Ludi Simpson, and Duncan Maclennan. Dordrecht: Springer.

Galster, George, Roger Andersson, and Sako Musterd. 2010. "Who Is Affected by Neighbourhood Income Mix? Gender, Age, Family, Employment, and Income Differences." *Urban Studies* 47(14): 2915–44.

Galster, George C., and Anna M. Santiago. 2006. "What's the 'Hood Got to Do with It? Parental Perceptions About How Neighborhood Mechanisms Affect Their Children." *Journal of Urban Affairs* 28(3): 201–26.

Gennetian, Lisa A., Lisa Sanbonmatsu, and Jens Ludwig. 2011. "An Overview of Moving to Opportunity: A Random Assignment Housing Mobility Study in Five U.S. Cities." In *Neighborhood and Life Chances: How Place Matters in Modern America*, edited by Harriet B. Newburger, Eugenie L. Birch, and Susan M. Wachter. Philadelphia: University of Pennsylvania Press.

Gephart, Martha A. 1997. "Neighborhoods and Communities as Contexts for Development." In *Neighborhood Poverty*, vol. 1: *Context and Consequences for Children*, 5th ed., edited by Jeanne Brooks-Gunn, Greg J. Duncan, and J. Lawrence Aber. New York: Russell Sage Foundation.

Gilliard-Matthews, Stacia, Robin Stevens, Madison Nilsen, and Jamie Dunaev. 2015. "'You See It Everywhere. It's Just Natural': Contextualizing the Role of Peers, Family, and Neighborhood in Initial Substance Use." *Deviant Behavior* 36(6): 492–509.

Goering, John M., and Judith D. Feins, eds. 2003. *Choosing a Better Life?: Evaluating the Moving to Opportunity Social Experiment*. Washington, D.C.: Urban Institute Press.

Harding, David, Lisa Gennetian, Christopher Winship, Lisa Sanbonmatsu, and Jeffrey Kling. 2010. "Unpacking Neighborhood Influences on Education Outcomes: Setting the Stage for Future Research." In *Whither Opportunity?: Rising Inequality, Schools, and Children's Life Chances*, edited by Greg J. Duncan and Richard. J. Murnane. New York: Russell Sage Foundation.

Haynie, Dana L., Richard J. Petts, David Maimon, and Alex R. Piquero. 2009. "Exposure to Violence in Adolescence and Precocious Role Exits." *Journal of Youth and Adolescence* 38(3): 269–86.

Hoffmann, John P. 2002. "The Community Context of Family Structure and Adolescent Drug Use." *Journal of Marriage and Family* 64(2): 314–30.

Jackson, Nicki, Simon Denny, and Shanthi Ameratunga. 2014. "Social and Socio-Demographic Neighborhood Effects on Adolescent Alcohol Use: A Systematic Review of Multi-Level Studies. *Social Science & Medicine* 115(1): 10–20.

Jacob, Brian A. 2004. "Public Housing, Housing Vouchers, and Student Achievement: Evidence from Public Housing Demolitions in Chicago." *American Economic Review* 94(1): 233–58.

Jargowsky, Paul A. 2013. *Concentration of Poverty in the New Millennium: Changes in the Prevalence, Composition, and Location of High-Poverty Neighborhoods*. New York and Camden, N.J.: The Century Foundation and Center for Urban Research and Education. Accessed June 13, 2015. http://www.tcf.org/assets/downloads/Concentration_of_Poverty_in_the_New_Millennium.pdf.

Jennings, Wesley G., Mildred M. Maldonado-Molina, Jennifer M. Reingle, and Kelli A. Komro. 2011. "A Multi-level Approach to Investigating Neighborhood Effects on Physical Aggression among Urban Chicago Youth." *American Journal of Criminal Justice* 36(4): 392–407.

Karriker-Jaffe, Katherine J. 2011. "Areas of Disadvantage: A Systematic Review of Effects of Area-Level Socioeconomic Status on Substance Use Outcomes." *Drug and Alcohol Review* 30(1): 84–95.

Kellam, Sheppard G., C. Hendricks Brown, Jeanne M. Poduska, Nicholas S. Ialongo, Wei Wang, Peter Toyinbo, Hanno Petras, Carla Ford, Amy Windham, and Holly C. Wilcox. 2008. "Effects of a Universal Classroom Behavior Management Program in First and Second Grades on Young Adult Behavioral, Psychiatric, and Social Outcomes." *Drug and Alcohol Dependence* 95(June): S5–28.

Kingsley, Tom, and Kathryn Pettit. 2007. "Destination Neighborhoods of Multi-Move Families in the Moving to Opportunity Demonstration." Paper presented at the Annual Meetings of the Urban Affairs Association, Cities and Migration: Opportunities and Challenges. Seattle, Wash. (April 26, 2007).

Lambert, Sharon F., Tamara L. Brown, Clarenda M. Phillips, and Nicholas S. Ialongo. 2004. "The Relationship Between Perceptions of Neighborhood Characteristics and Substance Use among Urban African American Adolescents." *American Journal of Community Psychology* 34(3–4): 205–18.

Leventhal, Tama, and Jeanne Brooks-Gunn. 2000. "The Neighborhoods They Live in: The Effect of Neighborhood Residence on Child and Adolescent Outcomes." *Psychological Bulletin* 126(2): 309–37.

Leventhal, Tama, Véronique Dupéré, and Jeanne Brooks-Gunn. 2009. "Neighborhood Influences on Adolescent Development." In *Handbook of Adolescent Psychology*, vol. 2: *Contextual Influences on Adolescent Development*, 3rd ed., edited by Richard M. Lerner and Laurence Steinberg, 411–43. Hoboken, N.J.: Wiley-Blackwell.

Lyle, David S. 2007. "Estimating and Interpreting Peer and Role Model Effects from Randomly Assigned Social Groups at West Point." *Review of Economics and Statistics* 89(2): 289–99.

Mennis, Jeremy, and Michael J. Mason. 2012. "Social and Geographic Contexts of Adolescent Substance Use: The Moderating Effects of Age and Gender." *Social Networks* 34(1): 150–57.

Molnar, Beth E., Magdalena Cerda, Andrea L. Roberts, and Stephen L. Buka. 2008. "Effects of Neighborhood Resources on Aggressive and Delinquent Behaviors Among Urban Youths." *American Journal of Public Health* 98(6): 1086–93.

Oakes, J. Michael. 2004. "The (Mis)estimation of Neighborhood Effects: Causal inference for a

Practicable Social Epidemiology." *Social Science and Medicine* 58(10): 1929-52.

Oakes, J. Michael, Kate E. Andrade, Ifrah M. Biyoow, and Logan T. Cowan. 2015. "Twenty Years of Neighborhood Effect Research: An Assessment." *Current Epidemiology Reports* 2(1): 80-87.

Oreopoulos, Philip. 2003. "The Long-Run Consequences of Living in a Poor Neighborhood." *Quarterly Journal of Economics* 118(4): 1533-75.

Partnership for Maternal, Newborn and Child Health. 2011. "PMNCH Knowledge Summary #15: Non-Communicable Diseases." Washington, D.C.: World Health Organization/PMNCH. Accessed July 7, 2016. http://www.who.int/entity/pmnch/knowledge/publications/summaries/ks15.pdf.

Pergamit, Michael R. 2010. "On the Lifetime Prevalence of Running Away from Home." Washington, D.C.: Urban Institute. Accessed July 7, 2016. http://www.urban.org/research/publication/lifetime-prevalence-running-away-home.

Poduska, Jeanne M., Sheppard G. Kellam, Wei Wang, C. Hendricks Brown, Nicholas S. Ialongo, and Peter Toyinbo. 2008. "Impact of the Good Behavior Game, a Universal Classroom-Based Behavior Intervention, on Young Adult Service Use for Problems with Emotions, Behavior, or Drugs or Alcohol." *Drug and Alcohol Dependence* 95(June): S29-44.

Rogerson, Peter A. 2001. *Statistical Methods for Geography*. London: Sage.

Rutter, Michael. 1989. "Pathways from Childhood to Adult Life." *Journal of Child Psychology and Psychiatry* 30(1): 23-51.

Sameroff, Arnold J., Ronald Seifer, Alfred Baldwin, and Clara Baldwin. 1993. "Stability of Intelligence from Preschool to Adolescence: The Influence of Social and Family Risk Factors." *Child Development* 64(1): 80-97.

Sampson, Robert J. 2001. "How Do Communities Undergird or Undermine Human Development? Relevant Contexts and Social Mechanisms." In *Does It Take a Village? Community Effects on Children, Adolescents, and Families*, edited by Alan Booth and Ann C. Crouter. Mahwah, N.J.: Lawrence Erlbaum Associates.

———. 2008. "Moving to Inequality: Neighborhood Effects and Experiments Meet Social Structure." *American Journal of Sociology* 114(1): 189-231.

Sampson, Robert J., Jeffrey D. Morenoff, and Thomas Gannon-Rowley. 2002. "Assessing 'Neighborhood Effects': Social Processes and New Directions in Research." *Annual Review of Sociology* 28(1): 443-78.

Sampson, Robert J, Patrick Sharkey, and Stephen W. Raudenbush. 2008. "Durable Effects of Concentrated Disadvantage on Verbal Ability Among African-American Children." *Proceedings of the National Academy of Sciences* 105(3): 845-82.

Sanbonmatsu, Lisa, Lawrence F. Katz, Jens Ludwig, Lisa A. Gennetian, Greg J. Duncan, Ronald C. Kessler, Emma Adam, Thomas W. McDade, and Stacy Tessler Lindau. 2011. "Moving to Opportunity for Fair Housing Demonstration Program—Final Impacts Evaluation." Washington: U.S. Department of Housing and Urban Development.

Santiago, Anna Maria, George C. Galster, Jessica L. Lucero, Karen J. Ishler, Eun Lye Lee, Georgios Kypriotakis, and Lisa Stack. 2014. "Opportunity Neighborhoods for Latino and African American Children." Washington: U.S. Department of Housing and Urban Development.

Sharkey, Patrick. 2013. *Stuck in Place: Urban Neighborhoods and the End of Progress toward Racial Equality*. Chicago: University of Chicago Press.

Sharkey, Patrick, and Jacob W. Faber. 2014. "Where, When, Why, and For Whom Do Residential Contexts Matter? Moving Away from the Dichotomous Understanding of Neighborhood Effects." *Annual Review of Sociology* 40(1): 559-79.

Small, Mario Luis, and Jessica Feldman. 2011. "Ethnographic Evidence, Heterogeneity, and Neighbourhood Effects after Moving to Opportunity." In *Neighbourhood Effects Research: New Perspectives*, edited by Maarten van Ham, David Manley, Nick Bailey, Ludi Simpson, and Duncan Maclennan. Dordrecht: Springer.

Snedker, Karen, Jerald R. Herting, and Emily Walton. 2009. "Contextual Effects and Adolescent Substance Use: Exploring the Role of Neighborhoods. *Social Science Quarterly* 90(5): 1272-97.

South, Scott J., Eric P. Baumer, and Amy Lutz. 2003. "Interpreting Community Effects on Youth Educational Attainment." *Youth & Society* 35(1): 3-36.

Substance Abuse and Mental Health Services Administration. 2013. "Behavioral Health Barometer: Colorado, 2013." *HHS Publication* no. SMA-13-4796CO. Rockville, Md.: Substance Abuse and Mental Health Services Administration.

Tyler, Kimberly A., and Bianca E. Bersani. 2008. "A

Longitudinal Study of Early Adolescent Precursors to Running Away." *Journal of Early Adolescence* 28(2): 230–51.

Vanfossen, Beth, C. Hendricks Brown, Sheppard Kellam, Natalie Sokoloff, and Susan Doering. 2010. "Neighborhood Context and the Development of Aggression in Boys and Girls." *Journal of Community Psychology* 38(3): 329–49.

Werner, Emmy E., and Ruth S. Smith. 1982. *Vulnerable but Invincible: A Study of Resilient Children and Youth*. New York: McGraw-Hill.

Wilson, William Julius. 1987. *The Truly Disadvantaged: The Inner City, the Underclass, and Public Policy*. Chicago: University of Chicago Press.

Wodtke, Geoffrey T., David J. Harding, and Felix Elwert. 2011. "Neighborhood Effects in Temporal Perspective: The Impact of Long-Term Exposure to Concentrated Disadvantage on High School Graduation." *American Sociological Review* 76(5): 713–36.

Zimmerman, Gregory M., and Steven F. Messner. 2010. "Neighborhood Context and the Gender Gap in Adolescent Violent Crime." *American Sociological Review* 75(6): 958–80.

Socioeconomic Segregation of Activity Spaces in Urban Neighborhoods: Does Shared Residence Mean Shared Routines?

CHRISTOPHER R. BROWNING, CATHERINE A. CALDER, LAUREN J. KRIVO, ANNA L. SMITH, AND BETHANY BOETTNER

Residential segregation by income and education is increasing alongside slowly declining black-white segregation. Segregation in urban neighborhood residents' nonhome activity spaces has not been explored. How integrated are the daily routines of people who live in the same neighborhood? Are people with different socioeconomic backgrounds that live near one another less likely to share routine activity locations than those of similar education or income? Do these patterns vary across the socioeconomic continuum or by neighborhood structure? The analyses draw on unique data from the Los Angeles Family and Neighborhood Survey that identify the location where residents engage in routine activities. Using multilevel p_2 (network) models, we analyze pairs of households in the same neighborhood and examine whether the dyad combinations across three levels of SES conduct routine activities in the same location, and whether neighbor socioeconomic similarity in the co-location of routine activities is dependent on the level of neighborhood socioeconomic inequality and trust. Results indicate that, on average, increasing SES diminishes the likelihood of sharing activity locations with any SES group. This pattern is most pronounced in neighborhoods characterized by high levels of socioeconomic inequality. Neighborhood trust explains a nontrivial proportion of the inequality effect on the extent of routine activity sorting by SES. Thus stark, visible neighborhood-level inequality by SES may lead to enhanced effects of distrust on the willingness to share routines across class.

Keywords: activity spaces, segregation, socioeconomic inequality, neighborhoods

Christopher R. Browning is professor of sociology at the Ohio State University. **Catherine A. Calder** is professor of statistics at the Ohio State University. **Lauren J. Krivo** is professor of sociology at Rutgers University. **Anna L. Smith** is a PhD candidate in statistics at the Ohio State University. **Bethany Boettner** is senior research associate at the Institute for Population Research at the Ohio State University.

© 2017 Russell Sage Foundation. Browning, Christopher R., Catherine A. Calder, Lauren J. Krivo, Anna L. Smith, and Bethany Boettner. 2017. "Socioeconomic Segregation of Activity Spaces in Urban Neighborhoods: Does Shared Residence Mean Shared Routines?" *RSF: The Russell Sage Foundation Journal of the Social Sciences* 3(2): 210–31. DOI: 10.7758/RSF.3.2.09. The authors wish to thank Jonathan Dirlam, Ruth Peterson, Mei-Po Kwan, Yanan Jia, and Samuel Bussmann. This research was supported by the National Institute on Drug Abuse R01 DA032371 03 ("Adolescent Health and Development in Context"), the National Science Foundation DMS-1209161 ("Bayesian Methods for Socio-Spatial Point Patterns and Networks"), and the Ohio State University Institute for Population Research (NICHD P2CHD058484). Direct correspondence to: Christopher R. Browning at browning.90@osu.edu, Department of Sociology, The Ohio State University, 238 Townshend Hall, 1885 Neil Ave Mall, Columbus, OH 43210; Catherine A. Calder at calder@stat.osu.edu, Department of Statistics, The Ohio State University, 429 Cockins Hall, 1958 Neil Ave., Columbus, OH 43221; Lauren J. Krivo at lkrivo @sociology.rutgers.edu, Department of Sociology, Rutgers, The State University of New Jersey, 26 Nichol Avenue, New Brunswick, NJ 08901; Anna L. Smith at smith.11066@buckeyemail.osu.edu, Department of Statistics, The Ohio State University, 404 Cockins Hall, 1958 Neil Ave., Columbus, OH 43221; and Bethany Boettner at boettner.6@osu.edu, Institute for Population Research, The Ohio State University, 65 Townshend Hall, 1885 Neil Ave Mall, Columbus, OH 43210.

Recent evidence indicates that residential segregation by income and education is increasing alongside trends of slowly but steadily declining black-white segregation (Domina 2006; Reardon and Bischoff 2011). Research on segregation patterns, however, focuses almost exclusively on where groups with varying economic statuses live, neglecting potential differences in the range of places people go during the course of their day. As such, segregation research often implicitly assumes that residents of the same neighborhood do not further sort themselves by socioeconomic status in the spaces where they conduct daily activities. Drawing on this expectation, some theories of intergroup contact and policies promoting mixed-income housing claim that residential integration by income and education has a range of benefits because integration extends beyond the walls of people's homes to the things that people do and the places they go (Jargowsky and Swanstrom 2009; Talen 2006).

Yet, few studies examine the extent of socioeconomic segregation in the activity spaces of neighborhood residents (but see Jones and Pebley 2014; Krivo et al. 2013). Are people with different socioeconomic backgrounds who live near one another just as likely to share routine activity locations as those of similar education or income? Or instead, are the activity locations of socioeconomically distinct households who live in the same neighborhood segregated? Residential propinquity should increase the extent to which individuals of different social classes encounter one another. However, social distance may trump such residential effects and make it unlikely that people with different socioeconomic statuses go to the same locations to conduct activities. No evidence to date evaluates the extent to which socioeconomic differences in households within the same neighborhood influence shared nonresidential routines.

Research is also silent about how household socioeconomic segregation in routine activity locations varies according to the character of the neighborhoods where people live. Drawing on competing perspectives regarding the influence of neighborhood heterogeneity on social interaction, we consider how neighborhood socioeconomic inequality affects the extent to which neighborhood residents from similar and dissimilar classes share activity locations. Extended to socioeconomic status (SES), the *contact hypothesis* would predict that high levels of diversity increase cross-group trust and social interaction, which should in turn increase the chances of neighbors of different statuses going to the same places (Allport 1954; Emerson, Kimbro, and Yancey 2002; Pettigrew 1998; Pettigrew and Tropp 2006). Alternative approaches, however, argue that neighborhood diversity fosters distrust, leading to either *generalized withdrawal* (reduced association with all groups) (Putnam 2007), or *conflict* (reduced trust and association with other SES groups but enhanced solidarity and association with one's own SES group).

In this paper, we draw on residential and activity space segregation research to develop and test hypotheses regarding the extent of, and variability in, socioeconomic (income, education) sorting in the routine activity locations of urban neighborhood residents. The analyses draw on unique data from the Los Angeles Family and Neighborhood Survey (L.A.FANS) that identify the locations where residents from a representative sample of neighborhoods in Los Angeles County live, work, shop, worship, visit the doctor, and spend other time. Extending p_2 models for network data (Zijlstra, van Duijn, and Snijders 2006) to the multilevel setting, we analyze pairs of households located in the same neighborhood (for a sample of sixty-five census tracts) and examine whether the dyads conduct routine activities in the same location (census block group). We then examine the extent to which observed activity location sorting patterns by SES vary across neighborhoods as a function of tract-level socioeconomic inequality and perceived trust. The study's innovations include use of novel activity space data to estimate the magnitude and multilevel sources of routine activity segregation—a largely neglected phenomenon in extant urban research.

THEORETICAL BACKGROUND

The focus on socioeconomic inequality in where neighborhood residents go stems from growing evidence that residential segregation by income and education is increasing (for example, Domina 2006; Fischer 2003; Massey and Fischer 2003; Reardon and Bischoff 2011). Segregation within metropolitan areas of the college educated from people with low education rose dramatically from 1970 through 2000 (Domina 2006), and the concentrations of poverty and affluence continue to climb (for example, Jargowsky 2013; Reardon and Bischoff 2011). These changes occurred alongside an overall decline in black-white segregation (Fischer 2003; Massey and Fischer 2003). Here, we move beyond analyses of tract-level patterns of integration or segregation to consider expectations regarding the extent to which routine activity patterns are shaped by social (SES) distance between residents of the same neighborhood; and neighborhood-level factors independently contribute to the tendency to share routines and modify the effects of social distance between households. We begin by discussing the potential for *household dyad* SES effects on spatial sorting in routines and then move to *neighborhood* effects on shared routines—both direct and through modifying dyad effects.

Household Dyad SES Effects on Shared Routines

An implicit assumption in studies of residential segregation is that identifying residence in a neighborhood (typically a census tract) and describing that neighborhood's sociodemographic composition captures day-to-day experiences of segregation or integration. Given this assumption, these analyses essentially assume a pattern of *random mixing* in nonresidential activity spaces. In this approach, households in the same neighborhood do not experience additional spatial sorting in the places they routinely go. Yet, the social structural factors that shape patterns of residential segregation may also operate to segregate routine activity locations such as places of employment, school, worship, child care, medical care, leisure, and other destinations (Palmer 2013). For example, differences in affordability, perceived acceptability, or bias in how people are treated, and information about where to get jobs, services, and other amenities may vary by economic status among residents of the same neighborhood, leading to segregation by SES in where people routinely go. Evidence of spatial sorting by socioeconomic status in routine activities among neighbors would support such notions and challenge the assumption of shared access to local resources (for example, schools, places of employment, and amenities such as parks) implicit in research on residential integration. Yet the extent to which activity spaces are segregated between households with different social characteristics within the same neighborhood is virtually unknown. Examining the degree of spatial sorting by socioeconomic status—a dominant social structural influence on social interaction more generally (Hipp and Perrin 2009)—in the daily routines of residents is a necessary step in understanding the mechanisms through which segregation affects access to resources and life outcomes.

The random mixing model may be seen as a relatively optimistic view—one that underlies mixed-income housing policies that assume residential socioeconomic integration will extend beyond simply living next to one another into the ways that residents spend their day and the places that they go (Jargowsky and Swanstrom 2009; Talen 2006). However, theory and research on mixed-income housing indicate that this may not be the case. Evidence suggests that people of different economic statuses carry out routine activities in different locations even if they reside in integrated neighborhoods (Lees 2008). First, *material constraints* may diminish the likelihood of shared routines across class. Material constraints limit the places lower-income residents go to shop, work, spend leisure time, and access social support services such as health care or child care due to affordability and accessibility (for example, transportation options). In contrast, higher-SES individuals have the resources to use more expensive services that may be in very different locations than those used by their lower-income counterparts. Further, their greater ability to afford an array of services and transportation costs may lead to a more extensive set of activity locations simply because they have resources to go wherever they want. As such, we hypothesize that higher-SES individuals will have a lower likelihood of contact during activities not only with coresidents of lower status but also with neighbors of any SES as routine activity locations increasingly reflect the unencumbered idiosyncratic preferences of individuals.

Beyond material constraints, *social distance* between residents of the same neighborhood may limit willingness to share routine activities. Differences in SES between residents may be associated with varying attitudes and lifestyles that could contribute to less willingness to share routines (Arthurson 2010; Kleit 2005; Levy, McDade, and Bertumen 2013; Tach 2009). To the extent that class similarity is associated with a sense of group identity, a preference for sharing routines with those of similar SES may enhance a feeling of belonging and inhibit sharing routines across SES (Hipp and Perrin 2009). Some people of higher status may hold stereotypes regarding the behavior and norms of lower-class individuals that lead them to avoid encounters with those of lower status even if they live near one another (Chaskin and Joseph 2013; Chaskin, Sichling, and Joseph 2013; Tach 2009). Lower-status individuals may also be less inclined to share routine activities with their higher-SES counterparts who live in their neighborhood because they think they might be poorly treated, discriminated against, or made to feel unwelcome (McCormick, Joseph, and Chaskin 2012; Tach 2014). Thus, we expect that the likelihood of shared routine activity locations across SES will be lower than for those of the same SES.

Neighborhood Effects on Shared Routines

We also explore how neighborhood characteristics shape where neighbors routinely go. Specifically, we examine how neighborhood socioeconomic inequality influences features of the social climate relevant for sharing routines—particularly collective trust. The ongoing debate regarding the role of social mixing in residential housing provides an important anchor point for understanding hypotheses regarding the role of SES inequality in routine activity patterns. In the optimistic view, social mixing across class brings people together in shared activities either through random mixing or through enhancing willingness to encounter others of different SES (see the discussion of the *contact hypothesis*). In contrast, over the last decade, a substantial literature questions social mixing as both an empirical outcome of neighborhood-SES diversity and a policy prescription for solving challenges in concentrated poverty neighborhoods (Galster 2007; Kleit and Carnegie 2011; Lees 2008; Walks and Maaranen 2008).

Extant theory suggests two mechanisms by which SES inequality might reduce the likelihood of shared routines across class. First, Robert Putnam argues—in an essay focused on race-ethnic composition—that diversity leads to a *generalized* decrease in trust (2007). When brought into proximity, he contends, residents of different groups experience increased distrust and social withdrawal. Putnam does not argue that diversity fosters conflict across groups but rather that it encourages an anomic tendency toward social isolation. He offers an array of evidence regarding diversity's negative short-term effects on collective trust. Applied to shared routines, withdrawal or "hunkering down" may involve an overall reduction in the use of nonhome space (for example, in elective activities such as spending leisure time in or near the home neighborhood) or a shift of activities away from local places shared with neighbors (for example, necessity-based activities such as grocery shopping might be diverted to places neighbors are less likely to frequent). This argument suggests that urban residents are less likely to share routine activity locations with any members of their own community as the level of neighborhood inequality by SES increases.

An alternative approach links neighborhood inequality with distrust and withdrawal only between households of different socioeconomic statuses. Consistent with conflict theory in studies of race and ethnicity (Blalock 1967; Bobo 1999; Quillian 1996; Taylor 1998), lower trust brought about by increasing SES inequality increases hostile relations across, but not within, SES groups (Zubrinsky and Bobo 1996). John Hipp (2007), for instance, finds that neighborhood socioeconomic inequality is associated with higher crime. He attributes this effect to the likely influence of inequality on cohesion (network ties) across classes. Reduced cohesion, in turn, is hypothesized to limit collective capacity to achieve shared goals, such as crime reduction (Hipp and Perrin 2009). Neighborhood-level socioeconomic inequality may enhance the salience of class differences and associated tensions, reducing trust overall, but amplifying the effects of distrust on the willingness of residents to share space with other SES groups. In turn, the likelihood of actual network tie formation across class may be diminished. Drawing on this logic, our analyses explore the possibility that SES inequality decreases the likelihood of shared routine locations for groups of different SES but does not affect (or even enhance) the chances of households of the same SES sharing locations for everyday activities.

Finally, the *contact hypothesis* offers the more optimistic expectation that neighborhood socioeconomic diversity may extend to shared routine activity locations (Allport 1954). Initially superficial exposures to neighbors of different backgrounds foster a perception that residents have common goals and can be counted on, thereby enhancing trust. Casual observation of neighbors engaged in familiar, conventional daily routines may increase trust and the progressive incorporation of similar local shopping, worship, and leisure options into daily routines (Emerson, Kimbro, and Yancey 2002; Sampson and Bartusch 1998). Greater socioeconomic diversity at the neighborhood level provides more opportunities for the types of trust-generating cross-SES observations that may amplify willingness to adopt socioeconomically diverse activity locations as part of routines (potentially further enhancing trust). This argument is consistent with research proposing social mixing by SES as a "positive public policy tool" promoting social cohesion across class (Cameron 2003; Lees, Slater, and Wyly 2008). Accordingly, neighborhood socioeconomic diversity is expected to increase trust relevant for the willingness to share routines across SES groups. In this view, greater SES inequality would increase the tendency of neighbors of different SES backgrounds to conduct routine activities in the same locations.

We assess these competing hypotheses by examining data on activity locations of residents of sixty-five Los Angeles census tracts using the Los Angeles Family and Neighborhood Study. We fit multilevel p_2 network models to dyadic tie data (shared activity locations among sampled households) to examine within-neighborhood household dyad, neighborhood, and neighborhood by household dyad (cross-level) interaction hypotheses. At the household dyad level, we explore whether higher SES reduces the likelihood of sharing routines with neighbors of any class (the material constraints and preferences hypothesis), and dissimilarity in the SES of household dyads decreases the likelihood of sharing an activity location (the social distance hypothesis). At the neighborhood level, we consider expectations that neighborhood-SES inequality decreases the overall likelihood of neighbors sharing an activity location (the generalized withdrawal hypothesis) and that this effect is mediated by collective trust. With respect to cross-level interactions, we consider whether neighborhood socioeconomic inequality moderates any observed tendency for routine activity location sorting by SES: decreasing shared activity location for households of different SES (consistent with conflict theory), or enhancing shared routines across SES (the contact hypothesis). Finally, we explore whether neighborhood-level trust amplifies the likelihood of sharing routines across SES and accounts for any observed moderating effects of neighborhood inequality on the likelihood of spatial sorting across and within SES groups.

DATA AND METHODS

We use data from the first wave of the Los Angeles Family and Neighborhood Survey. Collected between 2000 and 2002, the L.A.FANS is a stratified random sample of individuals residing in sixty-five census tracts in Los Angeles County, California (Sastry et al. 2006). Although high-poverty tracts were oversampled, the sample is representative of tracts across the income range of Los Angeles County. Within each tract, households were randomly selected and a randomly selected adult was interviewed within each household (N=2,619). We exclude households who did not indicate having at least one activity outside of their home, and those with no network ties to other households in their tract through activity locations (see dependent variable). Our sample includes remaining households with complete information on all independent variables (N=2,462).

Measures

Dependent variable. The outcome is a dichotomous indicator of whether two households living in the same neighborhood (census tract) go to the same location (block group) to conduct a routine activity. Respondents provided the address or the nearest intersection where household members commonly go for a range of routine activities—grocery shopping, school (if a child resides in the household), employment, attending religious institutions, relatives' homes, child care, health care, a place other than home or work where the responding adult spends the most time, and places other than home where the child spends the night. These locations were geocoded and associated with the census block group where the activity occurs.[1]

We use neighborhood-specific *activity locations* (unique block groups visited by one or more households) to construct our outcome using network methods. For each neighborhood, we constructed the two-mode household-by-activity location network, what we term the *ecological network* (Browning and Soller 2014), where households are tied to the activity locations they visit for one or more regular activities. Then we projected this two-mode household-by-activity ecological network onto the households, which gives several one-mode household-by-household networks. These one-mode networks indicate whether pairs of households (dyads) both have a regular activity in a specific block group. The binary variables indicating whether dyads are tied through each activity location in this collection of one-mode networks are the outcome in our statistical analyses. We predict this outcome based upon characteristics of the households in the dyad (for example, having the same or different SES) and of the census tract where they live (for example, SES inequality).[2]

Independent variables. We construct independent variables for *socioeconomic similarity* of the two households in a dyad based on whether they are in the bottom, middle, or top third of the socioeconomic status distribution of L.A.FANS respondents. Socioeconomic status is a scale combining household income and educational attainment. Household income is measured in dollars.[3] Educational attainment is measured in nineteen categories.[4] The correlation between logged income and education is 0.34. To measure household socioeconomic status, we standardize income and education across the households, average the z-scores to get a combined index, and divide the scale into thirds. The low-SES tertile has a median income of $15,000 and seven years of education. The middle-SES group has a median income of $24,000 and twelve years of education. The high-SES group has a median income of $70,000 and a bachelor's degree. In the multilevel models, we include a set of dummy variables indicating that households in each dyad are in the same specific category of SES (low, middle, or high SES) or different specific categories of household socioeconomic status (for example, one member of the dyad is low SES and the other is middle SES). The reference category is a pair of households that are both low SES.

We control for *race-ethnic similarity* within household dyads based on whether both respondents are white, black, Latino, or Asian-

---

1. We include only activity locations in block groups in California. On average, households reported 5.04 nonhome activities with valid block group locations.

2. Combining each household dyad with each possible tie through a block group location within a tract results in a total of 3,824,943 dyad-location records for analysis.

3. The income data include RAND-imputed values to deal with nonresponse using education, marital status, family composition, immigrant status, health status, and neighborhood poverty as predictors (Bitler and Peterson 2004).

4. Educational attainment is measured by nineteen categories including last year of school completed for those with less than a high school education and highest degree obtained.

Other race-ethnicity (two households with different racial-ethnic identities is the reference category). We also include a series of additional variables describing the respondent similarity of marital status, residential tenure (lived in the neighborhood for at least two years), and parental status. These controls contrast households having the same focal characteristic (for example, both households lived in the neighborhood for at least two years) with dissimilar dyads. The final dyad control variables measure the difference in age and the distance in geographic space between the two households in the dyad. The latter variable controls for the fact that physical proximity of households likely increases shared locations of routine activities. Estimating social distance effects on shared routines requires, at a minimum, a control for physical proximity of households in the dyad (Hipp and Perrin 2009).

We include four measures of structural characteristics of the census tract where the households in the dyad reside (using 2000 Census data) that are commonly used in neighborhood research. *Racial diversity* is the sum of the squared proportions of white, Latino, black, Asian, and other race-ethnic groups in the tract subtracted from one. Higher values indicate greater race-ethnic diversity. *Residential instability* is measured with the standardized percentage of residents age five and older who moved since 1995. *Immigrant concentration* is the mean of the standardized percentage of the tract population that is foreign born and of the tract population that does not speak English well or at all (among those age five and older). Also, in each neighborhood, we count the total number of unique census block groups visited by each household (regardless of how many activities may have taken place in those block groups) and use the median of this number, termed the *number of activity locations*, as a tract-level variable.

To measure neighborhood *socioeconomic inequality*, we separately compute a Gini index of income inequality and a Gini index of educational inequality for each census tract.[5] The income and education Gini coefficients are standardized separately, and then averaged to create a measure of combined socioeconomic inequality at the neighborhood level. Gini values are equal to one when one person has all the income-education in a neighborhood and zero if everyone has the same income-education, thus higher values of the SES inequality are indicative of more unequal income and education distributions in the tract. We include a measure of *neighborhood trust* based on respondents' expressed levels of agreement (on a 5-point scale) with the following statement: "People in this neighborhood can be trusted." The neighborhood-level measure is the mean value of the respondents in the neighborhood where they live.

ANALYTIC STRATEGY

In our analyses, the outcome is an indicator of a tie between pairs of individual households (dyads) based on the one-mode projected ecological network for households who reside in the same neighborhood. The complex nature of the data structure (cross-nesting of individuals and dyads within neighborhoods) requires an appropriate random effects approach to address multiple sources of dependency. To account for the nesting of dyads within neighborhoods, we fit multilevel regression models with neighborhood random effects. In addition, we include random effects at the individual (household) level to account for the fact that individuals are part of multiple dyads and, therefore, outcomes for pairs of dyads including the same

---

5. Income is measured by eleven categories ranging from less than $10,000 to $200,000 or more. The income Gini is constructed using the median income for each category, and the estimated median for the open-ended category at the top of the distribution (Parker and Fenwick 1983). For the tracts with no households in the top two categories, we use the average median value for all tracts in L.A. County. The mean of the unstandardized income Gini is 0.40 (s=0.05). To calculate the Gini coefficient for education, we follow Vinod Thomas, Yan Wang, and Xibo Fan (2001), midpoints used in parentheses: zero years, one to four years (2.5), five to six years (5.5), seven to eight years (7.5), nine years, ten years, eleven years, twelve years and no high school diploma, twelve years and diploma or equivalent, less than one year of college (12.5 years), one or more years of college but no degree (13.5), associate's degree (14), bachelor's degree (16), master's degree (18), professional degree (19), and doctoral degree (20 years). The mean of the unstandardized education Gini coefficient is 0.23 (s=0.09).

individual are dependent. Random effects models of this form, where the individual-level random effects are at a lower level than the (dyad-level) outcome, are nonstandard, but have been developed in the networks literature. Specifically, the network model accounts for dependence across dyadic outcomes using cross-nested random effects (van Duijn, Snijders, and Zijlstra 2004; Zijlstra, van Duijn, and Snijders 2006). We extend the p_2 model to the multilevel setting to account for the nesting of dyads within neighborhoods, as described.

The outcome of interest, Y_{ijk}, is an indicator that dyad i from neighborhood (tract) j is connected through activity location k. We model the log odds of dyad i in tract j being tied through activity location k as

$$\log\left(\frac{\mu_{ijk}}{1-\mu_{ijk}}\right) = \gamma_j + \alpha_{g_1(i,j)} + \alpha_{g_2(i,j)}$$
$$+ \sum_{p=1}^{P} \beta_p^H H_{ijp} + \sum_{q=1}^{Q} \beta_q^Z Z_{ijq}$$
$$+ \sum_{p=1}^{P} (\beta_p^{GH} G_j H_{ijp} + \beta_p^{TH} T_j H_{ijp}),$$

where Y_j is the tract-specific random intercept, $\alpha_{g_1(i,j)}$ and $\alpha_{g_2(i,j)}$ are random effects associated with individual one and individual two who make up dyad i in tract j (for example,, $g_{1(i,j)}$ is a function that maps the ith dyad in the jth tract to the index of the first individual in the dyad; $g_{2(i,j)}$ is defined similarly), H_{ijp} is an indicator of SES category p similarity in dyad i from tract j, β_p^H are corresponding fixed effects, the Z_{ijq}s are dyad-level control variables, and the β_q^Zs are corresponding fixed effects. The remaining terms capture cross-level interactions between the dyad-level SES similarity variables and tract-level measures of inequality (G_j) and trust (T_j).

We assume that

$$\gamma_j = \gamma^0 + \beta^G G_j + \beta^T T_j + \sum_{r=1}^{R} \beta_r^X X_{jr} + \varepsilon_j,$$

where $\varepsilon_j \sim$ iid $N(0,\tau^2)$, γ^0 is the overall mean, β^G and β^T are fixed effects corresponding to neighborhood levels of inequality and trust respectively, the X_{jr}s are tract-level control variables, and the β_r^Xs are the associated fixed effects. In addition, we assume that $\alpha_l = \alpha^0 + \nu_l$ where $\nu_l \sim$ iid $N(0,\sigma^2)$. To fit this model, we use the glmer function in the lme4 package (version .999999-0) in R (version 3.0.1). To accommodate the individual effects, it was necessary to edit the design matrix for the random effects. Neighborhood-level variables are mean-centered for ease of interpretation.

RESULTS

Table 1 presents the descriptive statistics for the households, neighborhoods, and household dyads in the analytic sample. The sample is majority Latino (56 percent) with a median income of $27,000 and a modal education level of high school diploma. Almost 60 percent of household dyads match on racial-ethnic identity; 39 percent are dyads in which both households are Latino. Sixty percent of dyads are two households with children. Approximately half of the neighbor pairs (dyads) have the same socioeconomic status, 15 percent low, 13 percent middle, and 21 percent high. The remaining dyads have different socioeconomic status with many more low-middle SES and middle-high SES than highly divergent low-high SES pairs of neighbors.

Household Dyad Effects

Table 2 reports results from multilevel p_2 models of whether two households living in the same neighborhood go to the same activity location. Model 1 includes only dyad-level SES and control variables. The tables present coefficients as log odds; in the discussion that follows we refer to the odds ratios for interpretation. The results show that two neighbors of low socioeconomic status are the most likely to routinely go to the same places. The odds of a routine activity tie for dyads with two middle-SES or two high-SES households are 13 percent ($p < 0.05$) and 15 percent ($p < 0.10$) lower, respectively, than for two low-SES neighbors. Pairs of households with different SES also have lower likelihoods of going to the same location than low-SES dyads; the odds of going to the same activity location for dyads with low- and middle-SES households are 14 percent lower ($p < 0.001$) than for low-SES dyads. Comparable figures for low-high and mid-high SES combinations are 21 percent ($p < 0.05$) and 16 percent lower ($p < 0.001$), respectively, than for

Table 1. Household and Neighborhood Descriptive Statistics

	Mean	SD
Household characteristics[a] (N=2,462)		
Less than high school diploma	0.35	
High school diploma	0.45	
College degree or more	0.19	
Median household income	$27,000	
Latino	0.56	
White	0.26	
Black	0.10	
Asian or other	0.08	
Married	0.50	
Residential tenure (two-plus years)	0.70	
Parents	0.76	
Age	−0.08	14.39
Neighborhood characteristics[b] (N=65)		
Immigrant concentration	0.00	1.10
Residential instability	0.00	0.88
Racial diversity	0.00	0.19
Activity locations[a]	3.91	0.54
Socioeconomic inequality	0.00	0.85
Neighborhood trust[a]	3.41	.44
Dyad characteristics[a] (N=3,824,943)		
Low-SES similarity	0.15	
Middle-SES similarity	0.13	
High-SES similarity	0.21	
Low-middle SES dissimilarity	0.24	
Low-high SES dissimilarity	0.09	
Middle-high SES dissimilarity	0.19	
Latino similarity	0.39	
White similarity	0.14	
Black similarity	0.03	
Asian or other similarity	0.02	
Married similarity	0.28	
Not married similarity	0.26	
Residential tenure (two-plus years) similarity	0.50	
Residential tenure (less than two years) similarity	0.10	
Parents similarity	0.59	
Not parents similarity	0.05	
Age difference	15.07	12.73
Distance	0.01	0.03

Source: Authors' calculations based on Los Angeles Neighborhood and Family Survey (Sastry et al. 2006) and U.S. Census data.
[a]Los Angeles Neighborhood and Family Survey.
[b]Neighborhood characteristics from the U.S. Census Bureau, except where noted.

Table 2. Coefficients from Multilevel p_2 Models of Eco-Network Tie Formation, Dyad and Neighborhood Level Predictors

	Model 1	Model 2	Model 3
Dyad-level predictors[a]			
Low-SES similarity (reference)			
Middle-SES similarity	-0.140**	-0.144**	-0.145**
	(0.07)	(0.08)	(0.07)
High-SES similarity	-0.158*	-0.168**	-0.188**
	(0.08)	(0.09)	(0.09)
Low-middle SES dissimilarity	-0.149***	-0.151***	-0.151***
	(0.04)	(0.04)	(0.04)
Low-high SES dissimilarity	-0.242***	-0.248***	-0.257***
	(0.05)	(0.05)	(0.05)
Middle-high SES dissimilarity	-0.171**	-0.178**	-0.188***
	(0.07)	(0.07)	(0.07)
Latino similarity	0.196***	0.192***	0.194***
	(0.04)	(0.04)	(0.04)
White similarity	0.140***	0.139***	0.133***
	(0.04)	(0.04)	(0.04)
Black similarity	-0.052	-0.046	-0.044
	(0.07)	(0.07)	(0.07)
Asian or other similarity	-0.029	-0.027	-0.027
	(0.07)	(0.07)	(0.07)
Married similarity	-0.082***	-0.085***	-0.086***
	(0.03)	(0.03)	(0.03)
Not married similarity	0.085***	0.089***	0.090***
	(0.03)	(0.03)	(0.02)
Tenure similarity (two-plus years)	0.155***	0.152***	0.150***
	(0.03)	(0.03)	(0.03)
Tenure similarity (less than two years)	-0.081**	-0.078**	0.076**
	(0.04)	(0.04)	(0.04)
Parents similarity	0.370***	0.372***	0.373***
	(0.03)	(0.03)	(0.03)
Not parents similarity	-0.280***	-0.283***	-0.283***
	(0.05)	(0.05)	(0.05)
Age difference	-0.001	-0.001	-0.001
	(0.00)	(0.00)	(0.00)
Distance	-2.076***	-2.067***	-2.060***
	(0.39)	(0.39)	(0.39)
Neighborhood predictors[b]			
Immigrant concentration		0.050	0.087
		(0.09)	(0.09)
Residential instability		-0.035	-0.048
		(0.10)	(0.10)
Racial diversity		-0.713*	-0.503
		(0.42)	(0.42)
Activity locations[a]		-0.350***	-0.394***
		(0.12)	(0.11)
Socioeconomic inequality		-0.224	-0.101
		(0.14)	(0.15)
Neighborhood trust[a]			0.374*
			(0.20)
Intercept	-5.562***	-5.554***	-5.547***
	(0.09)	(0.08)	(0.08)
Variance components			
Intercept	0.343	0.343	0.343
Tract	0.240	0.181	0.170

Source: Authors' calculations based on Los Angeles Neighborhood and Family Survey (Sastry et al. 2006) and U.S. Census data.
[a]Los Angeles Neighborhood and Family Survey.
[b]Neighborhood characteristics from the U.S. Census Bureau, except where noted.
*$p < .10$; **$p < .05$; ***$p < .01$

low-SES dyads. Consistent with the expectation that higher income offers more flexibility in activity locations, dyads involving higher-SES households (whether similar or dissimilar) are somewhat less likely to encounter other households from the same neighborhood of any SES than low-SES households are to encounter one another. Consistent with a social distance expectation, household pairs that are the most different in their SES (low—high) have the lowest likelihood of encountering one another. These results offer strong support for the hypothesis of spatial sorting in routine activities by SES, in contrast to the random mixing model.

Turning to dyad-level control variables, the odds of going to the same activity location for a dyad with two Latinos or two whites are 22 percent and 15 percent higher than for the average dyad where the households are of different race-ethnicities. Similarity on residential tenure and parental status also contribute to the likelihood of going to the same place; the odds of a location tie between two households with children are 45 percent higher than for a pair with a parent and a nonparent neighbor. The odds of going to the same location for a dyad with two nonparent households are 24 percent lower than neighbor pairs consisting of a parent and a nonparent.

An obvious potential explanation for the sorting patterns in model 1 is within-tract spatial segregation. In other words, the pattern may be due to the fact that the two households within each dyad live closer or farther from one another (Hipp and Perrin 2009). Accordingly, model 1 also includes the distance between the households in the dyad. The farther that households live from each other within their neighborhood, the less likely they are to go to the same routine activity location. However, analyses not presented indicate that inclusion of this measure does not alter the associations of other dyad characteristics with sharing activity locations.

Neighborhood Average Effects

Model 2 adds neighborhood socioeconomic inequality as well as tract indicators of immigrant concentration, residential instability, racial diversity, and the median number of activity locations per household. Two of the neighborhood characteristics are important. Greater racial diversity is associated with lower chances of going to the same place for routine activities ($p < 0.10$) (for additional discussion of race-ethnicity effects, see the sensitivity analyses section). The median number of activities is also negatively associated with location ties ($p < 0.001$), which indicates that the larger the number of distinct places households go to (on average), the lower the likelihood that household pairs share routines.[6] Neighborhood socioeconomic inequality is also negatively, but not significantly, associated with sharing routine activity locations. Although the average negative effect of racial diversity on the likelihood of a shared activity is consistent with Putnam's generalized withdrawal hypothesis, this association does not extend to socioeconomic inequality within neighborhoods. The effects of dyad characteristics, including SES similarity-difference, do not change substantially with the addition of tract-level factors.

Model 3 includes the average effect of neighborhood trust on the likelihood of a location tie and shows that trust increases the generalized tendency to share routines. A 1 standard deviation increase in neighborhood trust (0.44) is associated with a 17 percent increase in the odds of sharing a routine activity ($p < 0.10$). Of note, the coefficient for racial diversity is reduced by almost 30 percent (to nonsignificance) by including neighborhood trust. Although the coefficients for racial di-

---

6. Inclusion of the average household number of unique locations as a control is a somewhat conservative approach to assessing inequality effects because the increased number of locations traveled to is a possible mechanism linking inequality with the extent of shared locations. Although the magnitude of the main inequality effect is reduced somewhat with the inclusion of median number of activities, the effect is not significant with or without median number of activities included in the model. Moreover, the cross-level interactions between inequality and the dyad-SES similarity covariates are only nominally affected by inclusion of median number of activities.

versity (in model 2) and trust (in model 3) are marginally significant, the models offer suggestive evidence for the generalized withdrawal hypothesis with respect to racial diversity.

Neighborhood by Household Dyad Cross-Level Interactions

To assess whether the effects of SES household dyad similarity-dissimilarity differ by characteristics of neighborhoods, we test cross-level interactions between neighborhood socioeconomic inequality and household dyad SES similarity-dissimilarity. We then consider cross-level interactions between neighborhood trust and household dyad SES covariates. Table 3 presents the results of these models.

In model 1, the main effect of socioeconomic inequality, for two low-SES households, is not significant. For dyads with two middle- or high-SES households, the interactions with inequality are negative and significant ($p < 0.05$ and $p < 0.01$, respectively); as inequality increases, the likelihood of two neighbors of similar middle or higher SES going to the same location decreases. Both the average effects and the interaction terms are significant for dyads with one low- or middle-SES household and one high-SES household (at least $p < 0.05$). The likelihood of a location tie is lower for these dyads than for those with two low-SES households when inequality is average; as inequality increases, the odds of going to the same routine activity location decrease significantly. Only the pairs with one low- and one middle-SES household exhibit no such pattern by neighborhood socioeconomic inequality. The results show that increasing inequality reduces the likelihood of routinely going to the same place for all SES neighbor pairs except those with two low-SES or a low- and middle-SES household.

Figures 1 and 2 display these results clearly by presenting the predicted probability of two households in a randomly selected dyad visiting at least one of the same activity locations across levels of neighborhood inequality.[7] Figure 1 shows the chances of contact for similar SES dyads and figure 2 presents them for dissimilar SES dyads. For dyads with two low-SES households (figure 1), the predicted probability of sharing activity spaces is about 0.35, and does not vary significantly by neighborhood socioeconomic inequality. Among dyads with two similar middle- or high-SES households (figure 1), the probability of a shared routine location is about 0.40 when living in a neighborhood with very low socioeconomic inequality (1.5 standard deviations below the mean). The probability of going to the same place is significantly lower—about .29 for middle-SES dyads and .23 for high-SES dyads—if they reside in a neighborhood with very high inequality (1.5 standard deviations above the mean). Similar patterns are observed for dyads with one high-SES household (figure 2); the probability of a shared location at low levels of inequality is 0.33 for low-high SES pairs and declines to 0.26 in high inequality neighborhoods. For middle-high SES pairs, the probability of a shared location in low inequality neighborhoods is 0.39 and declines to 0.25 in high inequality neighborhoods.

The predicted probabilities reveal an overall pattern of more limited sharing of routine activity spaces as neighborhood socioeconomic inequality increases, for dyads involving higher-SES households (whether similar or dissimilar). At high inequality, higher-SES residents have a comparatively low likelihood of

---

7. The model estimates the probability of dyad i in neighborhood j having visited the *same specific activity location* k, $\hat{\mu}_{ijk}$, which we use to compute the probability of each dyad having visited *at least one of the same activity locations*. We use the empirical median of the number of unique activity locations across the tracts, N^A, in estimating this probability. We calculate predicted probabilities for each dyad-level covariate pattern (for example, similarity on race, marital status, and so on) and average these probabilities using weights that correspond to the frequency of each covariate pattern in the sample. Because our model includes no activity-specific terms, $\hat{\mu}_{ij1}$ does not depend on k.

$$P\left(\sum_{k=1}^{N^A} Y_{ijk} \geq 1\right) = 1 - P\left(\sum_{k=1}^{N^A} Y_{ijk} = 0\right) = 1 - \left[P(Y_{ij1} = 0)\right]^{N^A} = 1 - \left[1 - P(Y_{ij1} = 1)\right]^{N^A} = 1 - \left[1 - \hat{\mu}_{ij1}\right]^{N^A}$$

Table 3. Coefficients from Multilevel p_2 Models of Eco-Network Tie Formation, Dyad and Neighborhood Level Predictors with Cross-Level Interactions

	Model 1	Model 2
Dyad level predictors		
Low-SES similarity (reference)		
Middle-SES similarity	−0.070	0.000
	(0.08)	(0.08)
High-SES similarity	−0.182*	−0.112
	(0.10)	(0.10)
Low-middle SES dissimilarity	−0.128***	−0.081
	(0.05)	(0.05)
Low-high SES dissimilarity	−0.251***	−0.203***
	(0.06)	(0.06)
Middle-high SES dissimilarity	−0.158**	−0.096
	(0.08)	(0.08)
Latino similarity	0.193***	0.190***
	(0.04)	(0.04)
White similarity	0.132***	0.134***
	(0.04)	(0.04)
Black similarity	−0.041	−0.039
	(0.07)	(0.07)
Asian or other similarity	−0.031	−0.032
	(0.07)	(0.07)
Married similarity	−0.089***	−0.086***
	(0.03)	(0.03)
Not married similarity	0.092***	0.089***
	(0.03)	(0.03)
Tenure similarity (two-plus years)	0.149***	0.147***
	(0.06)	(0.03)
Tenure similarity (less than two yrs)	−0.074**	−0.072*
	(0.04)	(0.04)
Parents similarity	0.369***	0.369***
	(0.03)	(0.03)
Not parents similarity	−0.279***	−0.279***
	(0.05)	(0.05)
Age difference	−0.001	−0.001
	(0.00)	(0.00)
Distance	−2.061***	−2.059***
	(0.39)	(0.39)
Neighborhood predictors[b]		
Immigrant concentration	0.084	0.087
	(0.09)	(0.09)
Residential instability	−0.024	−0.027
	(0.10)	(0.10)
Racial diversity	−0.541	−0.560
	(0.41)	(0.42)
Activity locations[a]	−0.385***	−0.386***
	(0.11)	(0.11)
Socioeconomic inequality	0.049	−0.019
	(0.16)	(0.17)

Table 3. (cont.)

	Model 1	Model 2
Neighborhood trust[a]	0.363*	0.058
	(0.20)	(0.26)
Middle SES * inequality	−0.205**	−0.068
	(0.09)	(0.11)
High SES * inequality	−0.316***	−0.268**
	(0.11)	(0.14)
Low-middle SES * inequality	−0.059	0.019
	(0.06)	(0.06)
Low-high SES * inequality	−0.165**	−0.104
	(0.07)	(0.08)
Middle-high SES * inequality	−0.275***	−0.181
	(0.09)	(0.11)
Middle SES * trust[a]		0.534**
		(0.24)
High SES * trust		0.230
		(0.27)
Low-middle SES * trust		0.329**
		(0.14)
Low-high SES * trust		0.294*
		(0.18)
Middle-high SES * trust		0.396*
		(0.23)
Intercept	−5.624***	−0.567***
	(0.09)	(0.09)
Variance components		
Individual	0.342	0.341
Tract	0.159	0.162

Source: Authors' calculations based on Los Angeles Neighborhood and Family Survey (Sastry et al. 2006) and U.S. Census data.
[a]Los Angeles Neighborhood and Family Survey.
[b]Neighborhood characteristics from the U.S. Census Bureau, except where noted.
*$p < .10$; **$p < .05$; ***$p < .01$

encountering a low, middle, or another high-income household; this is also true for two middle-income households. This suggests a tendency toward withdrawal among higher-income groups that is amplified at higher levels of socioeconomic inequality.

Model 2 of table 3 includes cross-level interactions of neighborhood trust and dyad SES, to test whether the effect of socioeconomic inequality on sorting for dyads with higher-SES households is mediated by neighborhood trust. The findings show that the effect of trust for two households of low SES (main effect) is not significant. However, the interactions for dyads with two middle-SES households and for dyads of any dissimilar combination of SES are positive and significant. Therefore, as trust increases, the likelihood of middle-SES and SES-dissimilar dyads sharing routine locations increases. The average effects of the SES dyad combinations (when inequality and trust are at their means) by comparison to low-SES dyads are no longer significant with the exception of low-high SES dyads. The social distance

Figure 1. Predicted Probability, SES Gini Index, Similarity

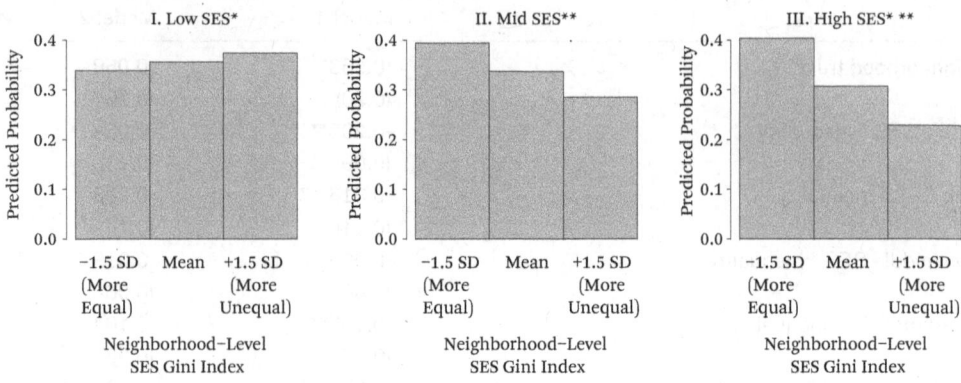

Source: Authors' calculations based on Los Angeles Neighborhood and Family Survey (Sastry et al. 2006) and U.S. Census data.
*based on a main effect that is significant.
**based on an interaction effect that is significant.

Figure 2. Predicted Probability, SES Gini Index, Dissimilarity

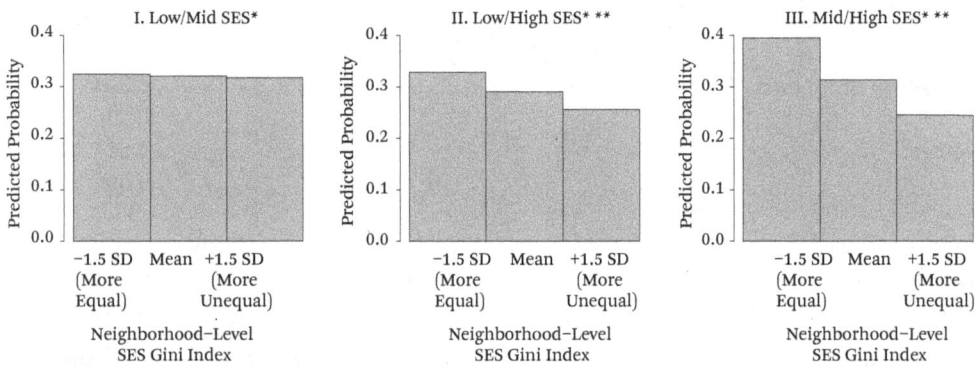

Source: Authors' calculations based on Los Angeles Neighborhood and Family Survey (Sastry et al. 2006) and U.S. Census data.
*based on a main effect that is significant.
**based on an interaction effect that is significant.

sorting effect for low-high SES dyads, in neighborhoods with average levels of trust, is nontrivial; these dyads are about 18 percent less likely to share routines than low-SES dyads. This lesser tendency to go to the same locations is significantly reduced at higher levels of neighborhood trust.

Figures 3 and 4 present the probability of the two households in a randomly selected dyad visiting at least one of the same activity locations for similar (figure 3) and dissimilar (figure 4) SES dyads across levels of neighborhood trust. The positive relationship between neighborhood trust and location sharing is particularly evident for dyads with two middle-SES households (figure 3), though it is seen for all pairs except those with two low-SES households. In neighborhoods with low perceived trust of neighbors, the probability of sharing a location is about 0.25 for all dyads other than the low-SES pairs. In high-trust neighborhoods, these probabilities of activity location contact are notably higher, between 0.35 and 0.40 for most combinations and a high of 0.46 for two middle-SES dyads. As a result, there are no statistically significant differences in the

Figure 3. Predicted Probability, Neighborhood-Level Trust, Similarity

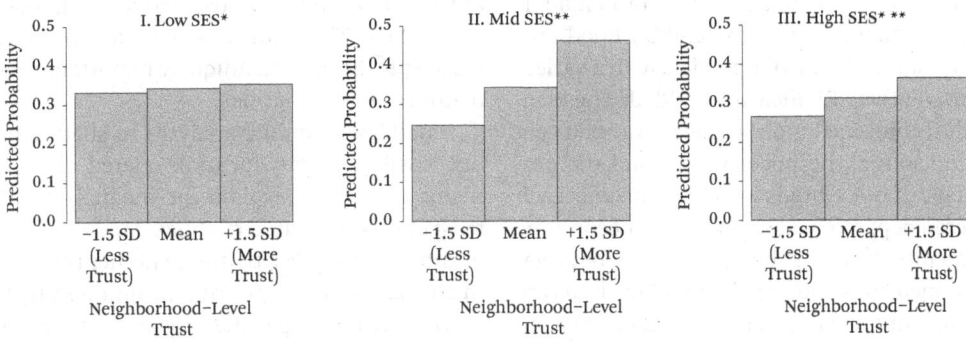

Source: Authors' calculations based on Los Angeles Neighborhood and Family Survey (Sastry et al. 2006) and U.S. Census data.
*based on a main effect that is significant.
**based on an interaction effect that is significant.

Figure 4. Predicted Probability, Neighborhood-Level Trust, Dissimilarity

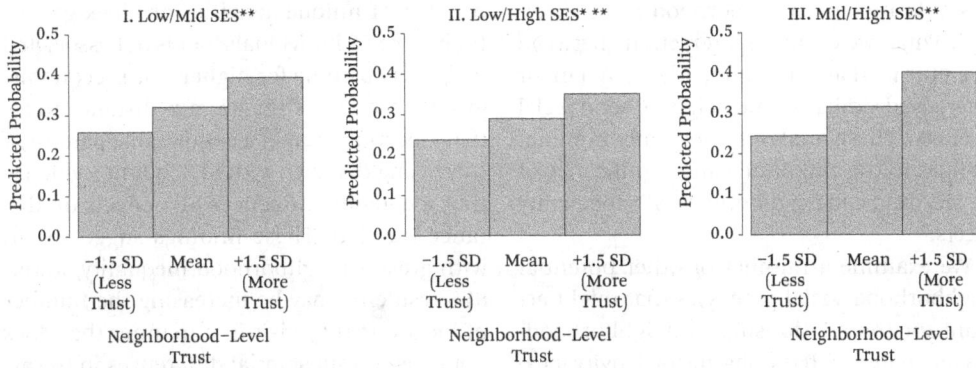

Source: Authors' calculations based on Los Angeles Neighborhood and Family Survey (Sastry et al. 2006) and U.S. Census data.
*based on a main effect that is significant.
**based on an interaction effect that is significant.

probability of shared routines by SES dyad characteristics in neighborhoods with high levels of trust, with the exception of middle-SES similar dyads, which have significantly higher chances of contact in activity locations. These results indicate that increases in neighborhood trust reduce the tendency toward sorting by SES. Moreover, introduction of trust in cross-level interactions with household dyad combinations accounts for a nontrivial portion of the inequality effects on SES sorting. Trust diminishes the magnitude of all of the inequality interactions, and to nonsignificance in three out of four cases.

In summary, the models offer evidence that SES inequality reduces the likelihood of shared routines but only for middle- and high-income similar dyads and dissimilar dyads involving a high-income household. The pattern exhibited is consistent with the notion of a SES group-specific withdrawal effect: inequality leads higher-income residents to withdraw from shared neighborhood spaces overall, including from each other. This effect is explained, in part, by diminished neighborhood trust for these dyad combinations, with the exception of high-SES similar dyads.

Sensitivity Analyses

To determine whether the effect of neighborhood inequality is due to neighborhood economic status, we also fit models with a variety of alternative SES measures added. These include a combined index of neighborhood economic status, the poverty rate, and the percentage of households with high income, each entered separately along with socioeconomic inequality. None of the interactions between these measures and the different SES dyads are significant showing that the effect of SES inequality is not due to its correlation with absolute SES.

We also consider the possibility that the average effects of dyad SES similarity-dissimilarity and the differential effects of neighborhood SES across various household-SES dyads are confounded by race-ethnic similarity-dissimilarity (and neighborhood racial diversity). Thus, we examine interactions between race-ethnic (Latino, white, black, Asian or other) dyad similarity and neighborhood racial diversity. These analyses show only nominal changes to the magnitude and significance of the SES dyad and neighborhood-SES inequality effects.[8]

We examine a number of other potential neighborhood social processes that might account for the relationship of neighborhood-SES inequality with the sharing of activity locations. These include social interaction and reciprocated exchange (frequency of favor exchange, advice giving across neighbors) and organizational density (examining whether the absence of institutions and services within people's neighborhoods might explain the tendency of higher-SES residents to go elsewhere). Neither social interaction and reciprocated exchange nor organizational density is significantly related to the tendency to share routines or to sorting by SES in this outcome. We also examine a combined measure of social cohesion (capturing the sense that neighbors are close-knit, helpful, get along, and share the same values, in addition to being trustworthy). Interactions of social cohesion with some of the SES dyad are significant, but these effects are weaker than those observed for neighborhood trust. This indicates that the sense of trust, specifically, is a uniquely important predictor of shared routines.

Finally, we conduct analyses to shed light on possible activity-location-related mechanisms that might explain the inequality and trust effects on shared routines. Models of the number of unique activities (whether they are in the same block group) and unique block groups visited (regardless of the number of activities) yield the same general conclusions. Consistent with expectations derived from the material constraints and preferences model, increasing SES is associated with more unique activities or block groups. However, cross-level interactions indicate that greater neighborhood-SES inequality increases the number of unique activities or block groups for lower-SES individuals, but is not associated with this outcome for higher status economic groups. Models of the average distance to activity locations reveal a comparable pattern of increasing distance with SES, but no evidence that inequality influences SES effects on distance traveled. These findings suggest that, with greater neighborhood inequality, lower-SES residents may be increasing the number of locations they visit in a manner that does not generate substantial differences in the average distance traveled but nevertheless produces fewer shared locations with higher-SES households. This somewhat counterintuitive result may be due to lower-SES groups adopting new nonhome activities (for example, child care or leisure activities away from home or its immediate vicinity) in response to amplified distrust of the local environment. Higher-SES groups do not appear to change the number of activities or the distance traveled with greater inequality, but may be choosing a more idiosyncratic set of destinations, perhaps due to the role of diminished trust on the willingness to share locations with neighbors of any class. These findings point to the need for more fine-grained analysis to determine the nature of

---

8. The impact of race-ethnicity on spatial sorting in routine activities within neighborhood and the effects of neighborhood diversity are significant substantive issues of their own. However, a full treatment of the role of race-ethnicity alone or in combination with socioeconomic influences is beyond the scope of this paper.

routine activity patterns by SES associated with greater inequality.

CONCLUSION

The voluminous literature on segregation has focused primarily on residential segregation within units of analysis such as census tracts, cities, and metropolitan regions. We extend this work to investigate patterns of integration and segregation by socioeconomic status in the activity locations neighborhood residents frequent in the course of their daily routines. We first consider the extent to which, conditional on residence in the same census tract, neighbors of the same or different SES frequent the same routine activity locations. We hypothesize that variation in material constraints and preferences by SES result in a lower likelihood of sharing routines for SES dyads involving higher-income households. Higher-SES residents have more extensive options for where they go (given greater affordability and accessibility). In turn, they may be less likely to share routine activity locations with neighbors of any SES. We also expect that social distance between residents of different economic statuses would lower the likelihood of sharing activity locations. Both hypotheses were supported in multilevel p_2 models. Unsurprisingly, neighbor dyads with one low- and one high-SES household are the least likely of all SES pairs to go to the same activity locations. The likelihood of sharing routine activity locations are also by far the greatest for two low-income neighbors.

These findings offer robust evidence of spatial sorting in routine activity locations by SES among residents of the same neighborhood, even after accounting for within-neighborhood residential segregation (as captured by variation in distance between home addresses). Approaches to segregation that go no further than residential location neglect systematic patterns of spatial sorting that limit the likelihood of cross-SES exposure. The results are consistent with the claims of social-mixing critics, who argue that spatial propinquity based on residence is not a sufficient condition to ensure exposures across economic lines in the course of daily routines (Lees 2008). They also complement Hipp and Perrin's (2009) finding that social distance in neighborhood ties exist, even after controlling for how close the residents live to one another.

Second, we investigate whether neighborhood conditions independently influence the likelihood of shared routines. We focus particularly on the role of neighborhood-SES inequality in generating overall differences in the likelihood of shared routines. Although the direction of the average SES-inequality effect is consistent with Putnam's (2007) hypothesis that diversity results in a generalized tendency toward withdrawal, only racial diversity achieves significance in the model. Further, considering the role of neighborhood trust in these relationships, we find reduced trust is an important reason why racial diversity diminishes the sharing of activity locations. Although beyond the scope of the current analysis, these results call for more attention to the role of race-ethnicity as a source of spatial sorting in daily routines.

Third, we examine whether the lesser tendency of dyads that include high-status households to share routine locations than other SES dyads varies depending on the extent of SES inequality in the neighborhood. Here we found consistent evidence that increases in neighborhood-SES inequality are associated with more pronounced spatial sorting in routine activity locations for higher-SES dyads. Under conditions of lower-SES inequality (versus higher-SES inequality), sorting in where neighbor households go is much more limited for middle- and higher-SES households. Thus, the assumption that residential integration is at least partly replicated in activity spaces appears to hold for residents of neighborhoods with low levels of inequality. In contrast, as SES inequality increases, middle- and higher-income residents are progressively less likely to encounter any neighborhood residents when they are away from home.

These findings have potentially important implications for understanding the conditions under which social mixing across SES—as manifest in spatial intersection—occur. More pronounced differences in the SES levels of neighborhood residents appear to interfere with the potential for cross-class mixing. Consistent with this finding, evidence suggests that cross-SES interactions are more likely when income heterogeneity is only moderate (Brophy and Smith 1997; Rosenbaum, Stroh, and Flynn 1998). Research on the impact of neighborhood income mix also shows that lower-income residents experience greater income growth if they live in neighborhoods that have larger percentages of middle-income but not high-income neighbors (Casciano and Massey 2008; Galster et al. 2008), reinforcing the importance of lower inequality for interclass relations. Of interest was the lack of evidence supporting an out-group avoidance explanation for the patterns of observed sorting by SES. We found no evidence that increases in SES inequality led to the diminished tendency to share activities with those of other classes versus those of the same class. The reduced likelihood appears to affect most dyad combinations involving higher-income households—whether similar or dissimilar.

These findings also provide some support for Putnam's expectation of an overall pattern of withdrawal as diversity in SES increases but with a class-specific manifestation of this tendency. Lower-SES residents were not significantly less likely to share routines with one another as inequality increased. Lower-SES residents are likely to have more limited flexibility in activity location choice—perhaps choosing (or adding) routine activities that limit contact with other SES groups, but not their own.

Also partially consistent with Putnam's expectations, we find relatively consistent evidence of neighborhood trust effects on the impact of dyad SES on sharing routing locations. As neighborhood trust increased, routine activity sharing among higher- and dissimilar-SES neighbors also generally increased. Indeed, at high levels of trust we found no significant evidence of spatial sorting by SES. Moreover, a nontrivial proportion of the SES inequality effect on the dyad-level SES sorting tendency was explained by trust. Trust appears to play an important role in the willingness of residents of different SES backgrounds to share daily routines. The findings also point to trust as a key pathway through which neighborhood socioeconomic inequality results in more limited sharing of routines. In combination, these results address the conditions under which, for instance, mixed-income housing and gentrifying neighborhoods will yield shared public space. To the extent that such public space sharing reinforces and enhances neighborhood social climates (Browning et al., forthcoming), these findings may shed light on extant research linking inequality with other negative outcomes such as crime (Hipp 2007) and poor health (Wilkinson and Pickett 2009).

Seen in the context of the increasing hollowing out of the middle class in the U.S. context (Bischoff and Reardon 2014; Galster, Cutsinger, and Booza 2006), these findings suggest that housing strategies seeking to place low-income residents in stable neighborhoods characterized by lower-middle residents and middle-income (as opposed to affluent) residents may be increasingly difficult to realize. To the extent that increasing SES inequality more generally is associated with reduced prevalence of middle-income communities, targeting such neighborhoods for placement of low-income housing may prove challenging. In addition, currently middle-income neighborhoods may be on a downward trajectory, diminishing the long-term benefits of mixed-income housing developments in these locations.

We emphasize the importance of seeking to develop strategies that buffer high-SES inequality neighborhoods (including gentrifying neighborhoods) from the pervasive mistrust that results in withdrawal from shared space. Socioeconomically disadvantaged residents of mixed-income housing developments should have the opportunity to benefit from exposure to neighborhoods composed of residents of all classes, not just middle-income residents with whom the development of trust is less complicated. Homogeneously high-SES urban areas also reduce exposure of affluent residents to the socioeconomic spectrum of urban areas, exacerbating class insularity. Further research on the conditions under which residentially proximate low- and high-income residents do not suffer trust deficits will promote the development of mixed-income housing strategies that counter increasingly prominent class-based spatial divisions.

Our analyses are characterized by a number

of limitations. First, our data are limited to the Los Angeles context. Thus, it is unclear whether these patterns extend to cities with different social, demographic, and economic structures. Second, information on the routine activity locations of L.A.FANS respondents is limited to a subset of common destinations. Currently, the L.A.FANS is the only available neighborhood-focused social survey data to also collect activity space information of any kind, though emerging projects are attempting to address limitations in the availability of rich information on routine activity locations (Browning and Soller 2014). Third, our sample of neighborhoods is somewhat small for investigating variability in neighborhood-level SES inequality. Nevertheless, the results of these analyses warrant future efforts to explore the effects of distinct types of SES distribution on household-level SES sorting tendencies. Finally, our data are cross-sectional, limiting our ability to infer causal effects. For instance, although trust is likely to foster shared routines, the reciprocal relationship is also likely—shared routines may lead to enhanced trust. Longitudinal data will provide an opportunity to more rigorously explore the mediating effects of trust in the link between inequality and shared routines.

The analyses reported here are among only a few studies to investigate activity space segregation and, to our knowledge, the only existing study to consider multilevel influences on routine activity sorting by SES. Although infrequently considered in the extant literature, patterns of shared exposure through activity routines is likely to be an increasingly common focus of investigation as richer data on urban activity spaces become more readily available. These data hold substantial promise to yield important insights into the nature of everyday patterns of social integration and isolation.

REFERENCES

Allport, Gordon W. 1954. *The Nature of Human Prejudice*. Boston, Mass.: Addison-Wesley.

Arthurson, Kathy. 2010. "Operationalising Social Mix: Spatial Scale, Lifestyle and Stigma as Mediating Points in Resident Interaction." *Urban Policy and Research* 28(1): 49–63.

Bischoff, Kendra, and Sean F. Reardon. 2014. "Residential Segregation by Income, 1970–2009." In *Diversity and Disparities: America Enters a New Century*, edited by John Logan. New York: Russell Sage Foundation.

Bitler, Marianne, and Christine Peterson. 2004. "LAFANS Income and Asset Imputations: Description of Imputed Income/Assets Data for LAFANS Wave 1." Santa Monica, Calif.: RAND Corporation.

Blalock, Hubert M., Jr. 1967. *Toward a Theory of Minority-Group Relations*. New York: John Wiley & Sons.

Bobo, Lawrence D. 1999. "Prejudice as Group Position: Microfoundations of a Sociological Approach to Racism and Race Relations." *Journal of Social Issues* 55(3): 445–72.

Brophy, Paul C., and Rhonda N. Smith. 1997. "Mixed-Income Housing: Factors for Success." *Cityscape* 3(2): 3–31.

Browning, Christopher R., Catherine A. Calder, Brian Soller, Aubrey L. Jackson, and Jonathan Dirlam. Forthcoming. "Ecological Networks and Neighborhood Social Organization." *American Journal of Sociology*.

Browning, Christopher R., and Brian Soller. 2014. "Moving Beyond Neighborhood: Activity Spaces and Ecological Networks as Contexts for Youth Development." *Cityscape* 16(1): 165–96.

Cameron, Stuart. 2003. "Gentrification, Housing Redifferentiation and Urban Regeneration: 'Going for Growth' in Newcastle upon Tyne." *Urban Studies* 40(12): 2367–82.

Casciano, Rebecca, and Douglas S. Massey. 2008. "Neighborhoods, Employment, and Welfare Use: Assessing the Influence of Neighborhood Socioeconomic Composition." *Social Science Research* 37(2): 544–58.

Chaskin, Robert J., and Mark L. Joseph. 2013. "'Positive' Gentrification, Social Control and the 'Right to the City' in Mixed-Income Communities: Uses and Expectations of Space and Place." *International Journal of Urban and Regional Research* 37(2): 480–502.

Chaskin, Robert J., Florian Sichling, and Mark L. Joseph. 2013. "Youth in Mixed-Income Communities Replacing Public Housing Complexes: Context, Dynamics and Response." *Cities* 35 (December): 423–31.

Domina, Thurston. 2006. "Brain Drain and Brain Gain: Rising Educational Segregation in the

United States, 1940–2000." *City & Community* 5(4): 387–407.

Emerson, Michael O., Rachel Tolbert Kimbro, and George Yancey. 2002. "Contact Theory Extended: The Effects of Prior Racial Contact on Current Social Ties." *Social Science Quarterly* 83(3): 745–61.

Fischer, Mary J. 2003. "The Relative Importance of Income and Race in Determining Residential Outcomes in U.S. Urban Areas, 1970–2000." *Urban Affairs Review* 38(5): 669–96.

Galster, George. 2007. "Neighbourhood Social Mix as a Goal of Housing Policy: A Theoretical Analysis." *International Journal of Housing Policy* 7(1): 19–43.

Galster, George, Roger Andersson, Sako Musterd, and Timo M. Kauppinen. 2008. "Does Neighborhood Income Mix Affect Earnings of Adults? New Evidence from Sweden." *Journal of Urban Economics* 63(3): 858–70.

Galster, George, Jackie Cutsinger, and Jason C. Booza. 2006. "Where Did They Go? The Decline of Middle-Income Neighborhoods in Metropolitan America." Metropolitan Policy Program. Washington, D.C.: Brookings Institution Press.

Hipp, John R. 2007. "Income Inequality, Race, and Place: Does the Distribution of Race and Class Within Neighborhoods Affect Crime Rates?" *Criminology* 45(3): 665–97.

Hipp, John R., and Andrew J. Perrin. 2009. "The Simultaneous Effect of Social Distance and Physical Distance on the Formation of Neighborhood Ties." *City & Community* 8(1): 5–25.

Jargowsky, Paul A. 2013. "Concentration of Poverty in the New Millennium: Changes in Prevalence, Composition, and Location of High-Poverty Neighborhoods." New York and Camden, N.J.: Century Foundation and the Center for Urban Research and Education.

Jargowsky, Paul A., and Todd Swanstrom. 2009. *Economic Integration: Why It Matters and How Cities Can Get More of It*. City Vitals Series. Chicago: CEOs for Cities.

Jones, Malia, and Anne R. Pebley. 2014. "Redefining Neighborhoods Using Common Destinations: Social Characteristics of Activity Spaces and Home Census Tracts Compared." *Demography* 51(3): 727–52.

Kleit, Rachel Garshick. 2005. "HOPE VI New Communities: Neighborhood Relationships in Mixed-Income Housing." *Environment and Planning A* 37(8): 1413–41.

Kleit, Rachel Garshick, and Nicole Bohme Carnegie. 2011. "Integrated or Isolated? The Impact of Public Housing Redevelopment on Social Network Homophily." *Social Networks* 33(2): 152–65.

Krivo, Lauren J., Heather M. Washington, Ruth D. Peterson, Christopher R. Browning, Catherine A. Calder, and Mei-Po Kwan. 2013. "Social Isolation of Disadvantage and Advantage: The Reproduction of Inequality in Urban Space." *Social Forces* 92(1): 141–64.

Lees, Loretta. 2008. "Gentrification and Social Mixing: Towards an Inclusive Urban Renaissance?" *Urban Studies* 45(12): 2449–70.

Lees, Loretta, Tom Slater, and Elvin Wyly. 2008. *Gentrification*. New York: Routledge.

Levy, Diane K., Zach McDade, and Kassie Bertumen. 2013. "Mixed-Income Living: Anticipated and Realized Benefits for Low-Income Households." *Cityscape* 15(2): 15–28.

Massey, Douglas S., and Mary J. Fischer. 2003. "The Geography of Inequality in the United States, 1950–2000." *Brookings-Wharton Papers on Urban Affairs* 2003(January): 1–40.

McCormick, Naomi J., Mark L. Joseph, and Robert J. Chaskin. 2012. "The New Stigma of Relocated Public Housing Residents: Challenges to Social Identity in Mixed-Income Developments." *City & Community* 11(3): 285–308.

Palmer, John R. B. 2013. "Activity-Space Segregation: Understanding Social Divisions in Space and Time." PhD diss., Princeton University.

Parker, Robert Nash, and Rudy Fenwick. 1983. "The Pareto Curve and Its Utility for Open-Ended Income Distributions in Survey Research." *Social Forces* 61(3): 872–85.

Pettigrew, Thomas F. 1998. "Intergroup Contact Theory." *Annual Review of Psychology* 49(1): 65–85.

Pettigrew, Thomas F., and Linda R. Tropp. 2006. "A Meta-Analytic Test of Intergroup Contact Theory." *Journal of Personality and Social Psychology* 90(5): 751–83.

Putnam, Robert D. 2007. "E Pluribus Unum: Diversity and Community in the Twenty-First Century." *Scandinavian Political Studies* 30(2): 137–74.

Quillian, Lincoln. 1996. "Group Threat and Regional Change in Attitudes Toward African-Americans." *American Journal of Sociology* 102(3): 816–60.

Reardon, Sean F., and Kendra Bischoff. 2011. "Income Inequality and Income Segregation." *American Journal of Sociology* 116(4): 1092–153.

Rosenbaum, James E., Linda K. Stroh, and Cathy A. Flynn. 1998. "Lake Parc Place: A Study of Mixed-income Housing." *Housing Policy Debate* 9(4): 703–40.

Sampson, Robert J., and Dawn Jeglum Bartusch. 1998. "Legal Cynicism and (subcultural?) Tolerance of Deviance: The Neighborhood Context of Racial Differences." *Law & Society Review* 32(4): 777–804.

Sastry, Narayan, Bonnie Ghosh-Dastidar, John Adams, and Anne R. Pebley. 2006. "The Design of a Multilevel Survey of Children, Families, and Communities: The Los Angeles Family and Neighborhood Survey." *Social Science Research* 35(4): 1000–24.

Tach, Laura M. 2009. "More Than Bricks and Mortar: Neighborhood Frames, Social Processes, and the Mixed-Income Redevelopment of a Public Housing Project." *City & Community* 8(3): 269–99.

———. "Diversity, Inequality, and Microsegregation: Dynamics of Inclusion and Exclusion in a Racially and Economically Diverse Community." *Cityscape* 16(3): 13–46.

Talen, Emily. 2006. "Design That Enables Diversity: The Complications of a Planning Ideal." *Journal of Planning Literature* 20(3): 233–49.

Taylor, Marylee C. 1998. "How White Attitudes Vary with the Racial Composition of Local Populations: Numbers Count." *American Sociological Review* 63(4): 512–35.

Thomas, Vinod, Yan Wang, and Xibo Fan. 2001. "Measuring Education Inequality: Gini Coefficients of Education." Working Paper no. 2525. Washington, D.C.: World Bank.

van Duijn, Marijtje A. J., Tom A. B. Snijders, and Bonne J. H. Zijlstra. 2004. "p2: A Random Effects Model with Covariates for Directed Graphs." *Statistica Neerlandica* 58(2): 234–54.

Walks, R. Alan, and Richard Maaranen. 2008. "Gentrification, Social Mix, and Social Polarization: Testing the Linkages in Large Canadian Cities." *Urban Geography* 29(4): 293–326.

Wilkinson, Richard G., and Kate E. Pickett. 2009. "Income Inequality and Social Dysfunction." *Annual Review of Sociology* 35(1): 493–511.

Zijlstra, Bonne J. H., Marijtje A. J. van Duijn, and Tom A. B. Snijders. 2006. "The Multilevel p2 Model." *Methodology: European Journal of Research Methods for the Behavioral and Social Sciences* 2(1): 42–47.

Zubrinsky, Camille L., and Lawrence Bobo. 1996. "Prismatic Metropolis: Race and Residential Segregation in the City of the Angels." *Social Science Research* 25(4): 335–74.